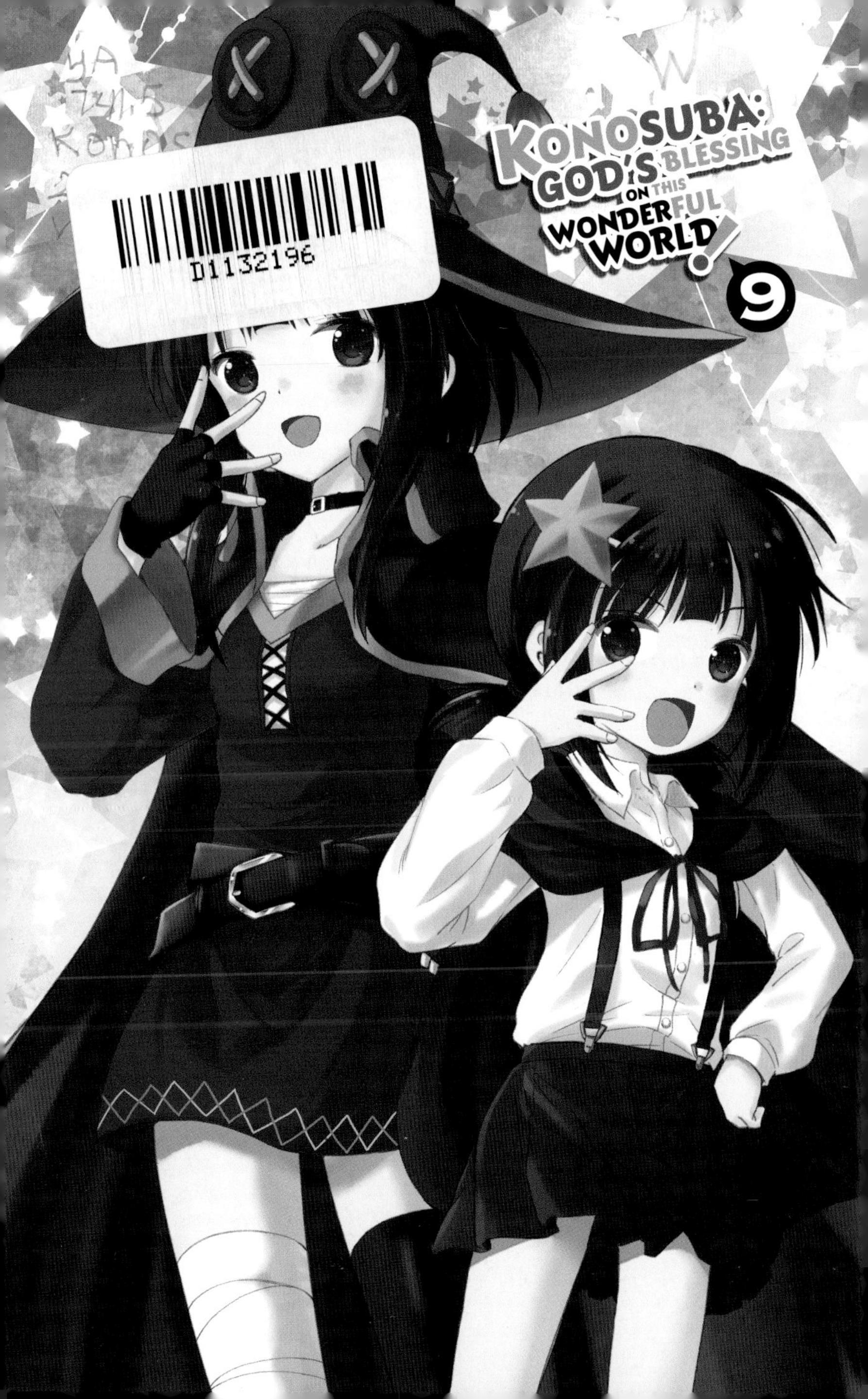
KONOSUBA: GOD'S BLESSING ON THIS WONDERFUL WORLD!
9
D1132196

# 9

## GOD'S BLESSING ON THIS WONDERFUL WORLD!
## CONTENTS

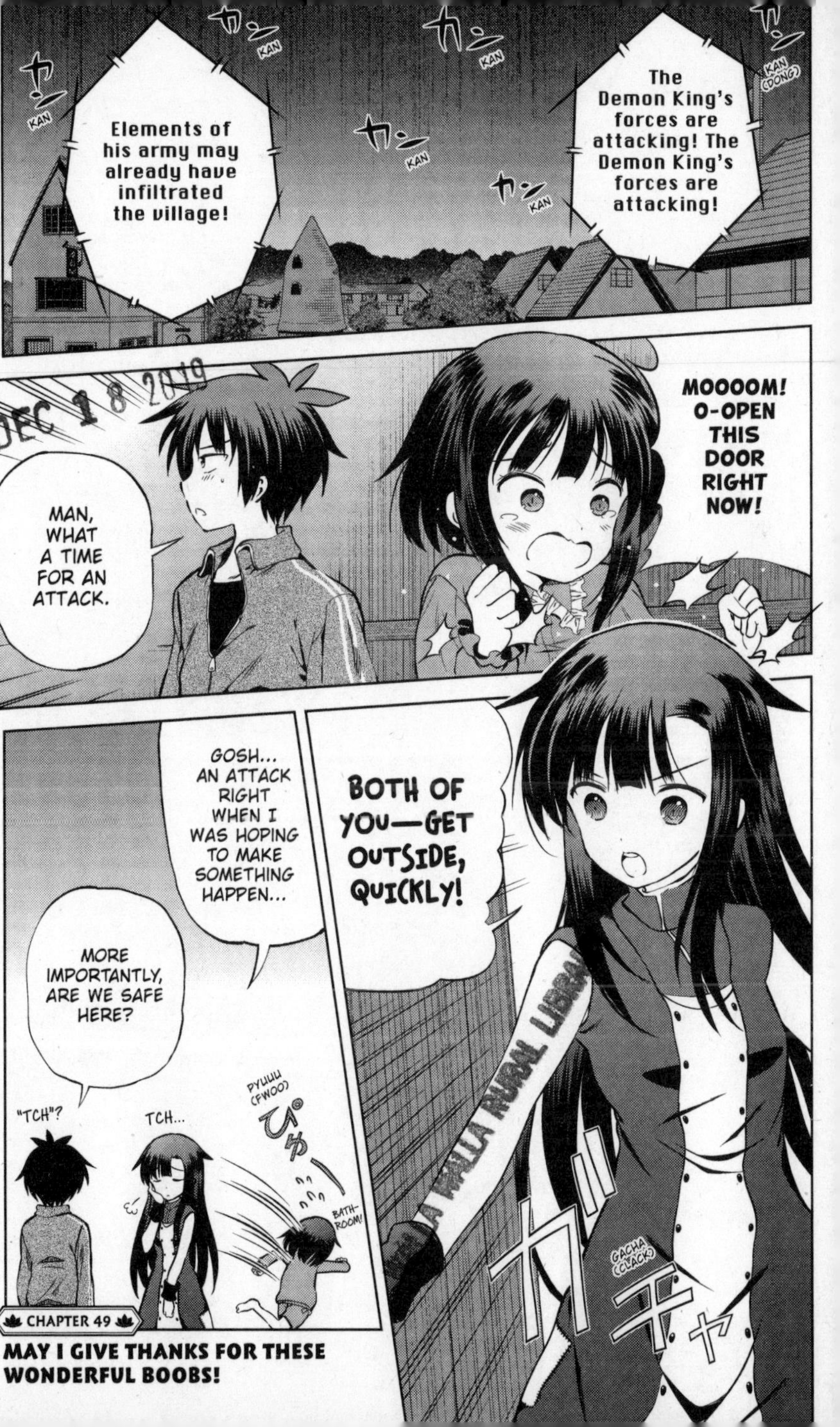
KAN (DONG)
The Demon King's forces are attacking! The Demon King's forces are attacking!
KAN
KAN
KAN
KAN
Elements of his army may already have infiltrated the village!
KAN
MOOOOM! O-OPEN THIS DOOR RIGHT NOW!
MAN, WHAT A TIME FOR AN ATTACK.
BOTH OF YOU—GET OUTSIDE, QUICKLY!
GACHA (CLACK)
GOSH... AN ATTACK RIGHT WHEN I WAS HOPING TO MAKE SOMETHING HAPPEN...
MORE IMPORTANTLY, ARE WE SAFE HERE?
TCH...
"TCH"?
PYUUU (FWOO)
BATH-ROOM!



CHAPTER 49

**MAY I GIVE THANKS FOR THESE WONDERFUL BOOBS!**

NOTE: "FUTAE NO KIWAMI! AAH!" IS A LINE IN THE ENGLISH DUB OF HIT ANIME *RUROUNI KENSHIN* THAT GAINED LEGENDARY STATUS AS A MEME IN JAPANESE ONLINE CIRCLES FOR ITS EXTREME CONTRAST TO THE ORIGINAL JAPANESE VERSION.

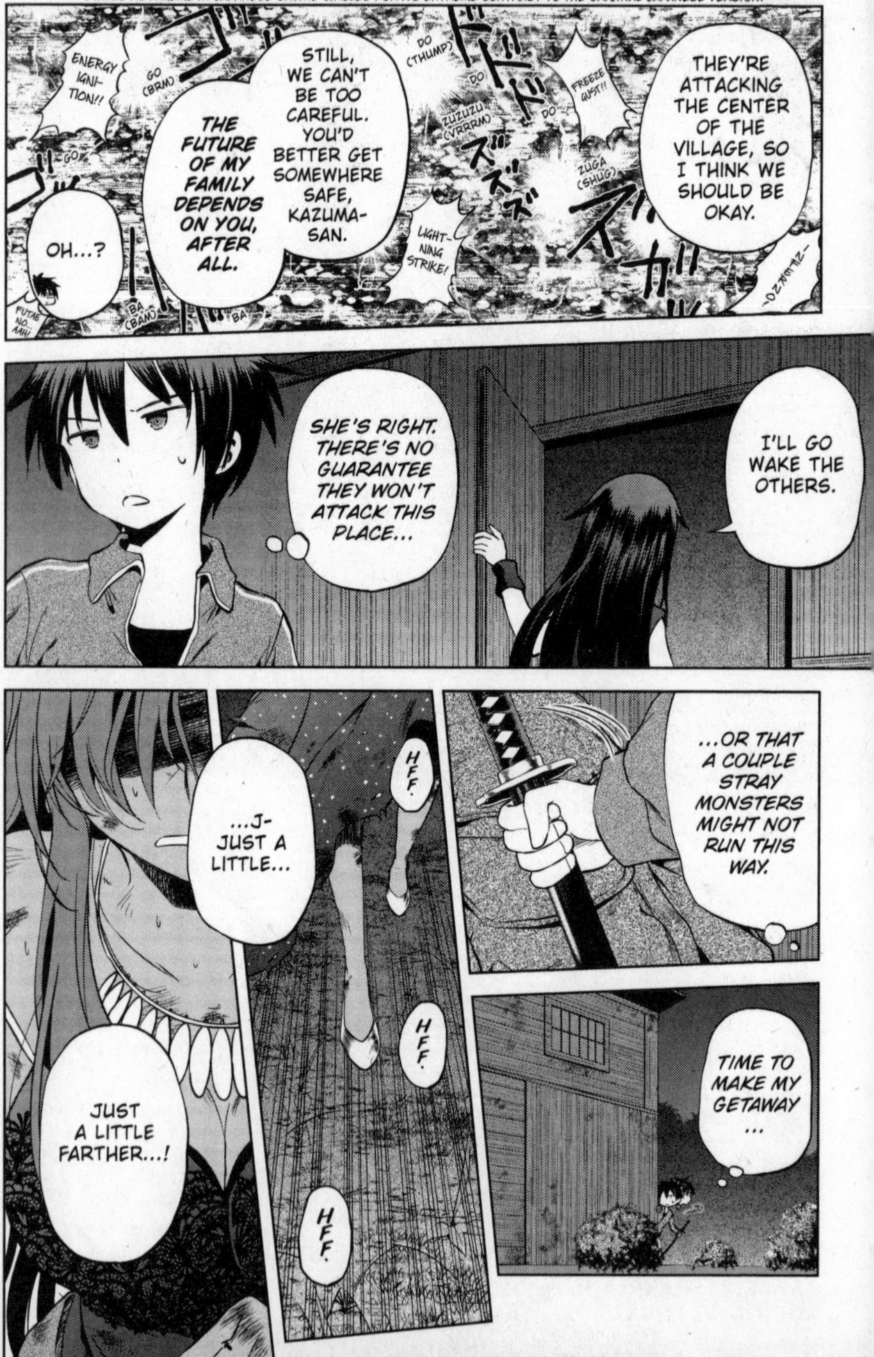

THEY'RE ATTACKING THE CENTER OF THE VILLAGE, SO I THINK WE SHOULD BE OKAY.
ZUGA (SHUG)
FREEZE GUST!!
DO
DO (THUMP)
DO
ZUZUZU (VRRRM)
LIGHTNING STRIKE!
STILL, WE CAN'T BE TOO CAREFUL. YOU'D BETTER GET SOMEWHERE SAFE, KAZUMA-SAN.
THE FUTURE OF MY FAMILY DEPENDS ON YOU, AFTER ALL.
GO (BRM)
ENERGY IGNITION!!
GO
BA (BAM)
BA
OH...?
FUTAE NO... AAH!
I'LL GO WAKE THE OTHERS.
SHE'S RIGHT. THERE'S NO GUARANTEE THEY WON'T ATTACK THIS PLACE...
...OR THAT A COUPLE STRAY MONSTERS MIGHT NOT RUN THIS WAY.
TIME TO MAKE MY GETAWAY...
HFF.
HFF.
HFF.
...J-JUST A LITTLE...
JUST A LITTLE FARTHER...!

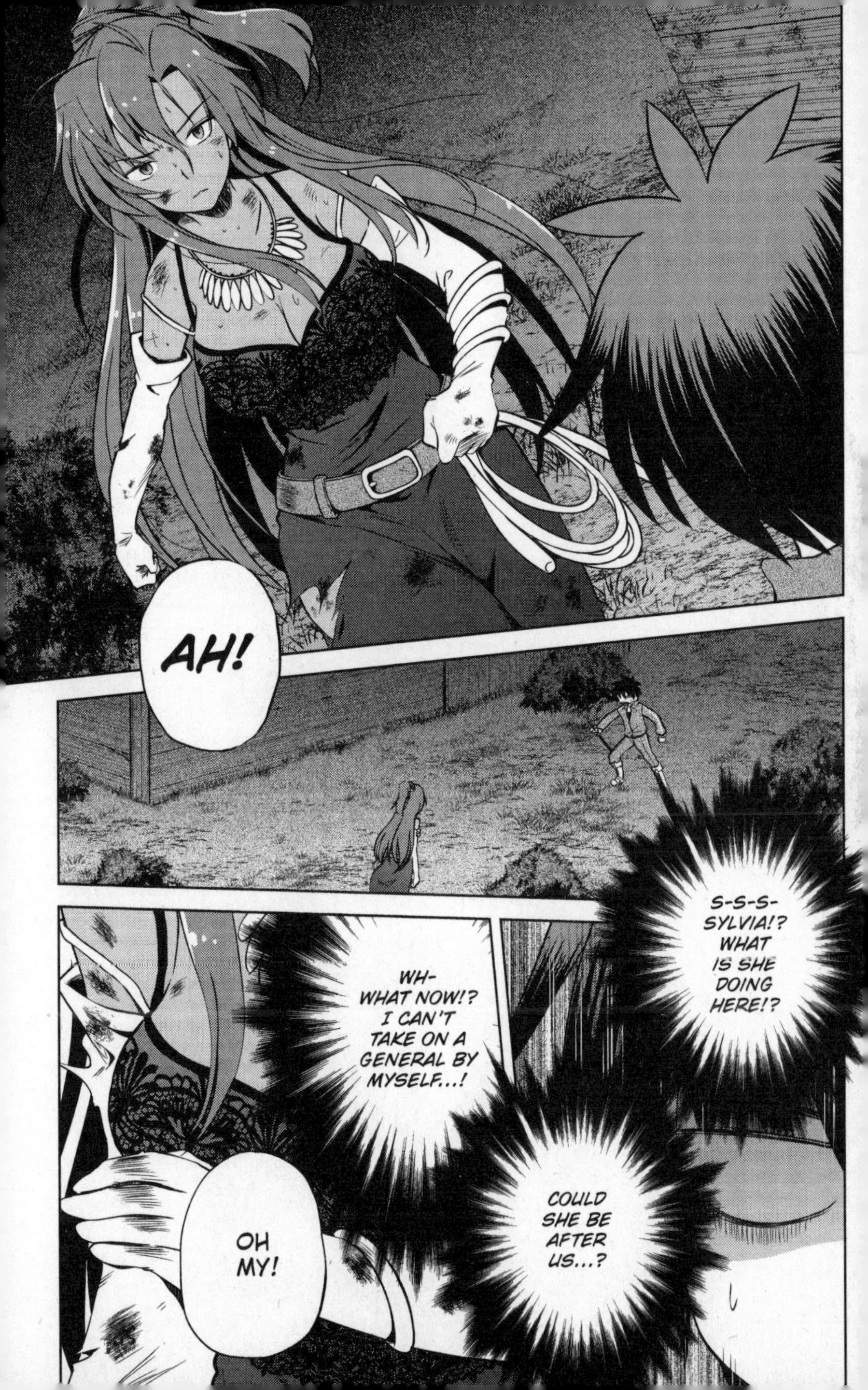
AH!
S-S-S-SYLVIA!? WHAT IS SHE DOING HERE!?
WH-WHAT NOW!? I CAN'T TAKE ON A GENERAL BY MYSELF...!
COULD SHE BE AFTER US...?
OH MY!

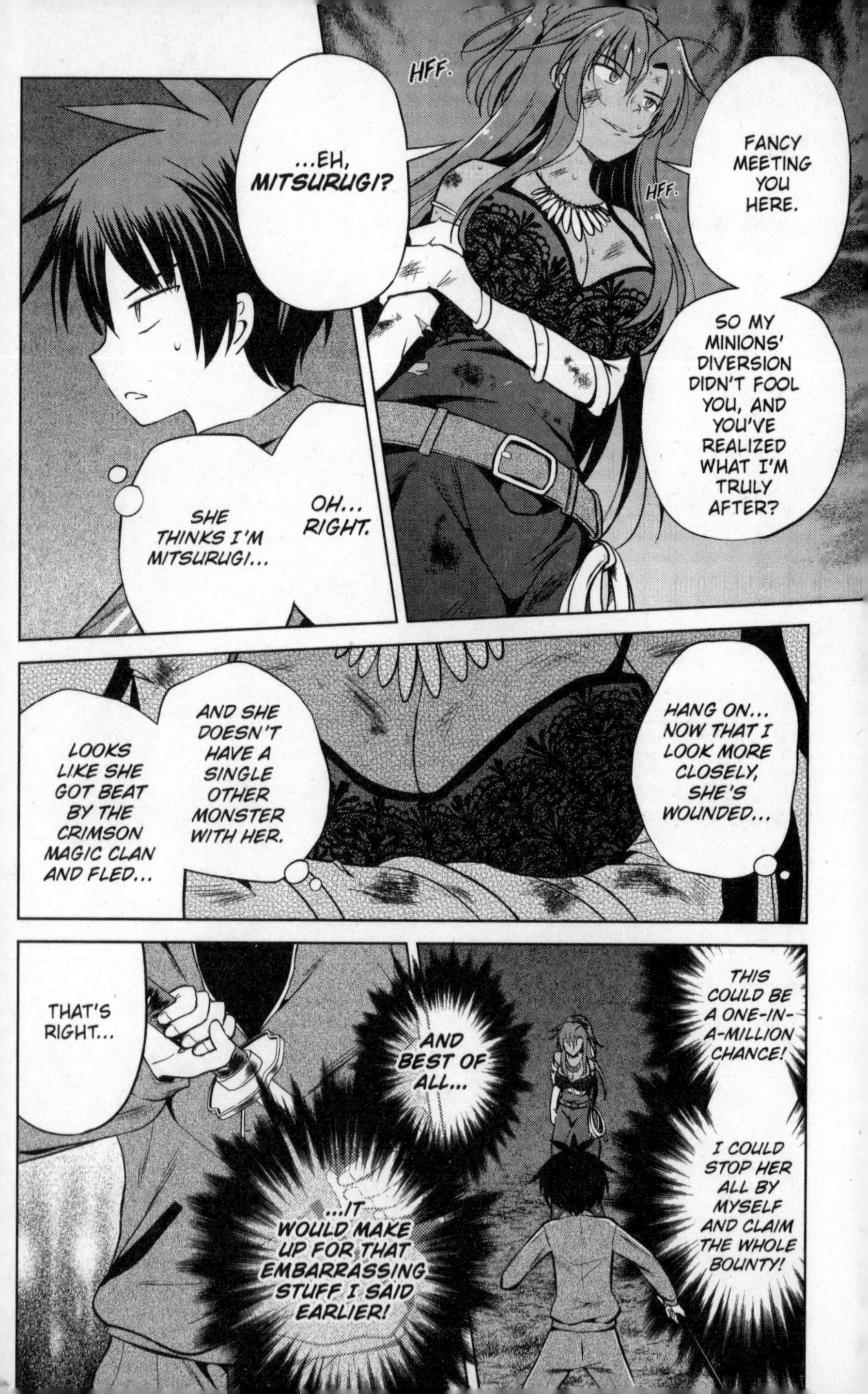
HFF.
FANCY MEETING YOU HERE.
HFF.
SO MY MINIONS' DIVERSION DIDN'T FOOL YOU, AND YOU'VE REALIZED WHAT I'M TRULY AFTER?
...EH, MITSURUGI?
OH... RIGHT.
SHE THINKS I'M MITSURUGI...
HANG ON... NOW THAT I LOOK MORE CLOSELY, SHE'S WOUNDED...
AND SHE DOESN'T HAVE A SINGLE OTHER MONSTER WITH HER.
LOOKS LIKE SHE GOT BEAT BY THE CRIMSON MAGIC CLAN AND FLED...
THIS COULD BE A ONE-IN-A-MILLION CHANCE!
I COULD STOP HER ALL BY MYSELF AND CLAIM THE WHOLE BOUNTY!
AND BEST OF ALL...
...IT WOULD MAKE UP FOR THAT EMBARRASSING STUFF I SAID EARLIER!
THAT'S RIGHT...

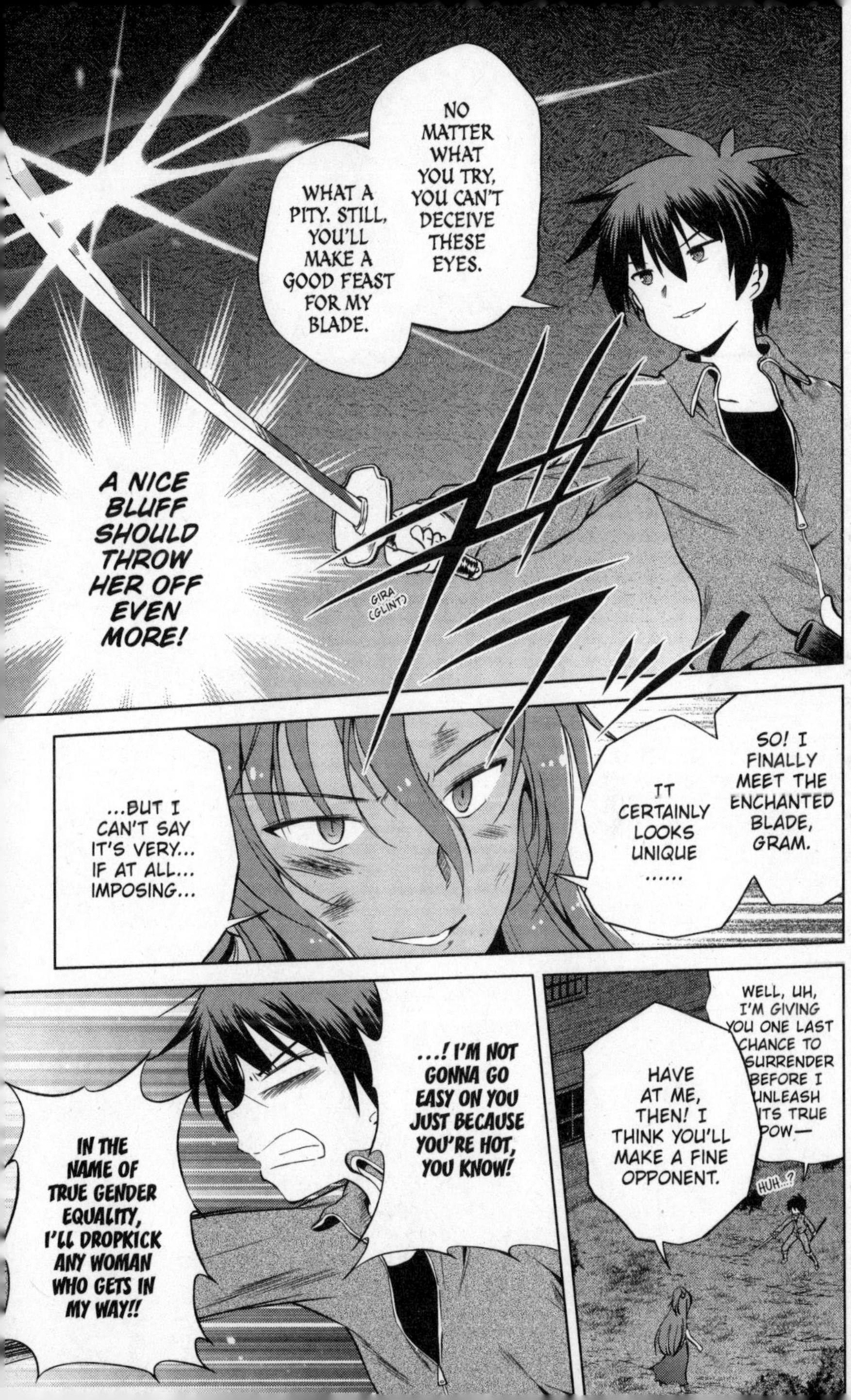
NO MATTER WHAT YOU TRY, YOU CAN'T DECEIVE THESE EYES.
WHAT A PITY. STILL, YOU'LL MAKE A GOOD FEAST FOR MY BLADE.
A NICE BLUFF SHOULD THROW HER OFF EVEN MORE!
GIRA (GLINT)
SO! I FINALLY MEET THE ENCHANTED BLADE, GRAM.
IT CERTAINLY LOOKS UNIQUE ......
...BUT I CAN'T SAY IT'S VERY... IF AT ALL... IMPOSING...
WELL, UH, I'M GIVING YOU ONE LAST CHANCE TO SURRENDER BEFORE I UNLEASH ITS TRUE POW—
HAVE AT ME, THEN! I THINK YOU'LL MAKE A FINE OPPONENT.
HUH...?
...! I'M NOT GONNA GO EASY ON YOU JUST BECAUSE YOU'RE HOT, YOU KNOW!
IN THE NAME OF TRUE GENDER EQUALITY, I'LL DROPKICK ANY WOMAN WHO GETS IN MY WAY!!

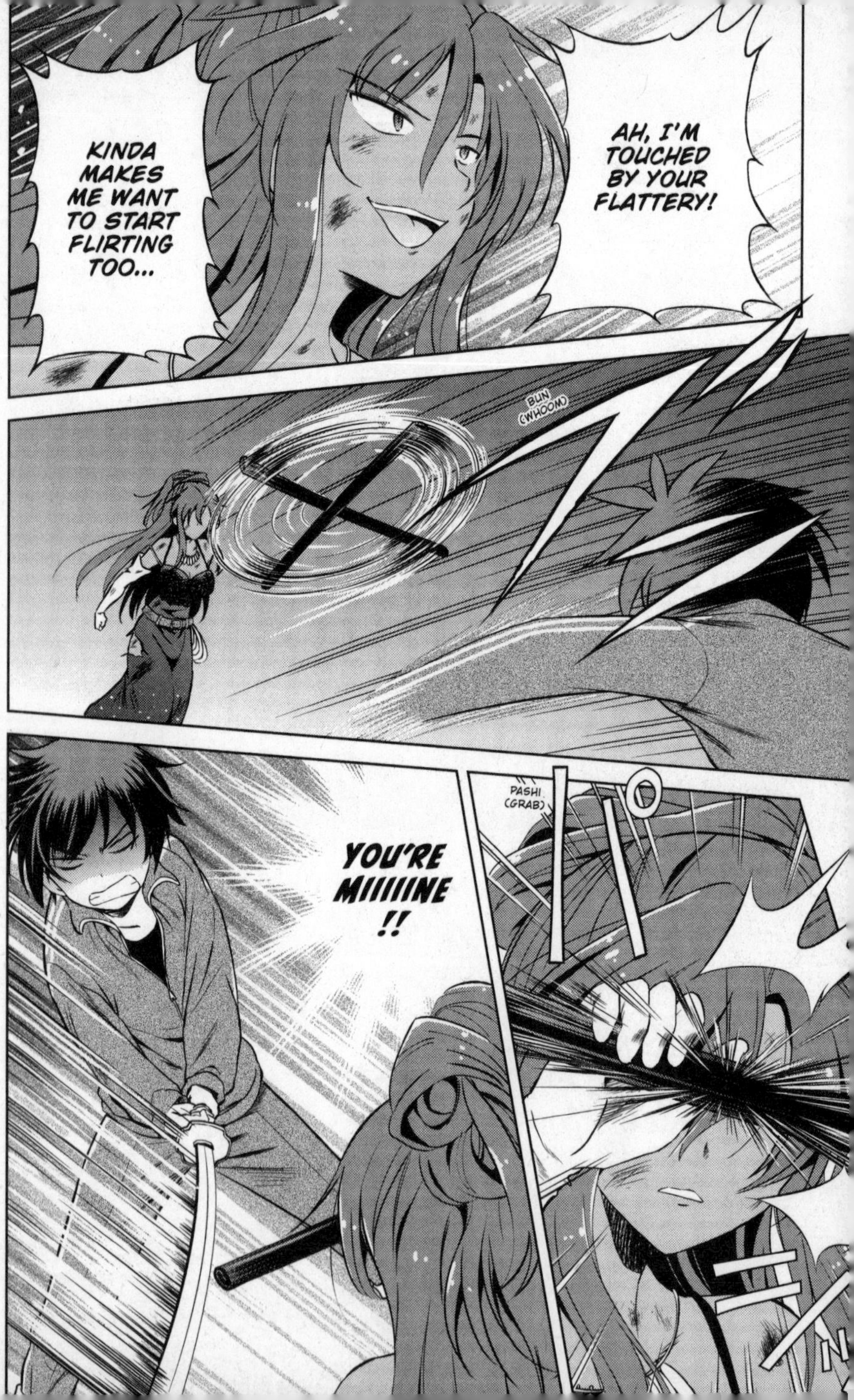
AH, I'M TOUCHED BY YOUR FLATTERY!
KINDA MAKES ME WANT TO START FLIRTING TOO...
BUN (WHOOM)
PASHI (GRAB)
YOU'RE MIIIIINE !!

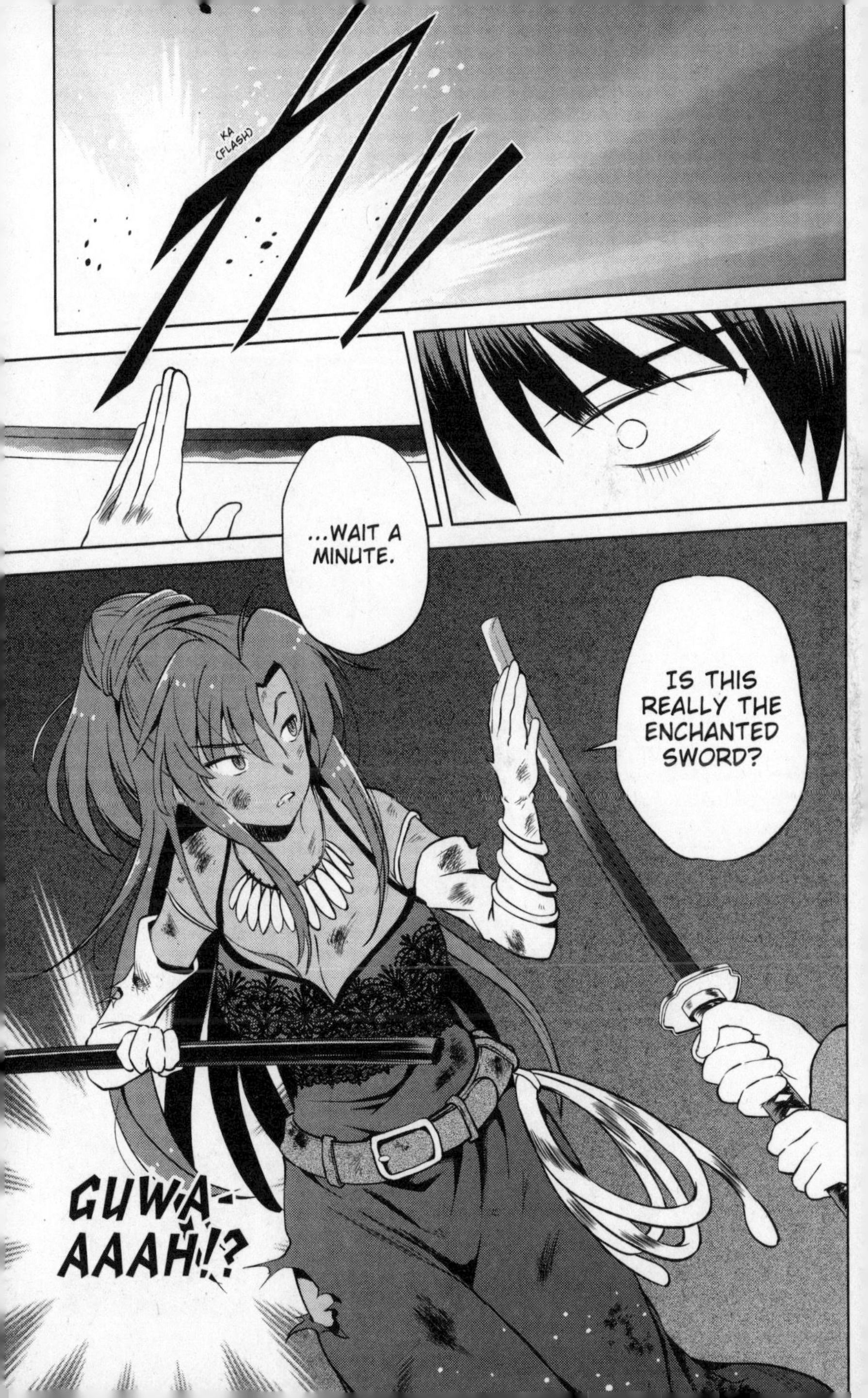
KA (FLASH)
...WAIT A MINUTE.
IS THIS REALLY THE ENCHANTED SWORD?
GUWAAAAH!!?

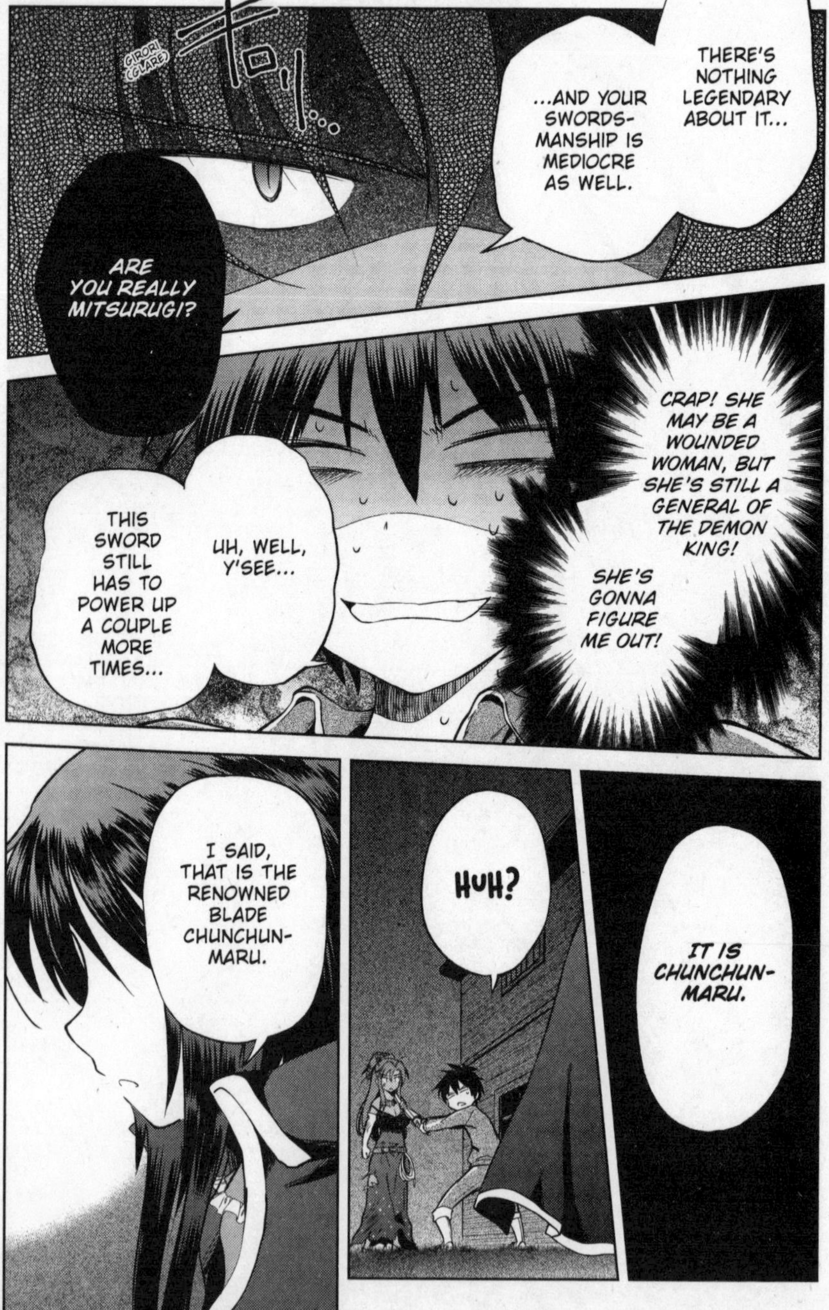
THERE'S NOTHING LEGENDARY ABOUT IT...
...AND YOUR SWORDS-MANSHIP IS MEDIOCRE AS WELL.
GIRORI (GLARE)
ARE YOU REALLY MITSURUGI?
CRAP! SHE MAY BE A WOUNDED WOMAN, BUT SHE'S STILL A GENERAL OF THE DEMON KING!
SHE'S GONNA FIGURE ME OUT!
UH, WELL, Y'SEE...
THIS SWORD STILL HAS TO POWER UP A COUPLE MORE TIMES...
IT IS CHUNCHUN-MARU.
HUH?
I SAID, THAT IS THE RENOWNED BLADE CHUNCHUN-MARU.

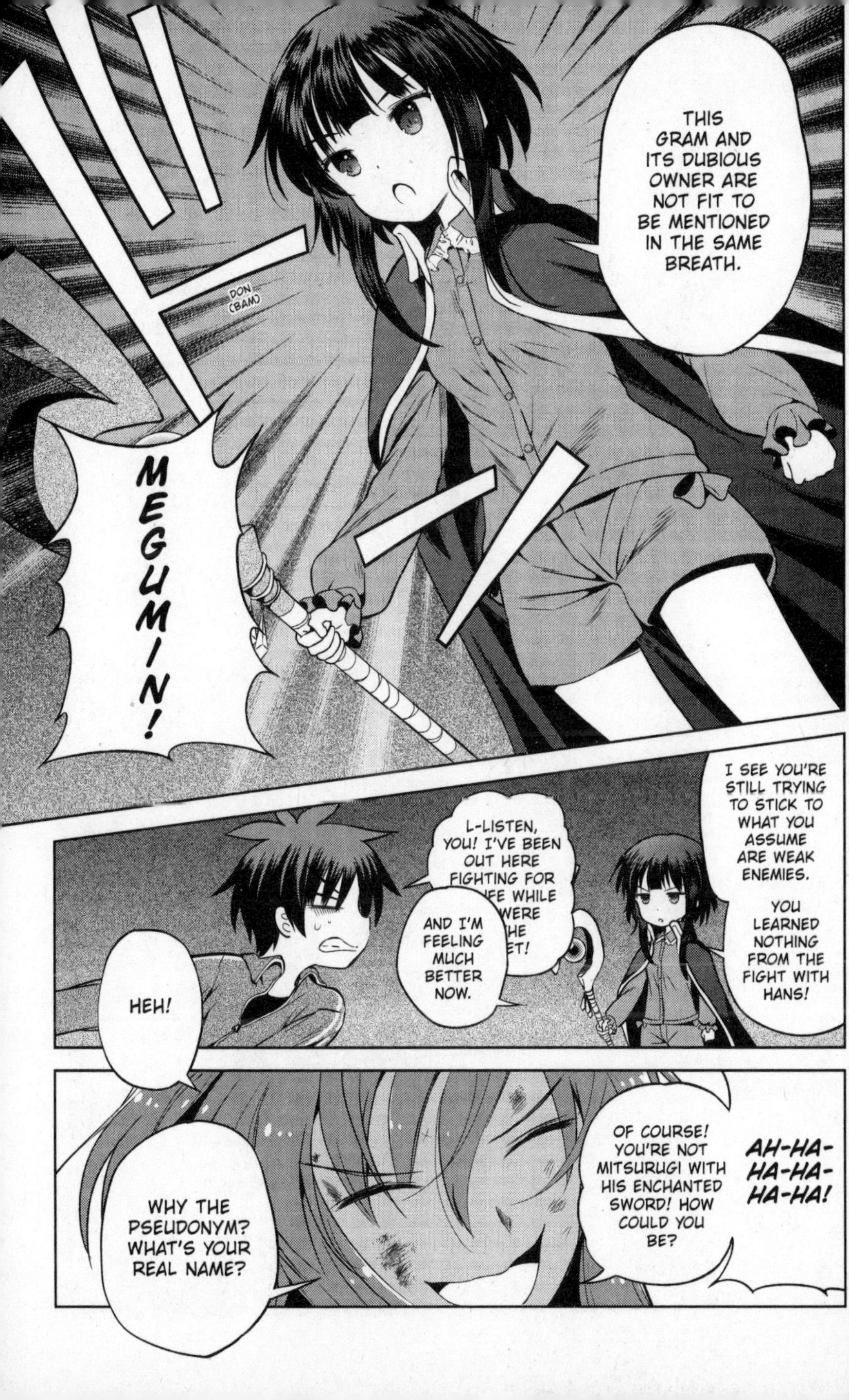
THIS GRAM AND ITS DUBIOUS OWNER ARE NOT FIT TO BE MENTIONED IN THE SAME BREATH.
DON (BAM)
MEGUMIN!
I SEE YOU'RE STILL TRYING TO STICK TO WHAT YOU ASSUME ARE WEAK ENEMIES.
YOU LEARNED NOTHING FROM THE FIGHT WITH HANS!
L-LISTEN, YOU! I'VE BEEN OUT HERE FIGHTING FOR
AND I'M FEELING MUCH BETTER NOW.
HEH!
AH-HA-HA-HA-HA-HA!
OF COURSE! YOU'RE NOT MITSURUGI WITH HIS ENCHANTED SWORD! HOW COULD YOU BE?
WHY THE PSEUDONYM? WHAT'S YOUR REAL NAME?

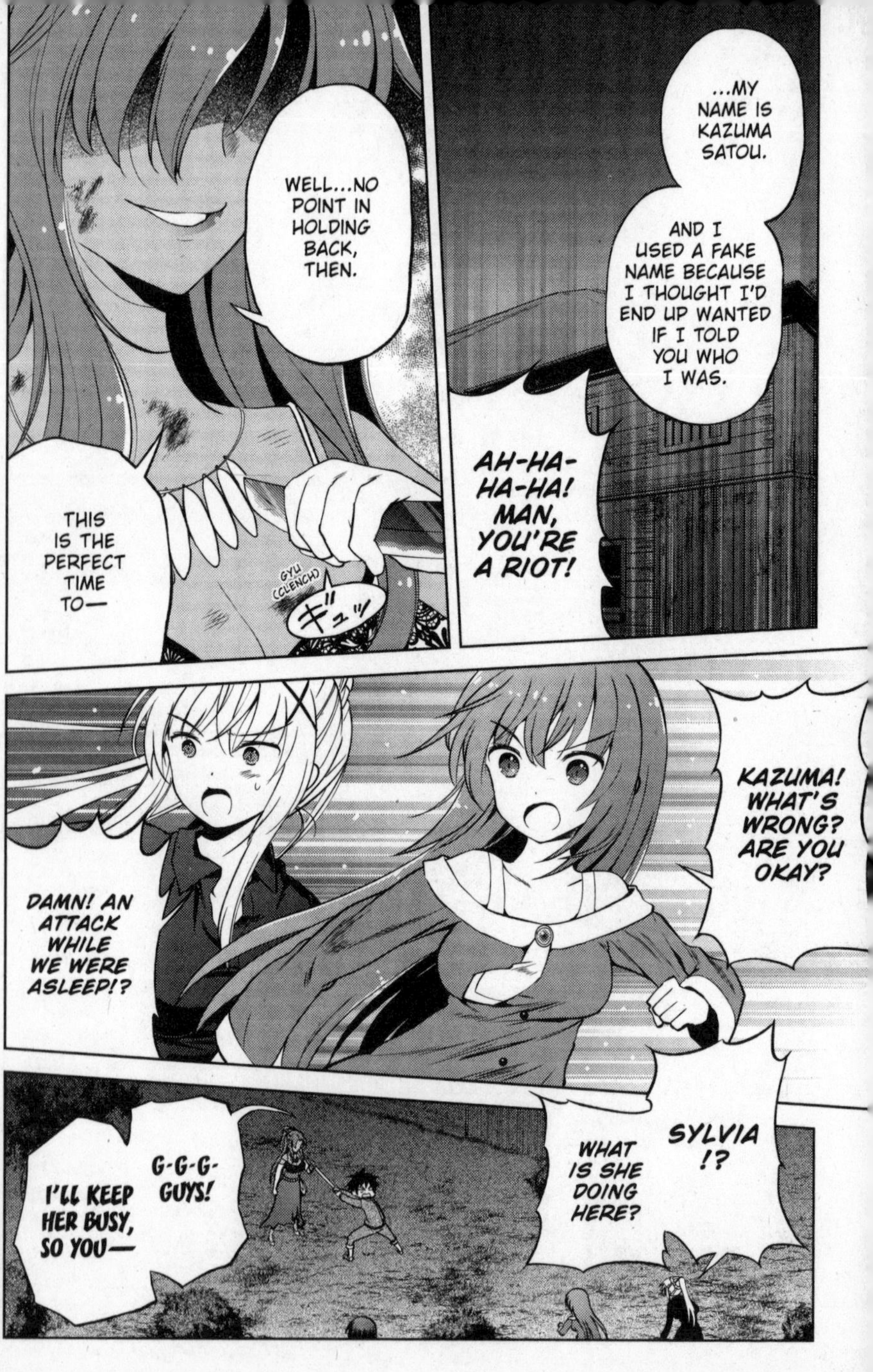
...MY NAME IS KAZUMA SATOU.
AND I USED A FAKE NAME BECAUSE I THOUGHT I'D END UP WANTED IF I TOLD YOU WHO I WAS.
AH-HA-HA-HA! MAN, YOU'RE A RIOT!
WELL...NO POINT IN HOLDING BACK, THEN.
THIS IS THE PERFECT TIME TO—
GYU (CLENCH)
ギュッ
KAZUMA! WHAT'S WRONG? ARE YOU OKAY?
DAMN! AN ATTACK WHILE WE WERE ASLEEP!?
SYLVIA!?
WHAT IS SHE DOING HERE?
G-G-G-GUYS!
I'LL KEEP HER BUSY, SO YOU—

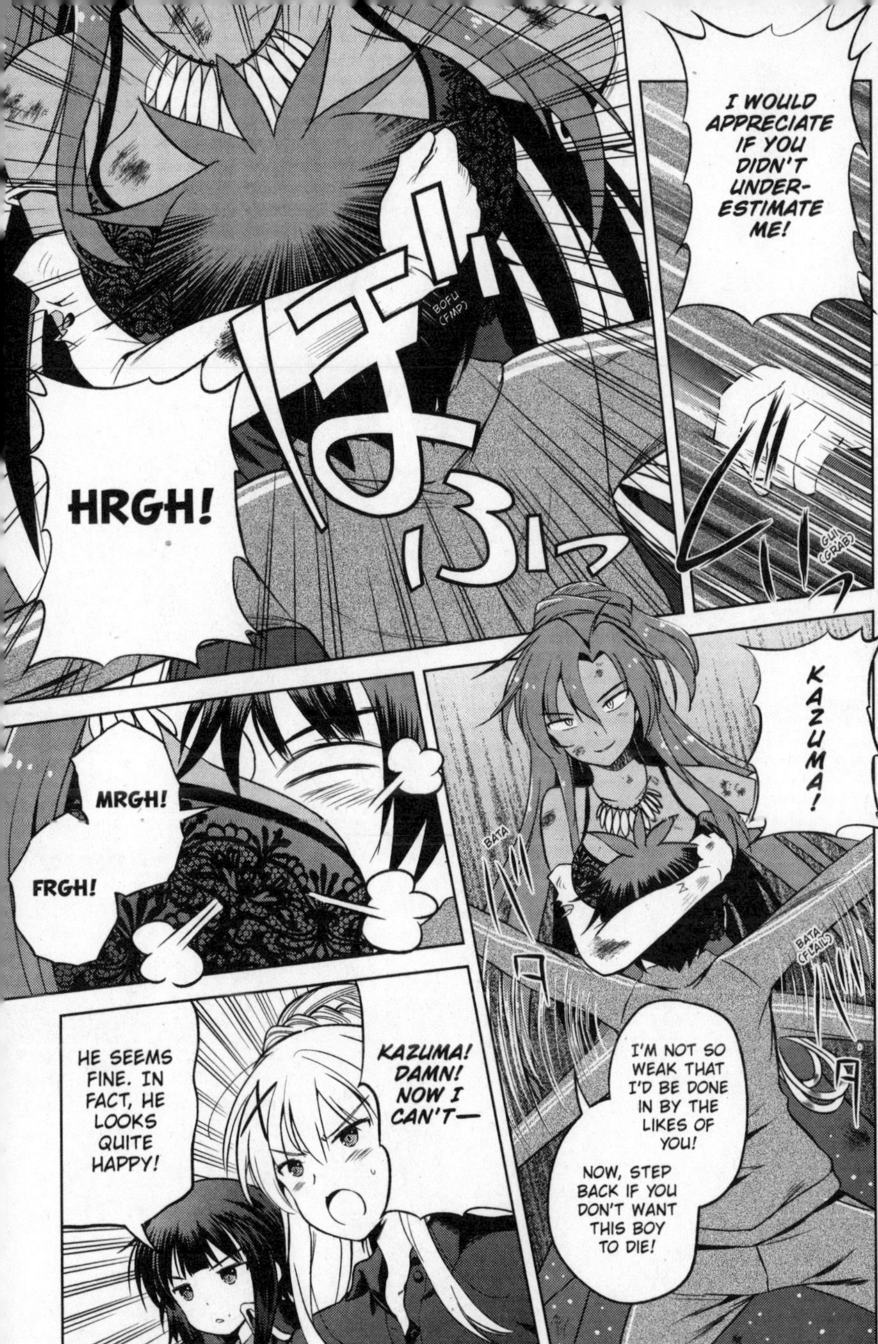
I WOULD APPRECIATE IF YOU DIDN'T UNDER-ESTIMATE ME!
GUI (GRAB)
BOFU (FMP)
HRGH!
KAZUMA!
BATA
BATA (FLAILS)
MRGH!
FRGH!
I'M NOT SO WEAK THAT I'D BE DONE IN BY THE LIKES OF YOU!
NOW, STEP BACK IF YOU DON'T WANT THIS BOY TO DIE!
KAZUMA! DAMN! NOW I CAN'T—
HE SEEMS FINE. IN FACT, HE LOOKS QUITE HAPPY!

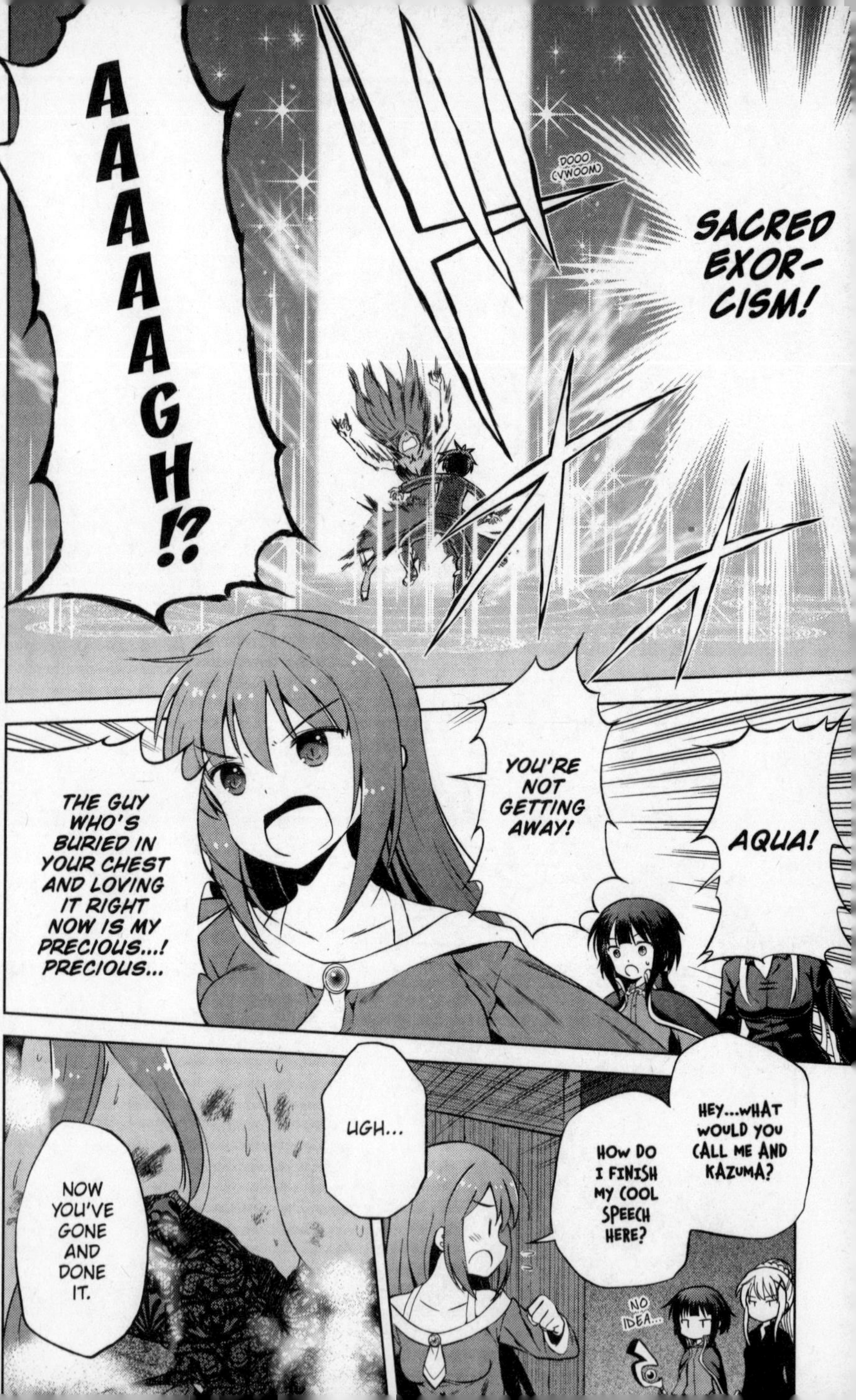
SACRED EXOR-CISM!
DOOO (VWOOM)
AAAAAGH!?
AQUA!
YOU'RE NOT GETTING AWAY!
THE GUY WHO'S BURIED IN YOUR CHEST AND LOVING IT RIGHT NOW IS MY PRECIOUS...! PRECIOUS...
HEY...WHAT WOULD YOU CALL ME AND KAZUMA?
HOW DO I FINISH MY COOL SPEECH HERE?
NO IDEA...
UGH...
NOW YOU'VE GONE AND DONE IT.

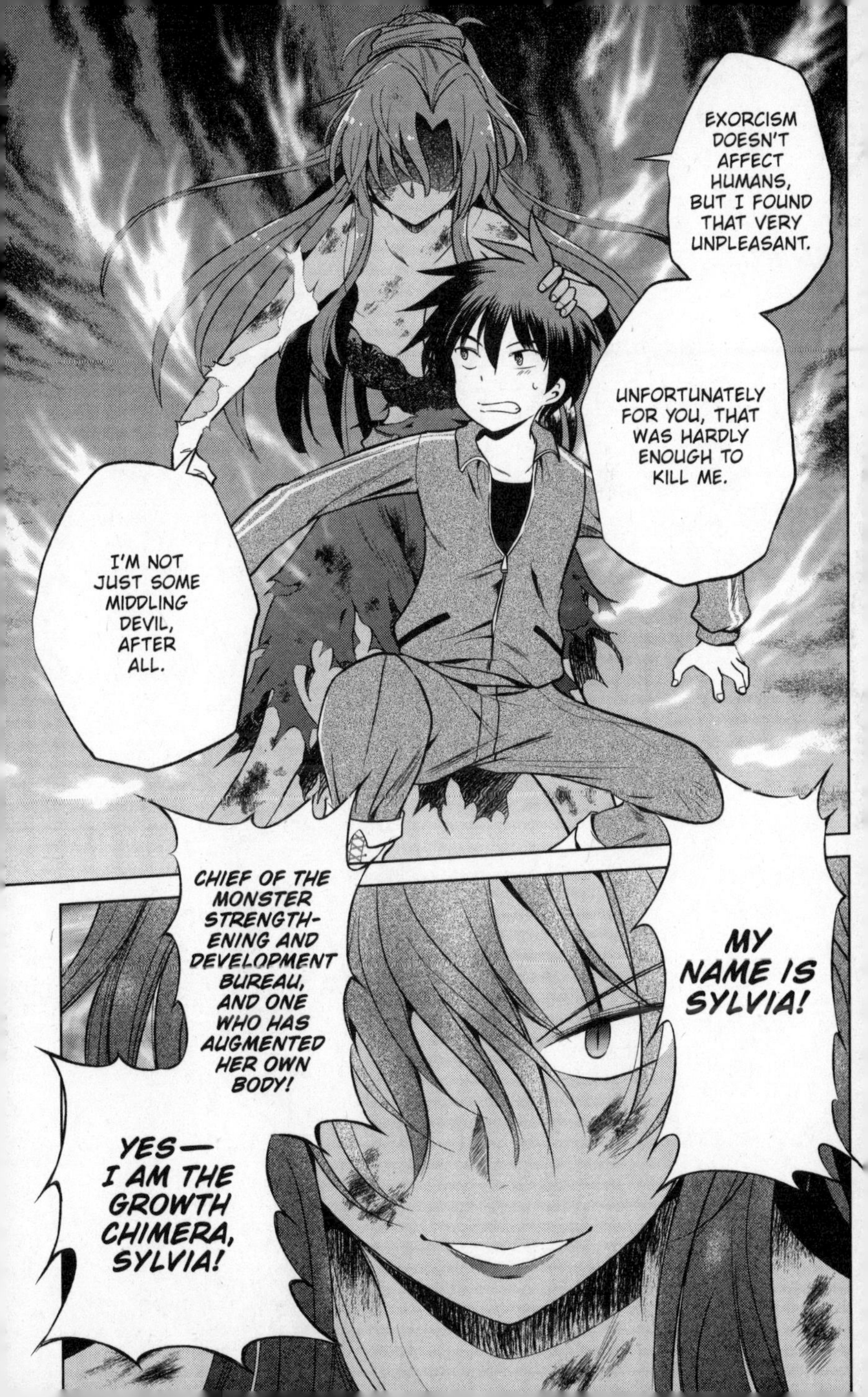
EXORCISM DOESN'T AFFECT HUMANS, BUT I FOUND THAT VERY UNPLEASANT.
UNFORTUNATELY FOR YOU, THAT WAS HARDLY ENOUGH TO KILL ME.
I'M NOT JUST SOME MIDDLING DEVIL, AFTER ALL.
MY NAME IS SYLVIA!
CHIEF OF THE MONSTER STRENGTH-ENING AND DEVELOPMENT BUREAU, AND ONE WHO HAS AUGMENTED HER OWN BODY!
YES— I AM THE GROWTH CHIMERA, SYLVIA!

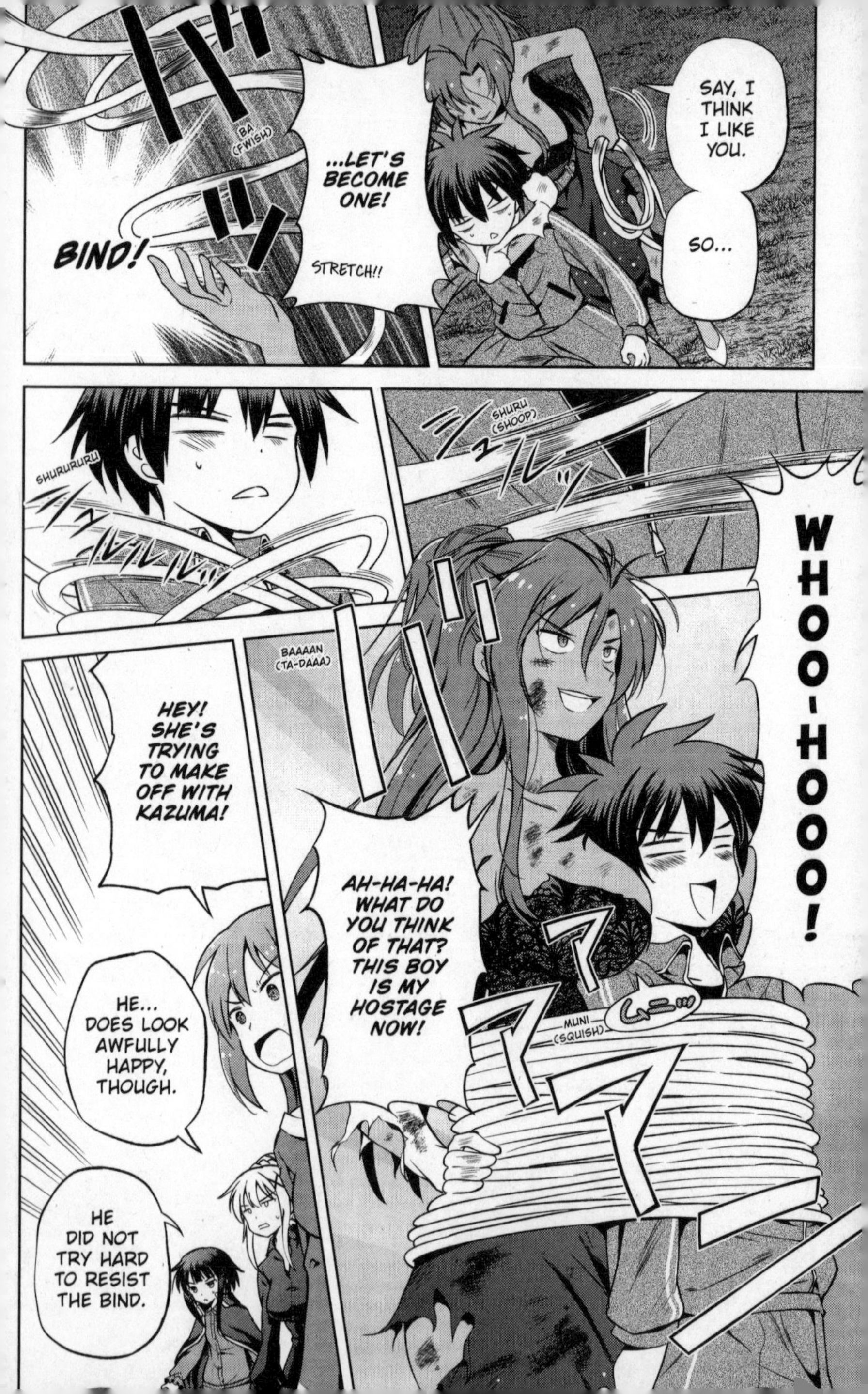
SAY, I THINK I LIKE YOU.
SO...
...LET'S BECOME ONE!
BA (FWISH)
BIND!
STRETCH!!
SHURU (SHOOP)
SHURURURU
WHOO-HOOOO!
BAAAAN (TA-DAAA)
AH-HA-HA! WHAT DO YOU THINK OF THAT? THIS BOY IS MY HOSTAGE NOW!
MUNI (SQUISH)
HEY! SHE'S TRYING TO MAKE OFF WITH KAZUMA!
HE... DOES LOOK AWFULLY HAPPY, THOUGH.
HE DID NOT TRY HARD TO RESIST THE BIND.

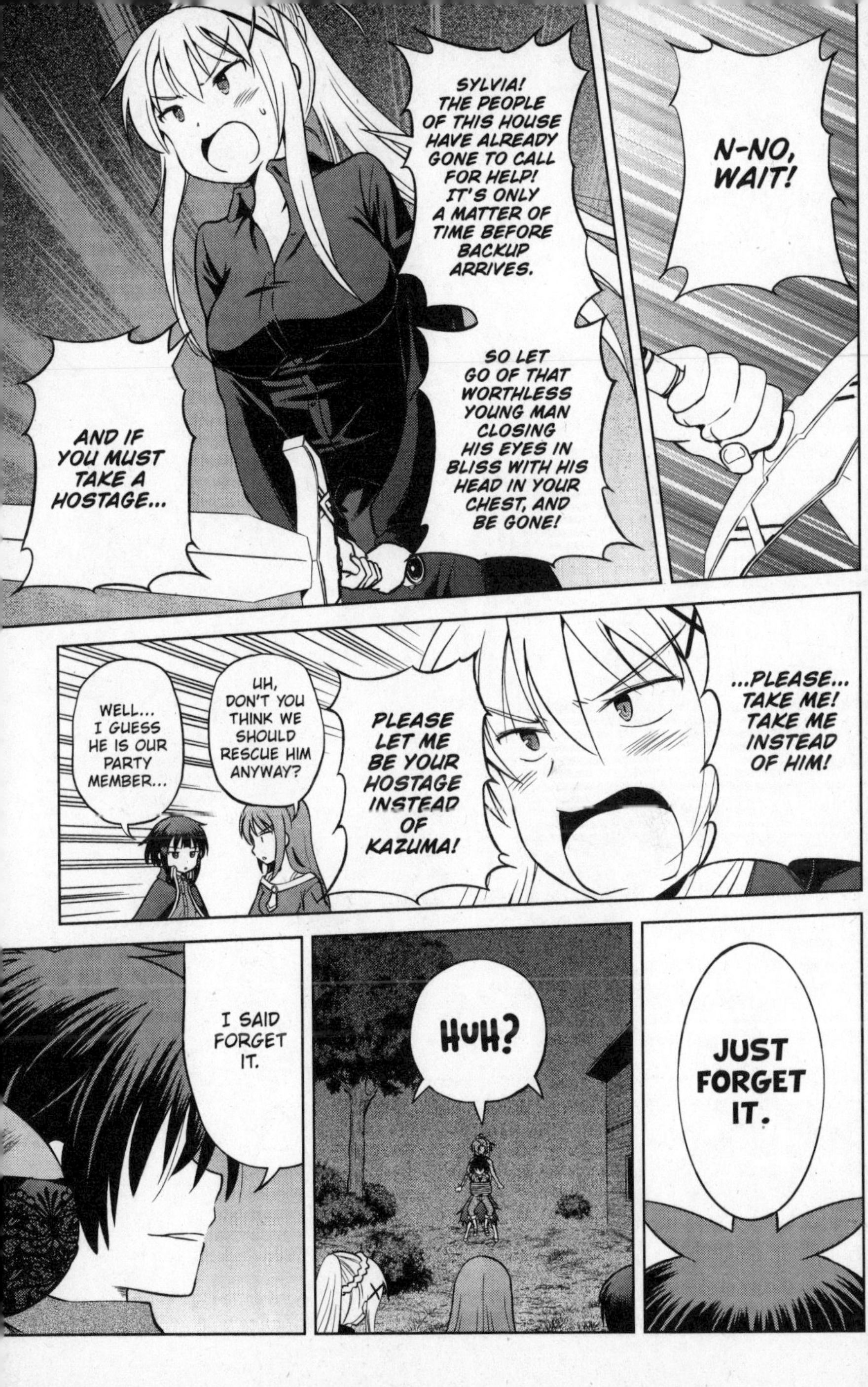
N-NO, WAIT!
SYLVIA! THE PEOPLE OF THIS HOUSE HAVE ALREADY GONE TO CALL FOR HELP! IT'S ONLY A MATTER OF TIME BEFORE BACKUP ARRIVES.
SO LET GO OF THAT WORTHLESS YOUNG MAN CLOSING HIS EYES IN BLISS WITH HIS HEAD IN YOUR CHEST, AND BE GONE!
AND IF YOU MUST TAKE A HOSTAGE...
...PLEASE... TAKE ME! TAKE ME INSTEAD OF HIM!
PLEASE LET ME BE YOUR HOSTAGE INSTEAD OF KAZUMA!
UH, DON'T YOU THINK WE SHOULD RESCUE HIM ANYWAY?
WELL... I GUESS HE IS OUR PARTY MEMBER...
JUST FORGET IT.
HUH?
I SAID FORGET IT.

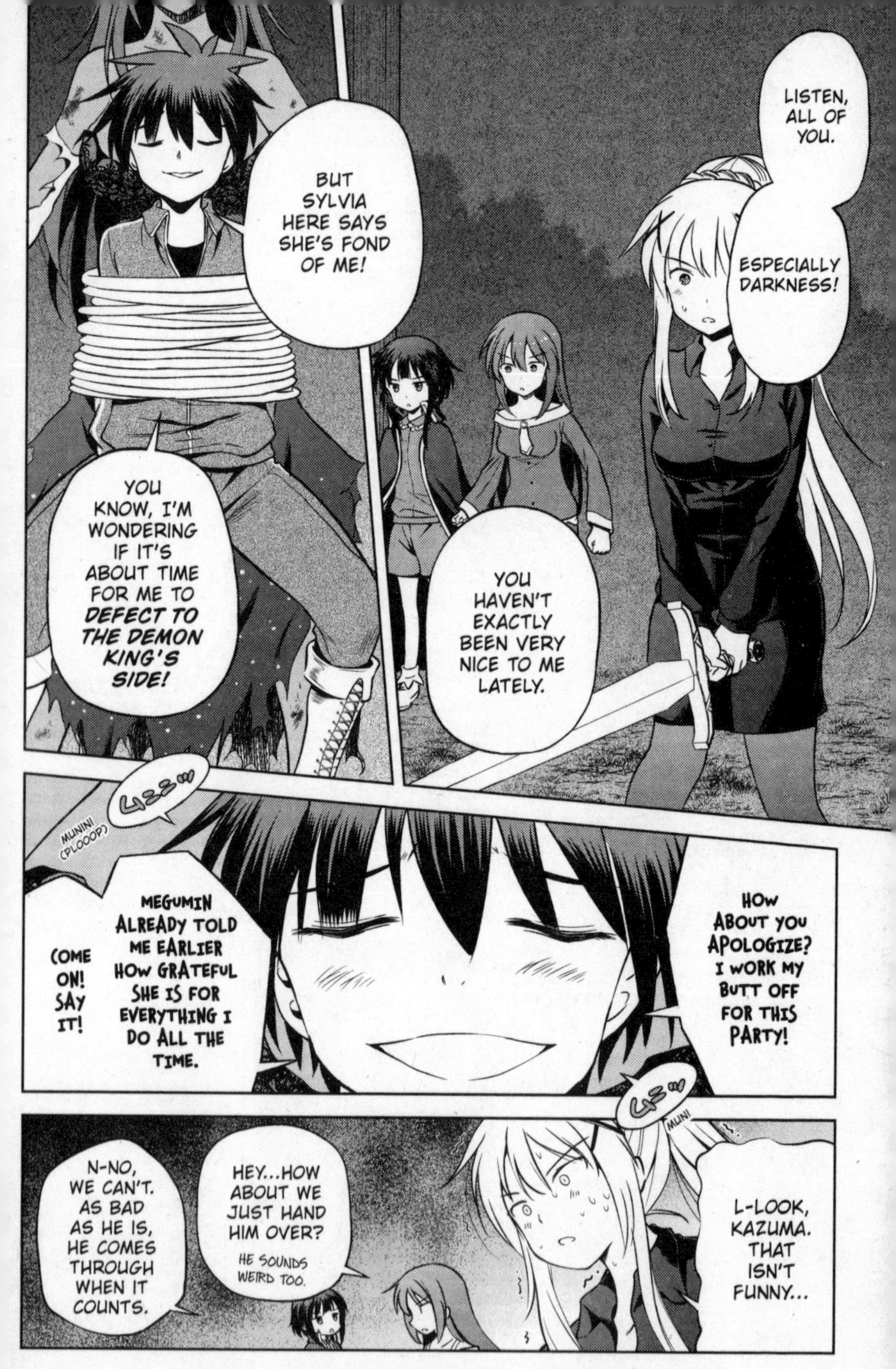
LISTEN, ALL OF YOU.
ESPECIALLY DARKNESS!
YOU HAVEN'T EXACTLY BEEN VERY NICE TO ME LATELY.
BUT SYLVIA HERE SAYS SHE'S FOND OF ME!
YOU KNOW, I'M WONDERING IF IT'S ABOUT TIME FOR ME TO ***DEFECT TO THE DEMON KING'S SIDE!***
MUNINI (PLOOOP)
HOW ABOUT YOU APOLOGIZE? I WORK MY BUTT OFF FOR THIS PARTY!
MEGUMIN ALREADY TOLD ME EARLIER HOW GRATEFUL SHE IS FOR EVERYTHING I DO ALL THE TIME.
COME ON! SAY IT!
MUNI
L-LOOK, KAZUMA. THAT ISN'T FUNNY...
HEY...HOW ABOUT WE JUST HAND HIM OVER?
HE SOUNDS WEIRD TOO.
N-NO, WE CAN'T. AS BAD AS HE IS, HE COMES THROUGH WHEN IT COUNTS.

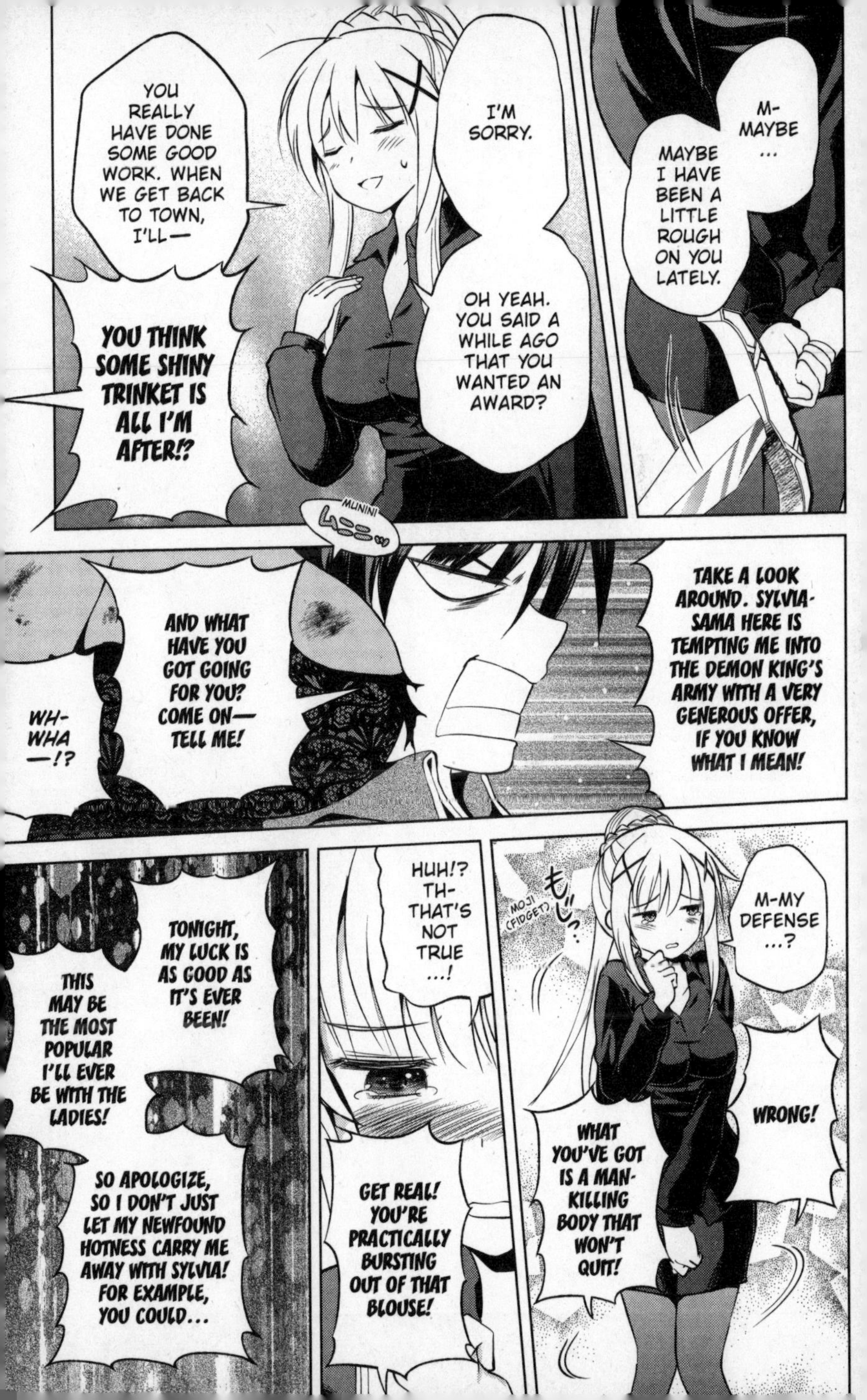
M-MAYBE...
MAYBE I HAVE BEEN A LITTLE ROUGH ON YOU LATELY.
I'M SORRY.
OH YEAH. YOU SAID A WHILE AGO THAT YOU WANTED AN AWARD?
YOU REALLY HAVE DONE SOME GOOD WORK. WHEN WE GET BACK TO TOWN, I'LL—
YOU THINK SOME SHINY TRINKET IS ALL I'M AFTER!?
MUNINI
TAKE A LOOK AROUND. SYLVIA-SAMA HERE IS TEMPTING ME INTO THE DEMON KING'S ARMY WITH A VERY GENEROUS OFFER, IF YOU KNOW WHAT I MEAN!
AND WHAT HAVE YOU GOT GOING FOR YOU? COME ON—TELL ME!
WH-WHA—!?
M-MY DEFENSE...?
MOJI (FIDGET)
WRONG!
WHAT YOU'VE GOT IS A MAN-KILLING BODY THAT WON'T QUIT!
HUH!? TH-THAT'S NOT TRUE...!
GET REAL! YOU'RE PRACTICALLY BURSTING OUT OF THAT BLOUSE!
TONIGHT, MY LUCK IS AS GOOD AS IT'S EVER BEEN!
THIS MAY BE THE MOST POPULAR I'LL EVER BE WITH THE LADIES!
SO APOLOGIZE, SO I DON'T JUST LET MY NEWFOUND HOTNESS CARRY ME AWAY WITH SYLVIA! FOR EXAMPLE, YOU COULD...

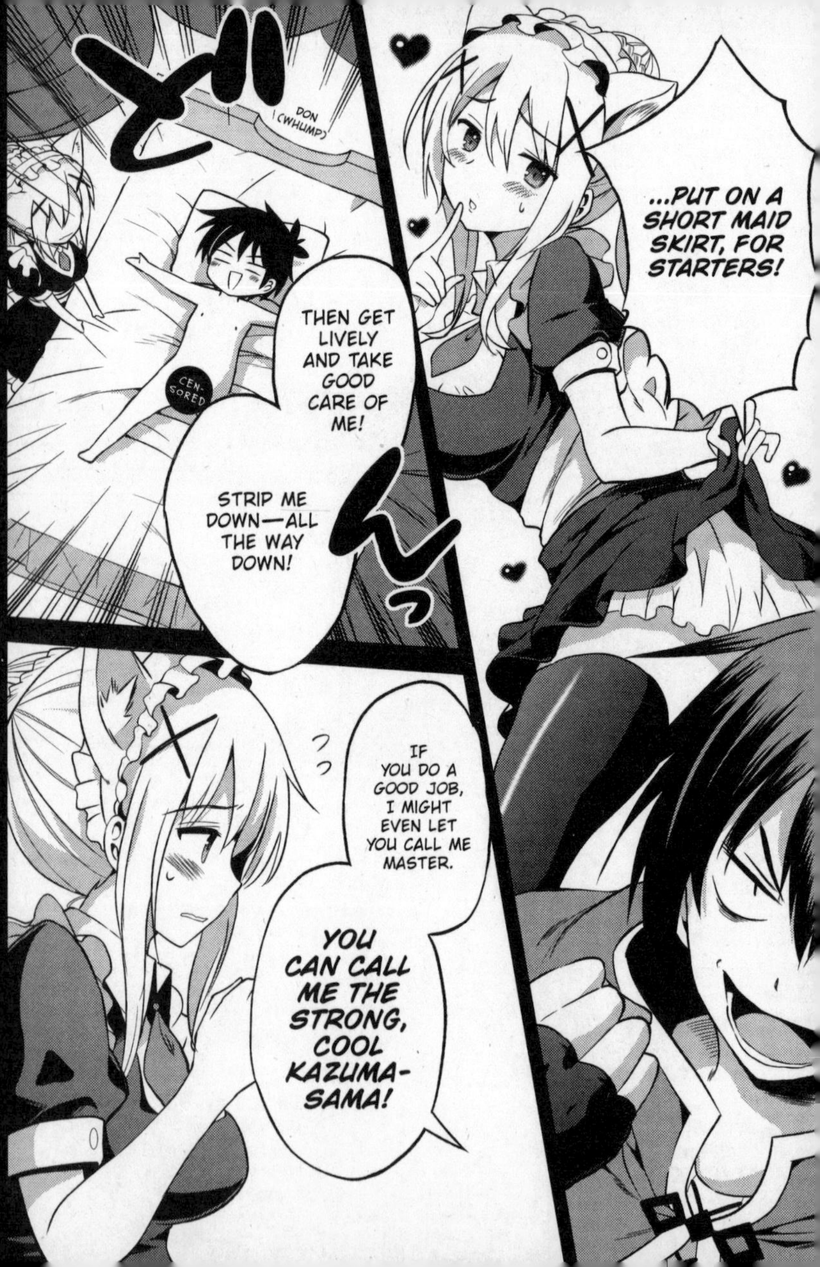
...PUT ON A SHORT MAID SKIRT, FOR STARTERS!
DON (WHUMP)
THEN GET LIVELY AND TAKE GOOD CARE OF ME!
STRIP ME DOWN—ALL THE WAY DOWN!
CEN-SORED
IF YOU DO A GOOD JOB, I MIGHT EVEN LET YOU CALL ME MASTER.
YOU CAN CALL ME THE STRONG, COOL KAZUMA-SAMA!

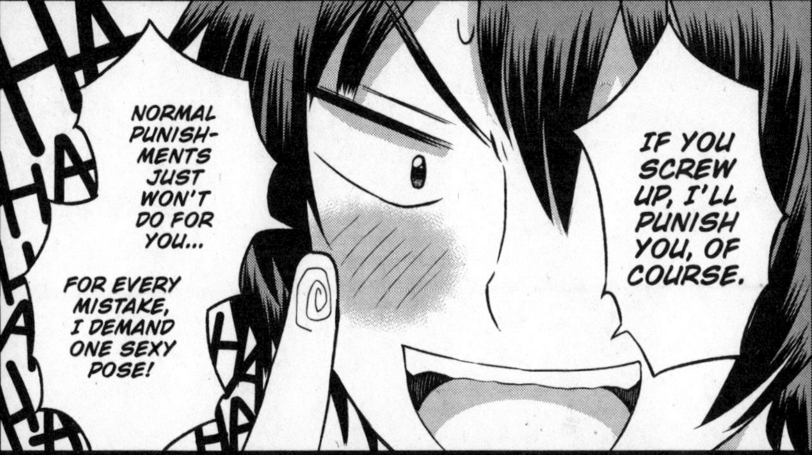
IF YOU SCREW UP, I'LL PUNISH YOU, OF COURSE.
NORMAL PUNISHMENTS JUST WON'T DO FOR YOU...
FOR EVERY MISTAKE, I DEMAND ONE SEXY POSE!
HAHAHA
HAHA
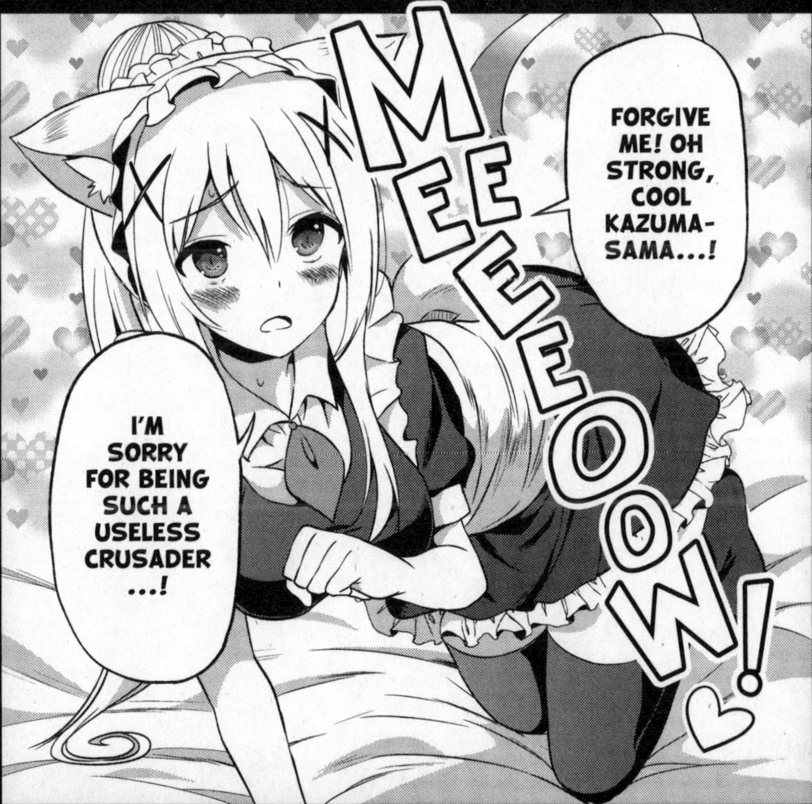
FORGIVE ME! OH STRONG, COOL KAZUMA-SAMA...!
MEEEEOOW!
I'M SORRY FOR BEING SUCH A USELESS CRUSADER ...!

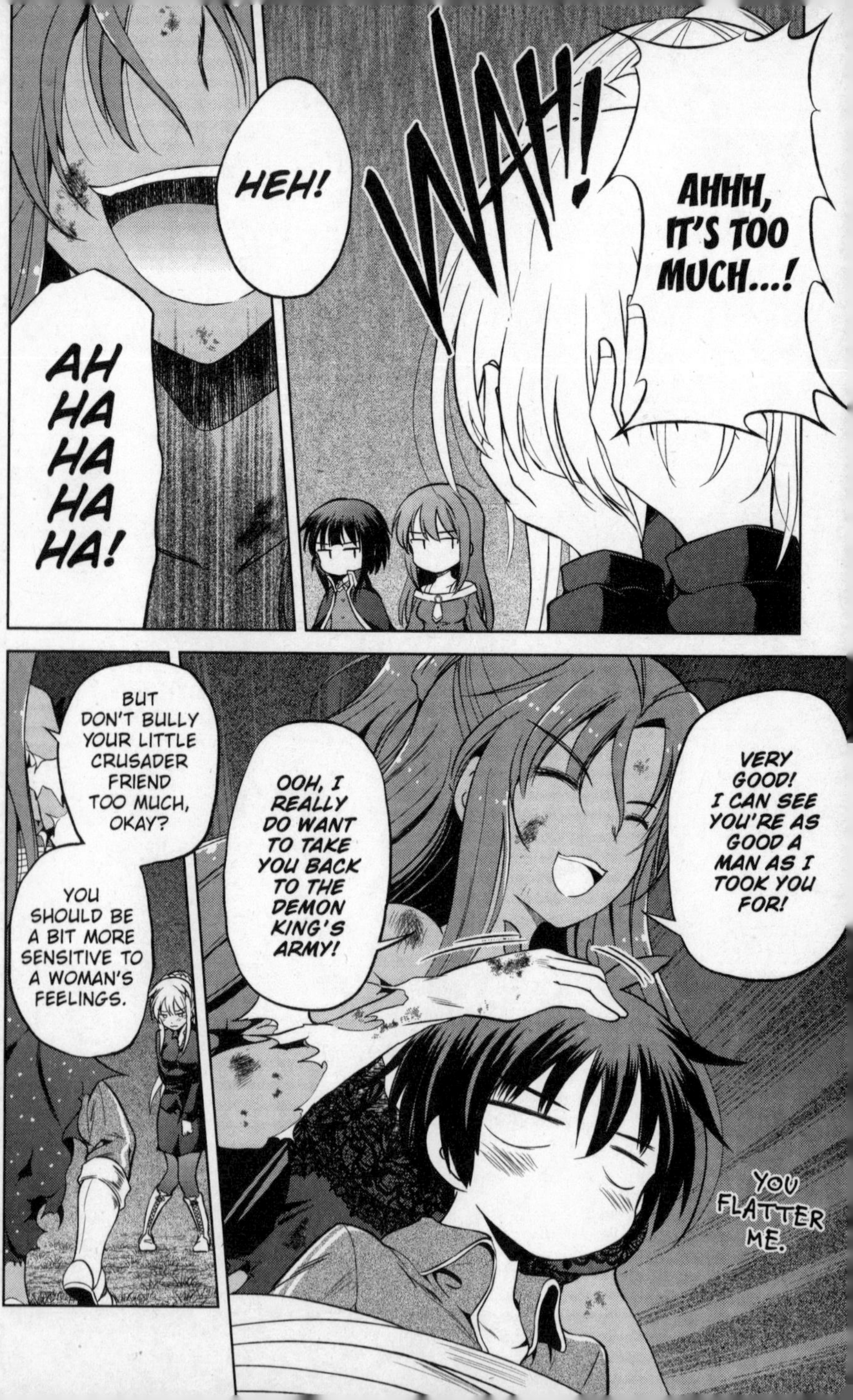
WAH!
AHHH, IT'S TOO MUCH...!
HEH!
AH HA HA HA HA HA!
VERY GOOD! I CAN SEE YOU'RE AS GOOD A MAN AS I TOOK YOU FOR!
OOH, I REALLY DO WANT TO TAKE YOU BACK TO THE DEMON KING'S ARMY!
BUT DON'T BULLY YOUR LITTLE CRUSADER FRIEND TOO MUCH, OKAY?
YOU SHOULD BE A BIT MORE SENSITIVE TO A WOMAN'S FEELINGS.
YOU FLATTER ME.

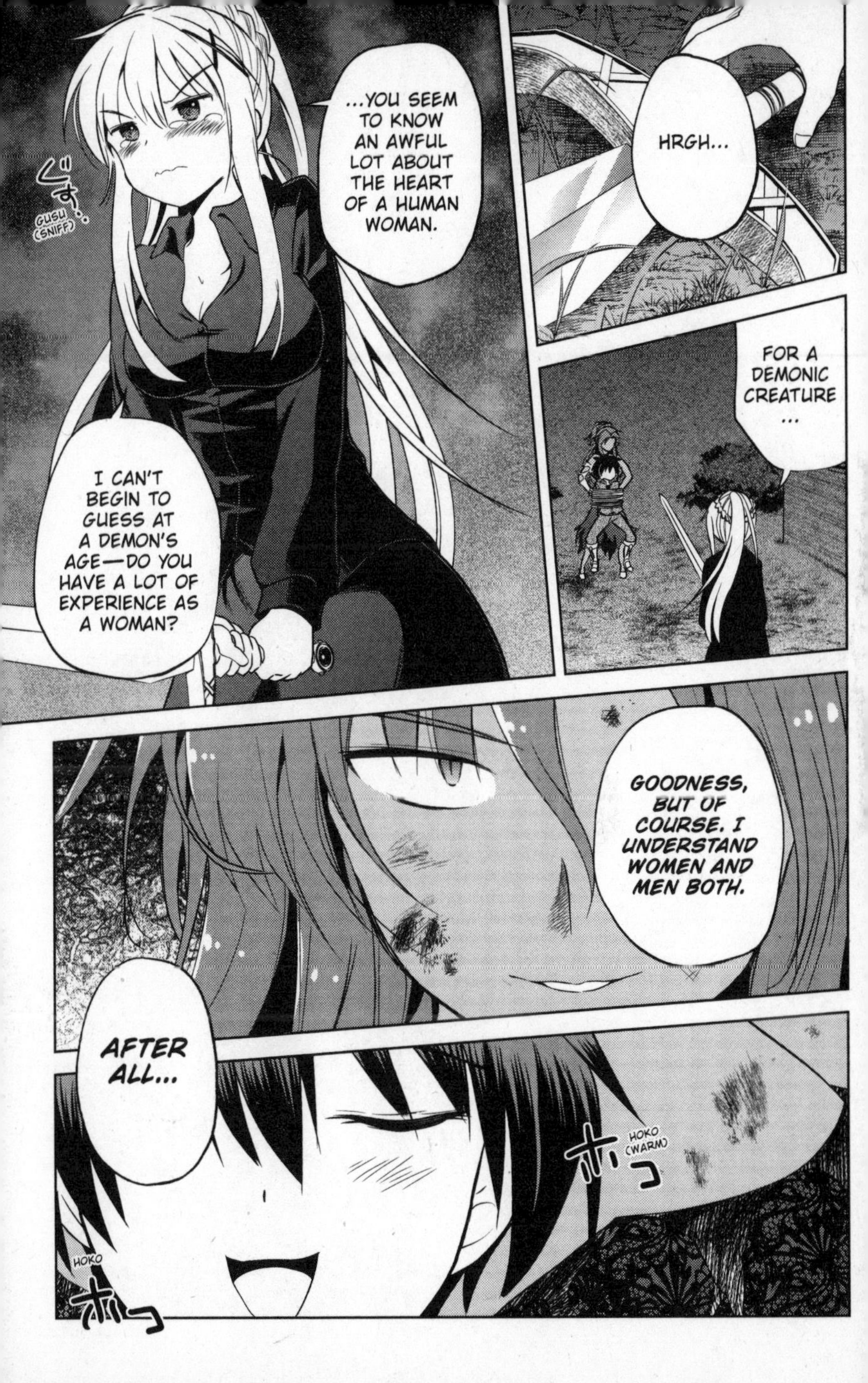
HRGH...
FOR A DEMONIC CREATURE ...
...YOU SEEM TO KNOW AN AWFUL LOT ABOUT THE HEART OF A HUMAN WOMAN.
ぐす・・
GUSU (SNIFF)
I CAN'T BEGIN TO GUESS AT A DEMON'S AGE—DO YOU HAVE A LOT OF EXPERIENCE AS A WOMAN?
GOODNESS, BUT OF COURSE. I UNDERSTAND WOMEN AND MEN BOTH.
AFTER ALL...
ホッ
HOKO (WARM)
ホッ
HOKO

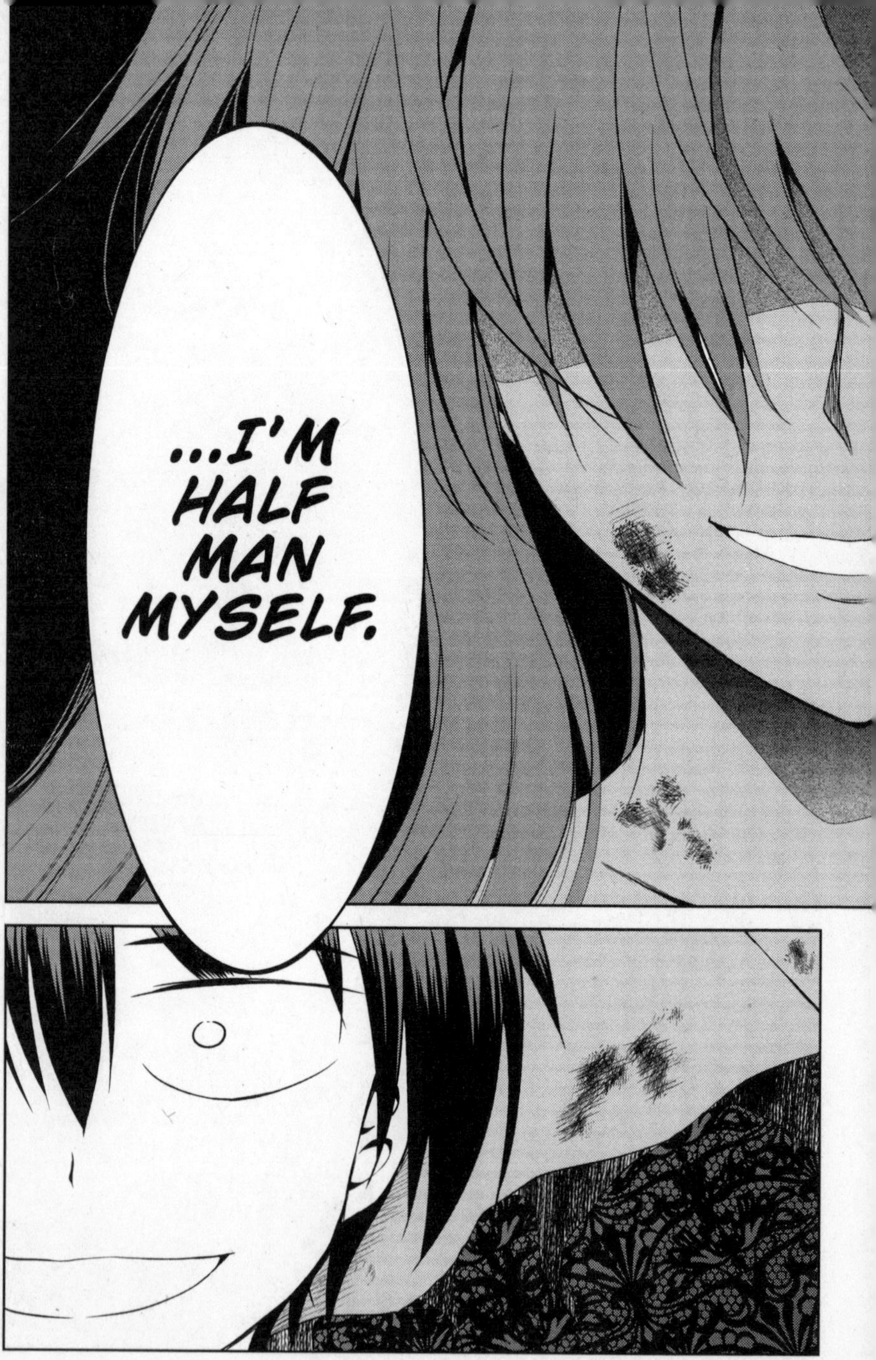
...I'M HALF MAN MYSELF.

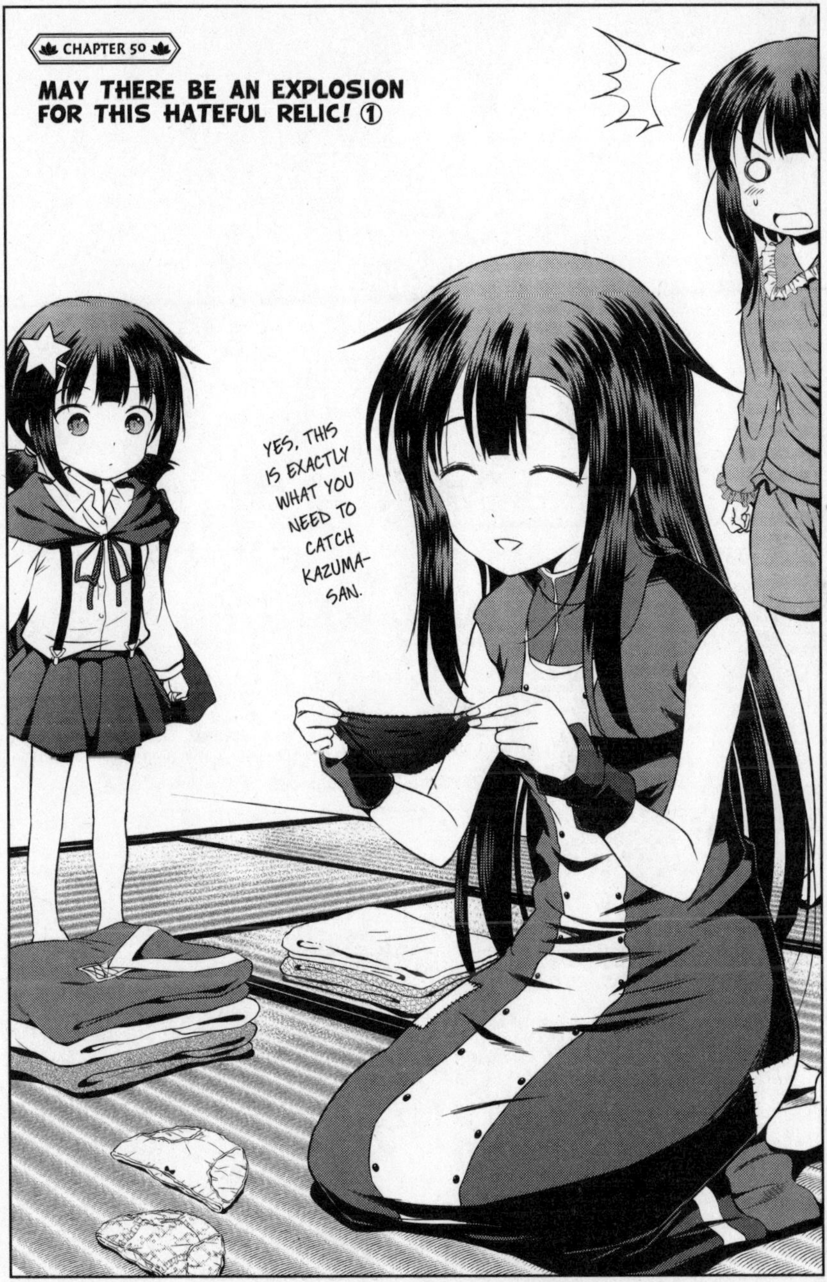
CHAPTER 50
MAY THERE BE AN EXPLOSION FOR THIS HATEFUL RELIC! ①
YES, THIS IS EXACTLY WHAT YOU NEED TO CATCH KAZUMA-SAN.

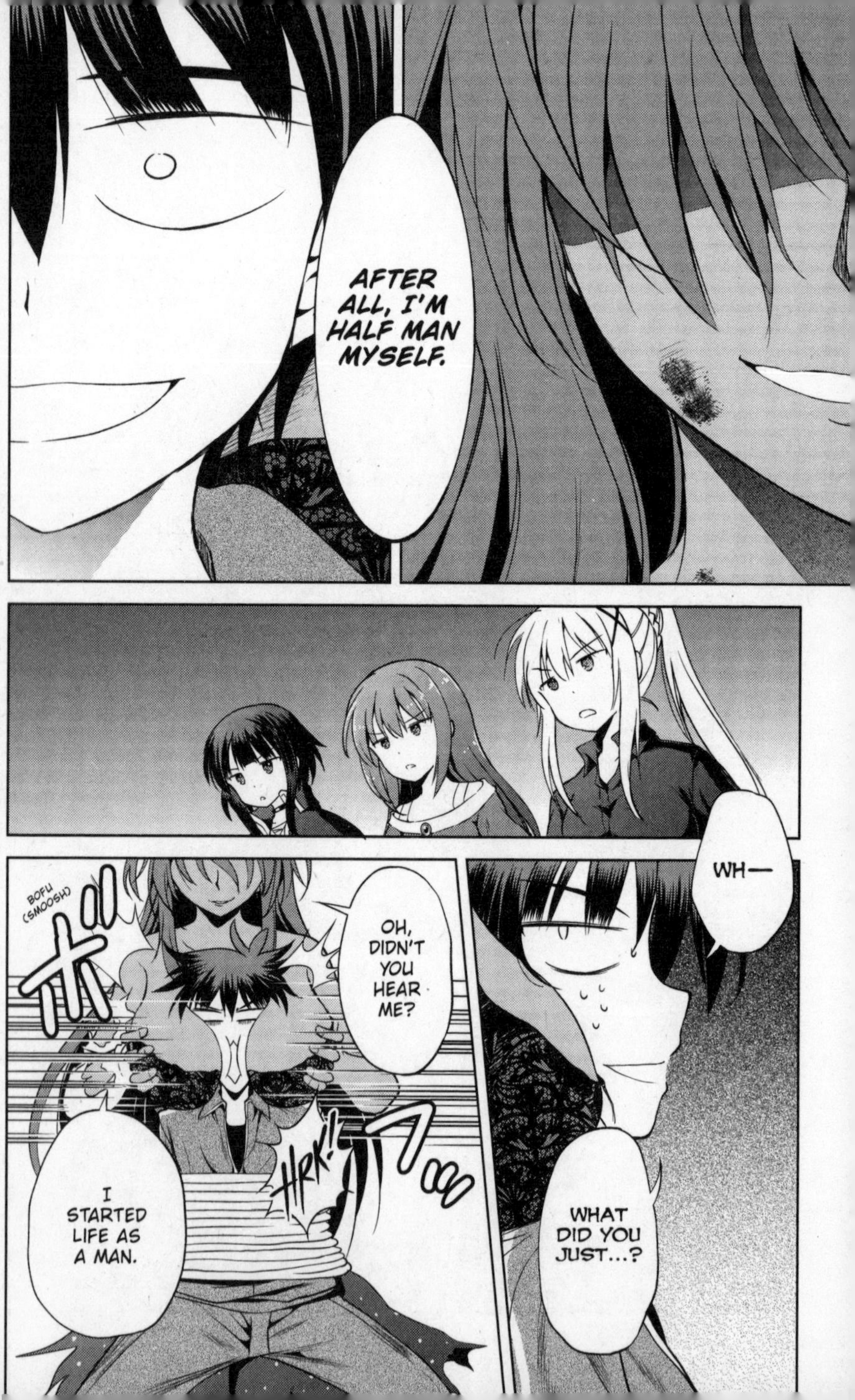
AFTER ALL, I'M HALF MAN MYSELF.
WH—
WHAT DID YOU JUST...?
OH, DIDN'T YOU HEAR ME?
BOFU (SMOOSH)
HRK!
I STARTED LIFE AS A MAN.

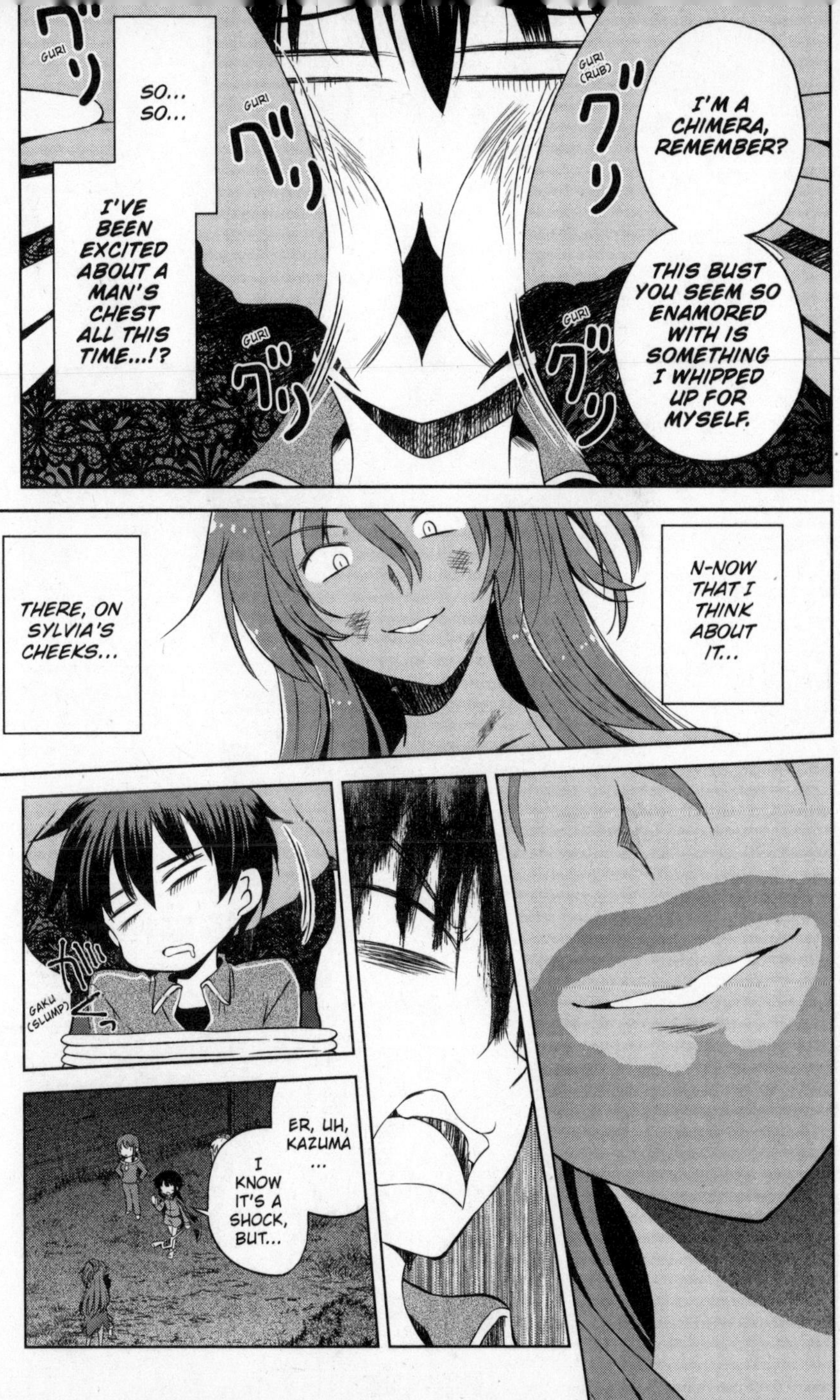
GURI (RUB)
GURI
GURI
I'M A CHIMERA, REMEMBER?
THIS BUST YOU SEEM SO ENAMORED WITH IS SOMETHING I WHIPPED UP FOR MYSELF.
GURI
GURI
GURI
SO... SO...
I'VE BEEN EXCITED ABOUT A MAN'S CHEST ALL THIS TIME...!?
N-NOW THAT I THINK ABOUT IT...
THERE, ON SYLVIA'S CHEEKS...
GAKU (SLUMP)
ER, UH, KAZUMA...
I KNOW IT'S A SHOCK, BUT...

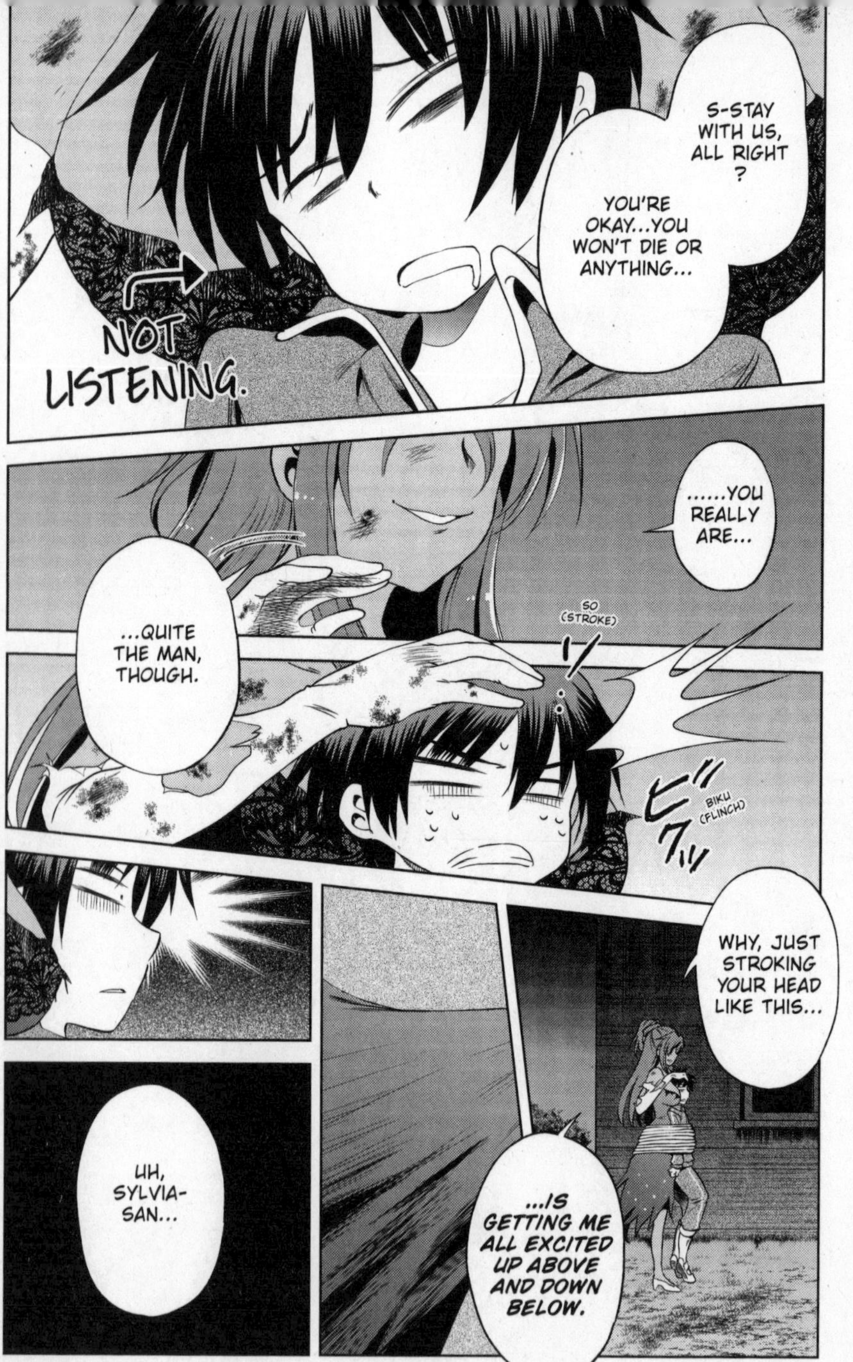
S-STAY WITH US, ALL RIGHT ?
YOU'RE OKAY...YOU WON'T DIE OR ANYTHING...
NOT LISTENING.
......YOU REALLY ARE...
...QUITE THE MAN, THOUGH.
SO (STROKE)
BIKU (FLINCH)
WHY, JUST STROKING YOUR HEAD LIKE THIS...
...IS GETTING ME ALL EXCITED UP ABOVE AND DOWN BELOW.
UH, SYLVIA-SAN...

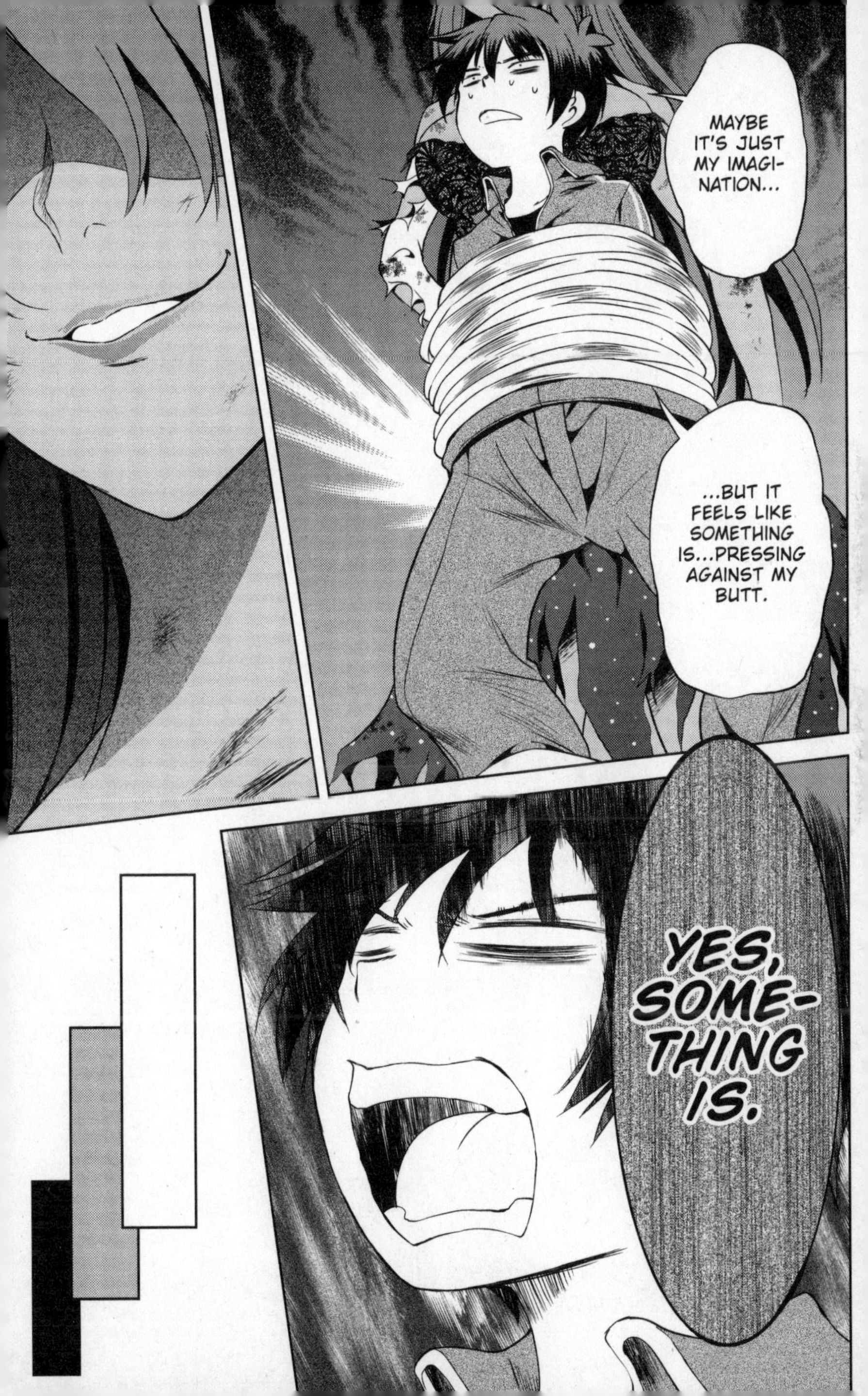
MAYBE IT'S JUST MY IMAGI-NATION...
...BUT IT FEELS LIKE SOMETHING IS...PRESSING AGAINST MY BUTT.
YES, SOME-THING IS.

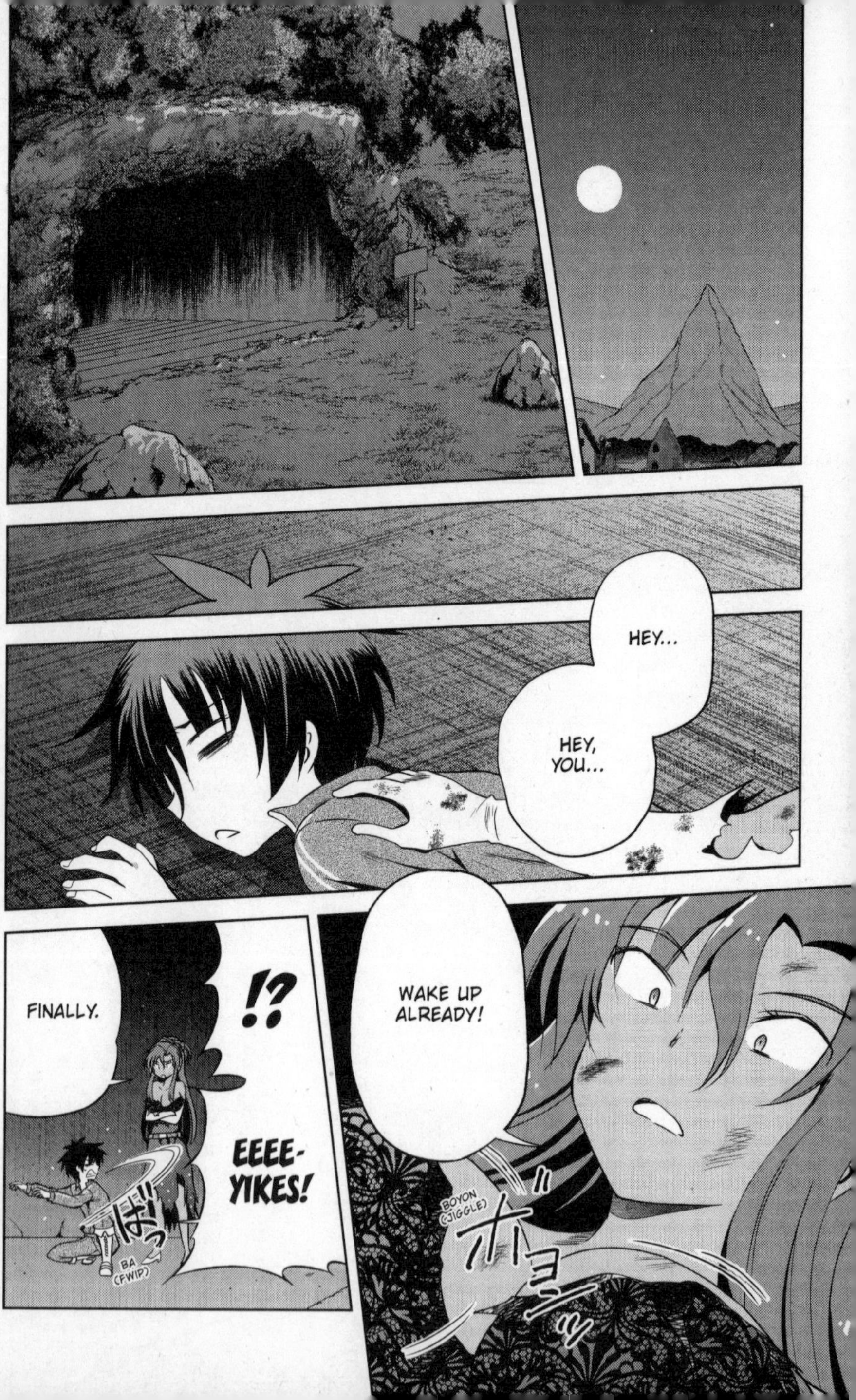
HEY...
HEY, YOU...
WAKE UP ALREADY!
BOYON (JIGGLE)
!?
FINALLY.
EEEE-YIKES!
BA (FWIP)

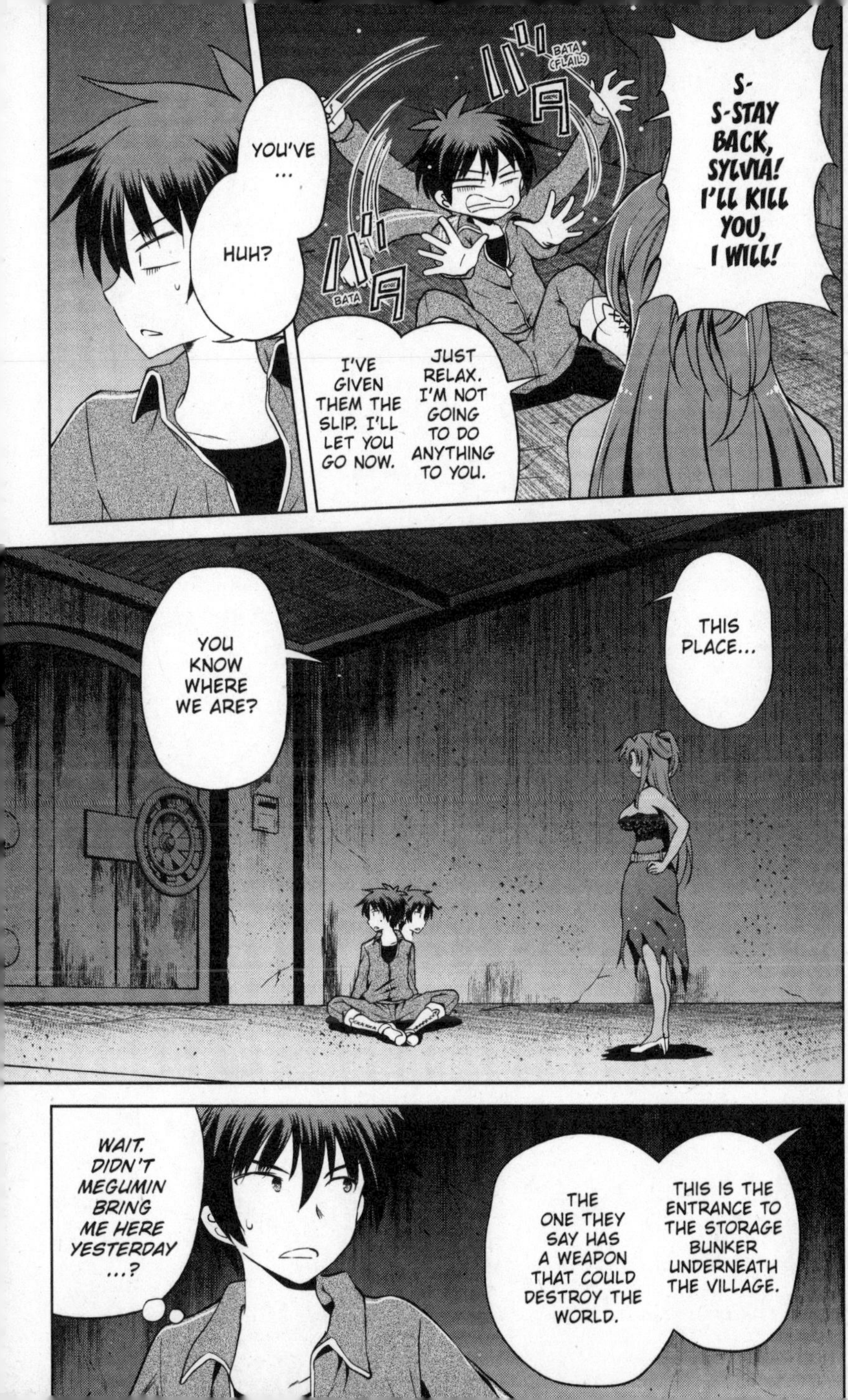
S-S-STAY BACK, SYLVIA! I'LL KILL YOU, I WILL!
BATA (FLAIL)
BATA
JUST RELAX. I'M NOT GOING TO DO ANYTHING TO YOU.
I'VE GIVEN THEM THE SLIP. I'LL LET YOU GO NOW.
YOU'VE ...
HUH?
THIS PLACE...
YOU KNOW WHERE WE ARE?
THIS IS THE ENTRANCE TO THE STORAGE BUNKER UNDERNEATH THE VILLAGE.
THE ONE THEY SAY HAS A WEAPON THAT COULD DESTROY THE WORLD.
WAIT. DIDN'T MEGUMIN BRING ME HERE YESTERDAY ...?

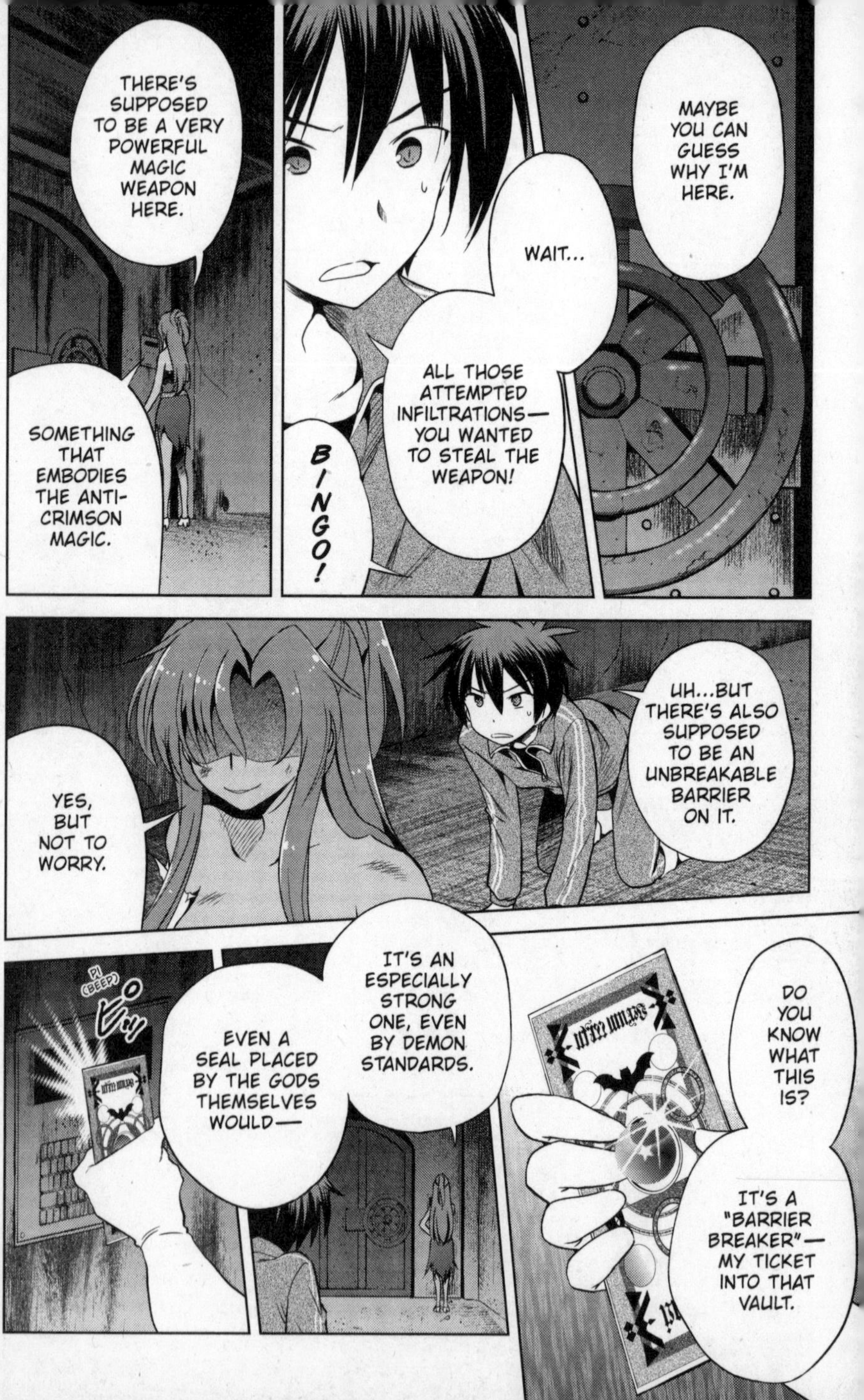
MAYBE YOU CAN GUESS WHY I'M HERE.
WAIT...
ALL THOSE ATTEMPTED INFILTRATIONS—YOU WANTED TO STEAL THE WEAPON!
BINGO!
THERE'S SUPPOSED TO BE A VERY POWERFUL MAGIC WEAPON HERE.
SOMETHING THAT EMBODIES THE ANTI-CRIMSON MAGIC.
UH...BUT THERE'S ALSO SUPPOSED TO BE AN UNBREAKABLE BARRIER ON IT.
YES, BUT NOT TO WORRY.
DO YOU KNOW WHAT THIS IS?
IT'S A "BARRIER BREAKER"—MY TICKET INTO THAT VAULT.
IT'S AN ESPECIALLY STRONG ONE, EVEN BY DEMON STANDARDS.
EVEN A SEAL PLACED BY THE GODS THEMSELVES WOULD—
PI (BEEP)

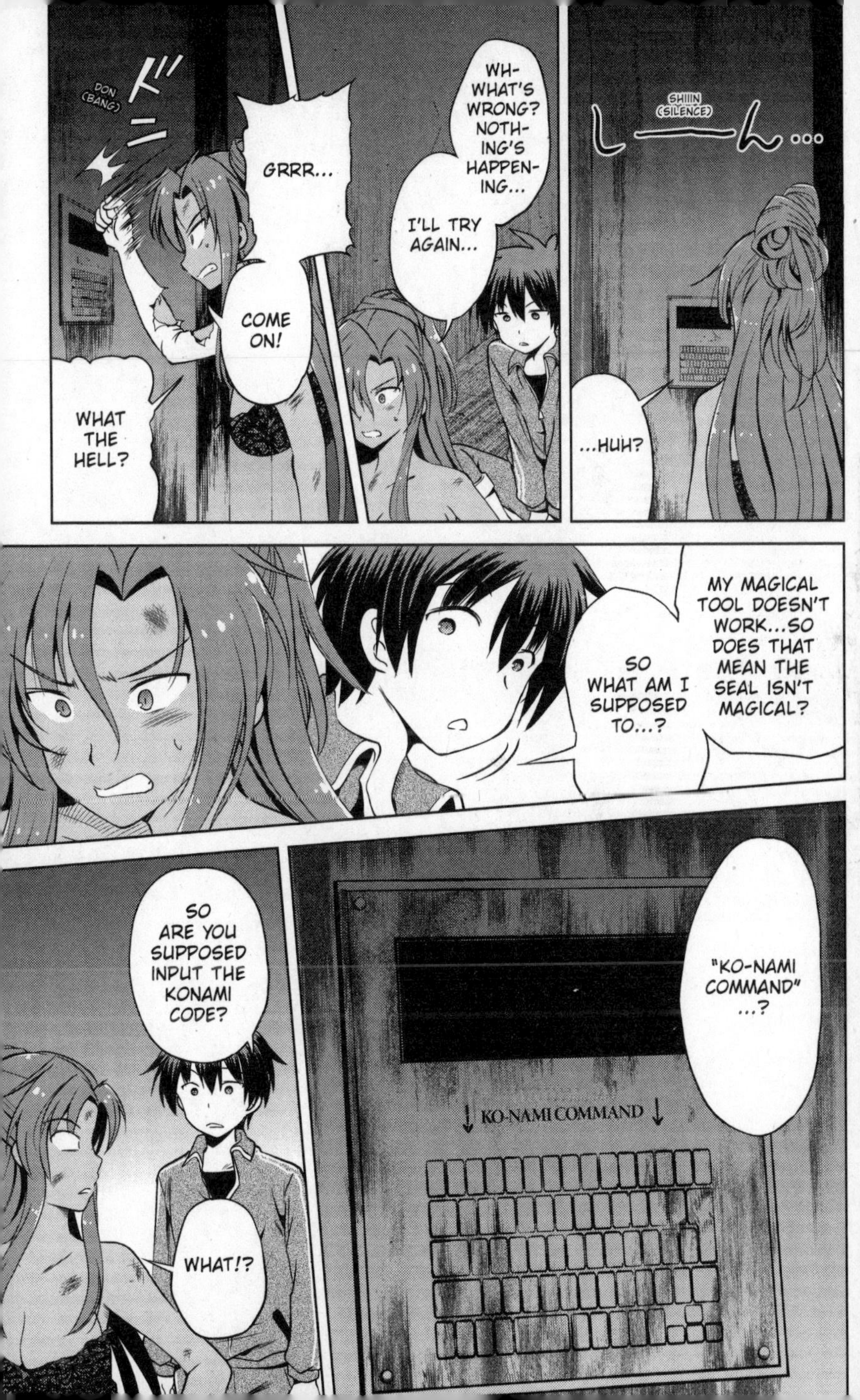
SHIIN (SILENCE)
...HUH?
WH-WHAT'S WRONG? NOTHING'S HAPPENING...
I'LL TRY AGAIN...
DON (BANG)
GRRR...
COME ON!
WHAT THE HELL?
MY MAGICAL TOOL DOESN'T WORK...SO DOES THAT MEAN THE SEAL ISN'T MAGICAL?
SO WHAT AM I SUPPOSED TO...?
"KO-NAMI COMMAND" ...?
↓ KO-NAMI COMMAND ↓
SO ARE YOU SUPPOSED INPUT THE KONAMI CODE?
WHAT!?

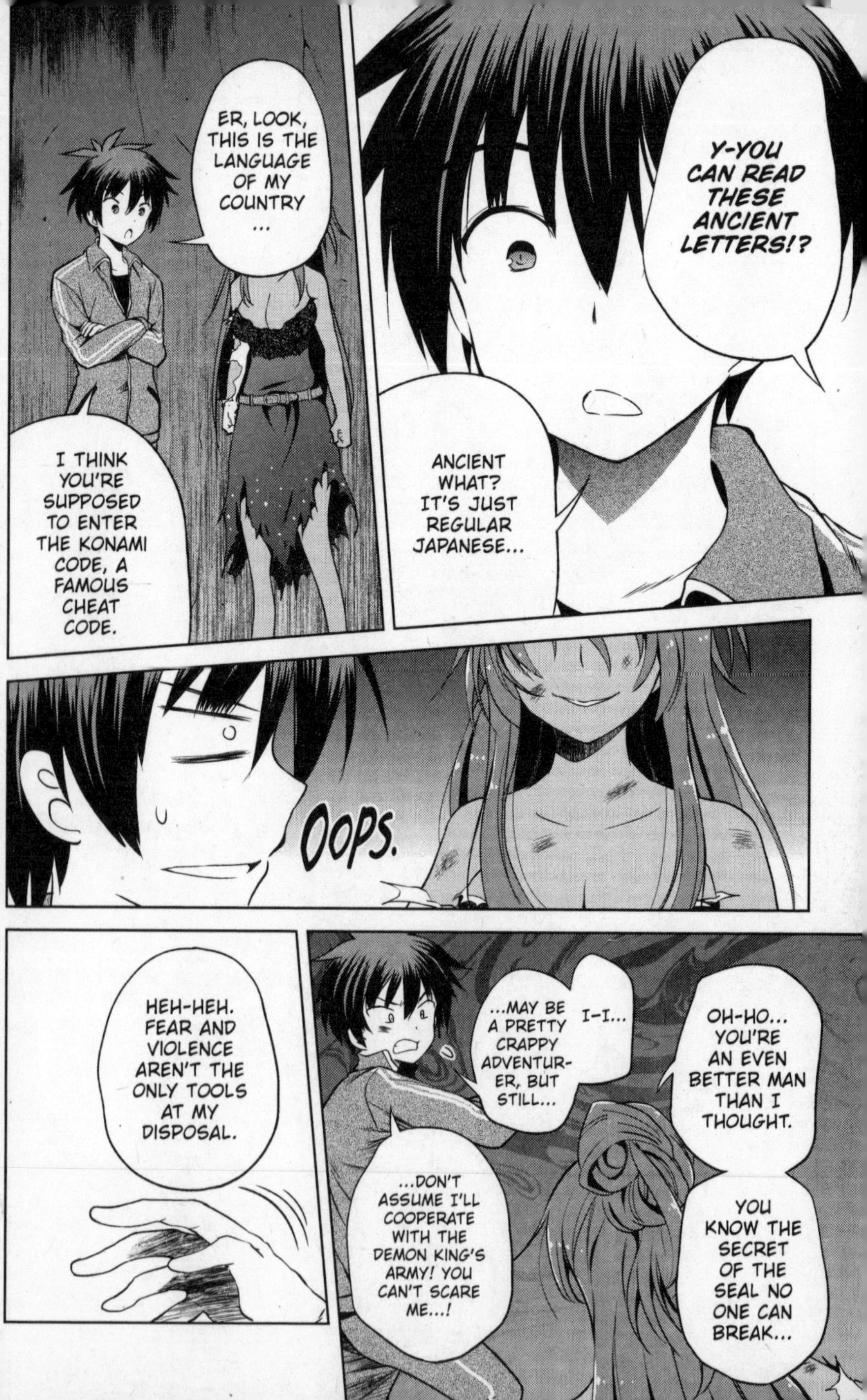
Y-YOU CAN READ THESE ANCIENT LETTERS!?
ANCIENT WHAT? IT'S JUST REGULAR JAPANESE...
ER, LOOK, THIS IS THE LANGUAGE OF MY COUNTRY...
I THINK YOU'RE SUPPOSED TO ENTER THE KONAMI CODE, A FAMOUS CHEAT CODE.
OOPS.
OH-HO... YOU'RE AN EVEN BETTER MAN THAN I THOUGHT.
YOU KNOW THE SECRET OF THE SEAL NO ONE CAN BREAK...
I-I...
...MAY BE A PRETTY CRAPPY ADVENTURER, BUT STILL...
...DON'T ASSUME I'LL COOPERATE WITH THE DEMON KING'S ARMY! YOU CAN'T SCARE ME...!
HEH-HEH. FEAR AND VIOLENCE AREN'T THE ONLY TOOLS AT MY DISPOSAL.

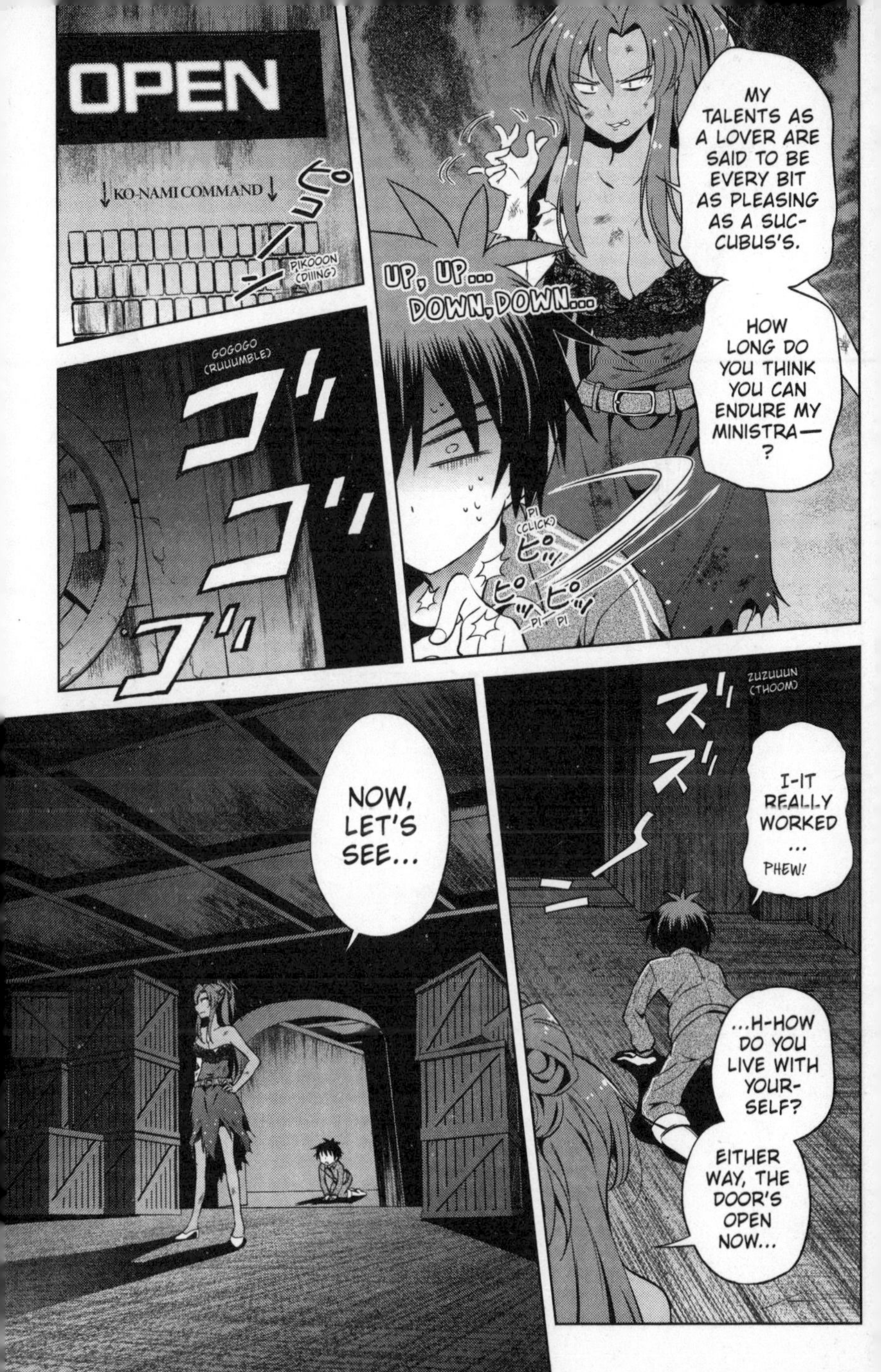
MY TALENTS AS A LOVER ARE SAID TO BE EVERY BIT AS PLEASING AS A SUC-CUBUS'S.
UP, UP... DOWN, DOWN...
HOW LONG DO YOU THINK YOU CAN ENDURE MY MINISTRA—?
PI (CLICK)
PI PI
OPEN
↓KO-NAMI COMMAND↓
PIKOOON (DIIING)
GOGOGO (RUUUMBLE)
ZUZUUUN (THOOM)
I-IT REALLY WORKED... PHEW!
...H-HOW DO YOU LIVE WITH YOUR-SELF?
EITHER WAY, THE DOOR'S OPEN NOW...
NOW, LET'S SEE...

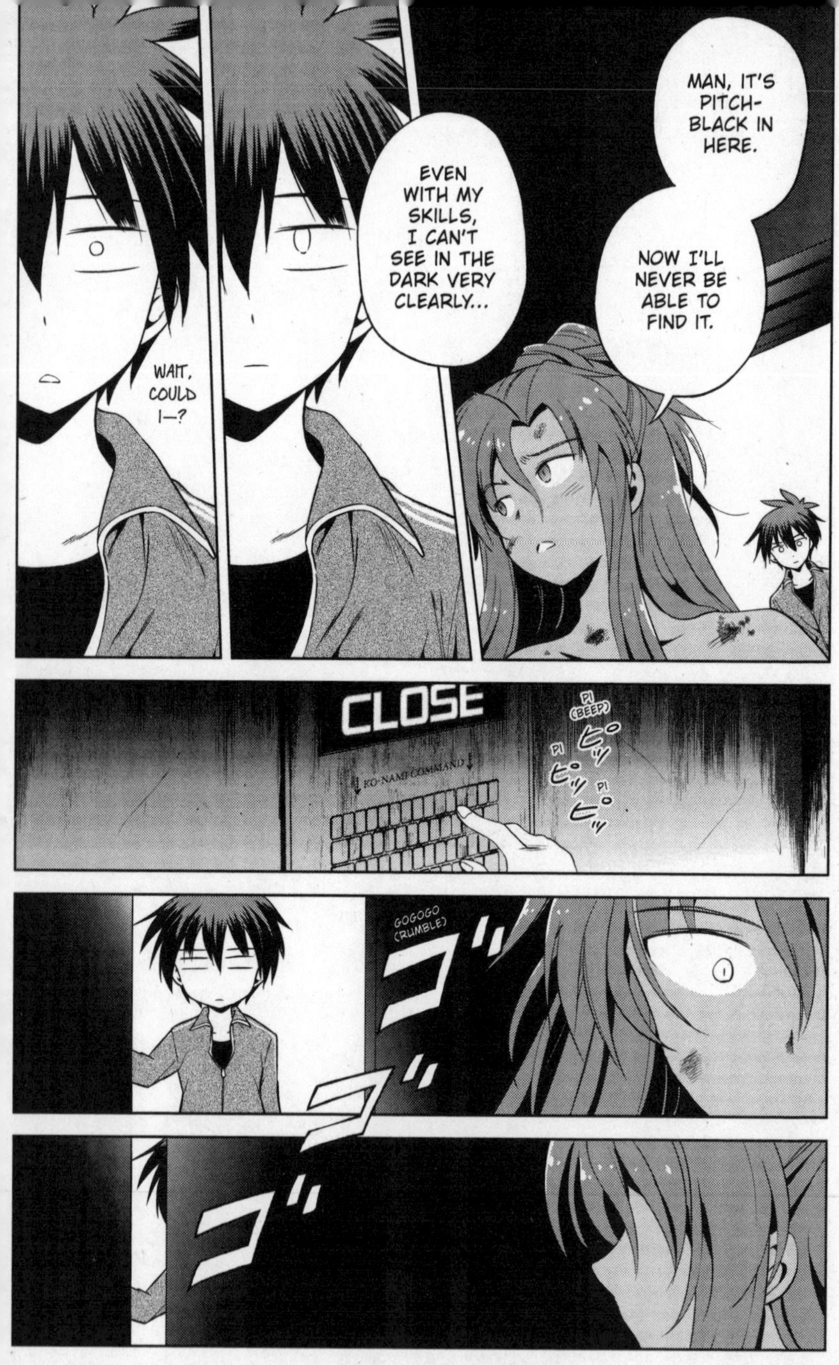
MAN, IT'S PITCH-BLACK IN HERE.
NOW I'LL NEVER BE ABLE TO FIND IT.
EVEN WITH MY SKILLS, I CAN'T SEE IN THE DARK VERY CLEARLY...
WAIT, COULD I—?
CLOSE
KO-NAMI COMMAND
PI (BEEP)
PI
PI
GOGOGO (RUMBLE)

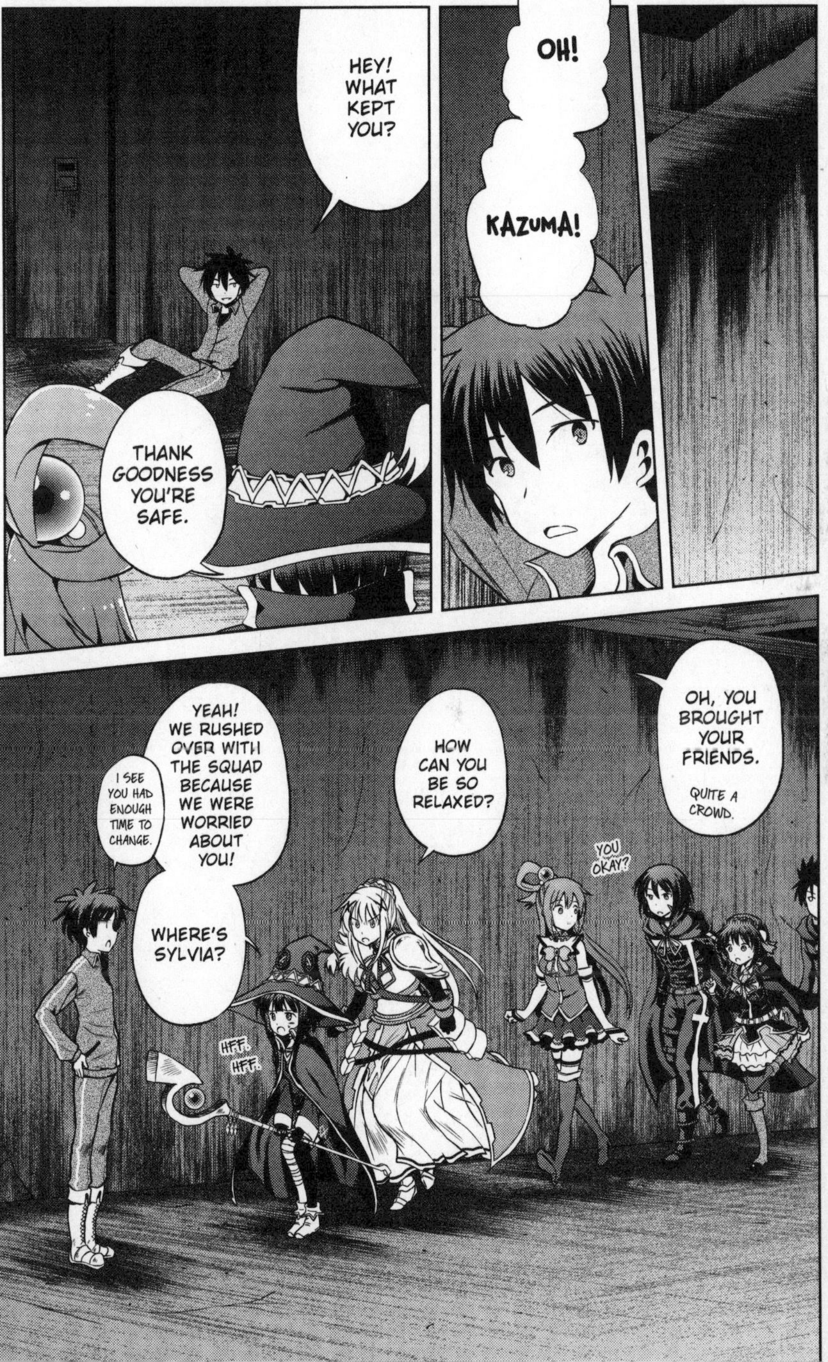
OH!
KAZUMA!
HEY! WHAT KEPT YOU?
THANK GOODNESS YOU'RE SAFE.
OH, YOU BROUGHT YOUR FRIENDS.
QUITE A CROWD.
YOU OKAY?
HOW CAN YOU BE SO RELAXED?
YEAH! WE RUSHED OVER WITH THE SQUAD BECAUSE WE WERE WORRIED ABOUT YOU!
I SEE YOU HAD ENOUGH TIME TO CHANGE.
WHERE'S SYLVIA?
HFF. HFF.

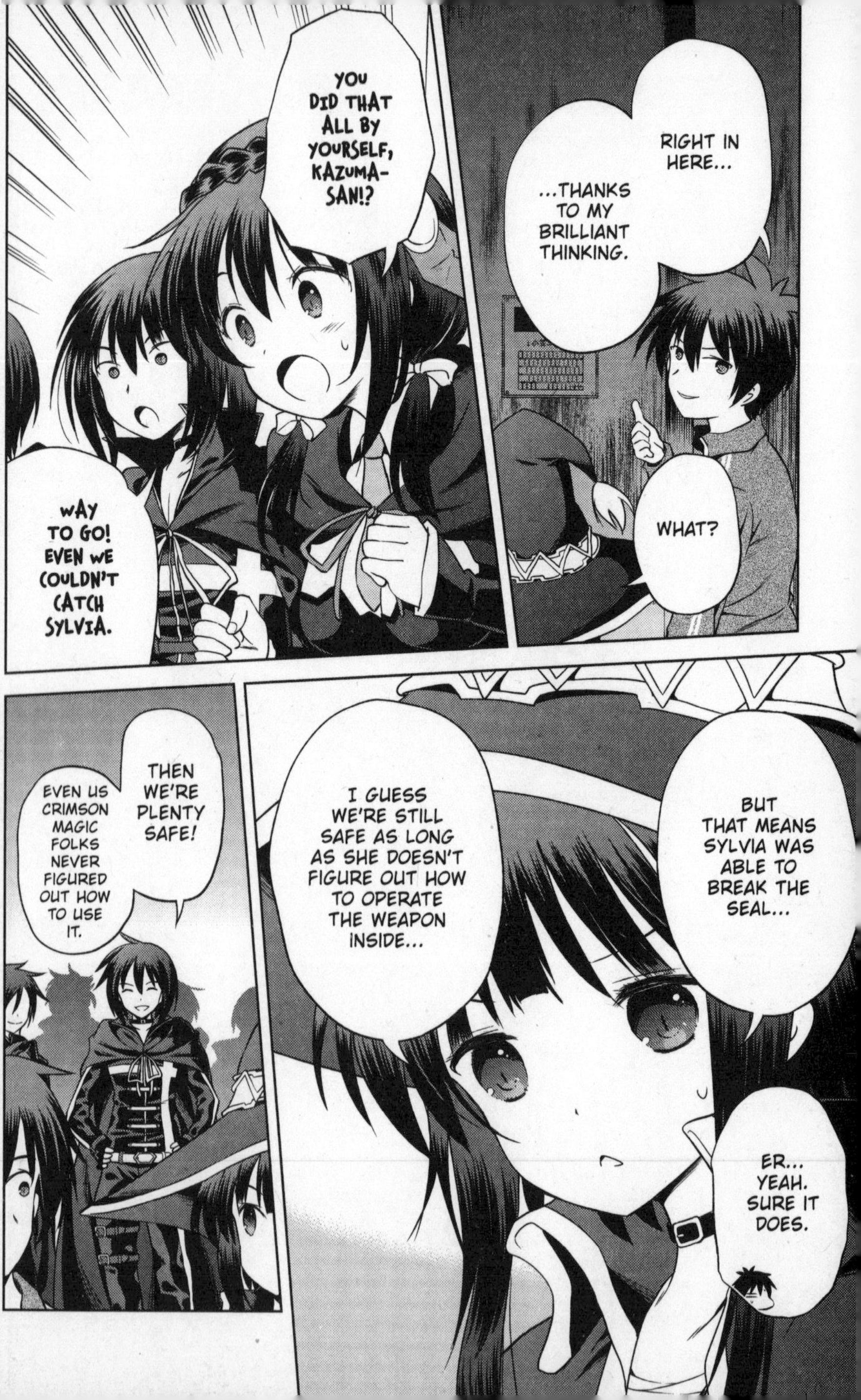
RIGHT IN HERE...
...THANKS TO MY BRILLIANT THINKING.
WHAT?
YOU DID THAT ALL BY YOURSELF, KAZUMA-SAN!?
WAY TO GO! EVEN WE COULDN'T CATCH SYLVIA.
BUT THAT MEANS SYLVIA WAS ABLE TO BREAK THE SEAL...
I GUESS WE'RE STILL SAFE AS LONG AS SHE DOESN'T FIGURE OUT HOW TO OPERATE THE WEAPON INSIDE...
ER... YEAH. SURE IT DOES.
THEN WE'RE PLENTY SAFE!
EVEN US CRIMSON MAGIC FOLKS NEVER FIGURED OUT HOW TO USE IT.

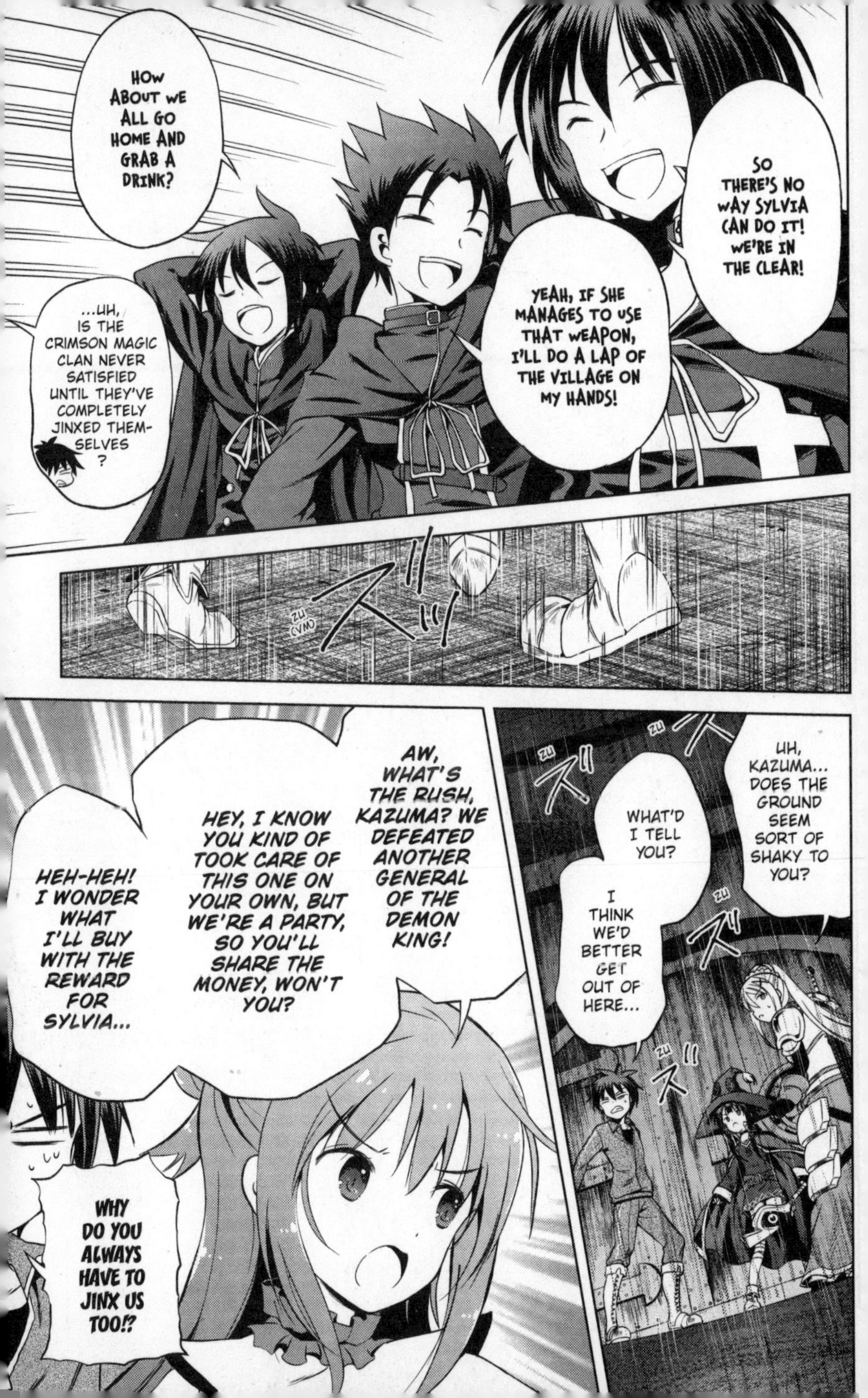
SO THERE'S NO WAY SYLVIA CAN DO IT! WE'RE IN THE CLEAR!
YEAH, IF SHE MANAGES TO USE THAT WEAPON, I'LL DO A LAP OF THE VILLAGE ON MY HANDS!
HOW ABOUT WE ALL GO HOME AND GRAB A DRINK?
...UH, IS THE CRIMSON MAGIC CLAN NEVER SATISFIED UNTIL THEY'VE COMPLETELY JINXED THEM-SELVES?
ZU (VM)
ZU
ZU
UH, KAZUMA... DOES THE GROUND SEEM SORT OF SHAKY TO YOU?
WHAT'D I TELL YOU?
I THINK WE'D BETTER GET OUT OF HERE...
ZU
ZU
AW, WHAT'S THE RUSH, KAZUMA? WE DEFEATED ANOTHER GENERAL OF THE DEMON KING!
HEY, I KNOW YOU KIND OF TOOK CARE OF THIS ONE ON YOUR OWN, BUT WE'RE A PARTY, SO YOU'LL SHARE THE MONEY, WON'T YOU?
HEH-HEH! I WONDER WHAT I'LL BUY WITH THE REWARD FOR SYLVIA...
WHY DO YOU ALWAYS HAVE TO JINX US TOO!?

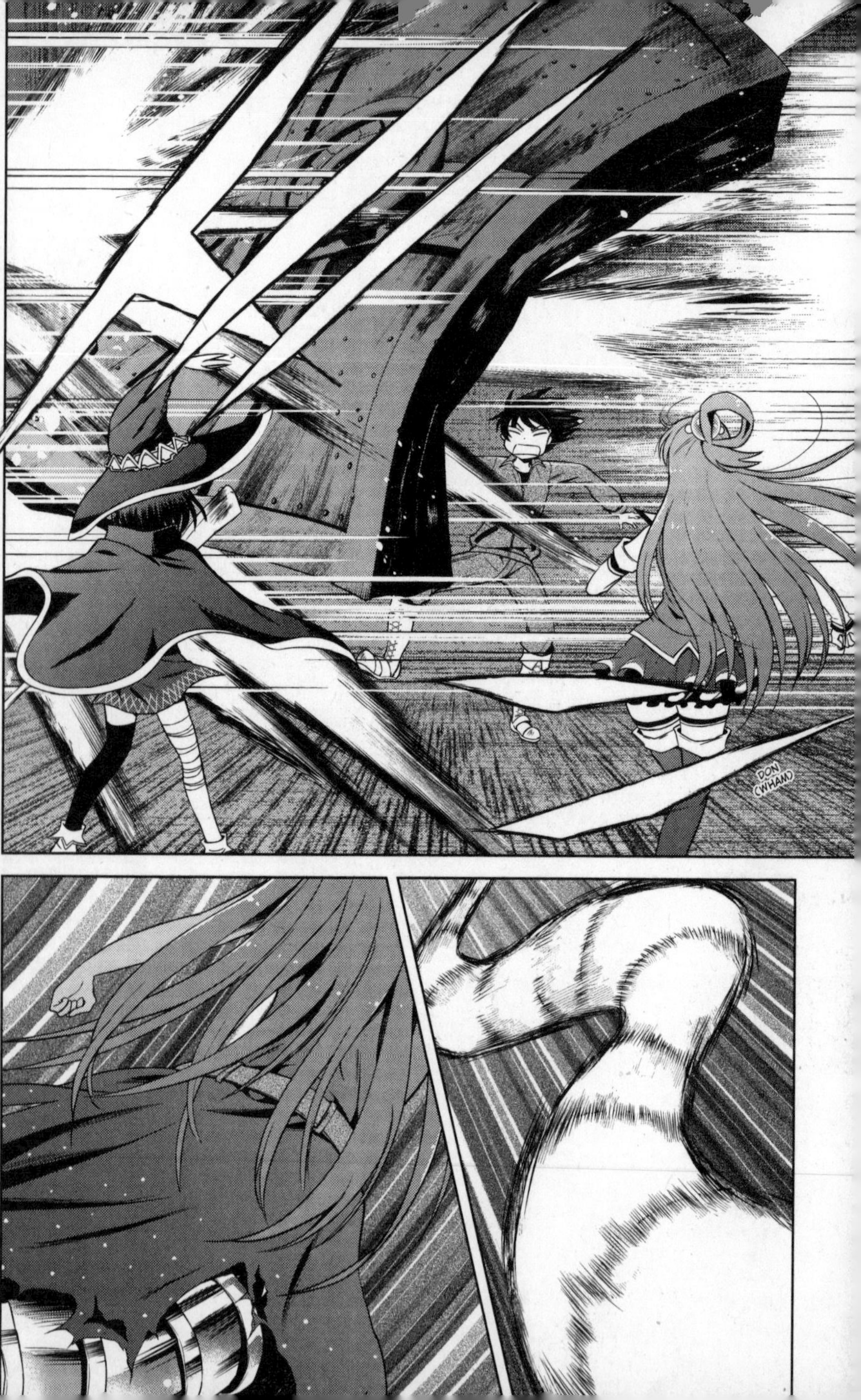
DON
(WHAM)

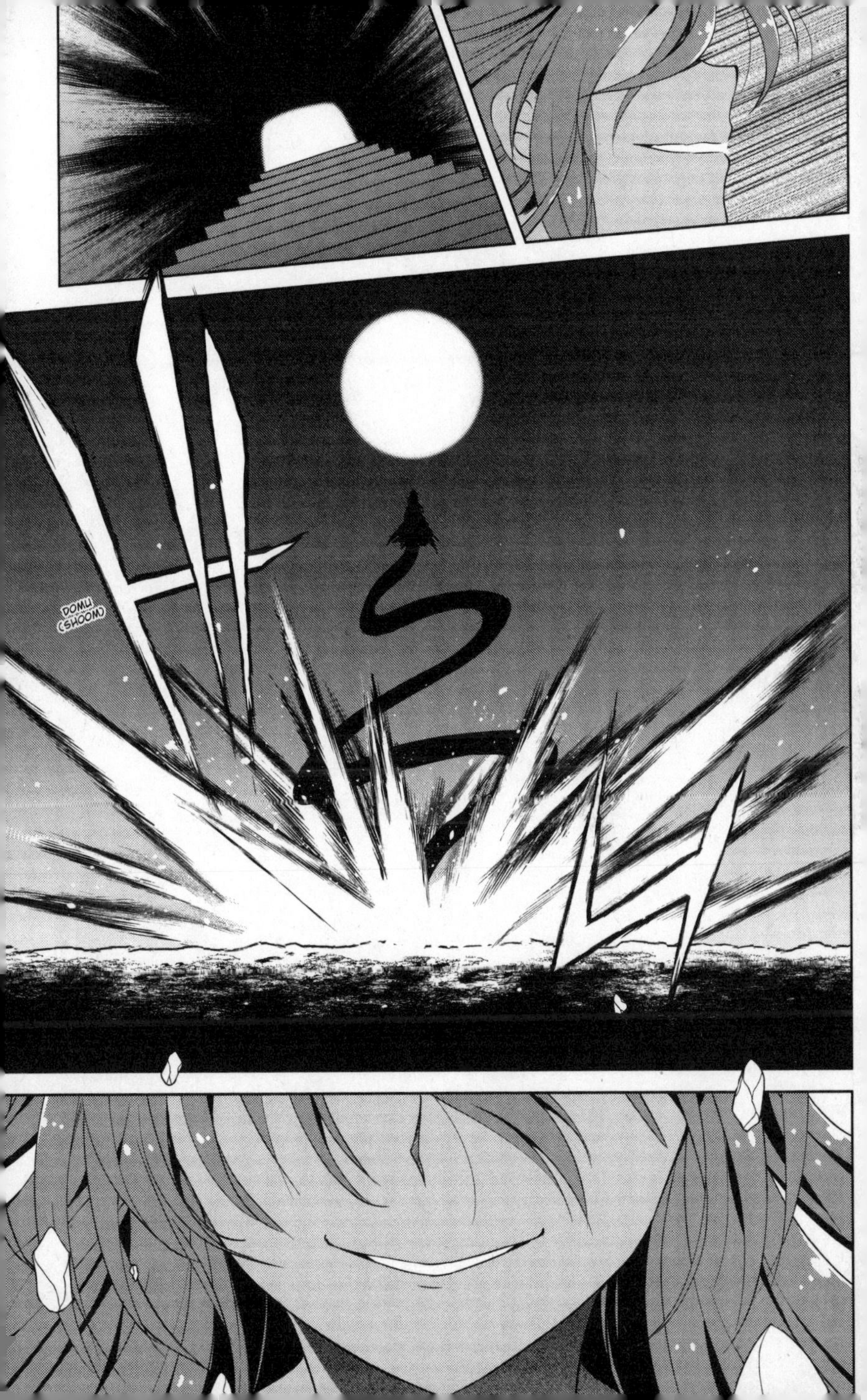
DOMU
(SHOOM)

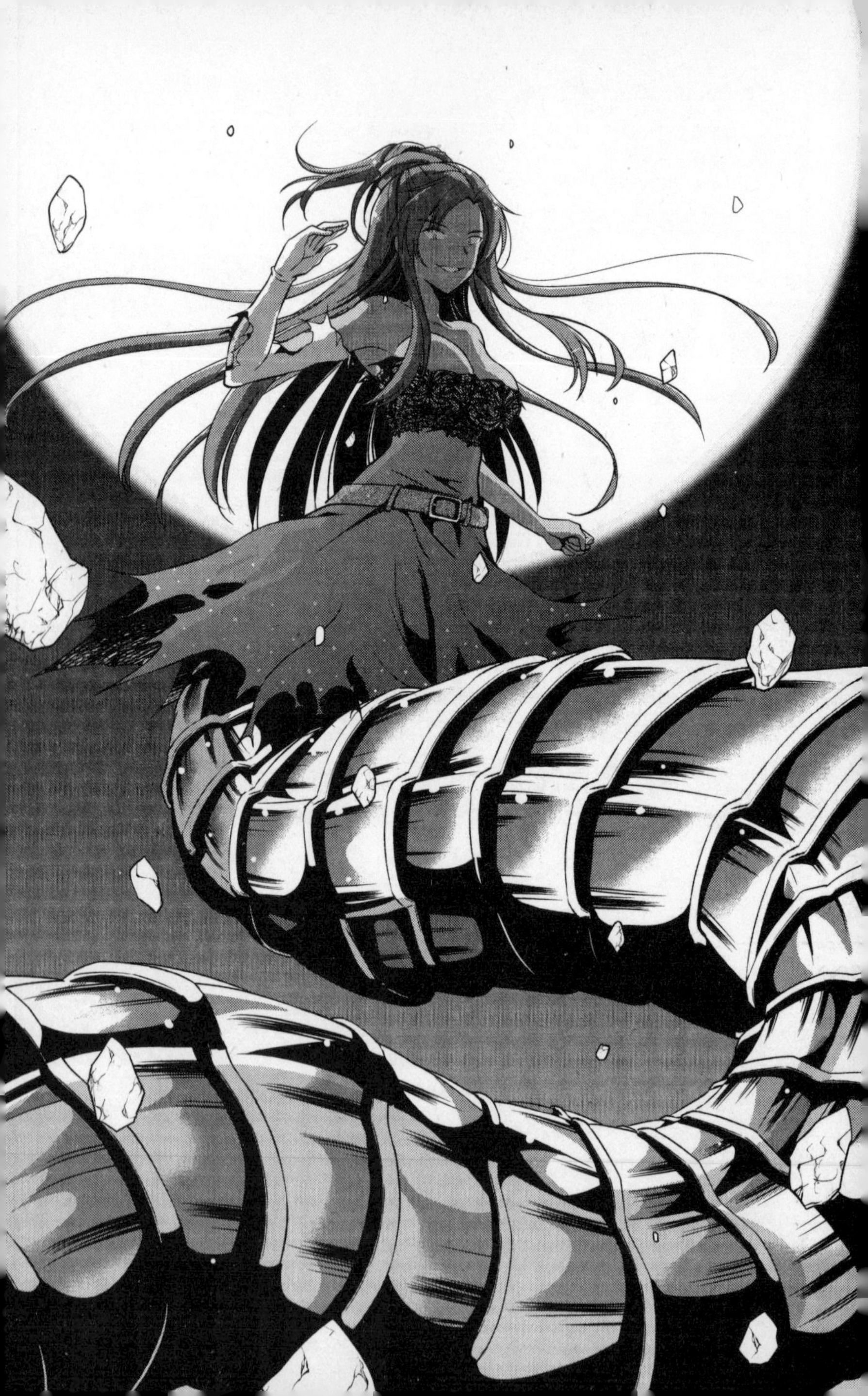

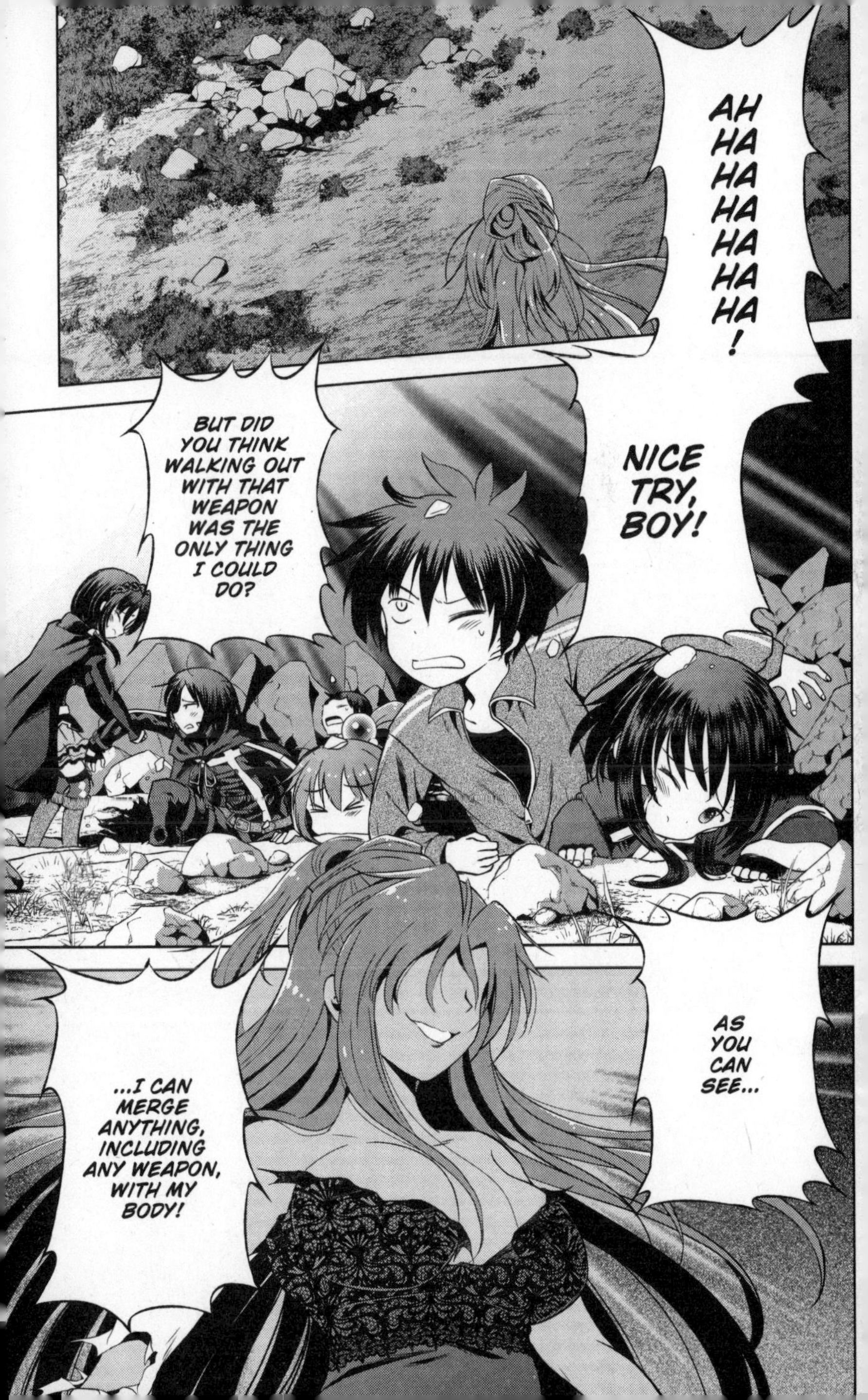

AH HA HA HA HA HA HA!
NICE TRY, BOY!
BUT DID YOU THINK WALKING OUT WITH THAT WEAPON WAS THE ONLY THING I COULD DO?
AS YOU CAN SEE...
...I CAN MERGE ANYTHING, INCLUDING ANY WEAPON, WITH MY BODY!

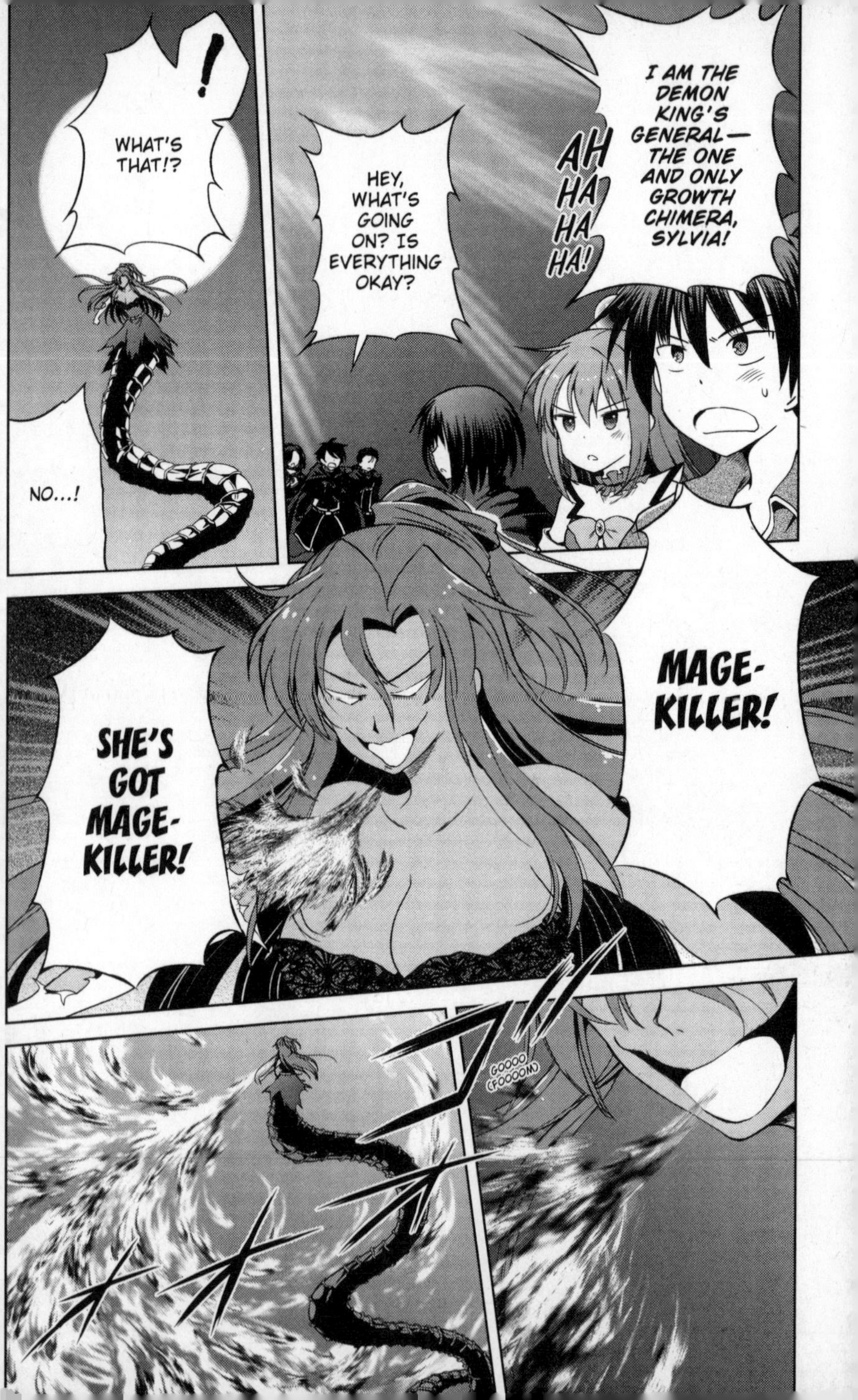

AH HA HA HA!
I AM THE DEMON KING'S GENERAL— THE ONE AND ONLY GROWTH CHIMERA, SYLVIA!
HEY, WHAT'S GOING ON? IS EVERYTHING OKAY?
!
WHAT'S THAT!?
NO...!
MAGE-KILLER!
SHE'S GOT MAGE-KILLER!
GOOOO (FOOOOM)

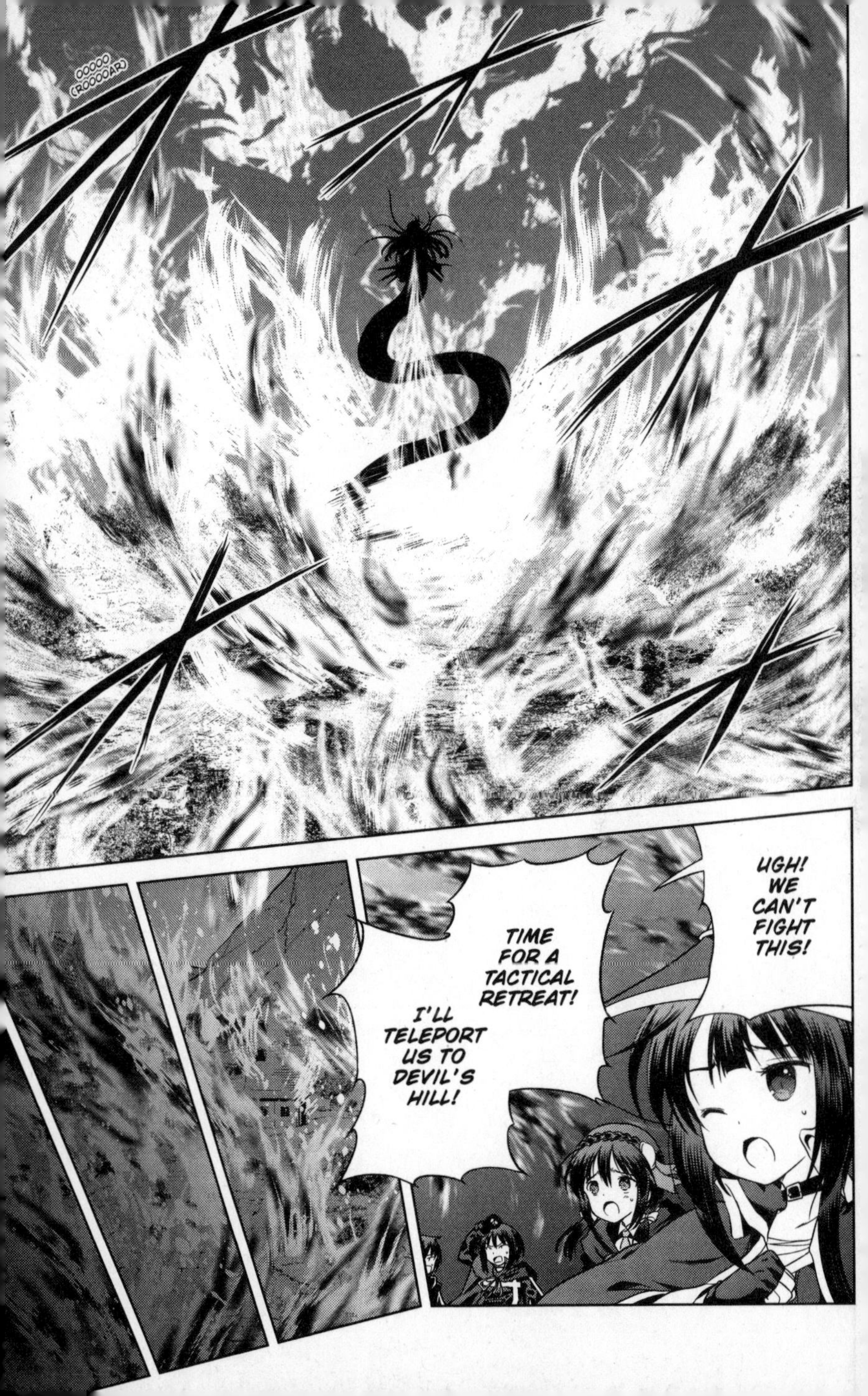
OOOOO (ROOOOAR)
UGH! WE CAN'T FIGHT THIS!
TIME FOR A TACTICAL RETREAT!
I'LL TELEPORT US TO DEVIL'S HILL!

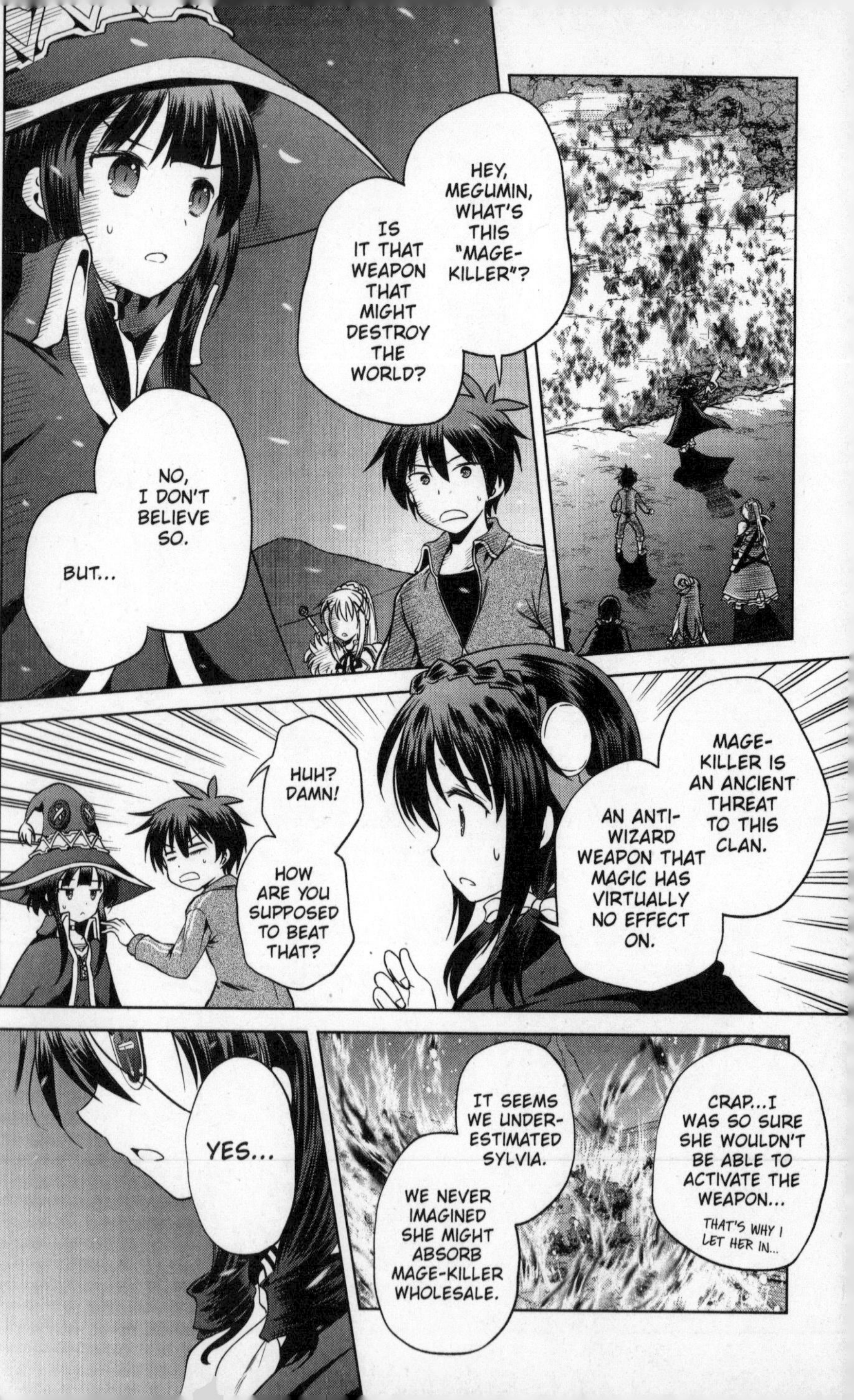
HEY, MEGUMIN, WHAT'S THIS "MAGE-KILLER"?
IS IT THAT WEAPON THAT MIGHT DESTROY THE WORLD?
NO, I DON'T BELIEVE SO.
BUT...
MAGE-KILLER IS AN ANCIENT THREAT TO THIS CLAN.
AN ANTI-WIZARD WEAPON THAT MAGIC HAS VIRTUALLY NO EFFECT ON.
HUH? DAMN!
HOW ARE YOU SUPPOSED TO BEAT THAT?
CRAP...I WAS SO SURE SHE WOULDN'T BE ABLE TO ACTIVATE THE WEAPON...
THAT'S WHY I LET HER IN...
IT SEEMS WE UNDER-ESTIMATED SYLVIA.
WE NEVER IMAGINED SHE MIGHT ABSORB MAGE-KILLER WHOLESALE.
YES...

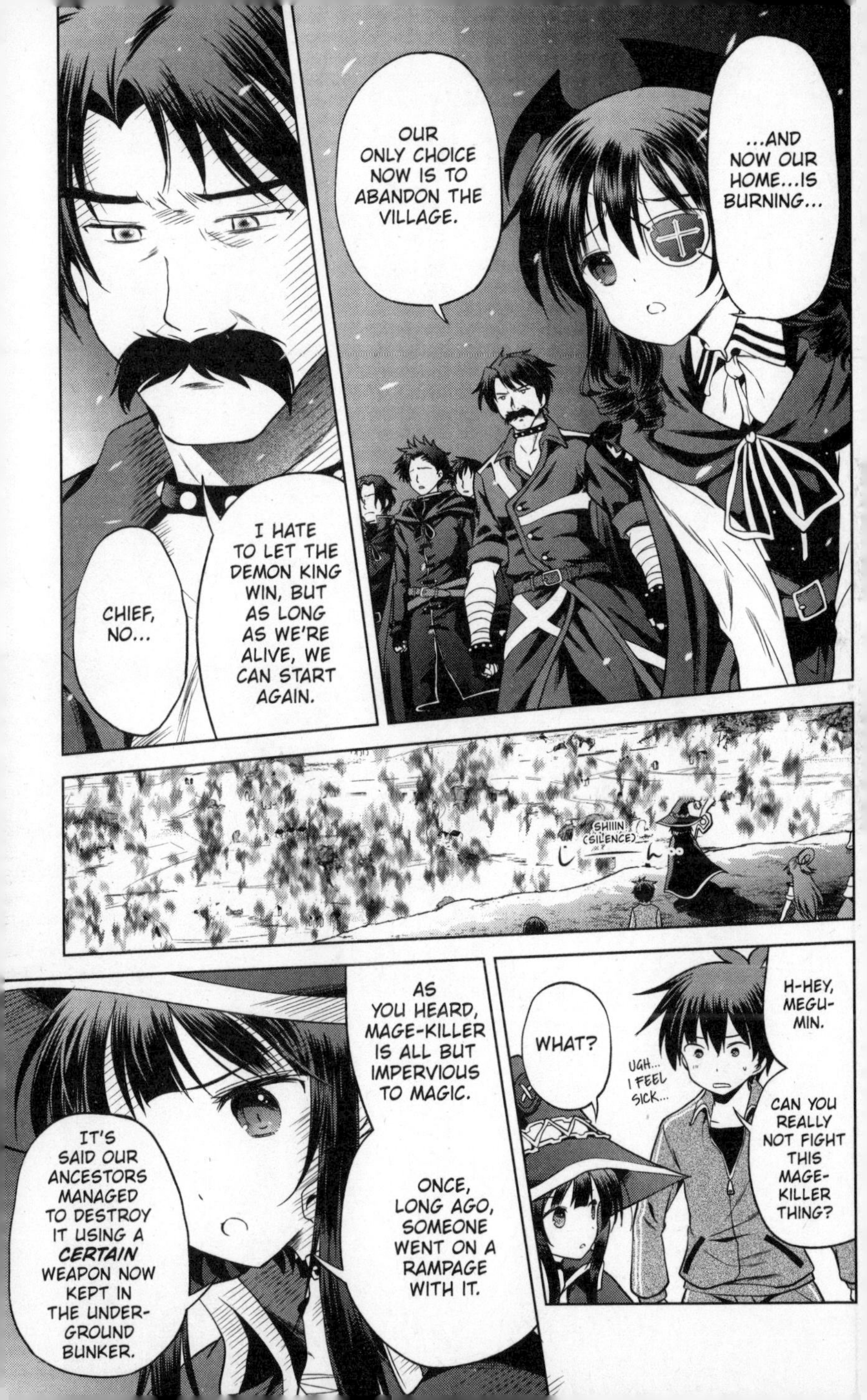
...AND NOW OUR HOME...IS BURNING...
OUR ONLY CHOICE NOW IS TO ABANDON THE VILLAGE.
I HATE TO LET THE DEMON KING WIN, BUT AS LONG AS WE'RE ALIVE, WE CAN START AGAIN.
CHIEF, NO...
SHIIIN (SILENCE)
H-HEY, MEGUMIN.
WHAT?
UGH... I FEEL SICK...
CAN YOU REALLY NOT FIGHT THIS MAGE-KILLER THING?
AS YOU HEARD, MAGE-KILLER IS ALL BUT IMPERVIOUS TO MAGIC.
ONCE, LONG AGO, SOMEONE WENT ON A RAMPAGE WITH IT.
IT'S SAID OUR ANCESTORS MANAGED TO DESTROY IT USING A ***CERTAIN*** WEAPON NOW KEPT IN THE UNDERGROUND BUNKER.

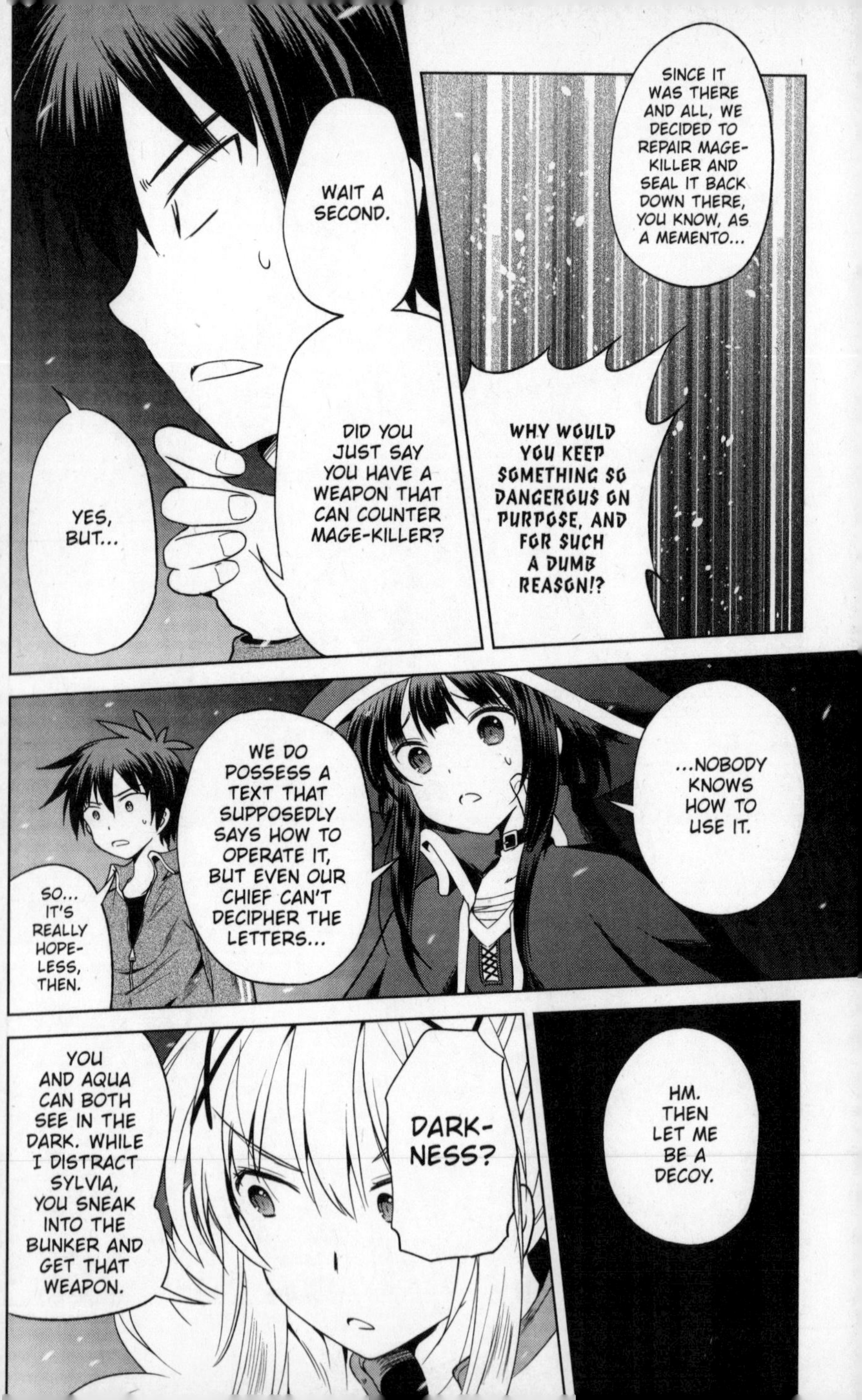
SINCE IT WAS THERE AND ALL, WE DECIDED TO REPAIR MAGE-KILLER AND SEAL IT BACK DOWN THERE, YOU KNOW, AS A MEMENTO...
WHY WOULD YOU KEEP SOMETHING SO DANGEROUS ON PURPOSE, AND FOR SUCH A DUMB REASON!?
WAIT A SECOND.
DID YOU JUST SAY YOU HAVE A WEAPON THAT CAN COUNTER MAGE-KILLER?
YES, BUT...
...NOBODY KNOWS HOW TO USE IT.
WE DO POSSESS A TEXT THAT SUPPOSEDLY SAYS HOW TO OPERATE IT, BUT EVEN OUR CHIEF CAN'T DECIPHER THE LETTERS...
SO... IT'S REALLY HOPE-LESS, THEN.
HM. THEN LET ME BE A DECOY.
DARK-NESS?
YOU AND AQUA CAN BOTH SEE IN THE DARK. WHILE I DISTRACT SYLVIA, YOU SNEAK INTO THE BUNKER AND GET THAT WEAPON.

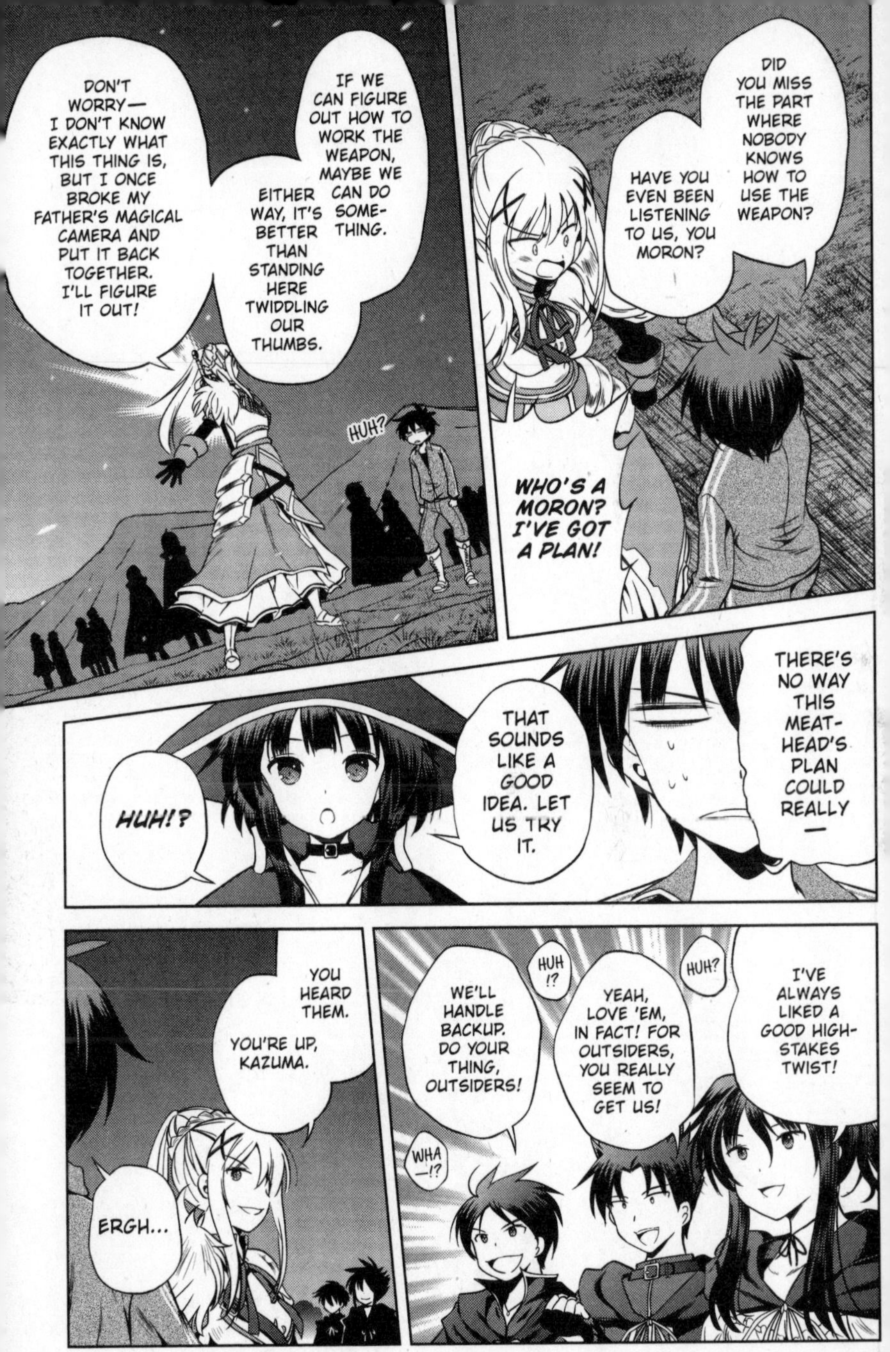
DID YOU MISS THE PART WHERE NOBODY KNOWS HOW TO USE THE WEAPON?
HAVE YOU EVEN BEEN LISTENING TO US, YOU MORON?
WHO'S A MORON? I'VE GOT A PLAN!
IF WE CAN FIGURE OUT HOW TO WORK THE WEAPON, MAYBE WE CAN DO SOMETHING.
EITHER WAY, IT'S BETTER THAN STANDING HERE TWIDDLING OUR THUMBS.
DON'T WORRY— I DON'T KNOW EXACTLY WHAT THIS THING IS, BUT I ONCE BROKE MY FATHER'S MAGICAL CAMERA AND PUT IT BACK TOGETHER. I'LL FIGURE IT OUT!
HUH?
THERE'S NO WAY THIS MEATHEAD'S PLAN COULD REALLY—
THAT SOUNDS LIKE A GOOD IDEA. LET US TRY IT.
HUH!?
I'VE ALWAYS LIKED A GOOD HIGH-STAKES TWIST!
HUH?
YEAH, LOVE 'EM, IN FACT! FOR OUTSIDERS, YOU REALLY SEEM TO GET US!
HUH!?
WE'LL HANDLE BACKUP. DO YOUR THING, OUTSIDERS!
WHA—!?
YOU HEARD THEM.
YOU'RE UP, KAZUMA.
ERGH...

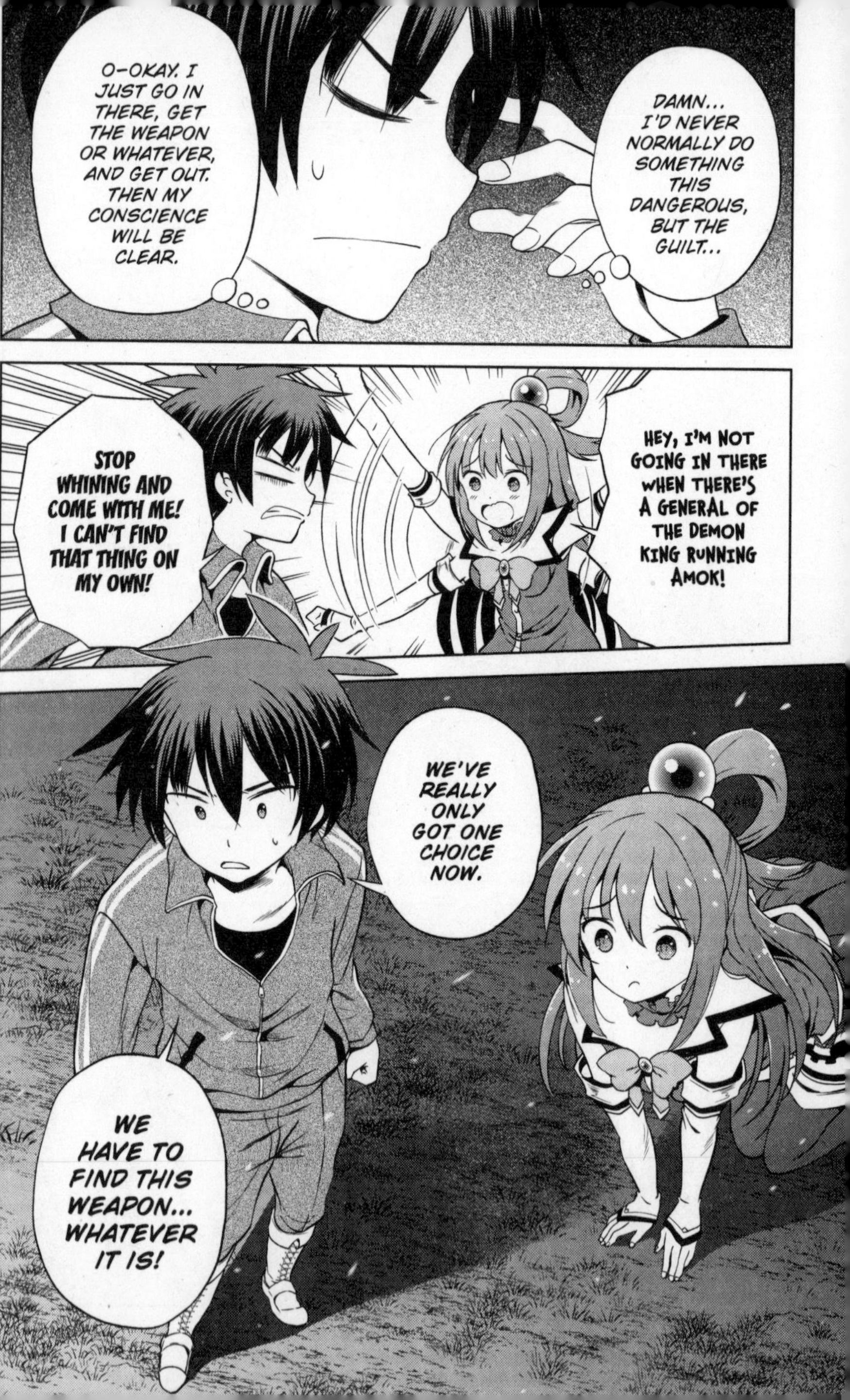
DAMN... I'D NEVER NORMALLY DO SOMETHING THIS DANGEROUS, BUT THE GUILT...
O-OKAY. I JUST GO IN THERE, GET THE WEAPON OR WHATEVER, AND GET OUT. THEN MY CONSCIENCE WILL BE CLEAR.
HEY, I'M NOT GOING IN THERE WHEN THERE'S A GENERAL OF THE DEMON KING RUNNING AMOK!
STOP WHINING AND COME WITH ME! I CAN'T FIND THAT THING ON MY OWN!
WE'VE REALLY ONLY GOT ONE CHOICE NOW.
WE HAVE TO FIND THIS WEAPON... WHATEVER IT IS!

CHAPTER 51

# MAY THERE BE AN EXPLOSION FOR THIS HATEFUL RELIC! ②

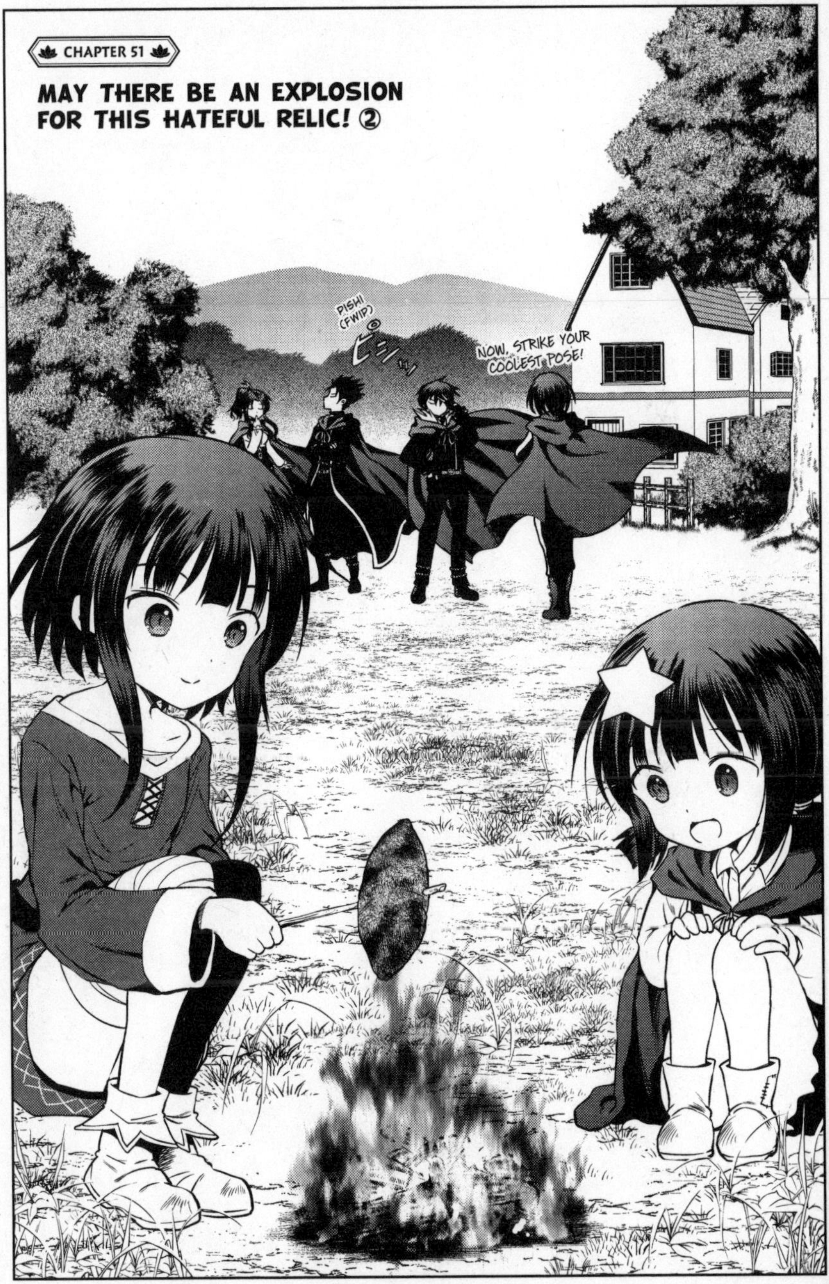
NOW, STRIKE YOUR COOLEST POSE!
PISHI (FWIP)

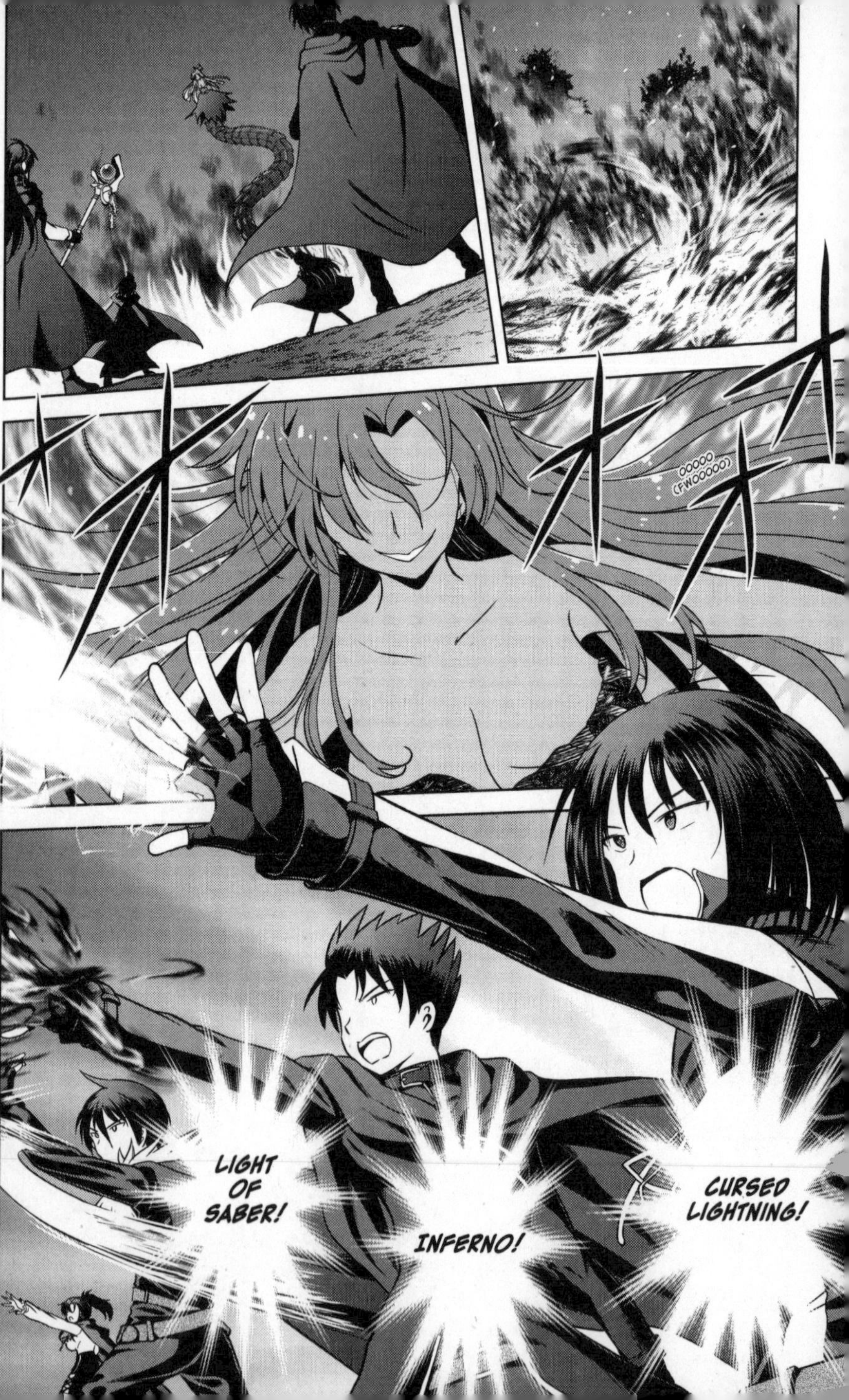
OOOOO
(FWOOOOO)
CURSED LIGHTNING!
INFERNO!
LIGHT OF SABER!

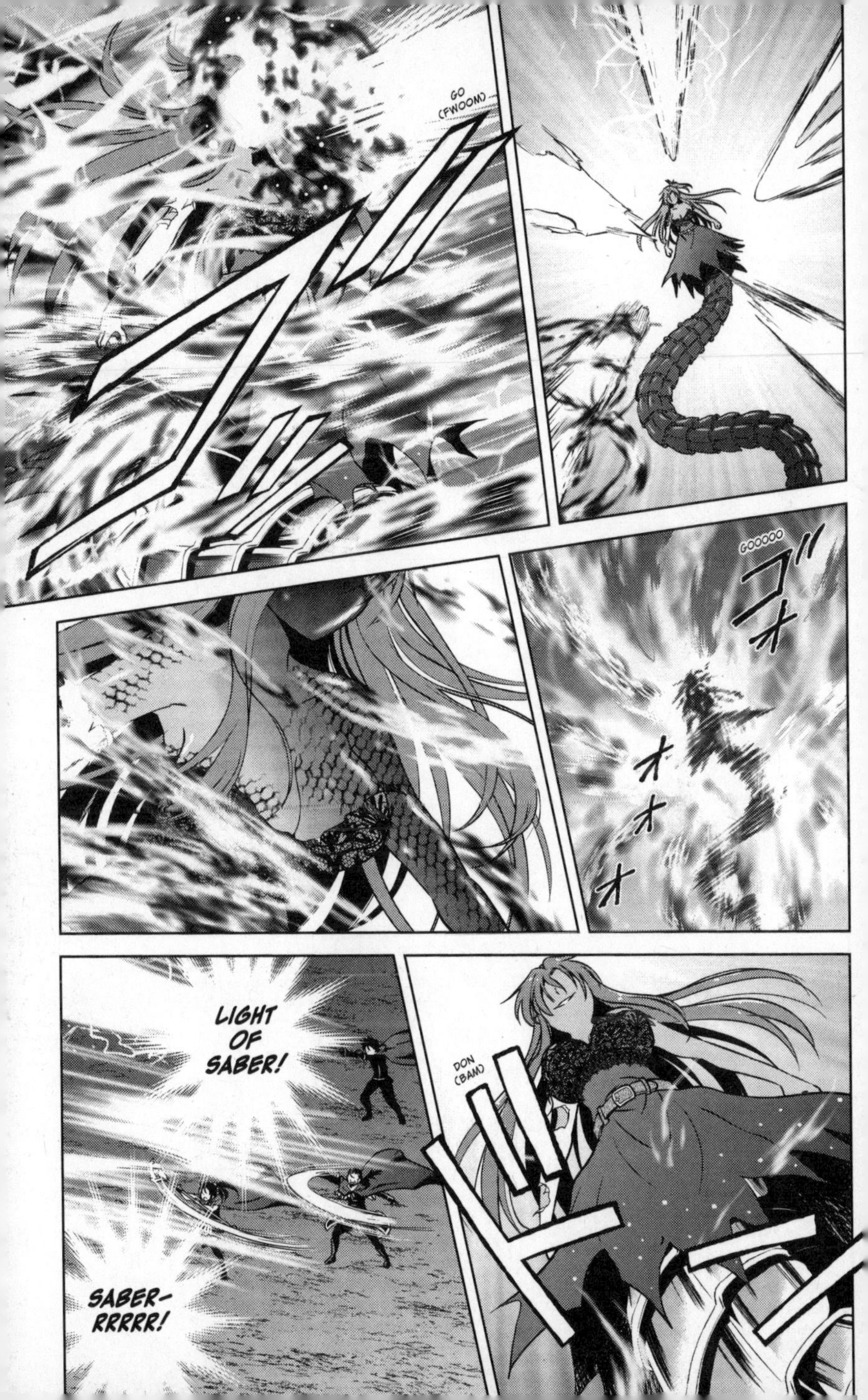
GO (FWOOM)
GOOOOO
ゴオオオオ
DON (BAM)
LIGHT OF SABER!
SABER-RRRRR!

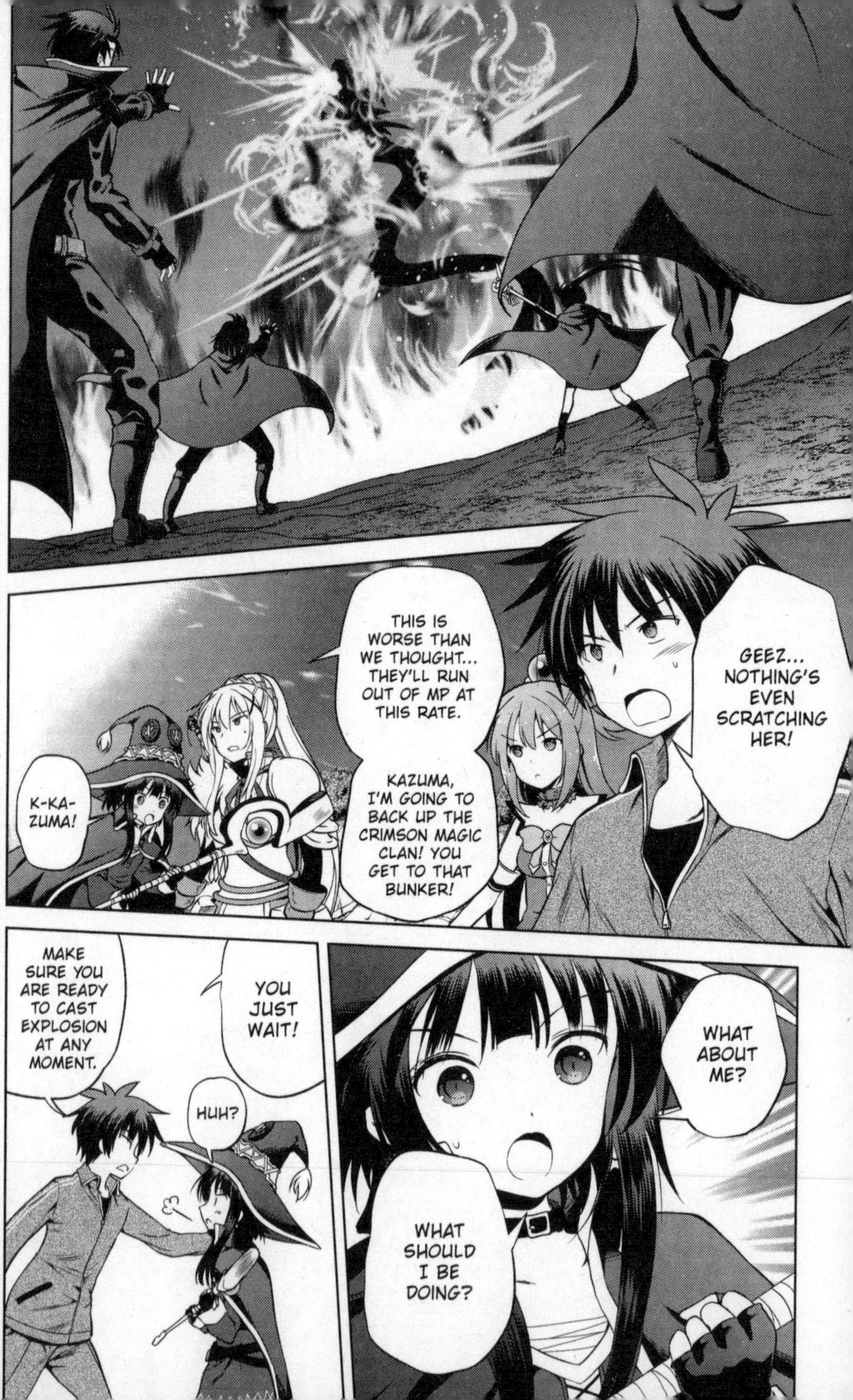
GEEZ... NOTHING'S EVEN SCRATCHING HER!
THIS IS WORSE THAN WE THOUGHT... THEY'LL RUN OUT OF MP AT THIS RATE.
KAZUMA, I'M GOING TO BACK UP THE CRIMSON MAGIC CLAN! YOU GET TO THAT BUNKER!
K-KA-ZUMA!
WHAT ABOUT ME?
WHAT SHOULD I BE DOING?
YOU JUST WAIT!
MAKE SURE YOU ARE READY TO CAST EXPLOSION AT ANY MOMENT.
HUH?

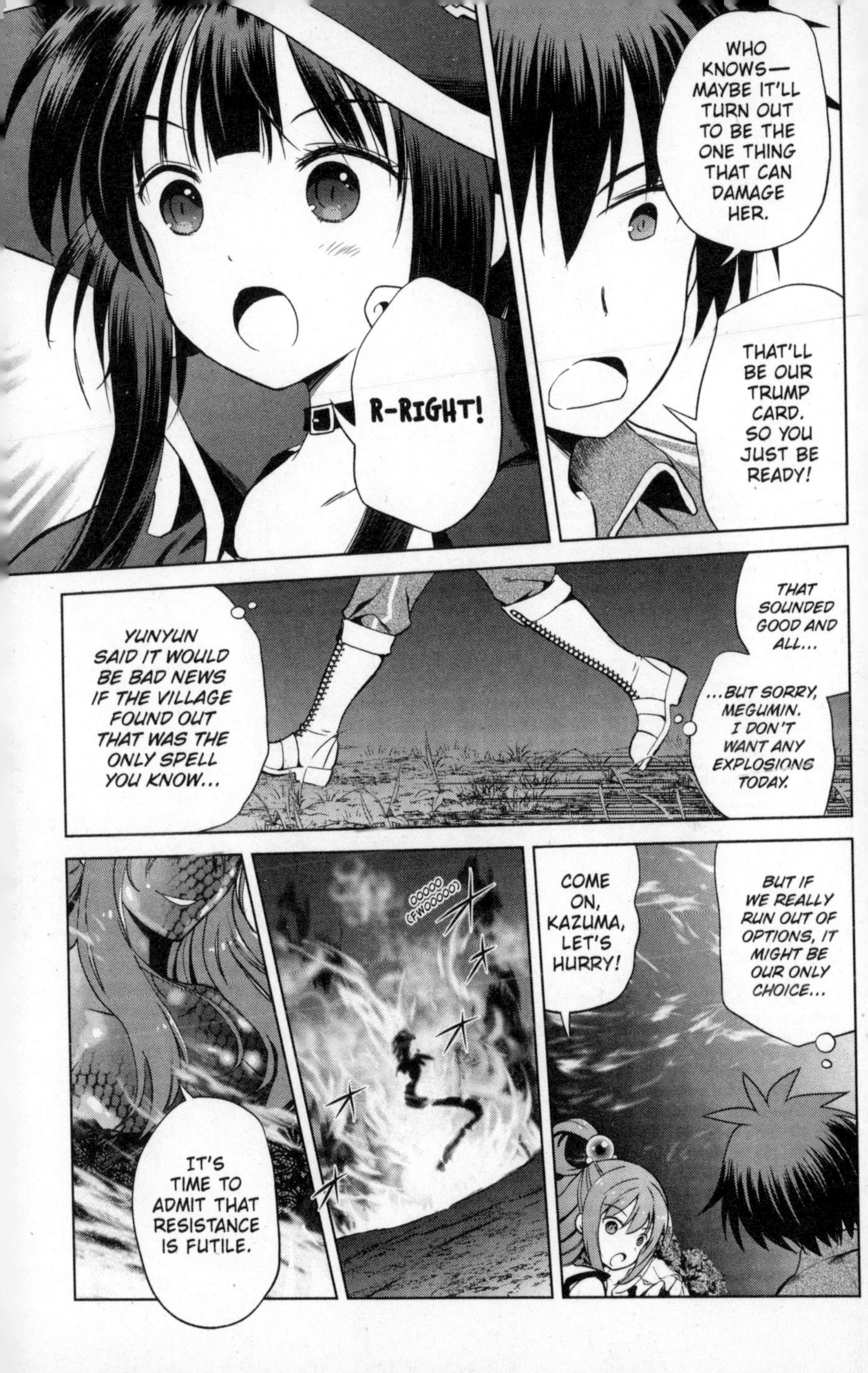
WHO KNOWS— MAYBE IT'LL TURN OUT TO BE THE ONE THING THAT CAN DAMAGE HER.
THAT'LL BE OUR TRUMP CARD. SO YOU JUST BE READY!
R-RIGHT!
THAT SOUNDED GOOD AND ALL...
...BUT SORRY, MEGUMIN. I DON'T WANT ANY EXPLOSIONS TODAY.
YUNYUN SAID IT WOULD BE BAD NEWS IF THE VILLAGE FOUND OUT THAT WAS THE ONLY SPELL YOU KNOW...
BUT IF WE REALLY RUN OUT OF OPTIONS, IT MIGHT BE OUR ONLY CHOICE...
COME ON, KAZUMA, LET'S HURRY!
(FWOOOOO)
IT'S TIME TO ADMIT THAT RESISTANCE IS FUTILE.

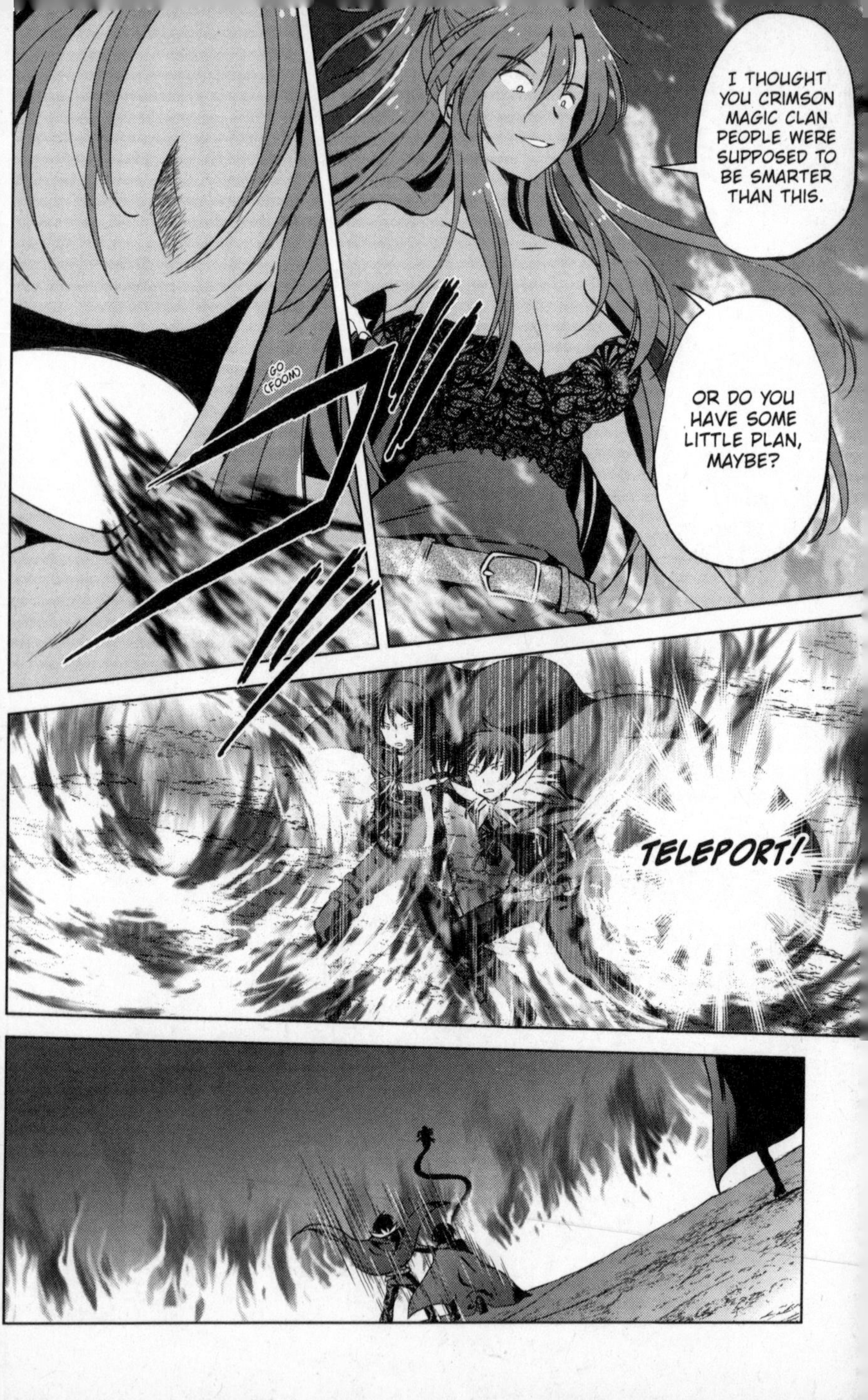
I THOUGHT YOU CRIMSON MAGIC CLAN PEOPLE WERE SUPPOSED TO BE SMARTER THAN THIS.
OR DO YOU HAVE SOME LITTLE PLAN, MAYBE?
GO (FOOM)
TELEPORT!

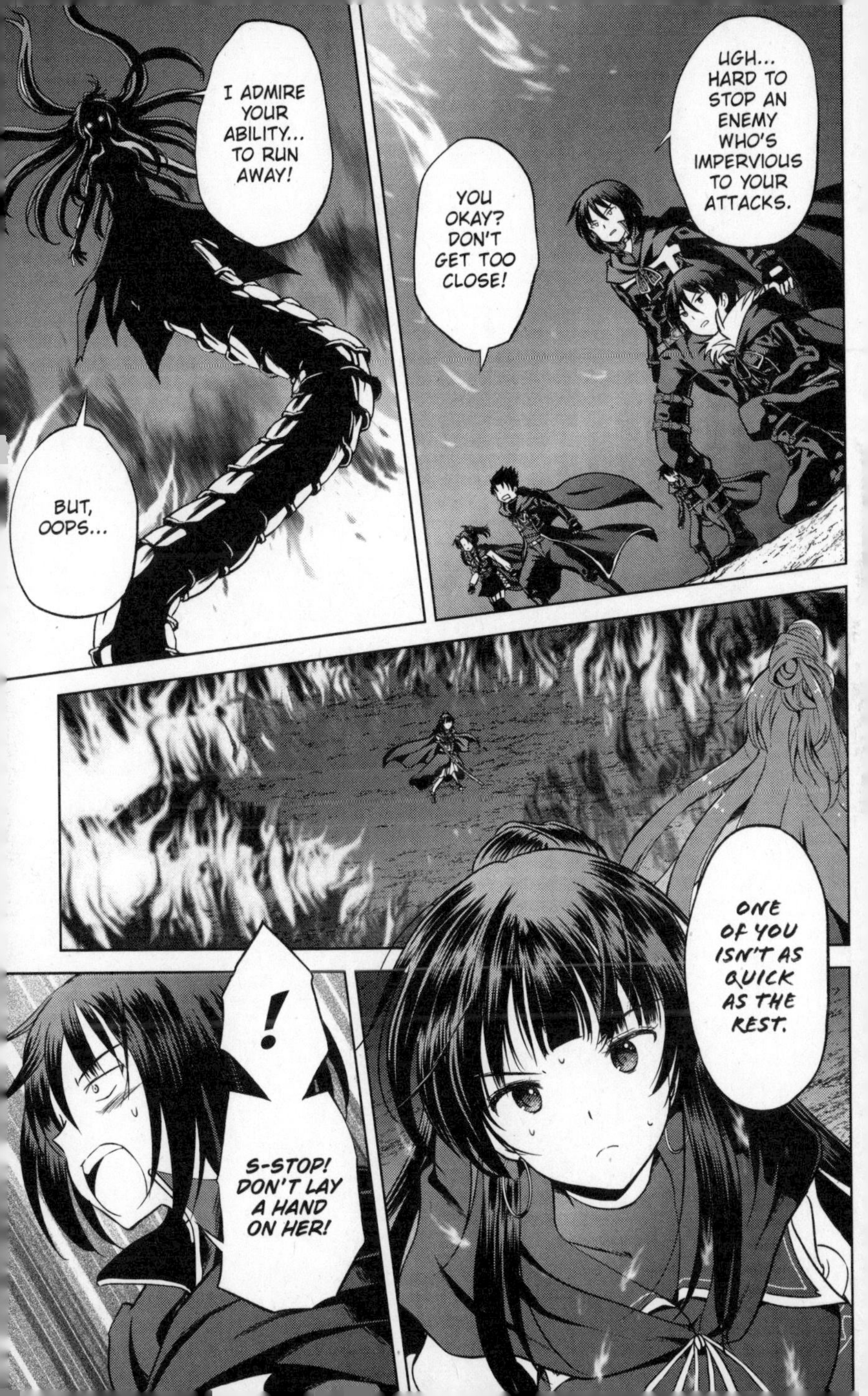
UGH... HARD TO STOP AN ENEMY WHO'S IMPERVIOUS TO YOUR ATTACKS.
YOU OKAY? DON'T GET TOO CLOSE!
I ADMIRE YOUR ABILITY... TO RUN AWAY!
BUT, OOPS...
ONE OF YOU ISN'T AS QUICK AS THE REST.
!
S-STOP! DON'T LAY A HAND ON HER!

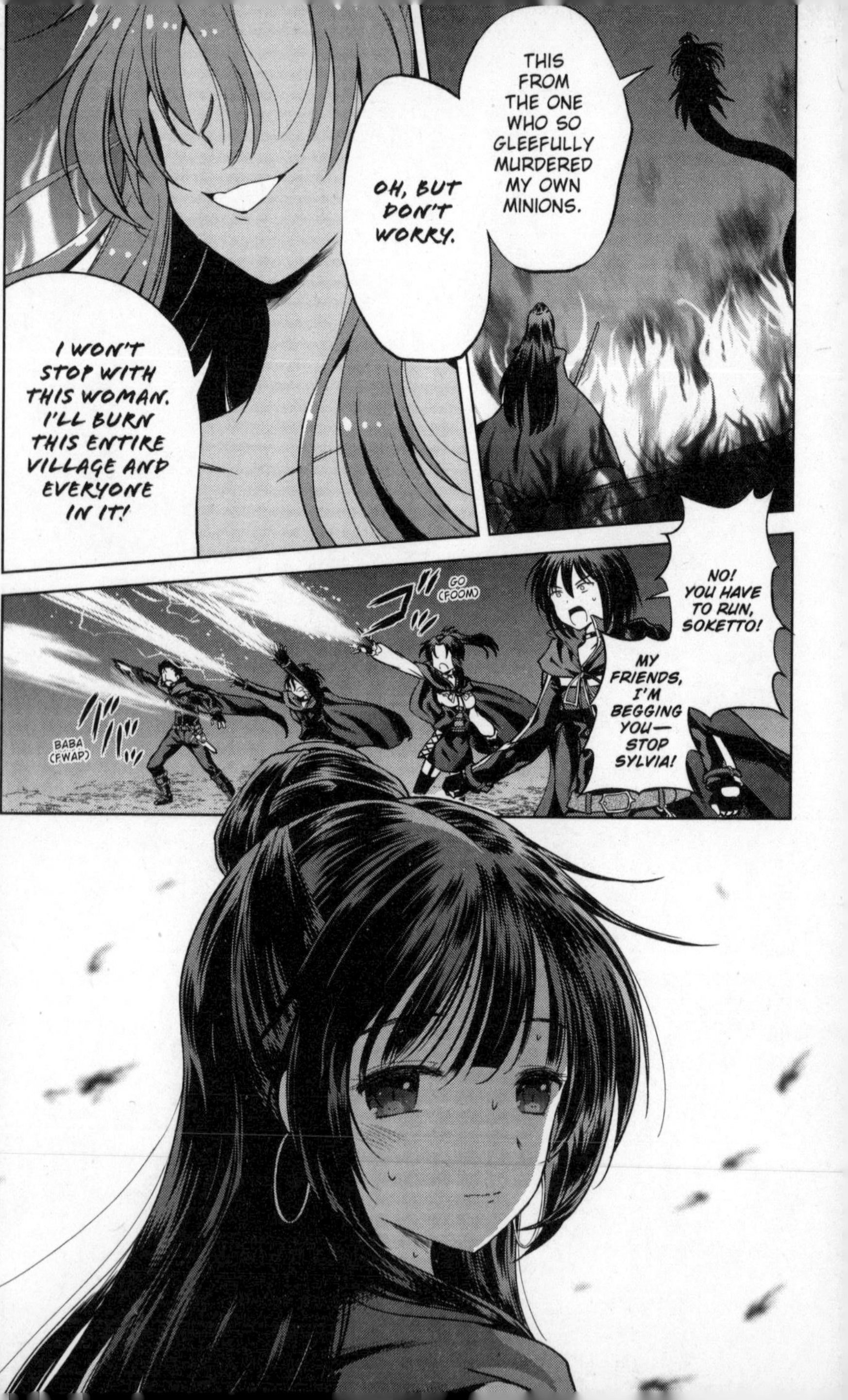
THIS FROM THE ONE WHO SO GLEEFULLY MURDERED MY OWN MINIONS.
OH, BUT DON'T WORRY.
I WON'T STOP WITH THIS WOMAN. I'LL BURN THIS ENTIRE VILLAGE AND EVERYONE IN IT!
NO! YOU HAVE TO RUN, SOKETTO!
MY FRIENDS, I'M BEGGING YOU—STOP SYLVIA!
GO (FOOM)
BABA (FWAP)

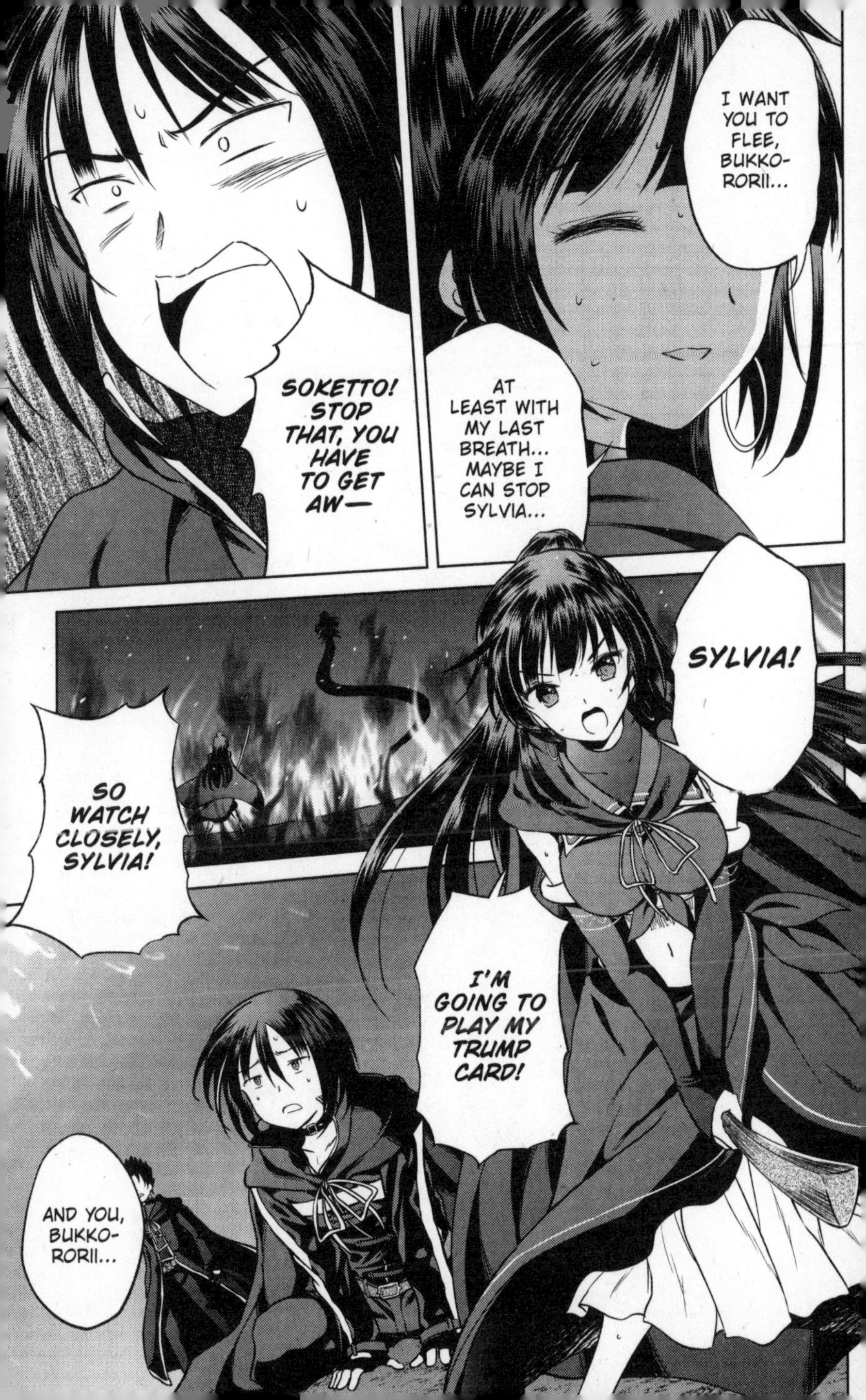
I WANT YOU TO FLEE, BUKKO-RORII...
AT LEAST WITH MY LAST BREATH... MAYBE I CAN STOP SYLVIA...
SOKETTO! STOP THAT, YOU HAVE TO GET AW—
SYLVIA!
I'M GOING TO PLAY MY TRUMP CARD!
SO WATCH CLOSELY, SYLVIA!
AND YOU, BUKKO-RORII...

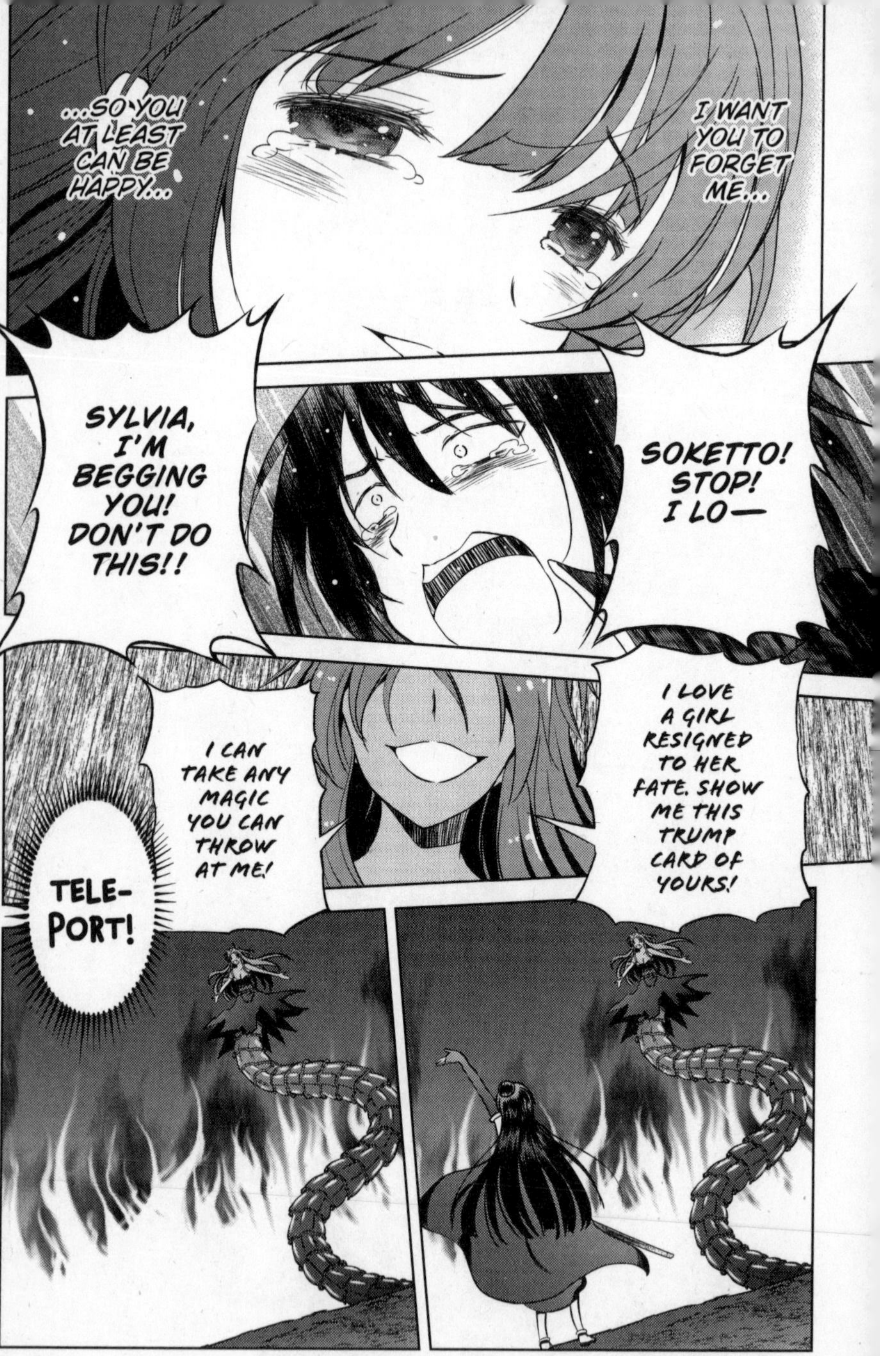
I WANT YOU TO FORGET ME...
...SO YOU AT LEAST CAN BE HAPPY...
SOKETTO! STOP! I LO—
SYLVIA, I'M BEGGING YOU! DON'T DO THIS!!
I LOVE A GIRL RESIGNED TO HER FATE. SHOW ME THIS TRUMP CARD OF YOURS!
I CAN TAKE ANY MAGIC YOU CAN THROW AT ME!
TELE-PORT!

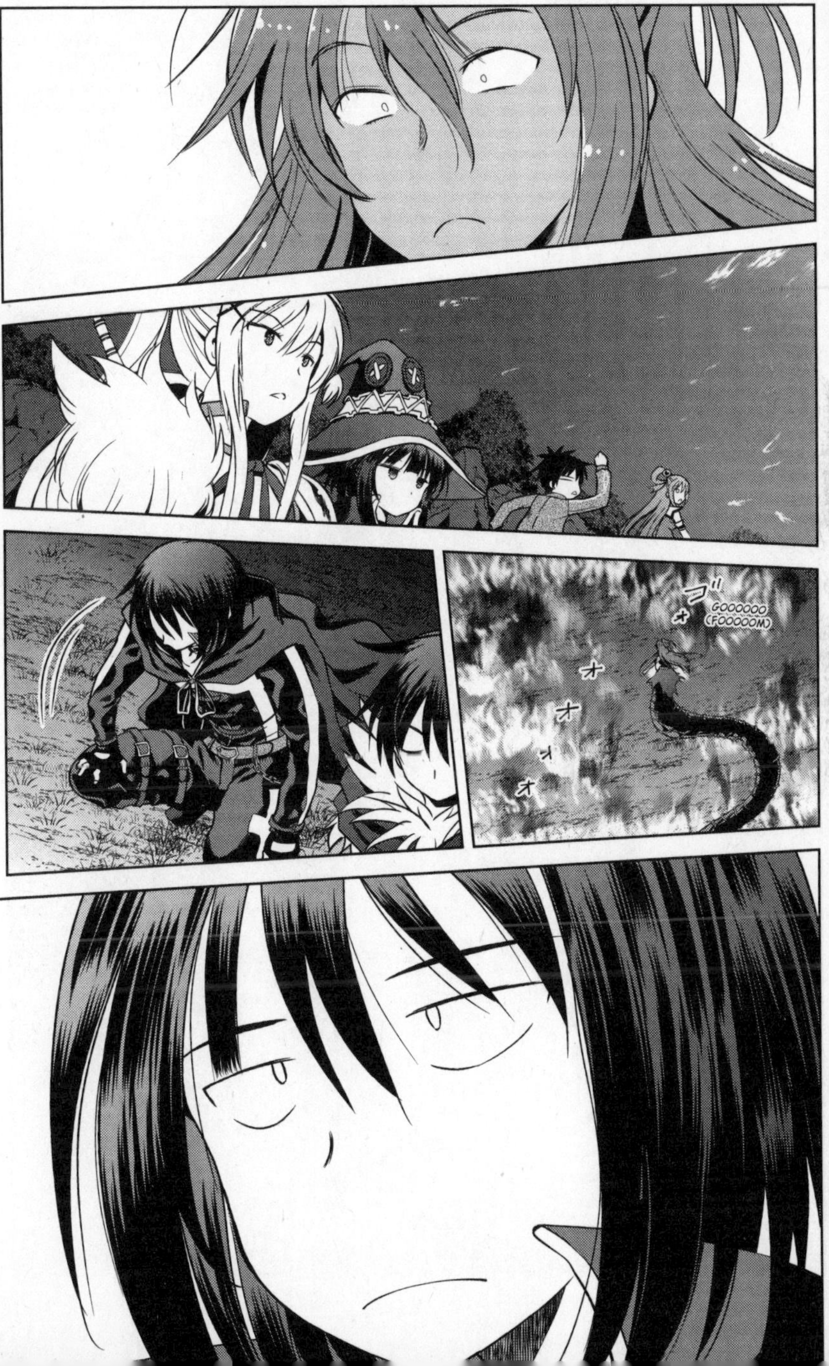
GOOOOOO
(FOOOOOM)

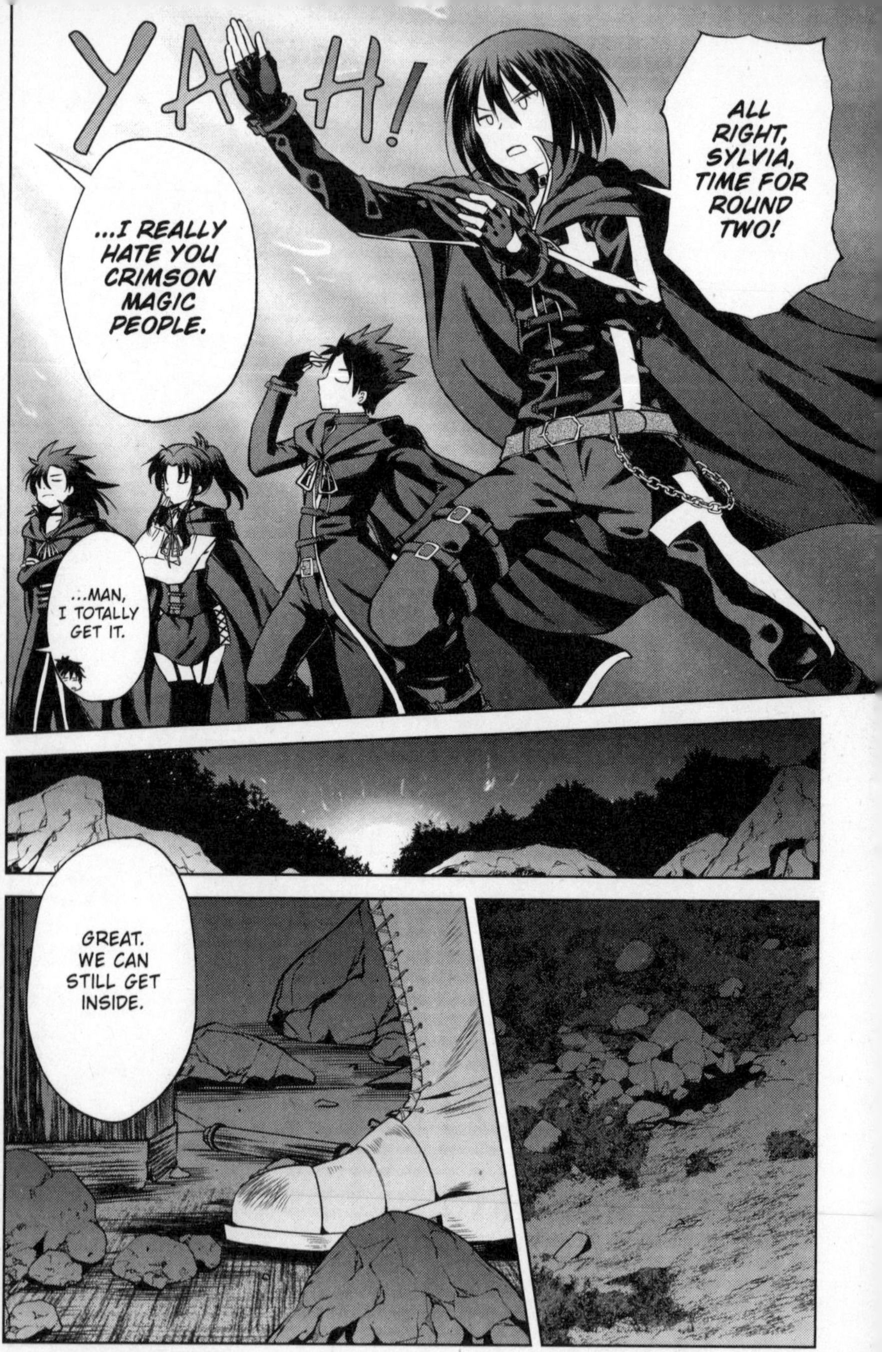
ALL RIGHT, SYLVIA, TIME FOR ROUND TWO!
YAH!
...I REALLY HATE YOU CRIMSON MAGIC PEOPLE.
...MAN, I TOTALLY GET IT.
GREAT. WE CAN STILL GET INSIDE.

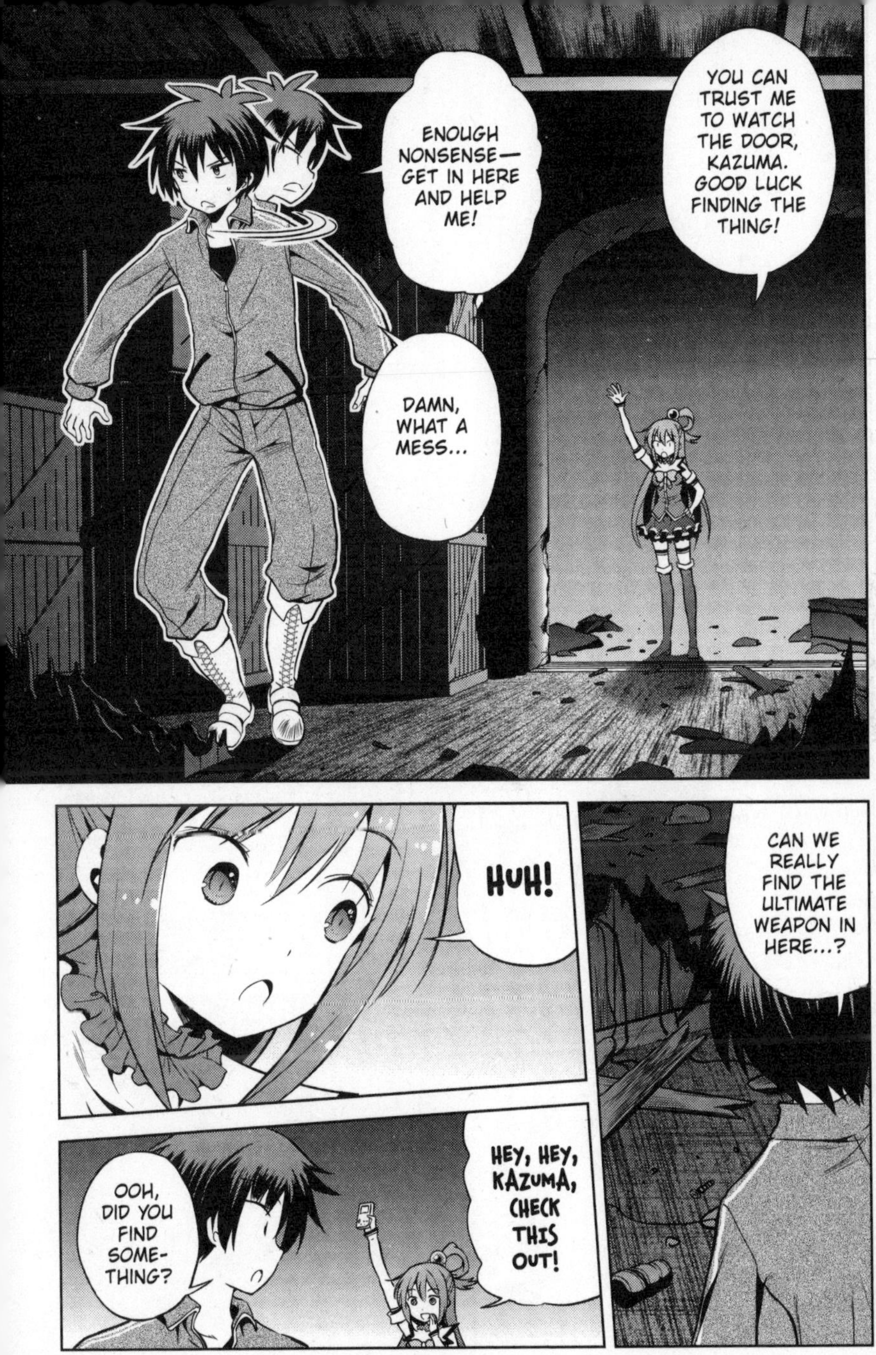
YOU CAN TRUST ME TO WATCH THE DOOR, KAZUMA. GOOD LUCK FINDING THE THING!
ENOUGH NONSENSE—GET IN HERE AND HELP ME!
DAMN, WHAT A MESS...
CAN WE REALLY FIND THE ULTIMATE WEAPON IN HERE...?
HUH!
HEY, HEY, KAZUMA, CHECK THIS OUT!
OOH, DID YOU FIND SOME-THING?

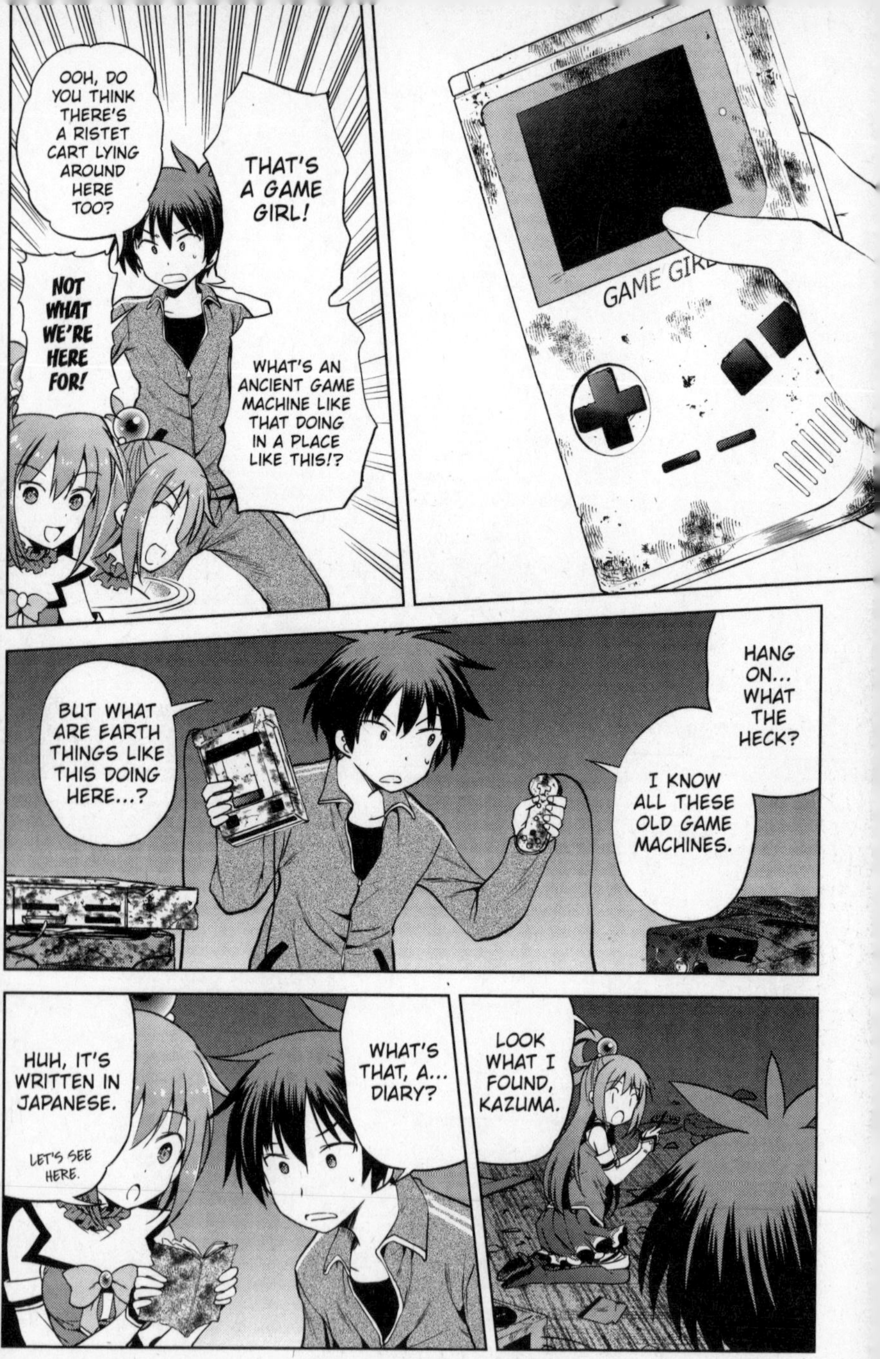
THAT'S A GAME GIRL!
WHAT'S AN ANCIENT GAME MACHINE LIKE THAT DOING IN A PLACE LIKE THIS!?
OOH, DO YOU THINK THERE'S A RISTET CART LYING AROUND HERE TOO?
NOT WHAT WE'RE HERE FOR!
HANG ON... WHAT THE HECK?
I KNOW ALL THESE OLD GAME MACHINES.
BUT WHAT ARE EARTH THINGS LIKE THIS DOING HERE...?
LOOK WHAT I FOUND, KAZUMA.
WHAT'S THAT, A... DIARY?
HUH, IT'S WRITTEN IN JAPANESE.
LET'S SEE HERE.

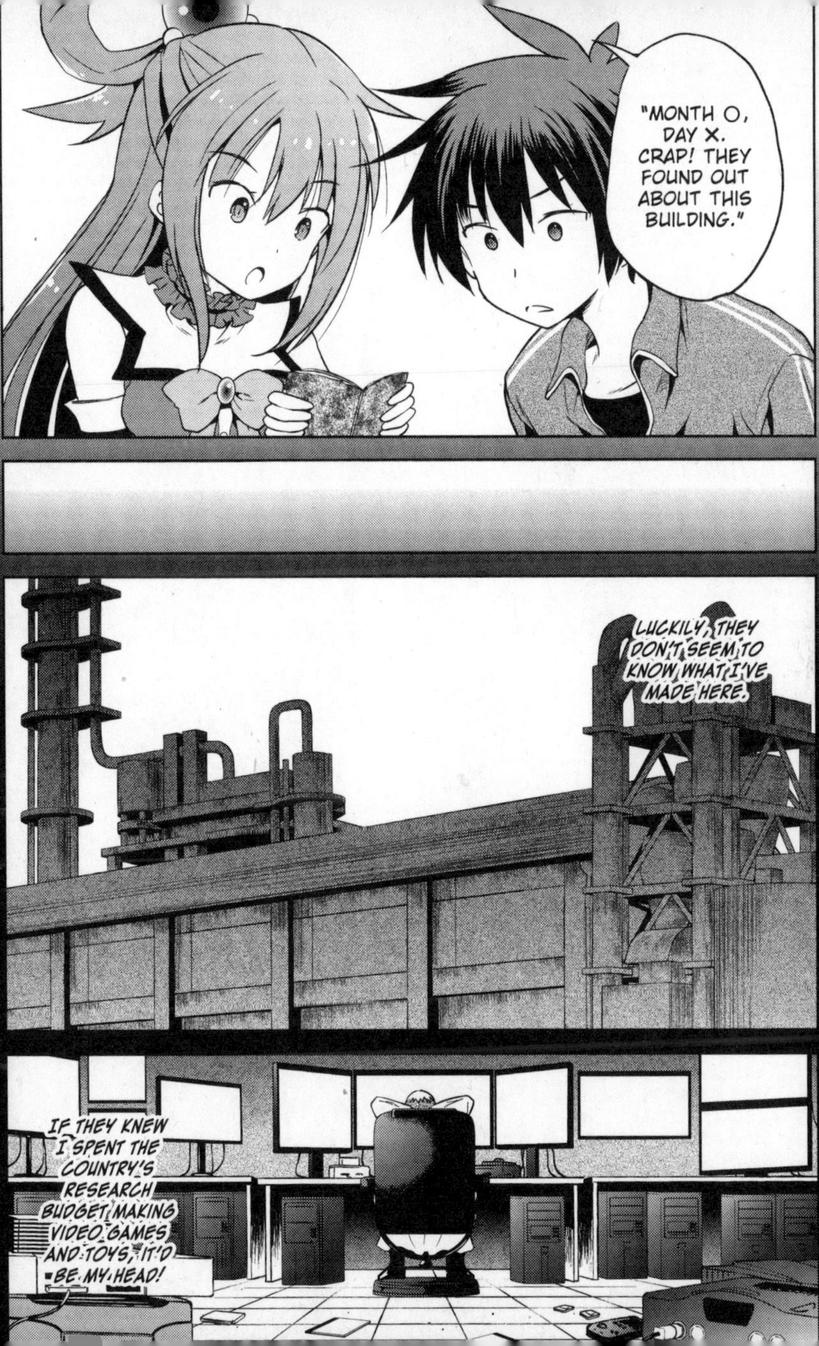
"MONTH O, DAY X. CRAP! THEY FOUND OUT ABOUT THIS BUILDING."
LUCKILY, THEY DON'T SEEM TO KNOW WHAT I'VE MADE HERE.
IF THEY KNEW I SPENT THE COUNTRY'S RESEARCH BUDGET MAKING VIDEO GAMES AND TOYS, IT'D BE MY HEAD!

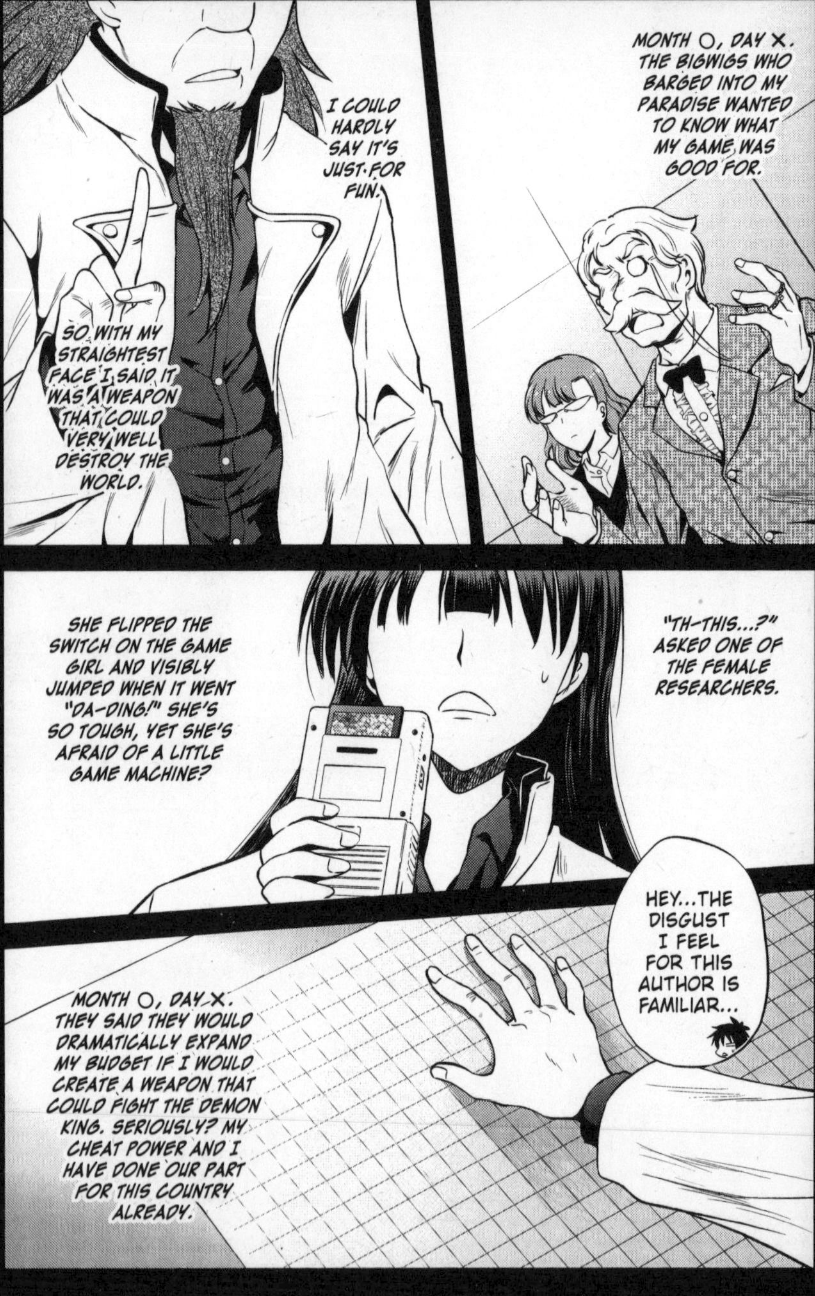
MONTH ○, DAY X. THE BIGWIGS WHO BARGED INTO MY PARADISE WANTED TO KNOW WHAT MY GAME WAS GOOD FOR.
I COULD HARDLY SAY IT'S JUST FOR FUN.
SO WITH MY STRAIGHTEST FACE I SAID IT WAS A WEAPON THAT COULD VERY WELL DESTROY THE WORLD.
"TH-THIS...?" ASKED ONE OF THE FEMALE RESEARCHERS.
SHE FLIPPED THE SWITCH ON THE GAME GIRL AND VISIBLY JUMPED WHEN IT WENT "DA-DING!" SHE'S SO TOUGH, YET SHE'S AFRAID OF A LITTLE GAME MACHINE?
HEY...THE DISGUST I FEEL FOR THIS AUTHOR IS FAMILIAR...
MONTH ○, DAY X. THEY SAID THEY WOULD DRAMATICALLY EXPAND MY BUDGET IF I WOULD CREATE A WEAPON THAT COULD FIGHT THE DEMON KING. SERIOUSLY? MY CHEAT POWER AND I HAVE DONE OUR PART FOR THIS COUNTRY ALREADY.

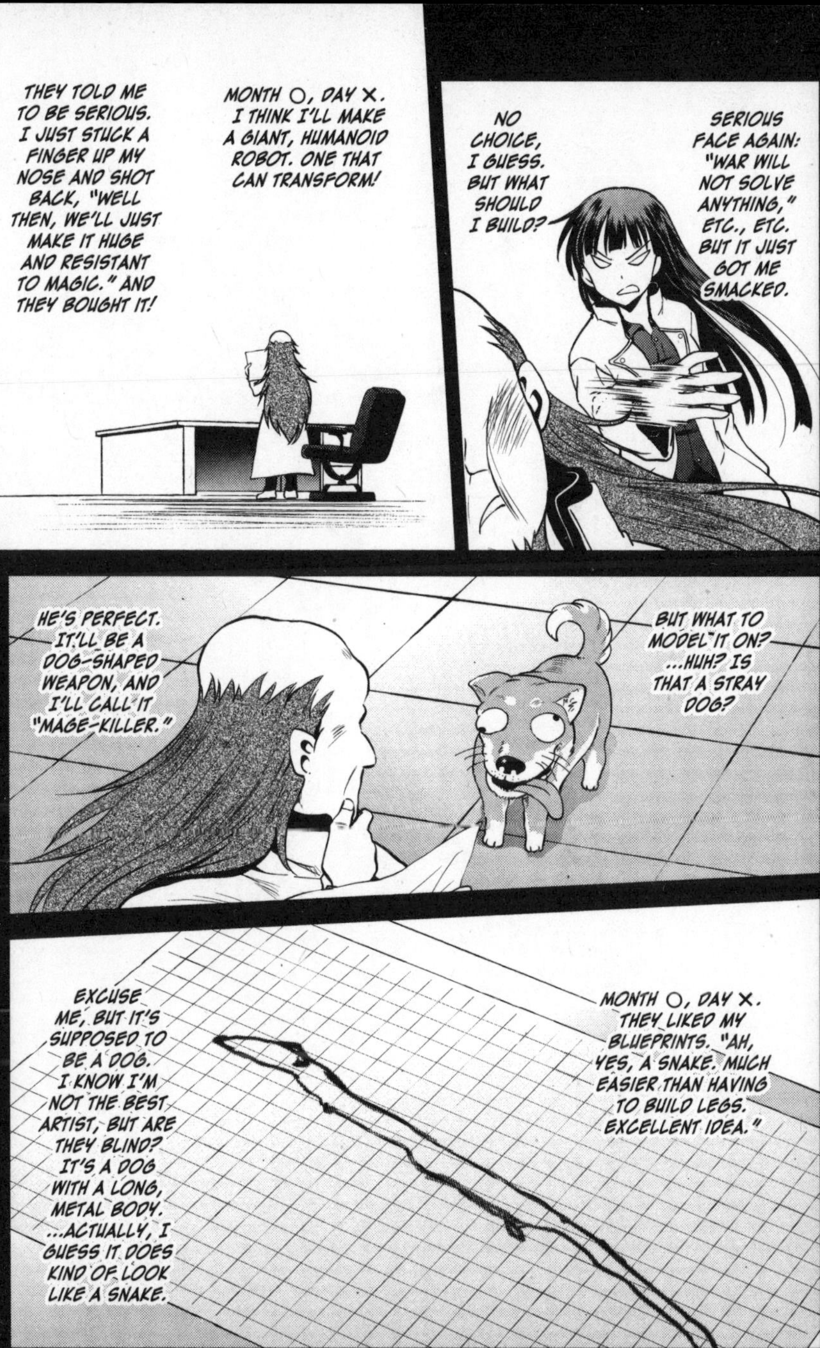
SERIOUS FACE AGAIN: "WAR WILL NOT SOLVE ANYTHING," ETC., ETC. BUT IT JUST GOT ME SMACKED.
NO CHOICE, I GUESS. BUT WHAT SHOULD I BUILD?
MONTH ○, DAY X. I THINK I'LL MAKE A GIANT, HUMANOID ROBOT. ONE THAT CAN TRANSFORM!
THEY TOLD ME TO BE SERIOUS. I JUST STUCK A FINGER UP MY NOSE AND SHOT BACK, "WELL THEN, WE'LL JUST MAKE IT HUGE AND RESISTANT TO MAGIC." AND THEY BOUGHT IT!
BUT WHAT TO MODEL IT ON? ...HUH? IS THAT A STRAY DOG?
HE'S PERFECT. IT'LL BE A DOG-SHAPED WEAPON, AND I'LL CALL IT "MAGE-KILLER."
MONTH ○, DAY X. THEY LIKED MY BLUEPRINTS. "AH, YES, A SNAKE. MUCH EASIER THAN HAVING TO BUILD LEGS. EXCELLENT IDEA."
EXCUSE ME, BUT IT'S SUPPOSED TO BE A DOG. I KNOW I'M NOT THE BEST ARTIST, BUT ARE THEY BLIND? IT'S A DOG WITH A LONG, METAL BODY. ...ACTUALLY, I GUESS IT DOES KIND OF LOOK LIKE A SNAKE.

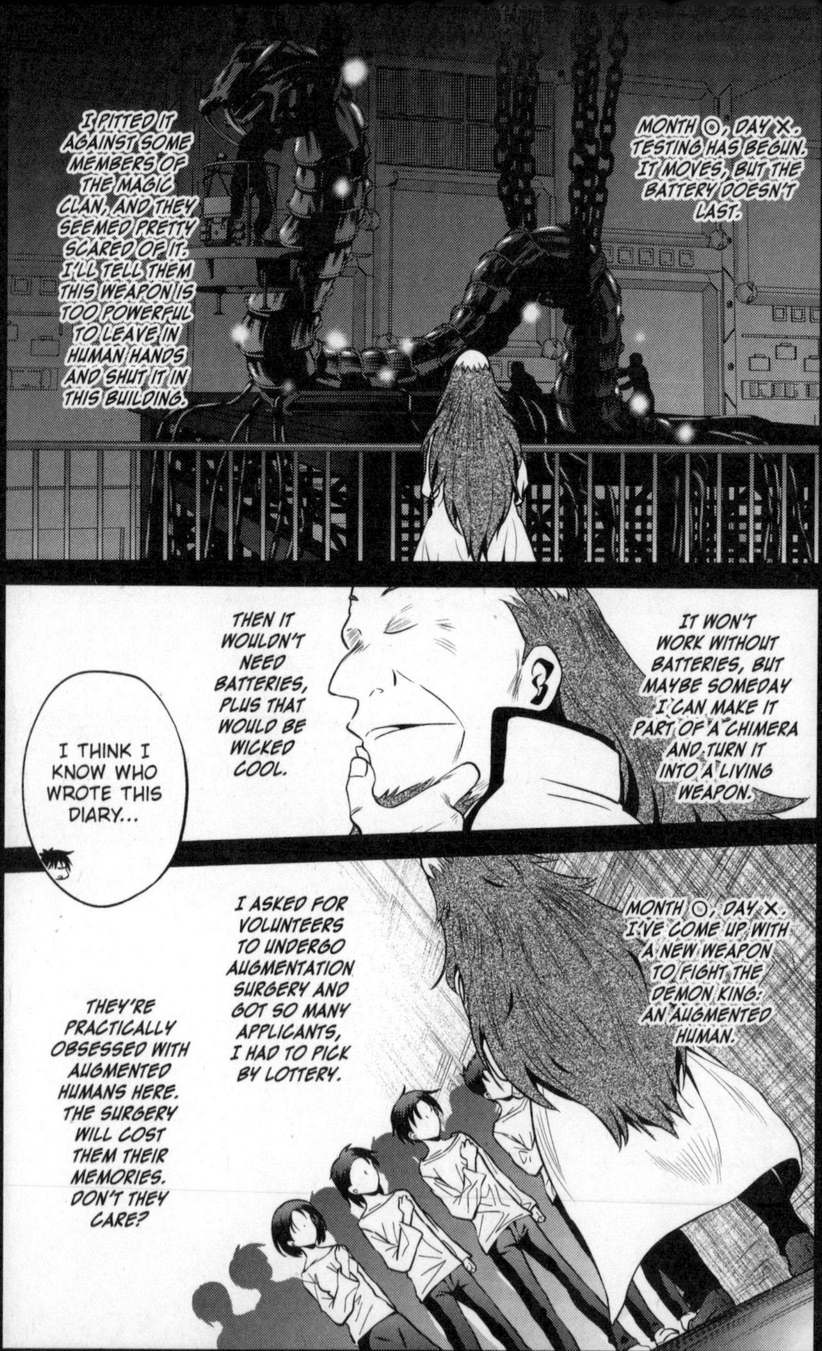
MONTH ◎, DAY X. TESTING HAS BEGUN. IT MOVES, BUT THE BATTERY DOESN'T LAST.
I PITTED IT AGAINST SOME MEMBERS OF THE MAGIC CLAN, AND THEY SEEMED PRETTY SCARED OF IT. I'LL TELL THEM THIS WEAPON IS TOO POWERFUL TO LEAVE IN HUMAN HANDS AND SHUT IT IN THIS BUILDING.
IT WON'T WORK WITHOUT BATTERIES, BUT MAYBE SOMEDAY I CAN MAKE IT PART OF A CHIMERA AND TURN IT INTO A LIVING WEAPON.
THEN IT WOULDN'T NEED BATTERIES, PLUS THAT WOULD BE WICKED COOL.
I THINK I KNOW WHO WROTE THIS DIARY...
MONTH ◎, DAY X. I'VE COME UP WITH A NEW WEAPON TO FIGHT THE DEMON KING: AN AUGMENTED HUMAN.
I ASKED FOR VOLUNTEERS TO UNDERGO AUGMENTATION SURGERY AND GOT SO MANY APPLICANTS, I HAD TO PICK BY LOTTERY.
THEY'RE PRACTICALLY OBSESSED WITH AUGMENTED HUMANS HERE. THE SURGERY WILL COST THEM THEIR MEMORIES. DON'T THEY CARE?

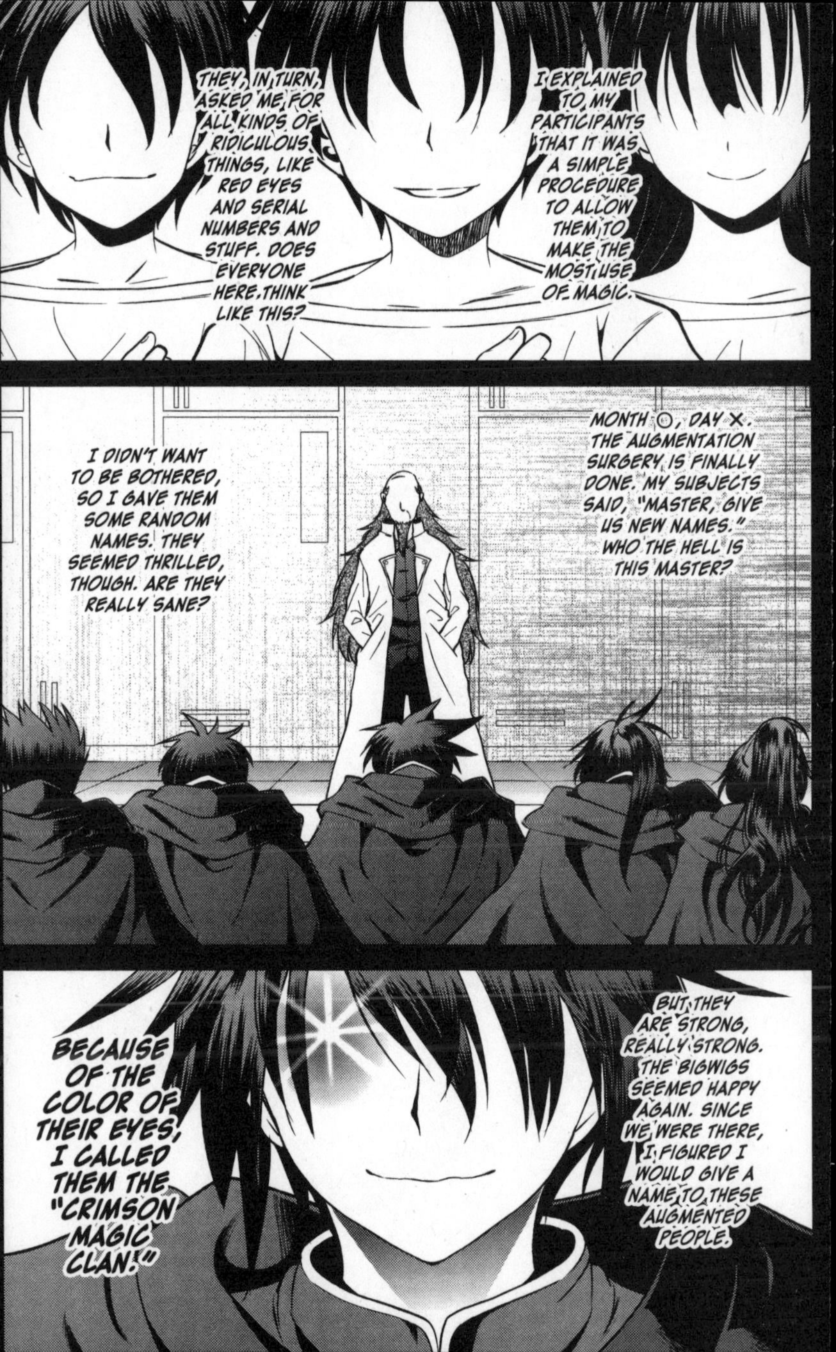
I EXPLAINED TO MY PARTICIPANTS THAT IT WAS A SIMPLE PROCEDURE TO ALLOW THEM TO MAKE THE MOST USE OF MAGIC.
THEY, IN TURN, ASKED ME FOR ALL KINDS OF RIDICULOUS THINGS, LIKE RED EYES AND SERIAL NUMBERS AND STUFF. DOES EVERYONE HERE THINK LIKE THIS?
MONTH ○, DAY X. THE AUGMENTATION SURGERY IS FINALLY DONE. MY SUBJECTS SAID, "MASTER, GIVE US NEW NAMES." WHO THE HELL IS THIS MASTER?
I DIDN'T WANT TO BE BOTHERED, SO I GAVE THEM SOME RANDOM NAMES. THEY SEEMED THRILLED, THOUGH. ARE THEY REALLY SANE?
BUT THEY ARE STRONG, REALLY STRONG. THE BIGWIGS SEEMED HAPPY AGAIN. SINCE WE WERE THERE, I FIGURED I WOULD GIVE A NAME TO THESE AUGMENTED PEOPLE.
BECAUSE OF THE COLOR OF THEIR EYES, I CALLED THEM THE "CRIMSON MAGIC CLAN."

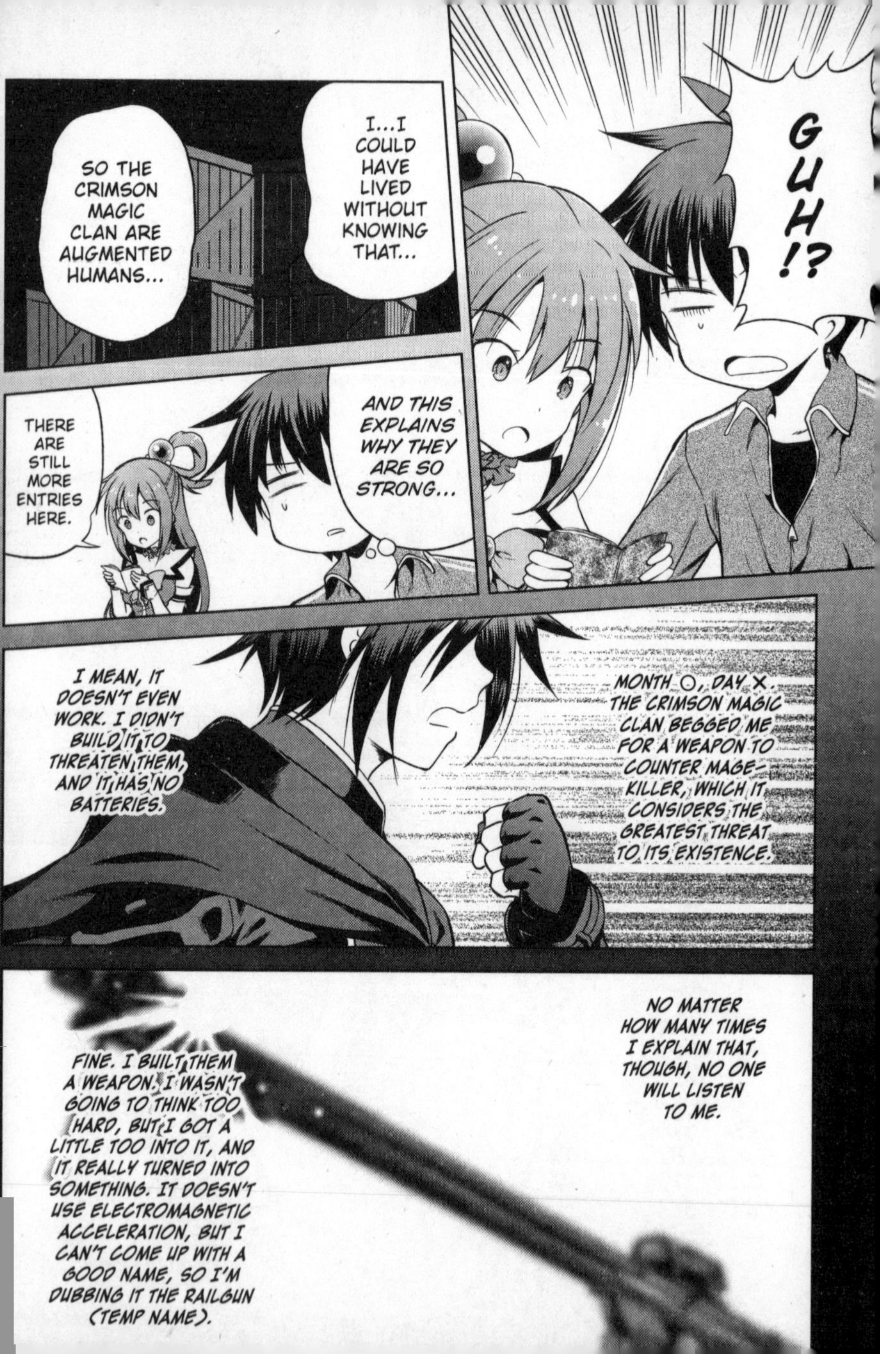
GUH!?
I...I COULD HAVE LIVED WITHOUT KNOWING THAT...
SO THE CRIMSON MAGIC CLAN ARE AUGMENTED HUMANS...
AND THIS EXPLAINS WHY THEY ARE SO STRONG...
THERE ARE STILL MORE ENTRIES HERE.
MONTH ○, DAY ×. THE CRIMSON MAGIC CLAN BEGGED ME FOR A WEAPON TO COUNTER MAGE-KILLER, WHICH IT CONSIDERS THE GREATEST THREAT TO ITS EXISTENCE.
I MEAN, IT DOESN'T EVEN WORK. I DIDN'T BUILD IT TO THREATEN THEM, AND IT HAS NO BATTERIES.
NO MATTER HOW MANY TIMES I EXPLAIN THAT, THOUGH, NO ONE WILL LISTEN TO ME.
FINE. I BUILT THEM A WEAPON. I WASN'T GOING TO THINK TOO HARD, BUT I GOT A LITTLE TOO INTO IT, AND IT REALLY TURNED INTO SOMETHING. IT DOESN'T USE ELECTROMAGNETIC ACCELERATION, BUT I CAN'T COME UP WITH A GOOD NAME, SO I'M DUBBING IT THE RAILGUN (TEMP NAME).

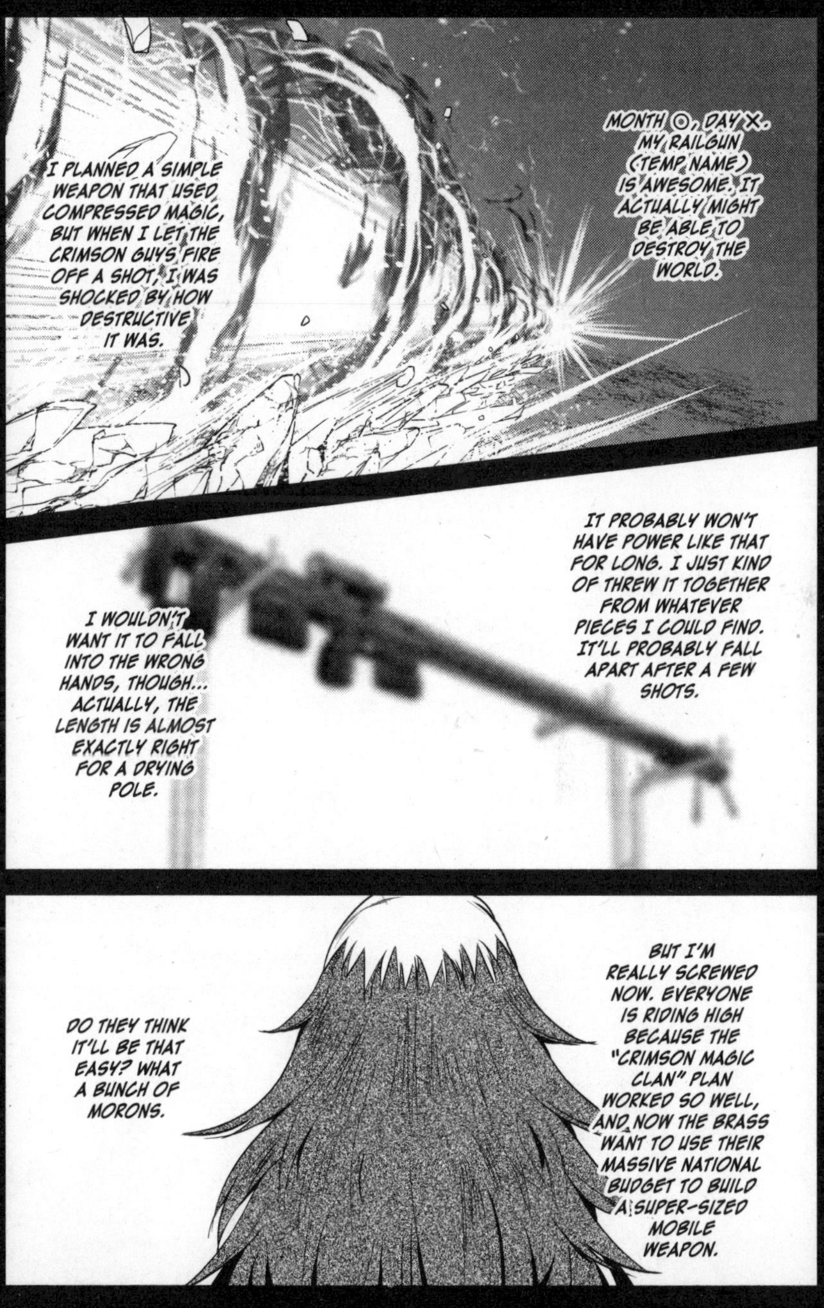
MONTH ◎, DAY X. MY RAILGUN (TEMP NAME) IS AWESOME. IT ACTUALLY MIGHT BE ABLE TO DESTROY THE WORLD.
I PLANNED A SIMPLE WEAPON THAT USED COMPRESSED MAGIC, BUT WHEN I LET THE CRIMSON GUYS FIRE OFF A SHOT, I WAS SHOCKED BY HOW DESTRUCTIVE IT WAS.
IT PROBABLY WON'T HAVE POWER LIKE THAT FOR LONG. I JUST KIND OF THREW IT TOGETHER FROM WHATEVER PIECES I COULD FIND. IT'LL PROBABLY FALL APART AFTER A FEW SHOTS.
I WOULDN'T WANT IT TO FALL INTO THE WRONG HANDS, THOUGH... ACTUALLY, THE LENGTH IS ALMOST EXACTLY RIGHT FOR A DRYING POLE.
BUT I'M REALLY SCREWED NOW. EVERYONE IS RIDING HIGH BECAUSE THE "CRIMSON MAGIC CLAN" PLAN WORKED SO WELL, AND NOW THE BRASS WANT TO USE THEIR MASSIVE NATIONAL BUDGET TO BUILD A SUPER-SIZED MOBILE WEAPON.
DO THEY THINK IT'LL BE THAT EASY? WHAT A BUNCH OF MORONS.

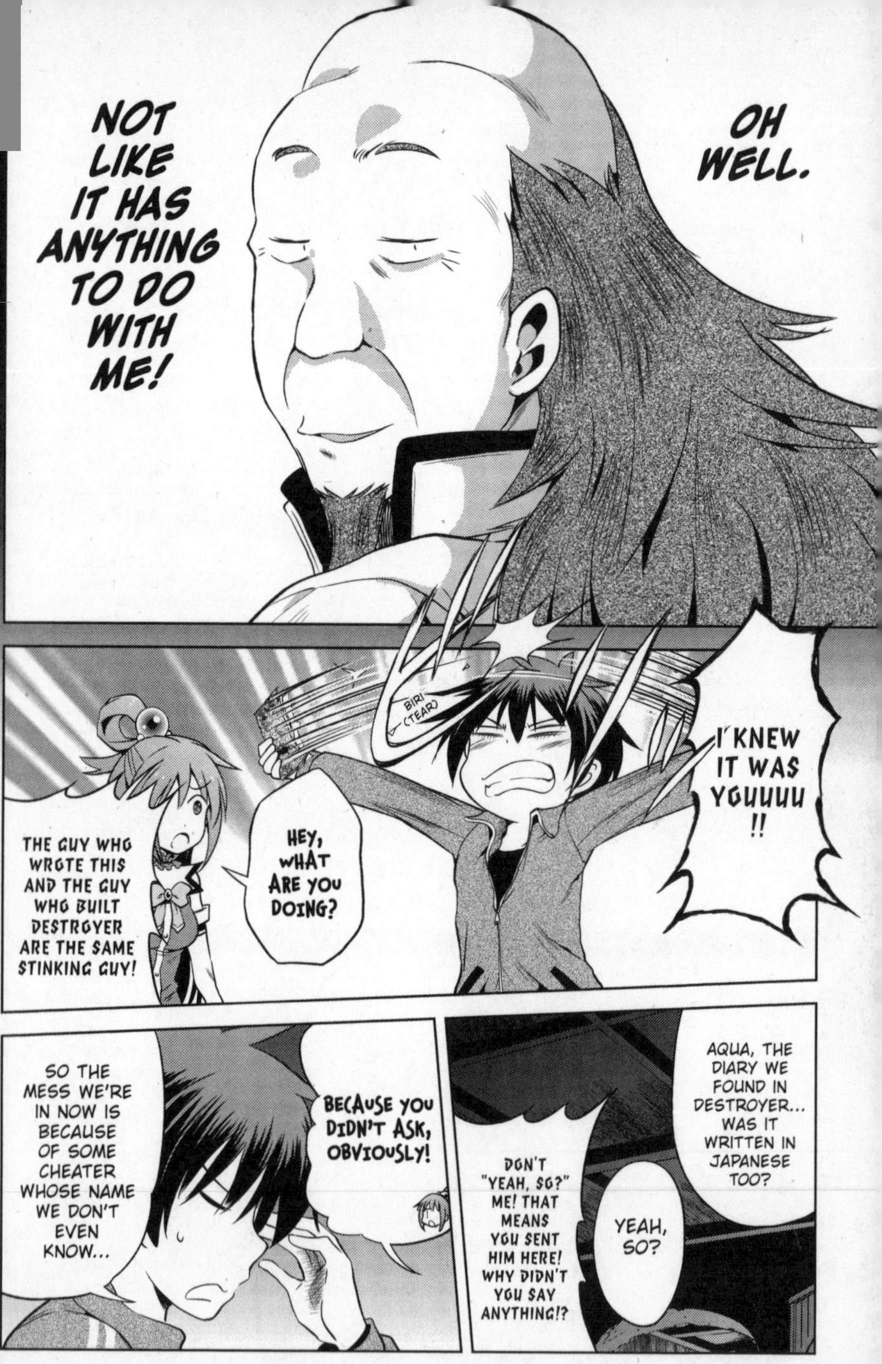
OH WELL.
NOT LIKE IT HAS ANYTHING TO DO WITH ME!
I KNEW IT WAS YOUUUU!!
BIRI (TEAR)
HEY, WHAT ARE YOU DOING?
THE GUY WHO WROTE THIS AND THE GUY WHO BUILT DESTROYER ARE THE SAME STINKING GUY!
AQUA, THE DIARY WE FOUND IN DESTROYER... WAS IT WRITTEN IN JAPANESE TOO?
YEAH, SO?
DON'T "YEAH, SO?" ME! THAT MEANS YOU SENT HIM HERE! WHY DIDN'T YOU SAY ANYTHING!?
BECAUSE YOU DIDN'T ASK, OBVIOUSLY!
SO THE MESS WE'RE IN NOW IS BECAUSE OF SOME CHEATER WHOSE NAME WE DON'T EVEN KNOW...

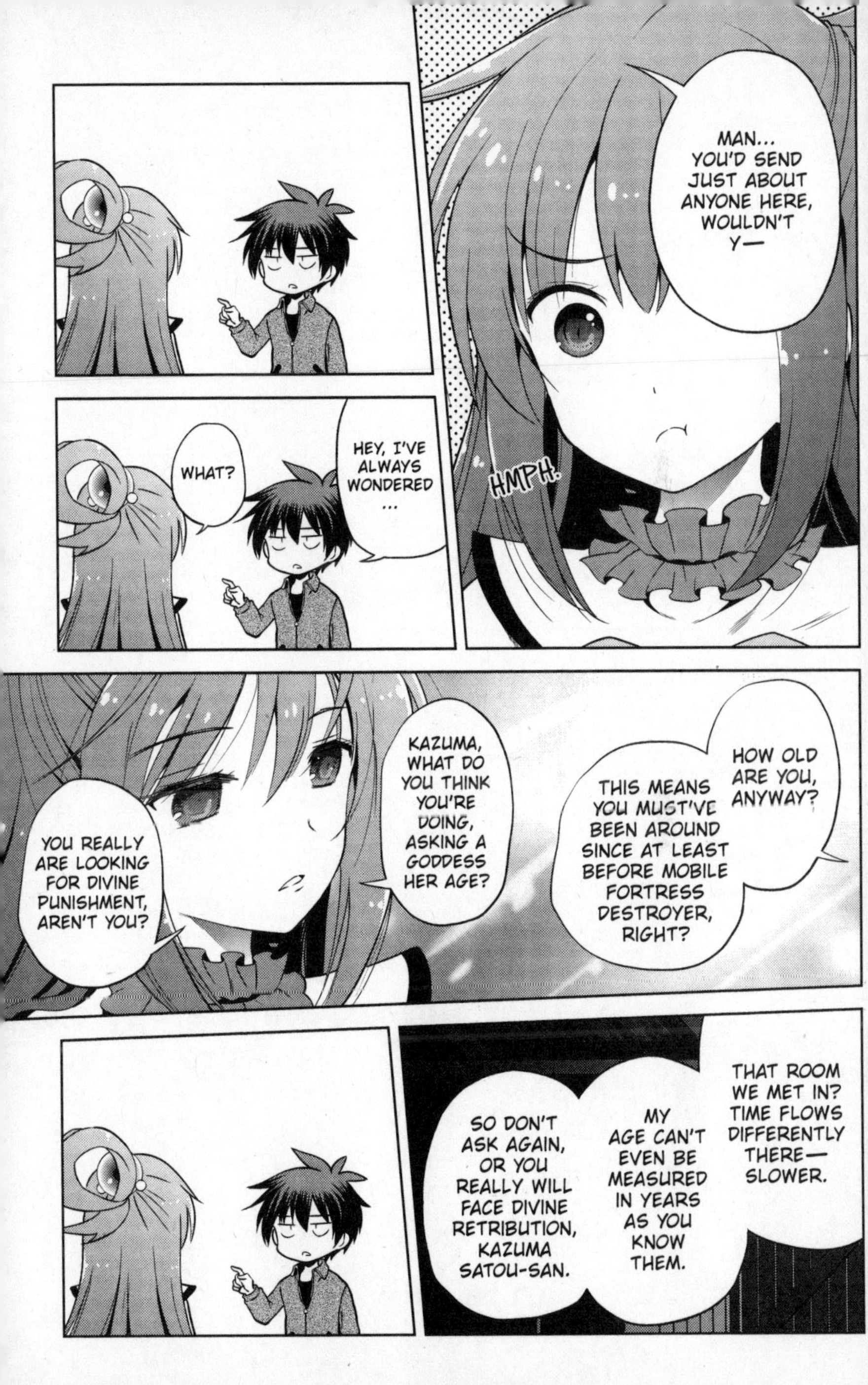
MAN... YOU'D SEND JUST ABOUT ANYONE HERE, WOULDN'T Y—
HMPH.
HEY, I'VE ALWAYS WONDERED ...
WHAT?
HOW OLD ARE YOU, ANYWAY?
THIS MEANS YOU MUST'VE BEEN AROUND SINCE AT LEAST BEFORE MOBILE FORTRESS DESTROYER, RIGHT?
KAZUMA, WHAT DO YOU THINK YOU'RE DOING, ASKING A GODDESS HER AGE?
YOU REALLY ARE LOOKING FOR DIVINE PUNISHMENT, AREN'T YOU?
THAT ROOM WE MET IN? TIME FLOWS DIFFERENTLY THERE—SLOWER.
MY AGE CAN'T EVEN BE MEASURED IN YEARS AS YOU KNOW THEM.
SO DON'T ASK AGAIN, OR YOU REALLY WILL FACE DIVINE RETRIBUTION, KAZUMA SATOU-SAN.

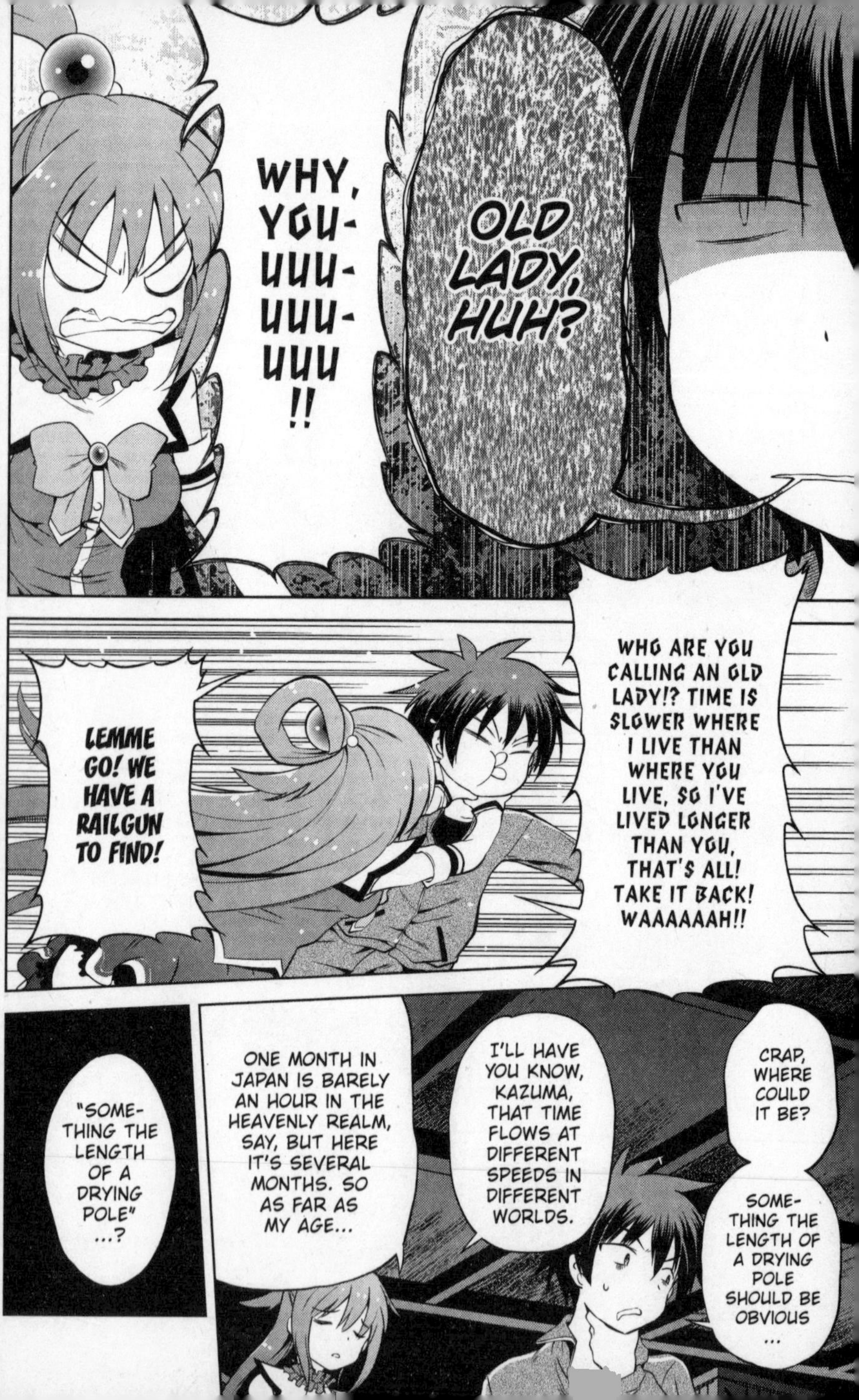
OLD LADY, HUH?
WHY, YOUUUUUUUUUUU!!
WHO ARE YOU CALLING AN OLD LADY!? TIME IS SLOWER WHERE I LIVE THAN WHERE YOU LIVE, SO I'VE LIVED LONGER THAN YOU, THAT'S ALL! TAKE IT BACK! WAAAAAAH!!
LEMME GO! WE HAVE A RAILGUN TO FIND!
CRAP, WHERE COULD IT BE?
SOMETHING THE LENGTH OF A DRYING POLE SHOULD BE OBVIOUS...
I'LL HAVE YOU KNOW, KAZUMA, THAT TIME FLOWS AT DIFFERENT SPEEDS IN DIFFERENT WORLDS.
ONE MONTH IN JAPAN IS BARELY AN HOUR IN THE HEAVENLY REALM, SAY, BUT HERE IT'S SEVERAL MONTHS. SO AS FAR AS MY AGE...
"SOMETHING THE LENGTH OF A DRYING POLE"...?

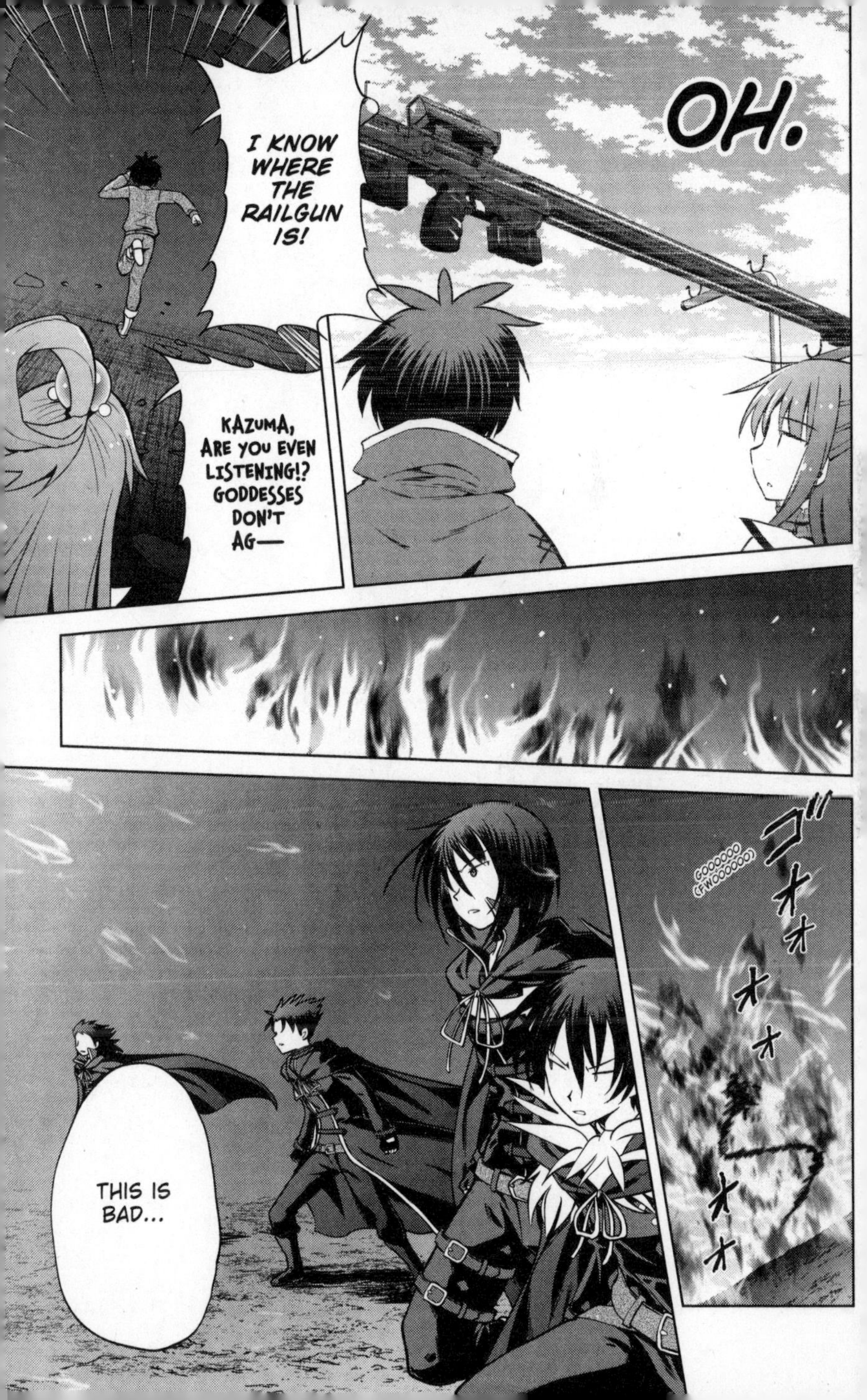
OH.
I KNOW WHERE THE RAILGUN IS!
KAZUMA, ARE YOU EVEN LISTENING!? GODDESSES DON'T AG—
ゴオオオオオオ
GOOOOOO (FWOOOOOO)
THIS IS BAD...

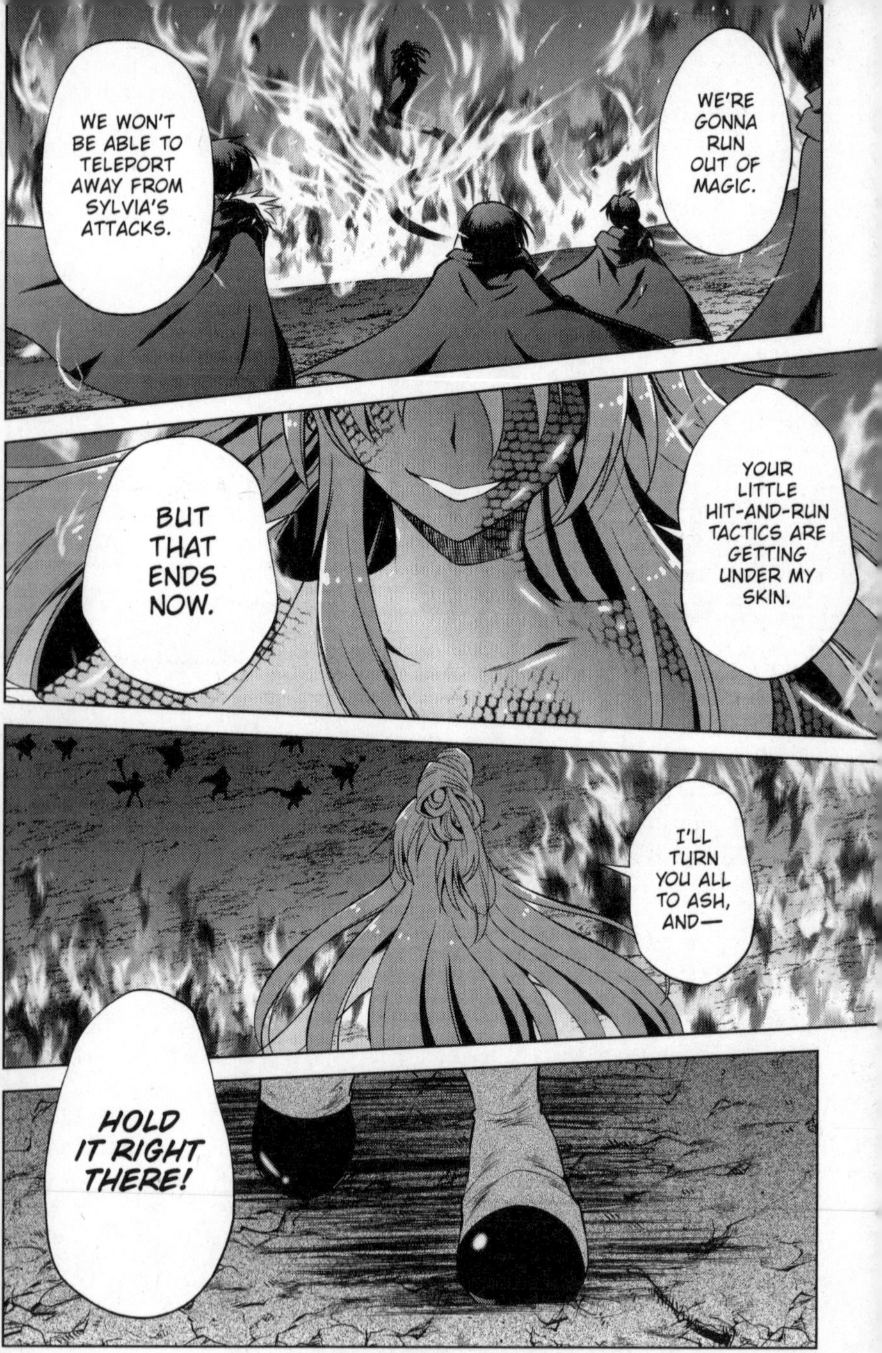
WE'RE GONNA RUN OUT OF MAGIC.
WE WON'T BE ABLE TO TELEPORT AWAY FROM SYLVIA'S ATTACKS.
YOUR LITTLE HIT-AND-RUN TACTICS ARE GETTING UNDER MY SKIN.
BUT THAT ENDS NOW.
I'LL TURN YOU ALL TO ASH, AND—
HOLD IT RIGHT THERE!

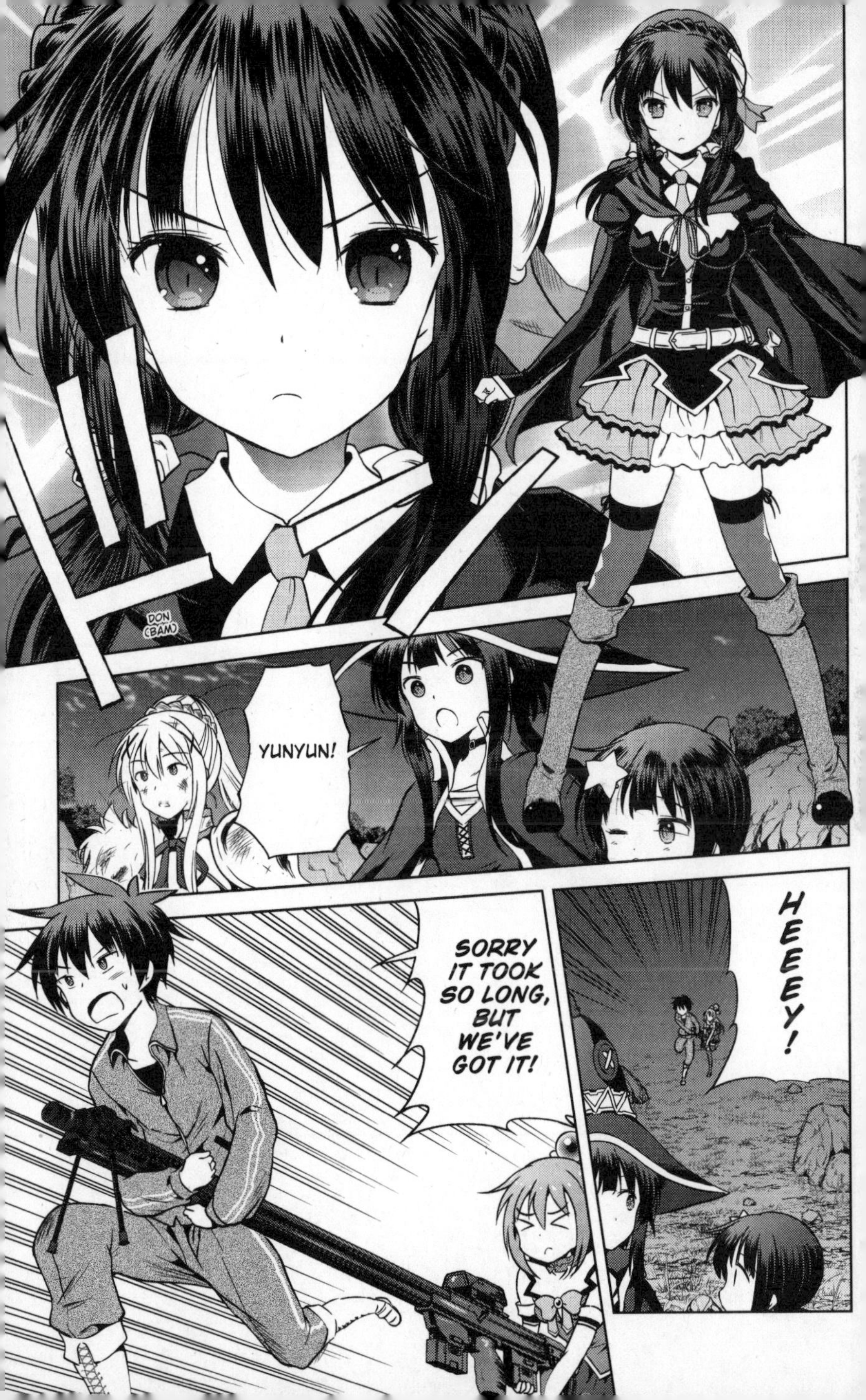
DON (BAM)
YUNYUN!
HEEEY!
SORRY IT TOOK SO LONG, BUT WE'VE GOT IT!

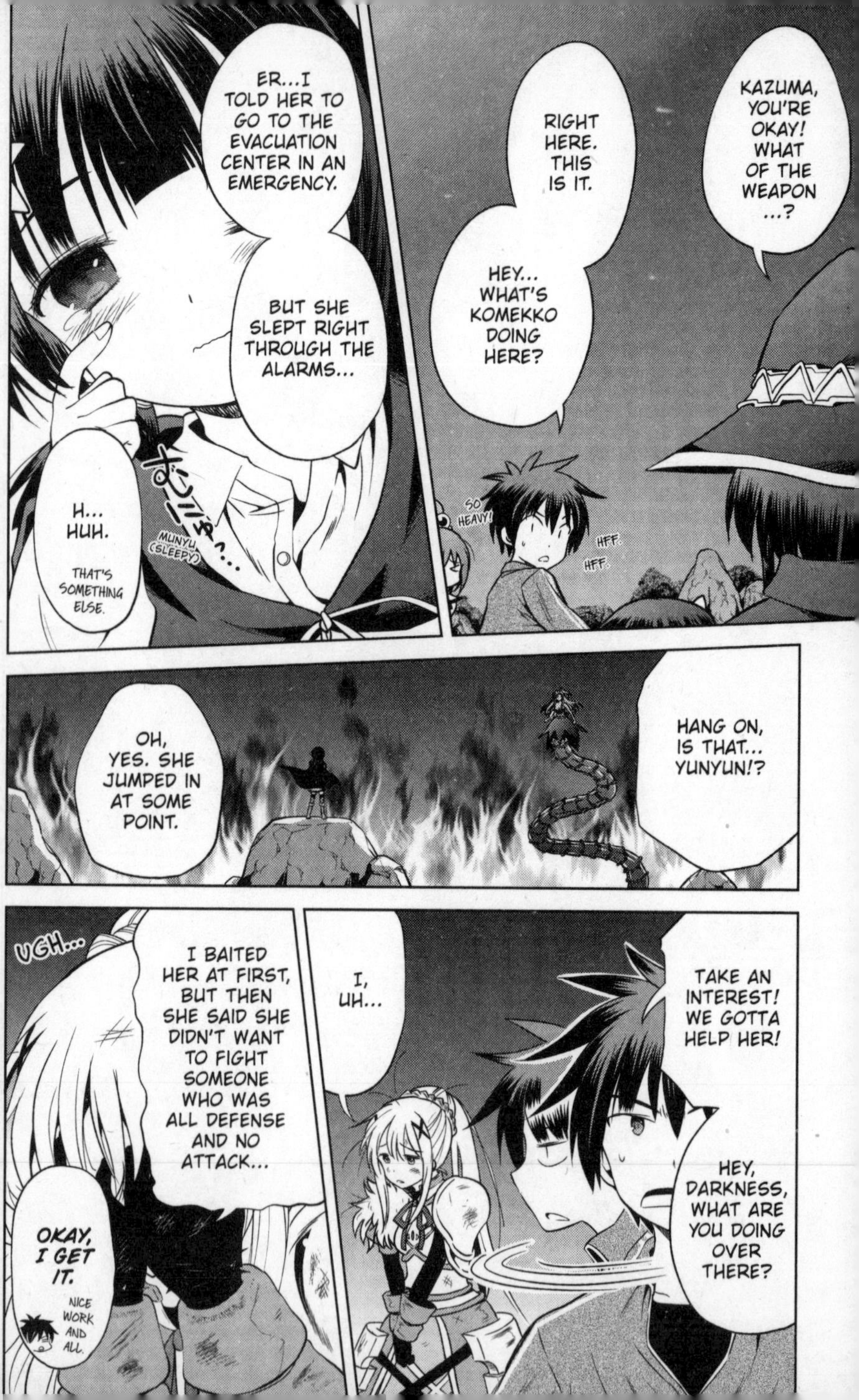
KAZUMA, YOU'RE OKAY! WHAT OF THE WEAPON ...?
RIGHT HERE. THIS IS IT.
HEY... WHAT'S KOMEKKO DOING HERE?
SO HEAVY!
HFF. HFF.
ER...I TOLD HER TO GO TO THE EVACUATION CENTER IN AN EMERGENCY.
BUT SHE SLEPT RIGHT THROUGH THE ALARMS...
MUNYU (SLEEPY)
H... HUH.
THAT'S SOMETHING ELSE.
HANG ON, IS THAT... YUNYUN!?
OH, YES. SHE JUMPED IN AT SOME POINT.
TAKE AN INTEREST! WE GOTTA HELP HER!
HEY, DARKNESS, WHAT ARE YOU DOING OVER THERE?
I, UH...
UGH...
I BAITED HER AT FIRST, BUT THEN SHE SAID SHE DIDN'T WANT TO FIGHT SOMEONE WHO WAS ALL DEFENSE AND NO ATTACK...
OKAY, I GET IT.
NICE WORK AND ALL.

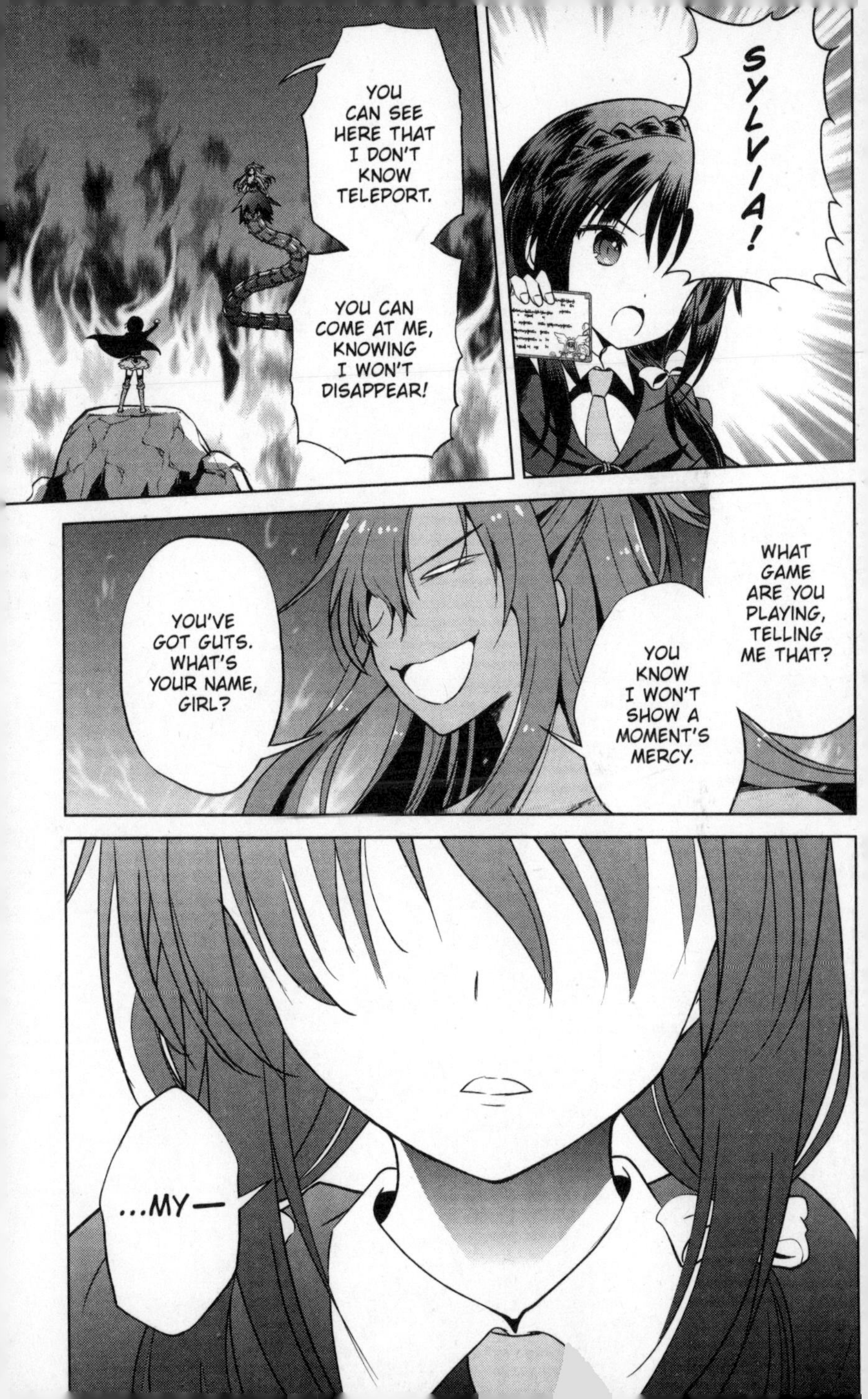
SYLVIA!
YOU CAN SEE HERE THAT I DON'T KNOW TELEPORT.
YOU CAN COME AT ME, KNOWING I WON'T DISAPPEAR!
WHAT GAME ARE YOU PLAYING, TELLING ME THAT?
YOU KNOW I WON'T SHOW A MOMENT'S MERCY.
YOU'VE GOT GUTS. WHAT'S YOUR NAME, GIRL?
...MY—

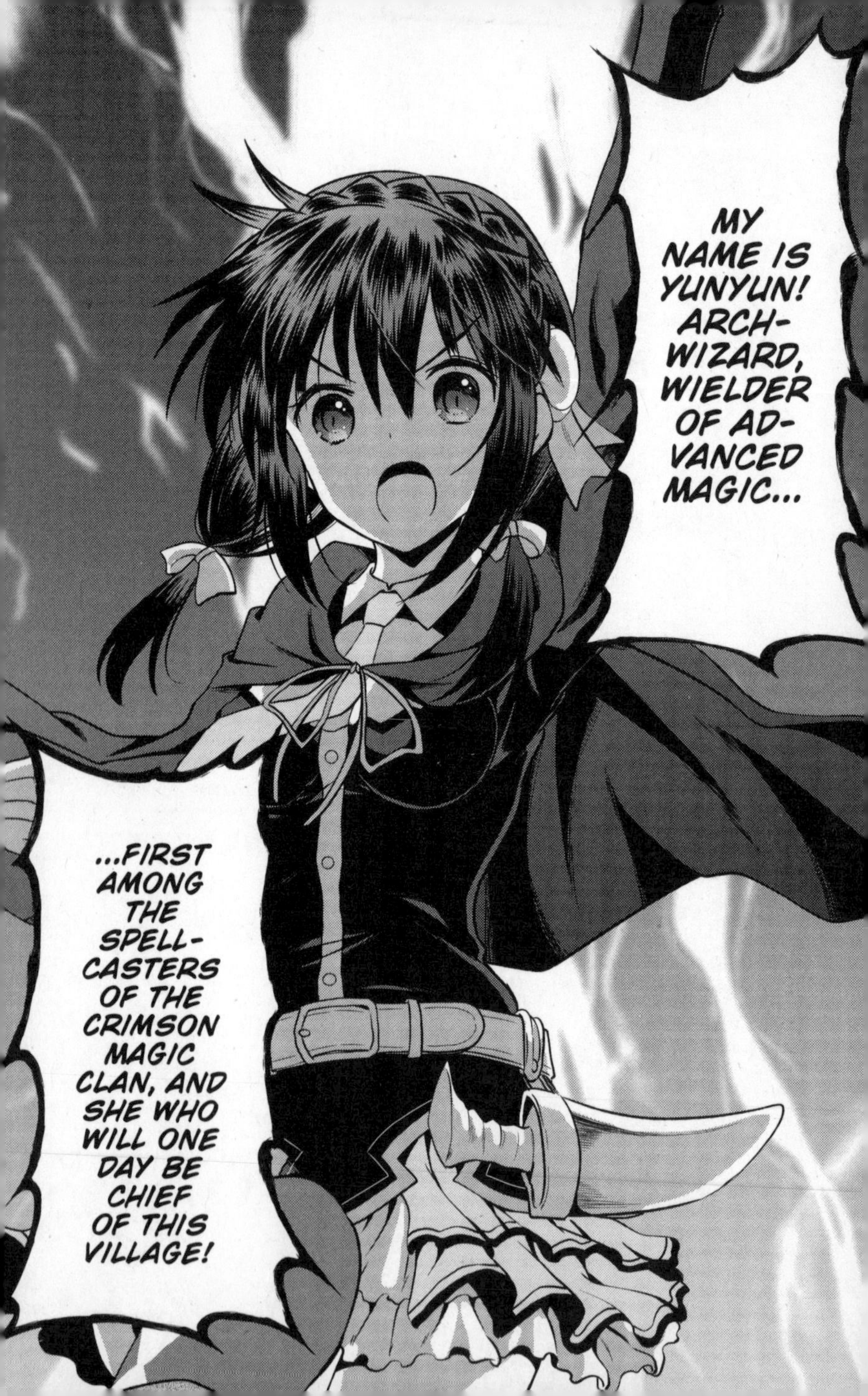
MY NAME IS YUNYUN! ARCH-WIZARD, WIELDER OF AD-VANCED MAGIC...
...FIRST AMONG THE SPELL-CASTERS OF THE CRIMSON MAGIC CLAN, AND SHE WHO WILL ONE DAY BE CHIEF OF THIS VILLAGE!

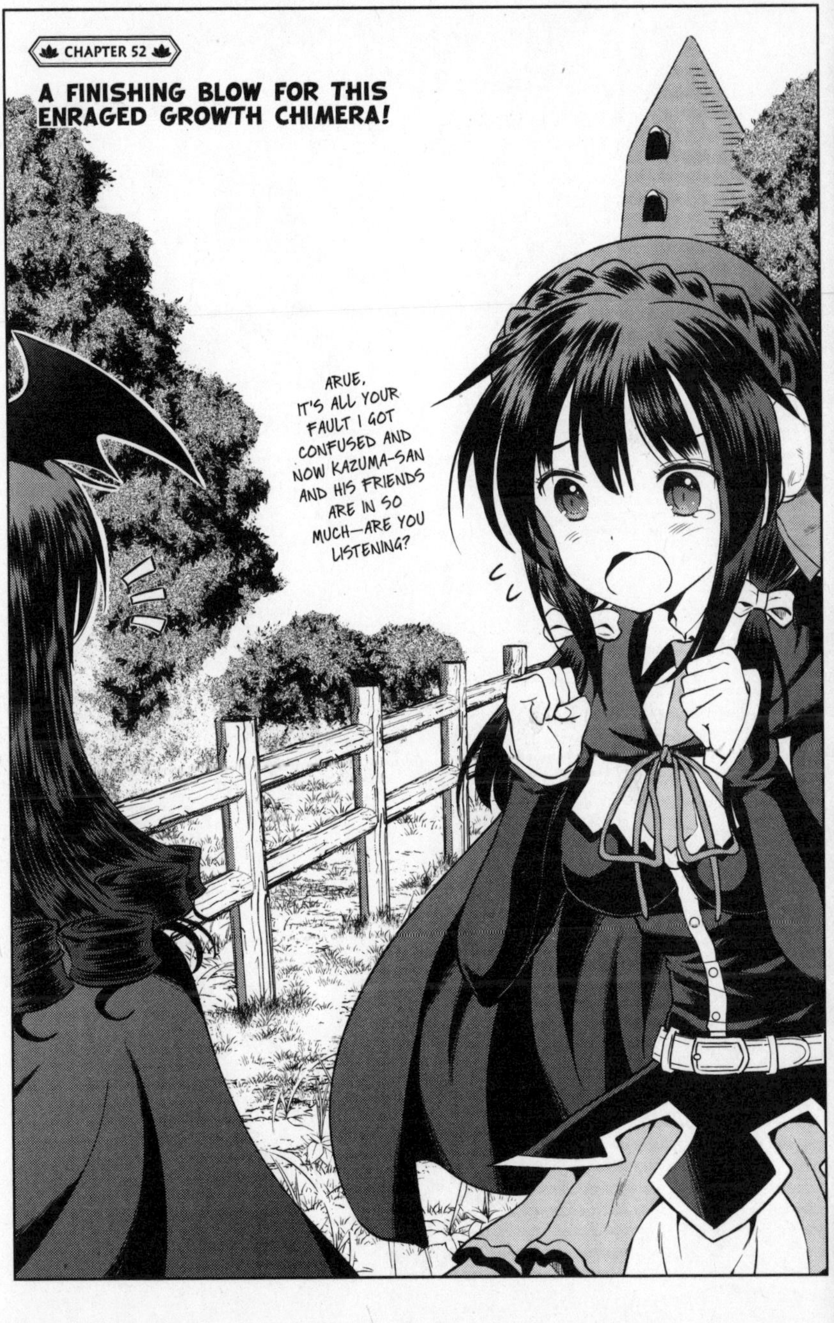
CHAPTER 52
A FINISHING BLOW FOR THIS ENRAGED GROWTH CHIMERA!
ARUE, IT'S ALL YOUR FAULT I GOT CONFUSED AND NOW KAZUMA-SAN AND HIS FRIENDS ARE IN SO MUCH—ARE YOU LISTENING?

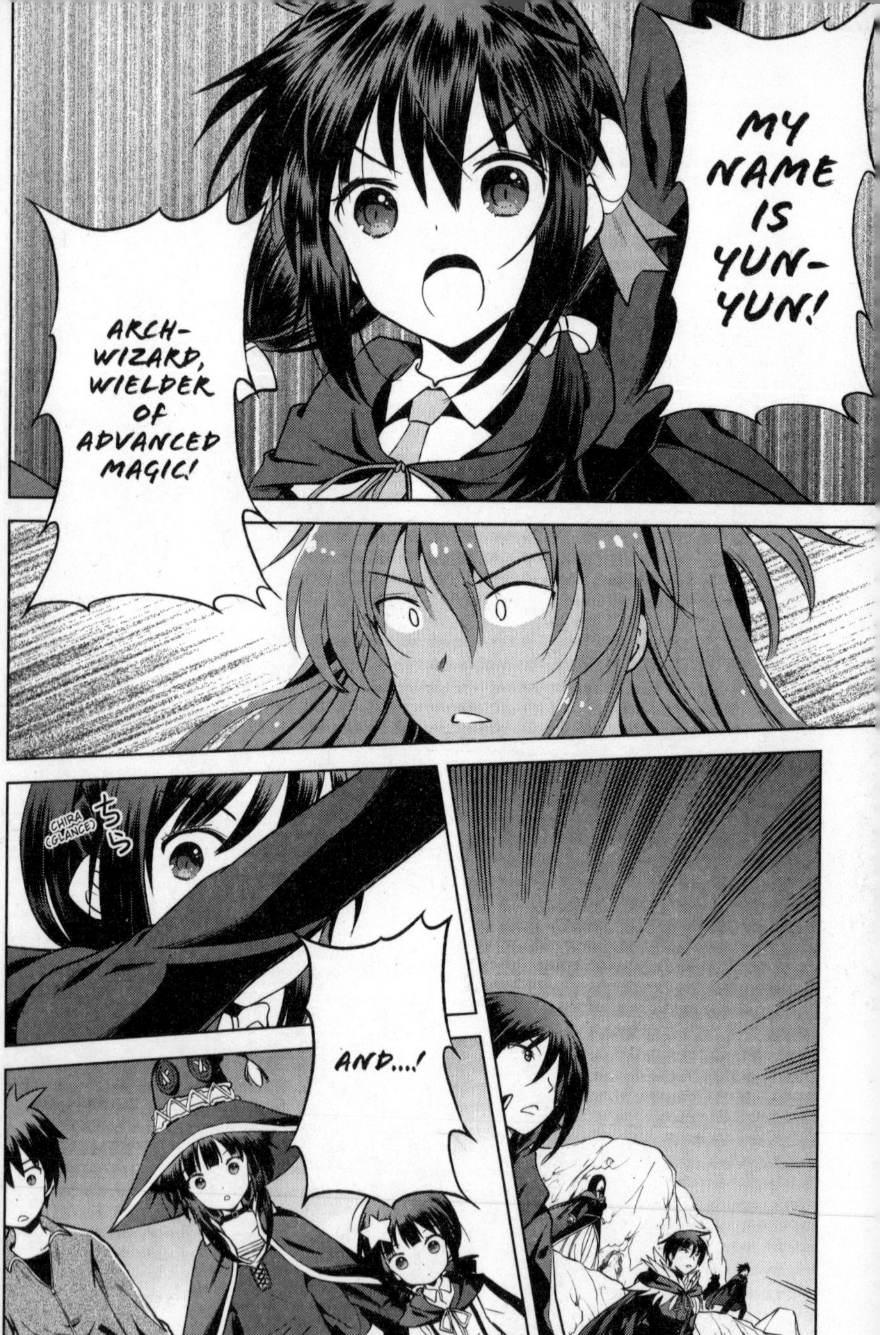
MY NAME IS YUN-YUN!
ARCH-WIZARD, WIELDER OF ADVANCED MAGIC!
ちら
CHIRA (GLANCE)
AND...!

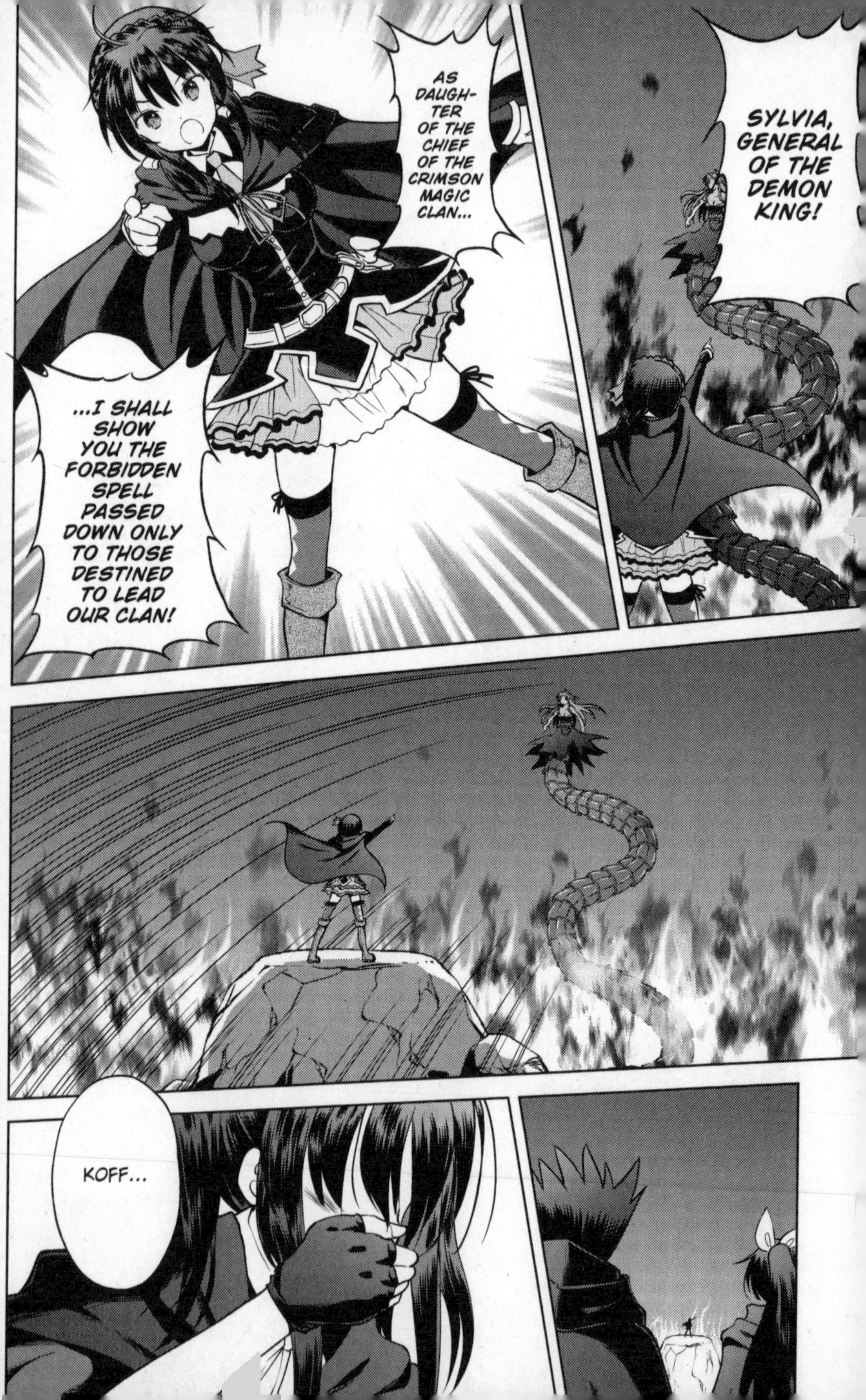
SYLVIA, GENERAL OF THE DEMON KING!
AS DAUGHTER OF THE CHIEF OF THE CRIMSON MAGIC CLAN...
...I SHALL SHOW YOU THE FORBIDDEN SPELL PASSED DOWN ONLY TO THOSE DESTINED TO LEAD OUR CLAN!
KOFF...

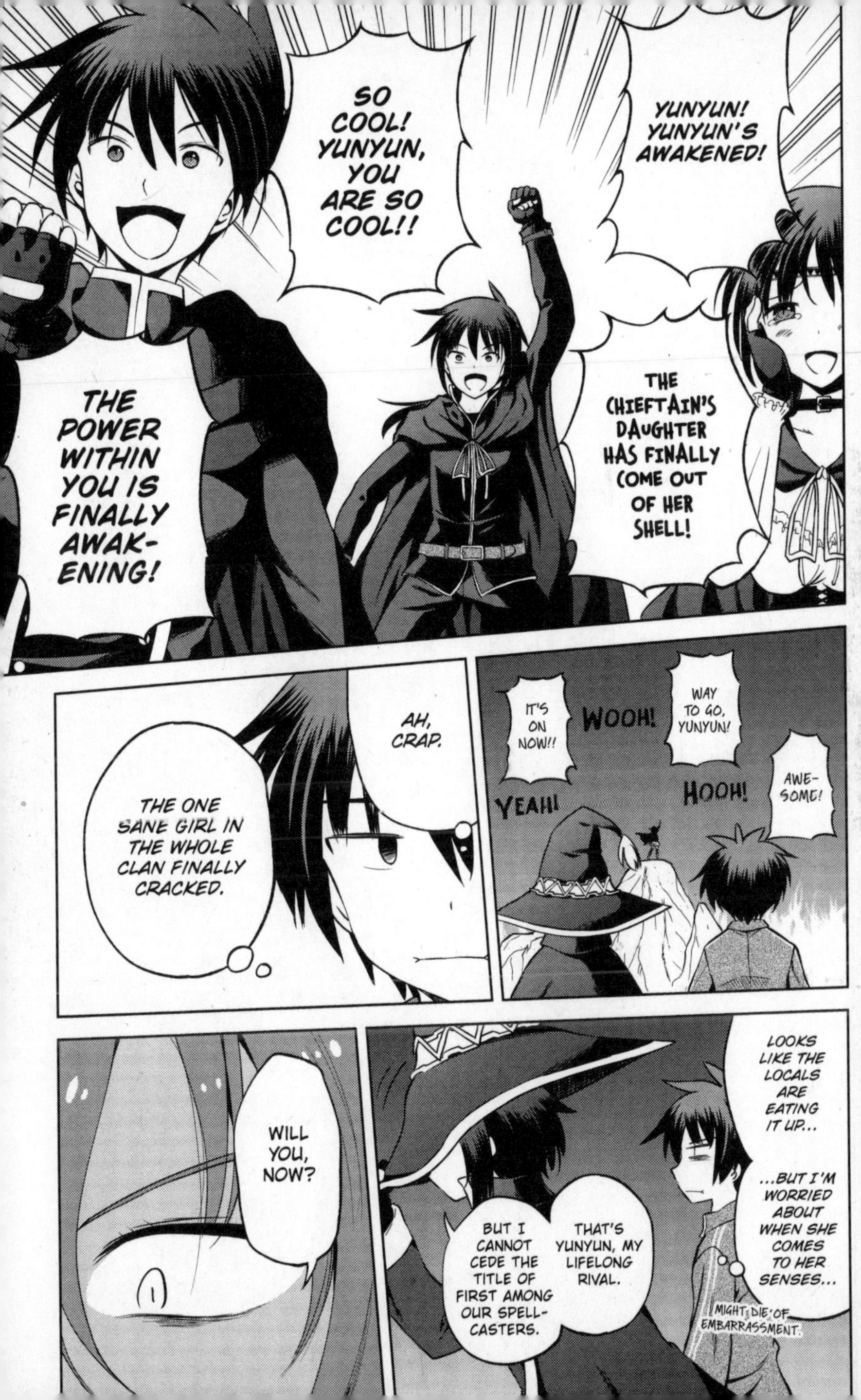
YUNYUN! YUNYUN'S AWAKENED!
SO COOL! YUNYUN, YOU ARE SO COOL!!
THE CHIEFTAIN'S DAUGHTER HAS FINALLY COME OUT OF HER SHELL!
THE POWER WITHIN YOU IS FINALLY AWAK-ENING!
WAY TO GO, YUNYUN!
WOOH!
IT'S ON NOW!!
AWE-SOME!
HOOH!
YEAH!
AH, CRAP.
THE ONE SANE GIRL IN THE WHOLE CLAN FINALLY CRACKED.
LOOKS LIKE THE LOCALS ARE EATING IT UP...
...BUT I'M WORRIED ABOUT WHEN SHE COMES TO HER SENSES...
MIGHT DIE OF EMBARRASSMENT.
THAT'S YUNYUN, MY LIFELONG RIVAL.
BUT I CANNOT CEDE THE TITLE OF FIRST AMONG OUR SPELL-CASTERS.
WILL YOU, NOW?

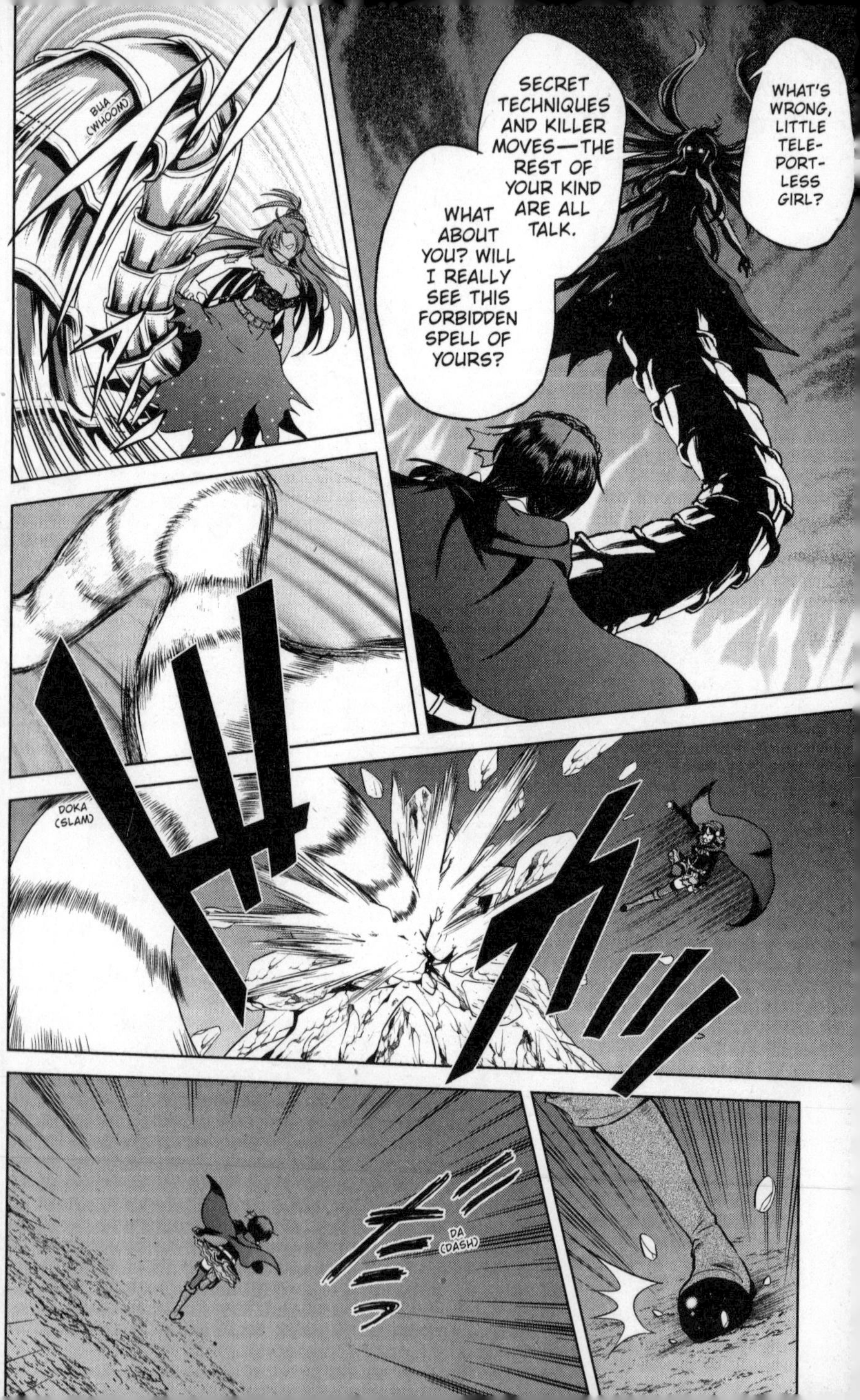
WHAT'S WRONG, LITTLE TELE-PORT-LESS GIRL?
SECRET TECHNIQUES AND KILLER MOVES—THE REST OF YOUR KIND ARE ALL TALK.
WHAT ABOUT YOU? WILL I REALLY SEE THIS FORBIDDEN SPELL OF YOURS?
BUA (WHOOM)
DOKA (SLAM)
DA (DASH)

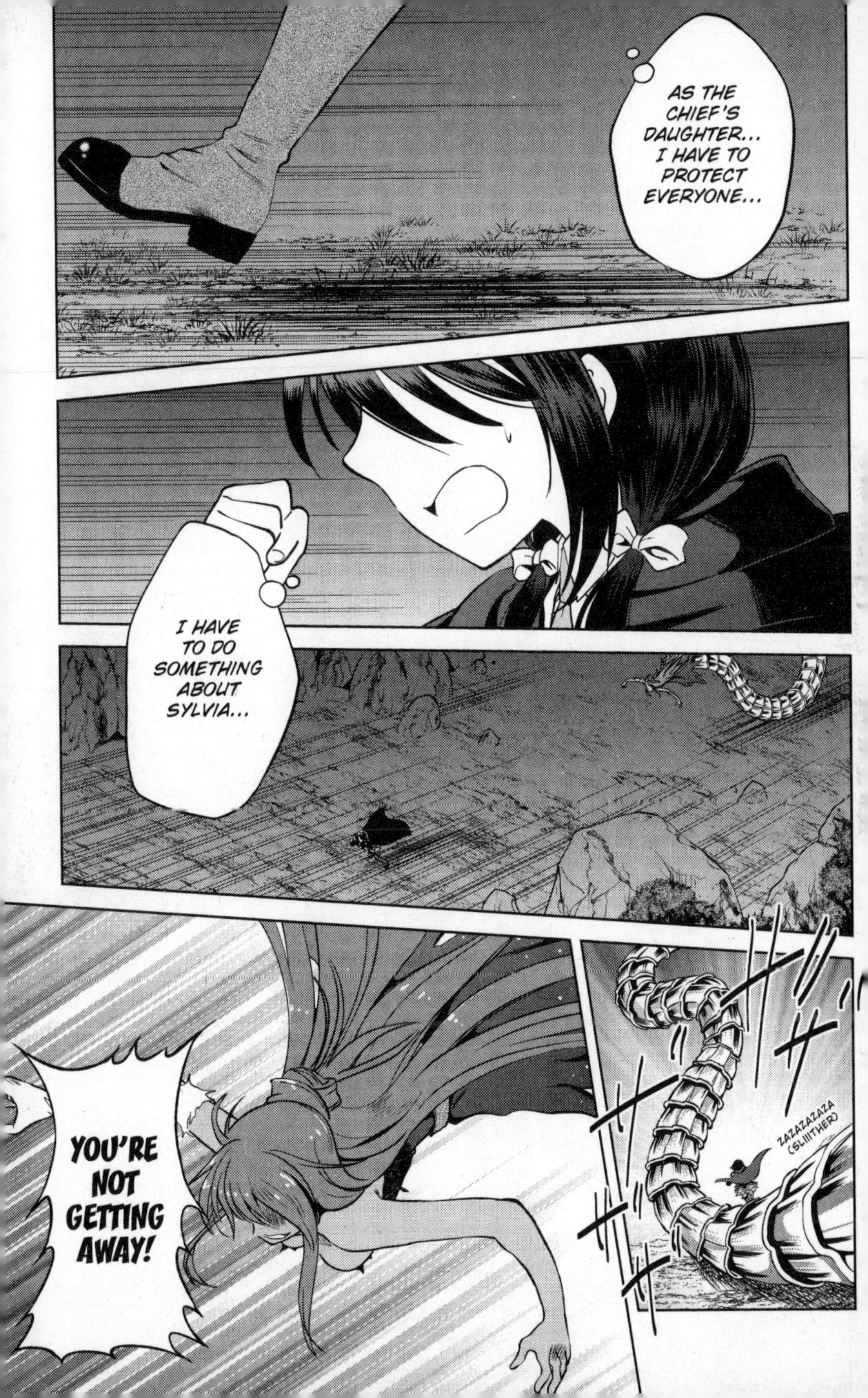
AS THE CHIEF'S DAUGHTER... I HAVE TO PROTECT EVERYONE...
I HAVE TO DO SOMETHING ABOUT SYLVIA...
ZAZAZAZAZA (SLIIITHER)
YOU'RE NOT GETTING AWAY!

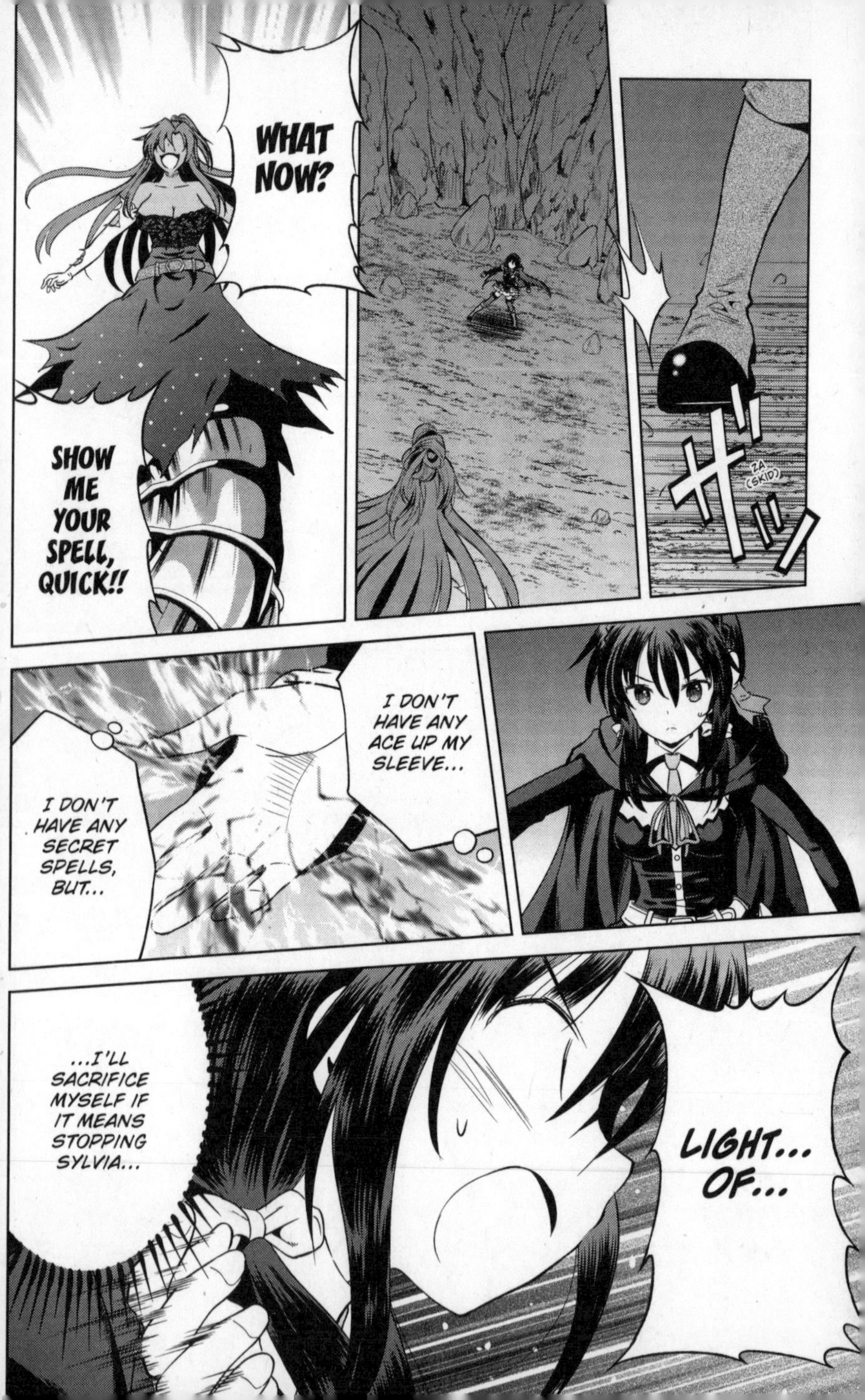
ZA (SKID)
WHAT NOW?
SHOW ME YOUR SPELL, QUICK!!
I DON'T HAVE ANY ACE UP MY SLEEVE...
I DON'T HAVE ANY SECRET SPELLS, BUT...
...I'LL SACRIFICE MYSELF IF IT MEANS STOPPING SYLVIA...
LIGHT... OF...

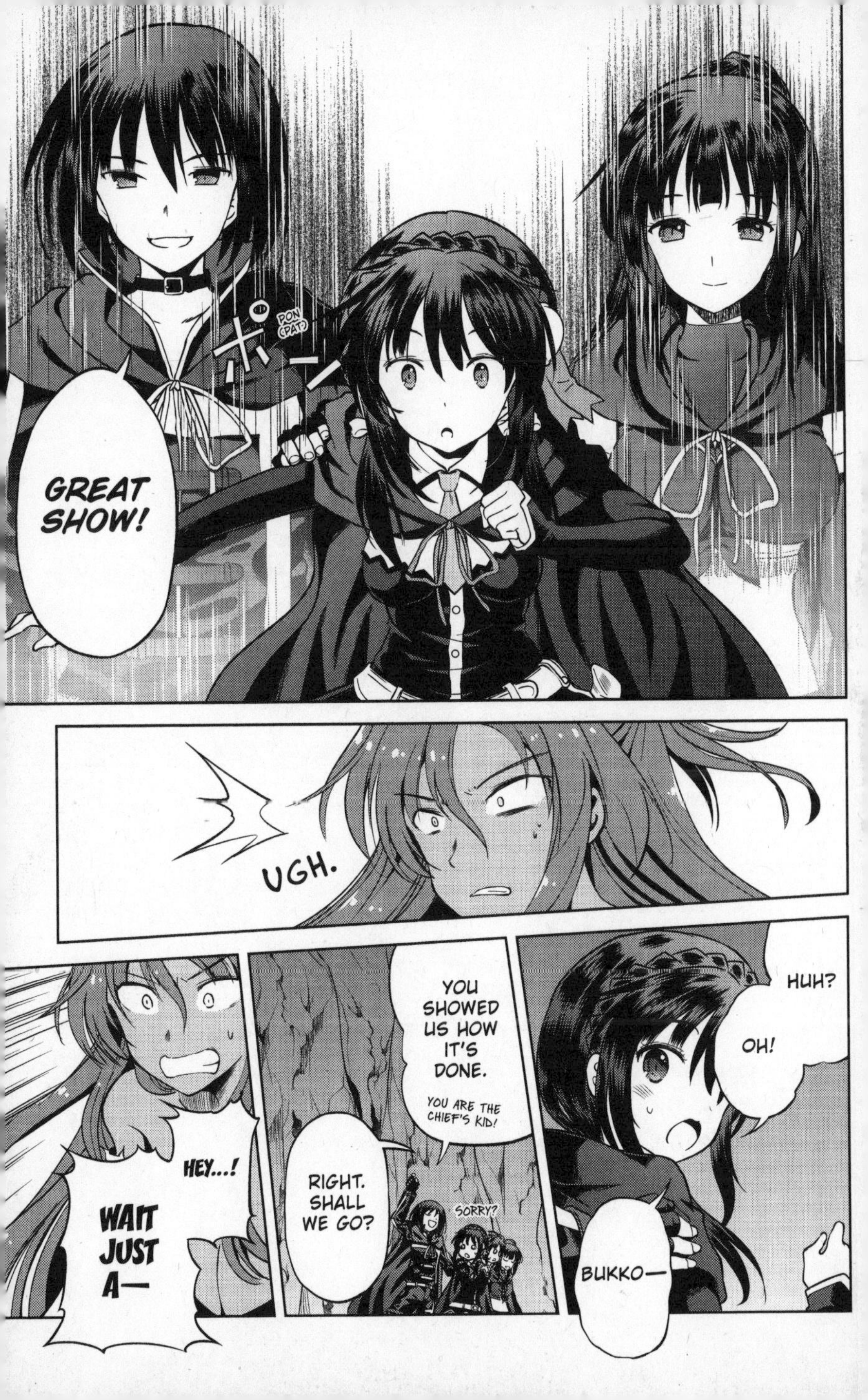
PON (PAT)
GREAT SHOW!
UGH.
HUH?
OH!
BUKKO—
YOU SHOWED US HOW IT'S DONE.
YOU ARE THE CHIEF'S KID!
RIGHT. SHALL WE GO?
SORRY?
HEY...!
WAIT JUST A—

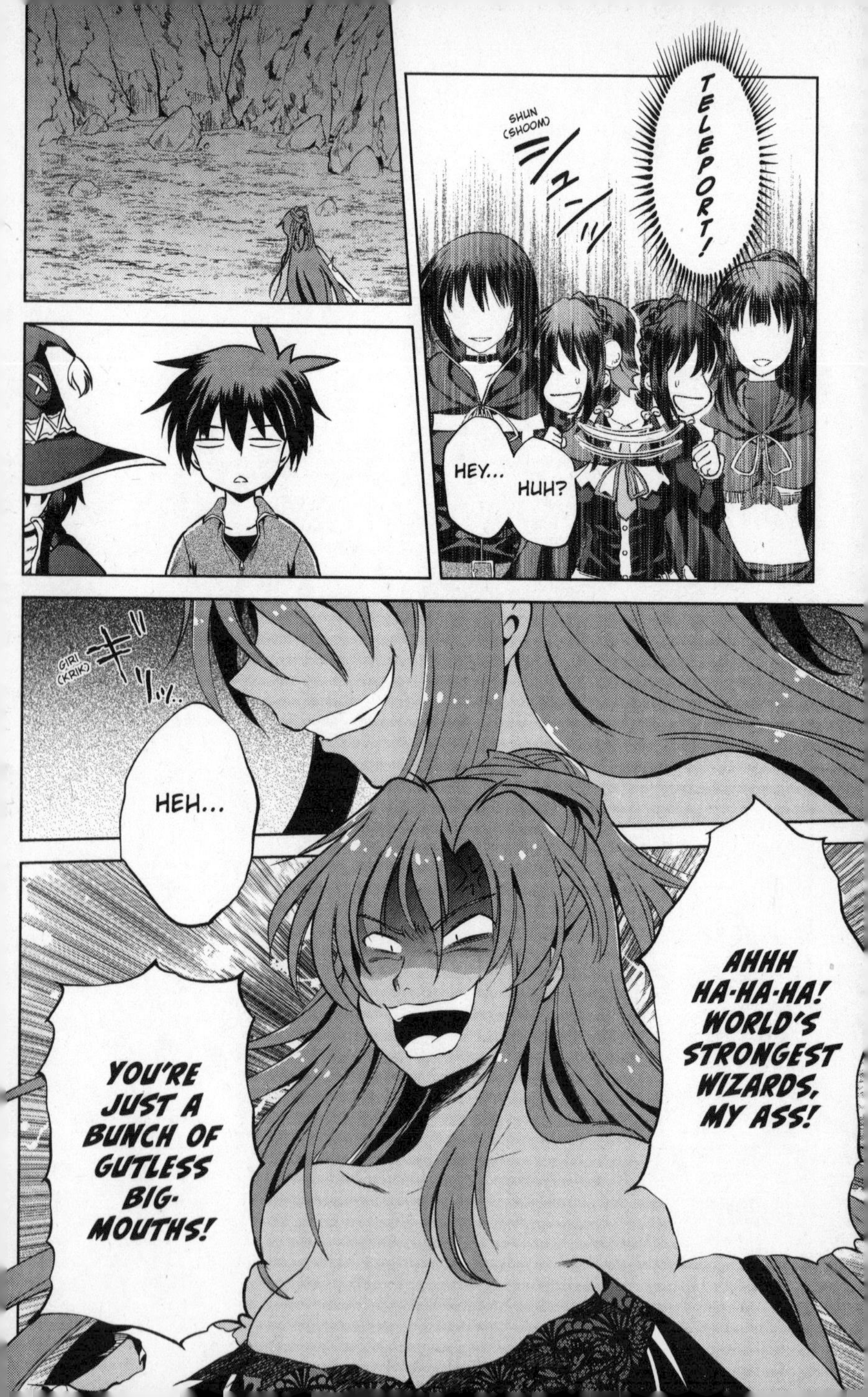
TELEPORT!
SHUN (SHOOM)
HEY...
HUH?
GIRI (KRIK)
HEH...
AHHH HA-HA-HA! WORLD'S STRONGEST WIZARDS, MY ASS!
YOU'RE JUST A BUNCH OF GUTLESS BIG-MOUTHS!

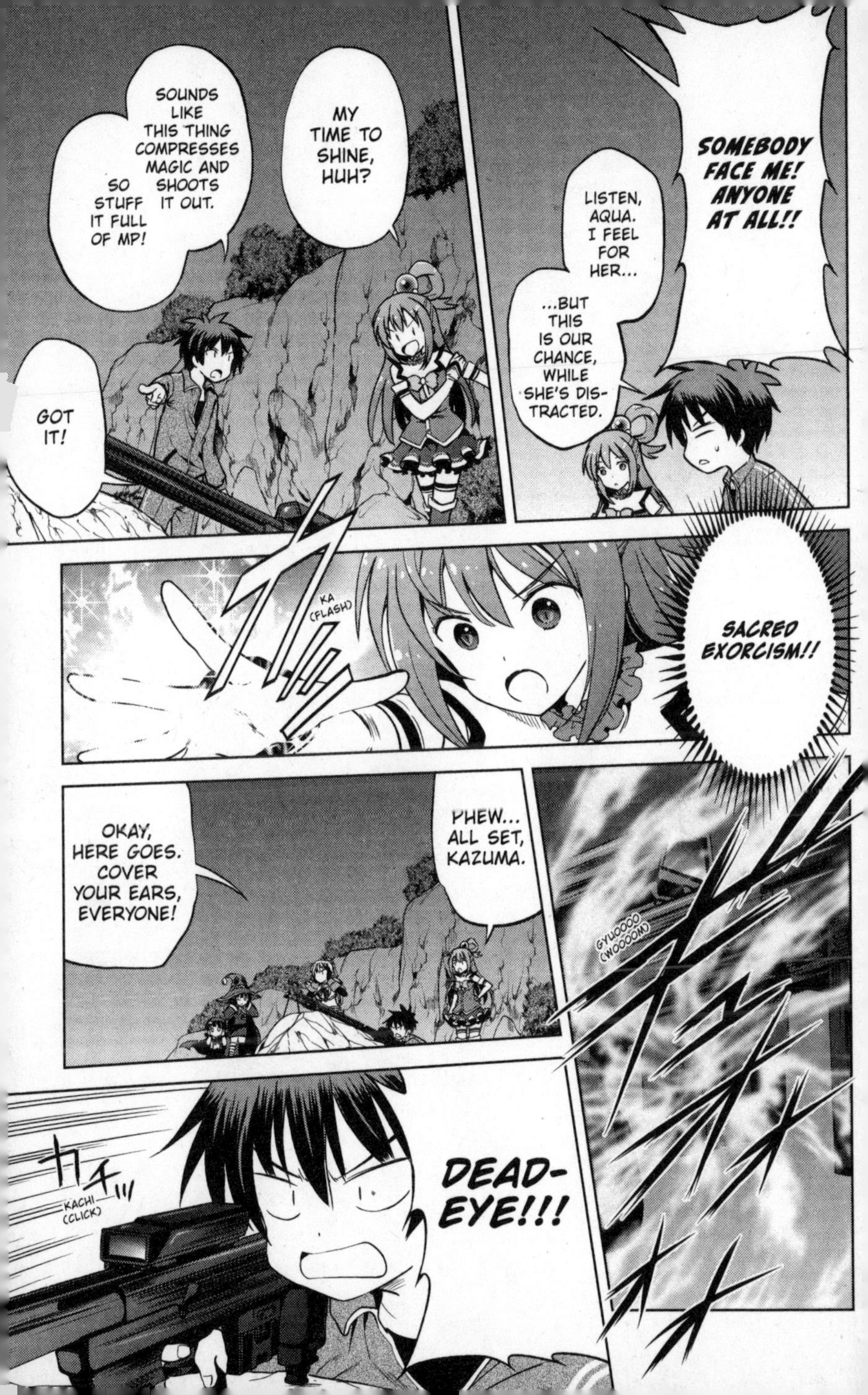
SOMEBODY FACE ME! ANYONE AT ALL!!
LISTEN, AQUA. I FEEL FOR HER...
...BUT THIS IS OUR CHANCE, WHILE SHE'S DIS-TRACTED.
MY TIME TO SHINE, HUH?
SOUNDS LIKE THIS THING COMPRESSES MAGIC AND SHOOTS IT OUT.
SO STUFF IT FULL OF MP!
GOT IT!
SACRED EXORCISM!!
KA (FLASH)
GYUOOOO (WOOOOM)
PHEW... ALL SET, KAZUMA.
OKAY, HERE GOES. COVER YOUR EARS, EVERYONE!
DEAD-EYE!!!
カチッ
KACHI (CLICK)

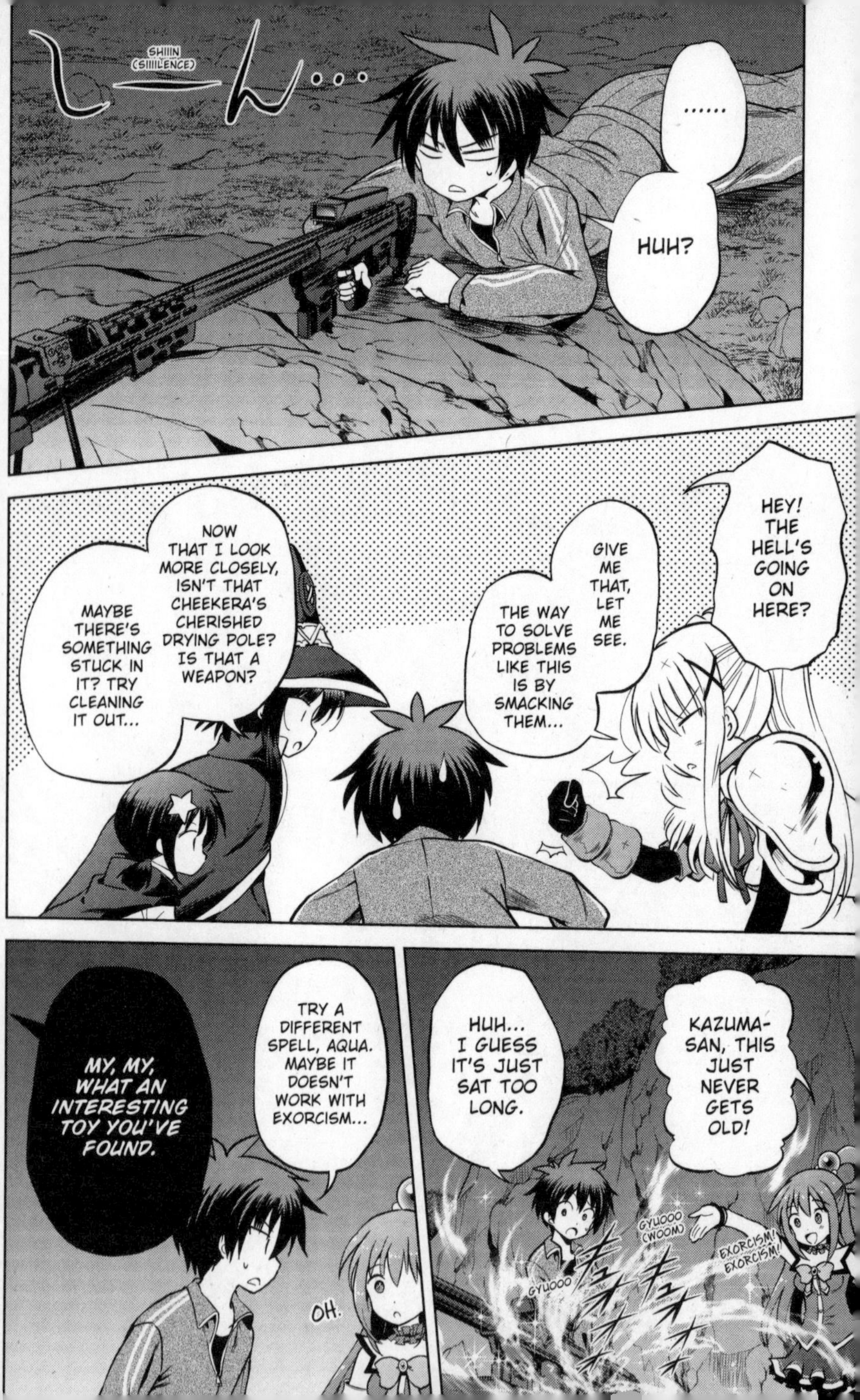
......
HUH?
しーん...
SHIIN (SIIIILENCE)
HEY! THE HELL'S GOING ON HERE?
GIVE ME THAT, LET ME SEE.
THE WAY TO SOLVE PROBLEMS LIKE THIS IS BY SMACKING THEM...
NOW THAT I LOOK MORE CLOSELY, ISN'T THAT CHEEKERA'S CHERISHED DRYING POLE? IS THAT A WEAPON?
MAYBE THERE'S SOMETHING STUCK IN IT? TRY CLEANING IT OUT...
KAZUMA-SAN, THIS JUST NEVER GETS OLD!
EXORCISM! EXORCISM!
GYUOOO (WOOM)
GYUOOO
HUH... I GUESS IT'S JUST SAT TOO LONG.
TRY A DIFFERENT SPELL, AQUA. MAYBE IT DOESN'T WORK WITH EXORCISM...
MY, MY, WHAT AN INTERESTING TOY YOU'VE FOUND.
OH.

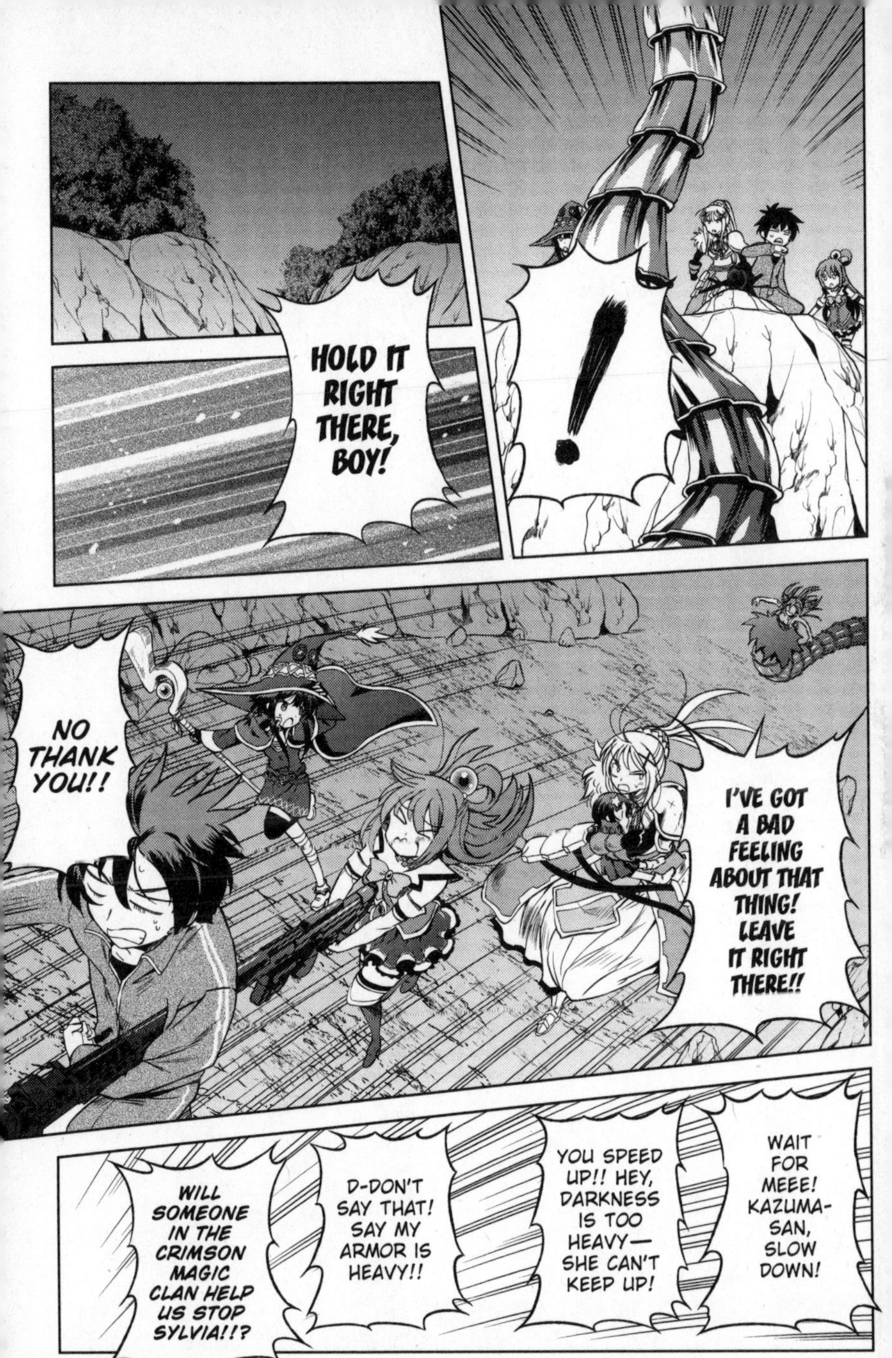
!
HOLD IT RIGHT THERE, BOY!
I'VE GOT A BAD FEELING ABOUT THAT THING! LEAVE IT RIGHT THERE!!
NO THANK YOU!!
WAIT FOR MEEE! KAZUMA-SAN, SLOW DOWN!
YOU SPEED UP!! HEY, DARKNESS IS TOO HEAVY—SHE CAN'T KEEP UP!
D-DON'T SAY THAT! SAY MY ARMOR IS HEAVY!!
WILL SOMEONE IN THE CRIMSON MAGIC CLAN HELP US STOP SYLVIA!!?

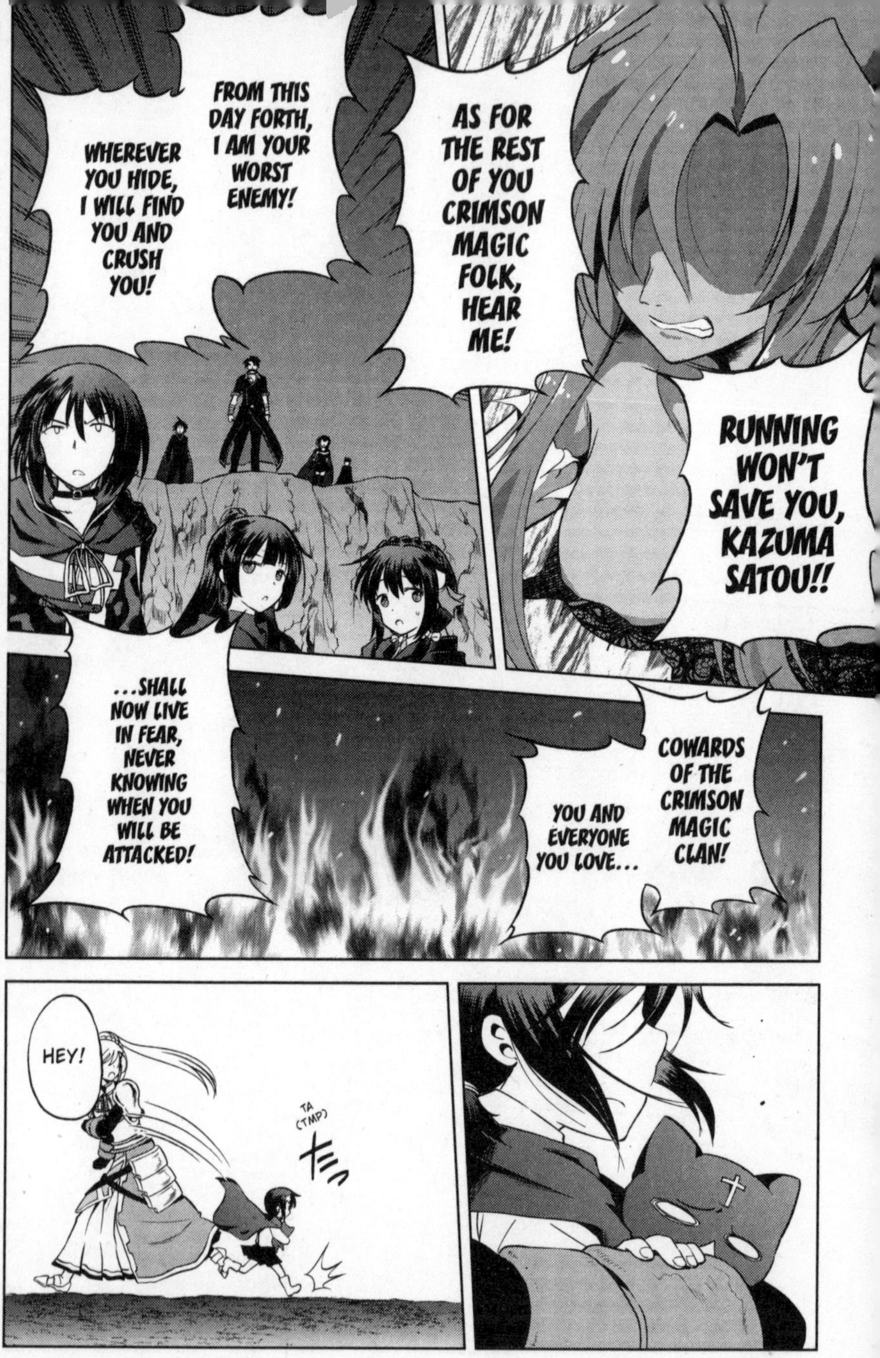
RUNNING WON'T SAVE YOU, KAZUMA SATOU!!
FROM THIS DAY FORTH, I AM YOUR WORST ENEMY!
WHEREVER YOU HIDE, I WILL FIND YOU AND CRUSH YOU!
AS FOR THE REST OF YOU CRIMSON MAGIC FOLK, HEAR ME!
COWARDS OF THE CRIMSON MAGIC CLAN!
YOU AND EVERYONE YOU LOVE...
...SHALL NOW LIVE IN FEAR, NEVER KNOWING WHEN YOU WILL BE ATTACKED!
HEY!
TA (TMP)

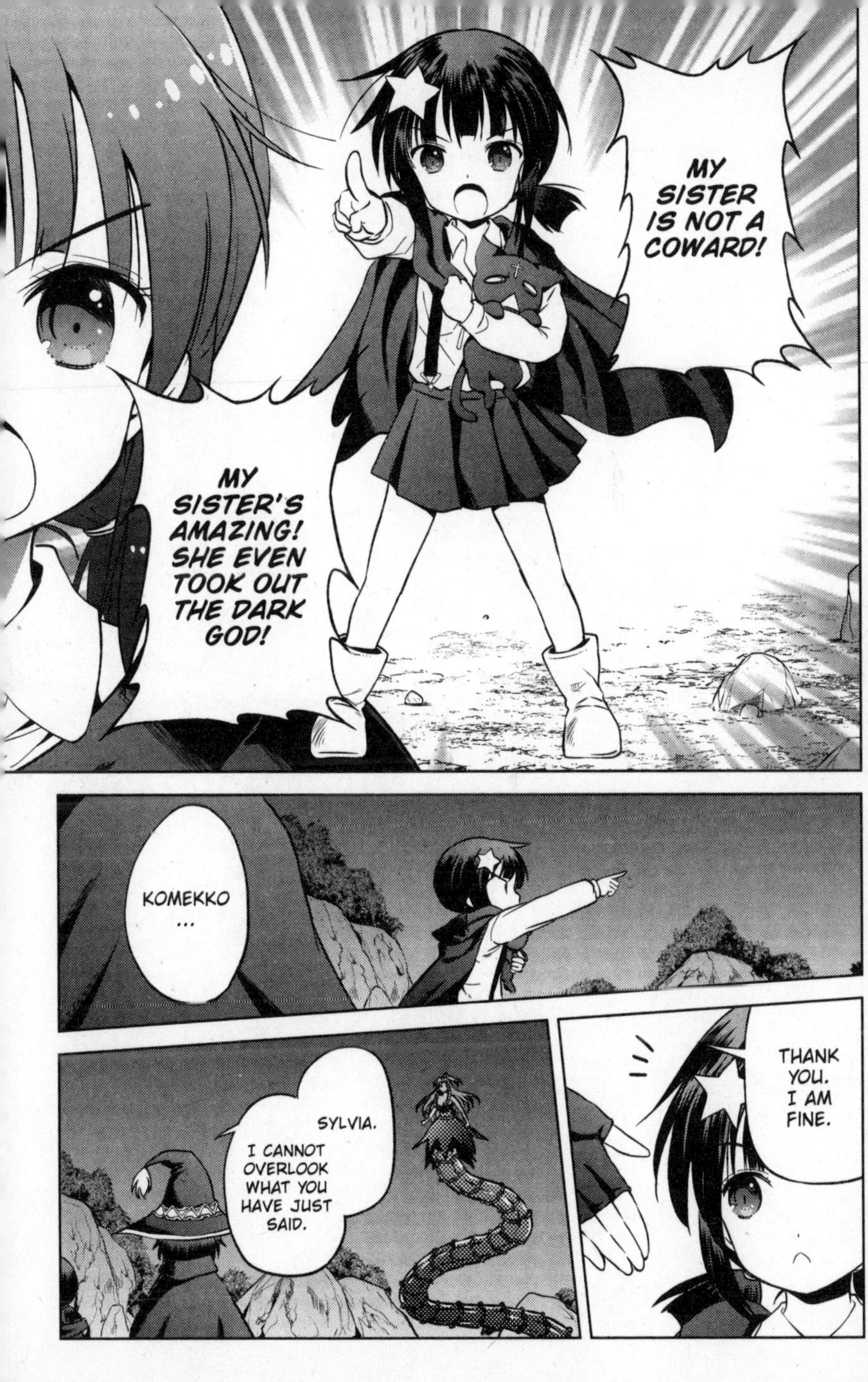
MY SISTER IS NOT A COWARD!
MY SISTER'S AMAZING! SHE EVEN TOOK OUT THE DARK GOD!
KOMEKKO ...
THANK YOU. I AM FINE.
SYLVIA.
I CANNOT OVERLOOK WHAT YOU HAVE JUST SAID.

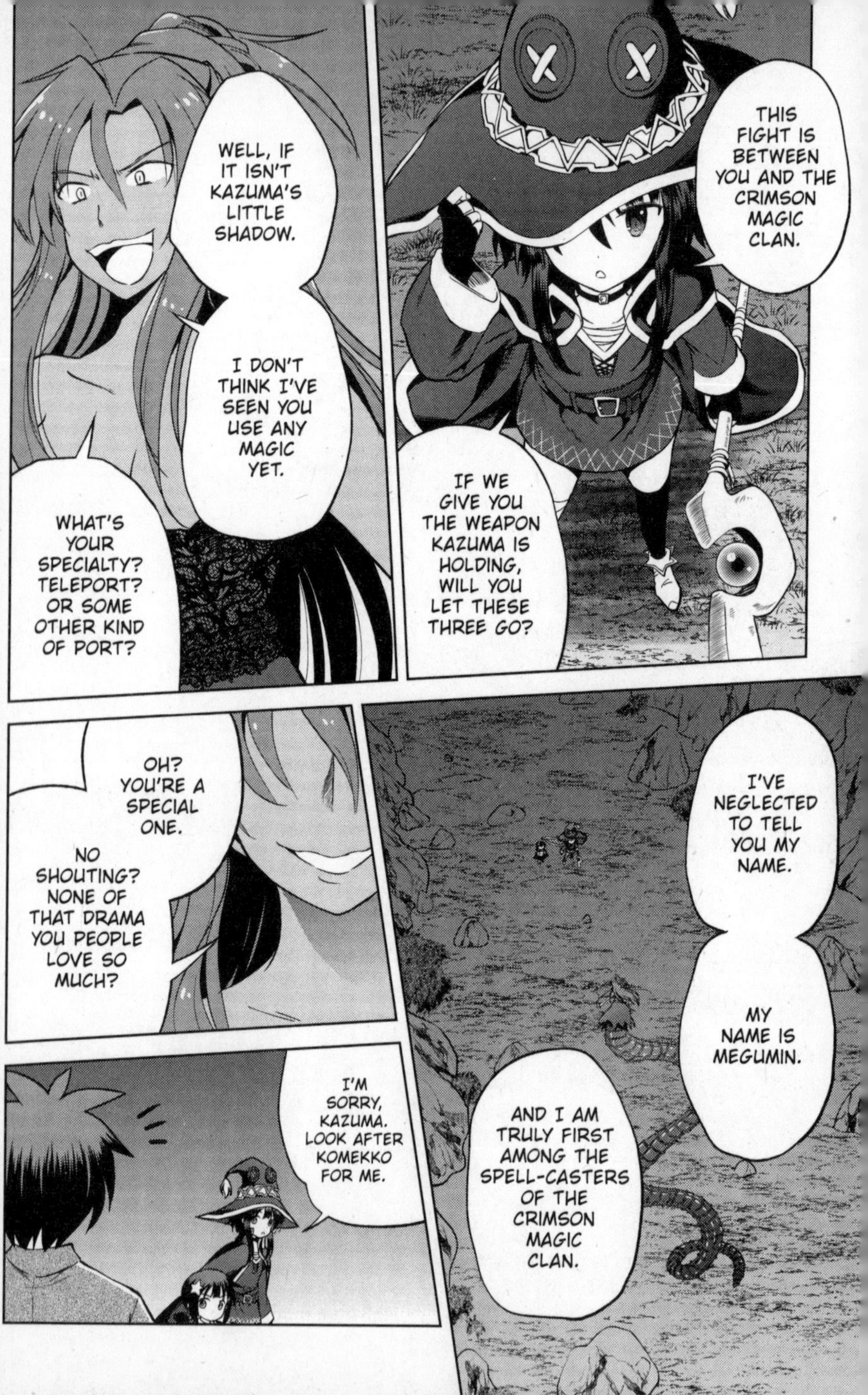
THIS FIGHT IS BETWEEN YOU AND THE CRIMSON MAGIC CLAN.
IF WE GIVE YOU THE WEAPON KAZUMA IS HOLDING, WILL YOU LET THESE THREE GO?
WELL, IF IT ISN'T KAZUMA'S LITTLE SHADOW.
I DON'T THINK I'VE SEEN YOU USE ANY MAGIC YET.
WHAT'S YOUR SPECIALTY? TELEPORT? OR SOME OTHER KIND OF PORT?
I'VE NEGLECTED TO TELL YOU MY NAME.
MY NAME IS MEGUMIN.
AND I AM TRULY FIRST AMONG THE SPELL-CASTERS OF THE CRIMSON MAGIC CLAN.
OH? YOU'RE A SPECIAL ONE.
NO SHOUTING? NONE OF THAT DRAMA YOU PEOPLE LOVE SO MUCH?
I'M SORRY, KAZUMA. LOOK AFTER KOMEKKO FOR ME.

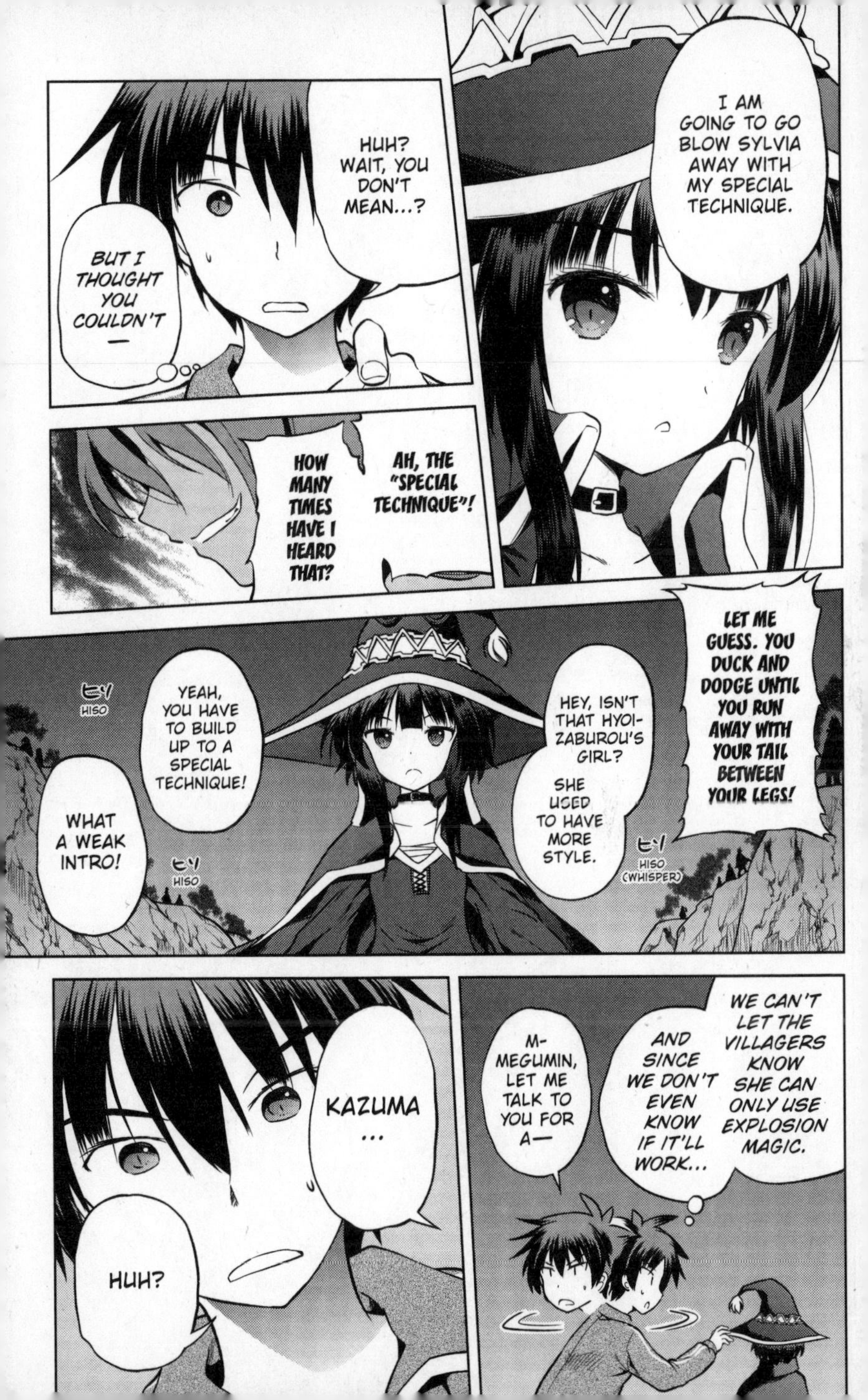
I AM GOING TO GO BLOW SYLVIA AWAY WITH MY SPECIAL TECHNIQUE.
HUH? WAIT, YOU DON'T MEAN...?
BUT I THOUGHT YOU COULDN'T —
AH, THE "SPECIAL TECHNIQUE"!
HOW MANY TIMES HAVE I HEARD THAT?
LET ME GUESS. YOU DUCK AND DODGE UNTIL YOU RUN AWAY WITH YOUR TAIL BETWEEN YOUR LEGS!
ヒソ HISO (WHISPER)
HEY, ISN'T THAT HYOI-ZABUROU'S GIRL?
SHE USED TO HAVE MORE STYLE.
YEAH, YOU HAVE TO BUILD UP TO A SPECIAL TECHNIQUE!
ヒソ HISO
WHAT A WEAK INTRO!
ヒソ HISO
WE CAN'T LET THE VILLAGERS KNOW SHE CAN ONLY USE EXPLOSION MAGIC.
AND SINCE WE DON'T EVEN KNOW IF IT'LL WORK...
M-MEGUMIN, LET ME TALK TO YOU FOR A—
KAZUMA...
HUH?

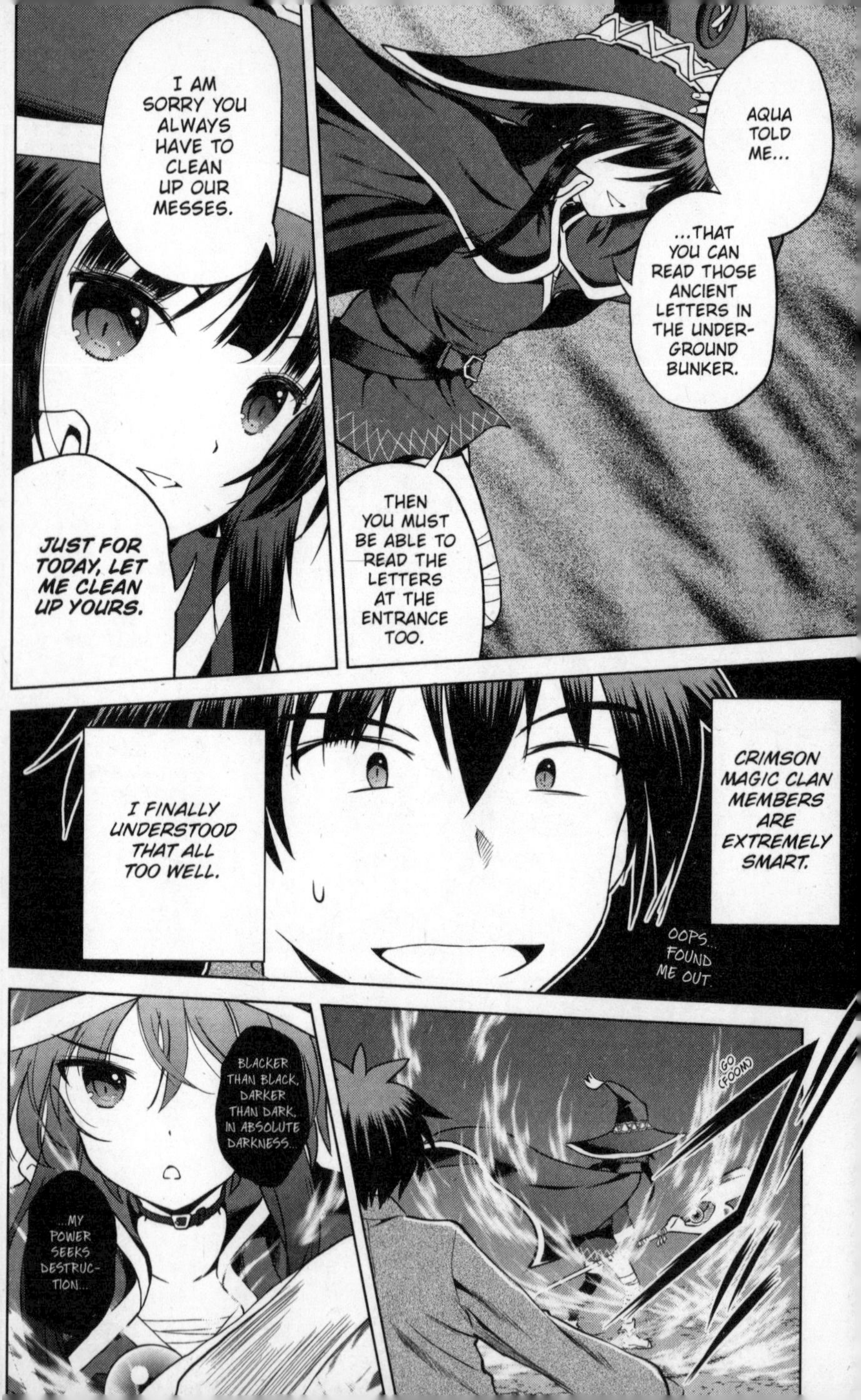
AQUA TOLD ME...
...THAT YOU CAN READ THOSE ANCIENT LETTERS IN THE UNDERGROUND BUNKER.
THEN YOU MUST BE ABLE TO READ THE LETTERS AT THE ENTRANCE TOO.
I AM SORRY YOU ALWAYS HAVE TO CLEAN UP OUR MESSES.
JUST FOR TODAY, LET ME CLEAN UP YOURS.
CRIMSON MAGIC CLAN MEMBERS ARE EXTREMELY SMART.
OOPS... FOUND ME OUT.
I FINALLY UNDERSTOOD THAT ALL TOO WELL.
GO (FOOM)
BLACKER THAN BLACK, DARKER THAN DARK, IN ABSOLUTE DARKNESS...
...MY POWER SEEKS DESTRUCTION...

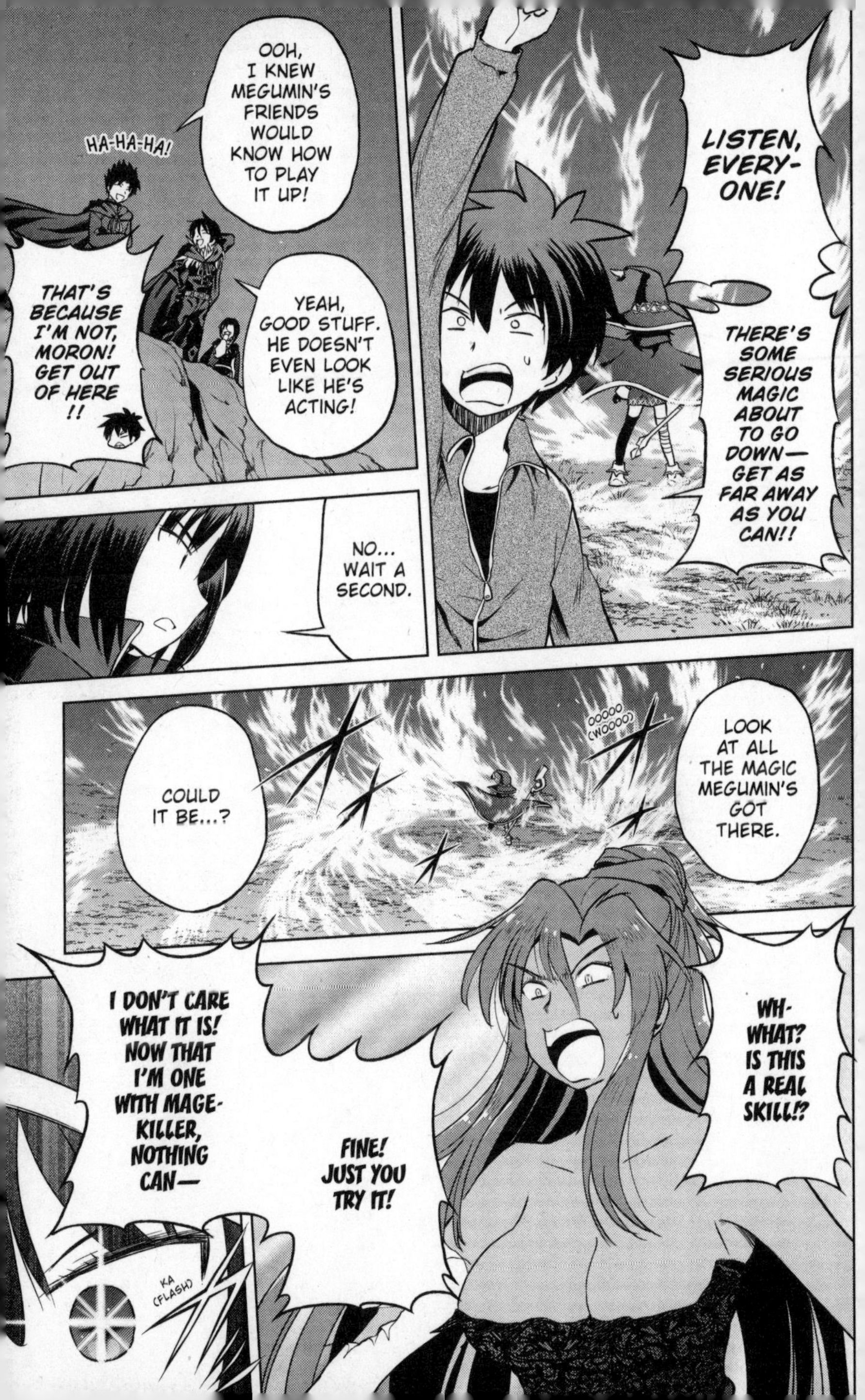
LISTEN, EVERY-ONE!
THERE'S SOME SERIOUS MAGIC ABOUT TO GO DOWN—GET AS FAR AWAY AS YOU CAN!!
OOH, I KNEW MEGUMIN'S FRIENDS WOULD KNOW HOW TO PLAY IT UP!
HA-HA-HA!
YEAH, GOOD STUFF. HE DOESN'T EVEN LOOK LIKE HE'S ACTING!
THAT'S BECAUSE I'M NOT, MORON! GET OUT OF HERE!!
NO... WAIT A SECOND.
LOOK AT ALL THE MAGIC MEGUMIN'S GOT THERE.
OOOOO (WOOOO)
COULD IT BE...?
WH-WHAT? IS THIS A REAL SKILL!?
FINE! JUST YOU TRY IT!
I DON'T CARE WHAT IT IS! NOW THAT I'M ONE WITH MAGE-KILLER, NOTHING CAN—
KA (FLASH)

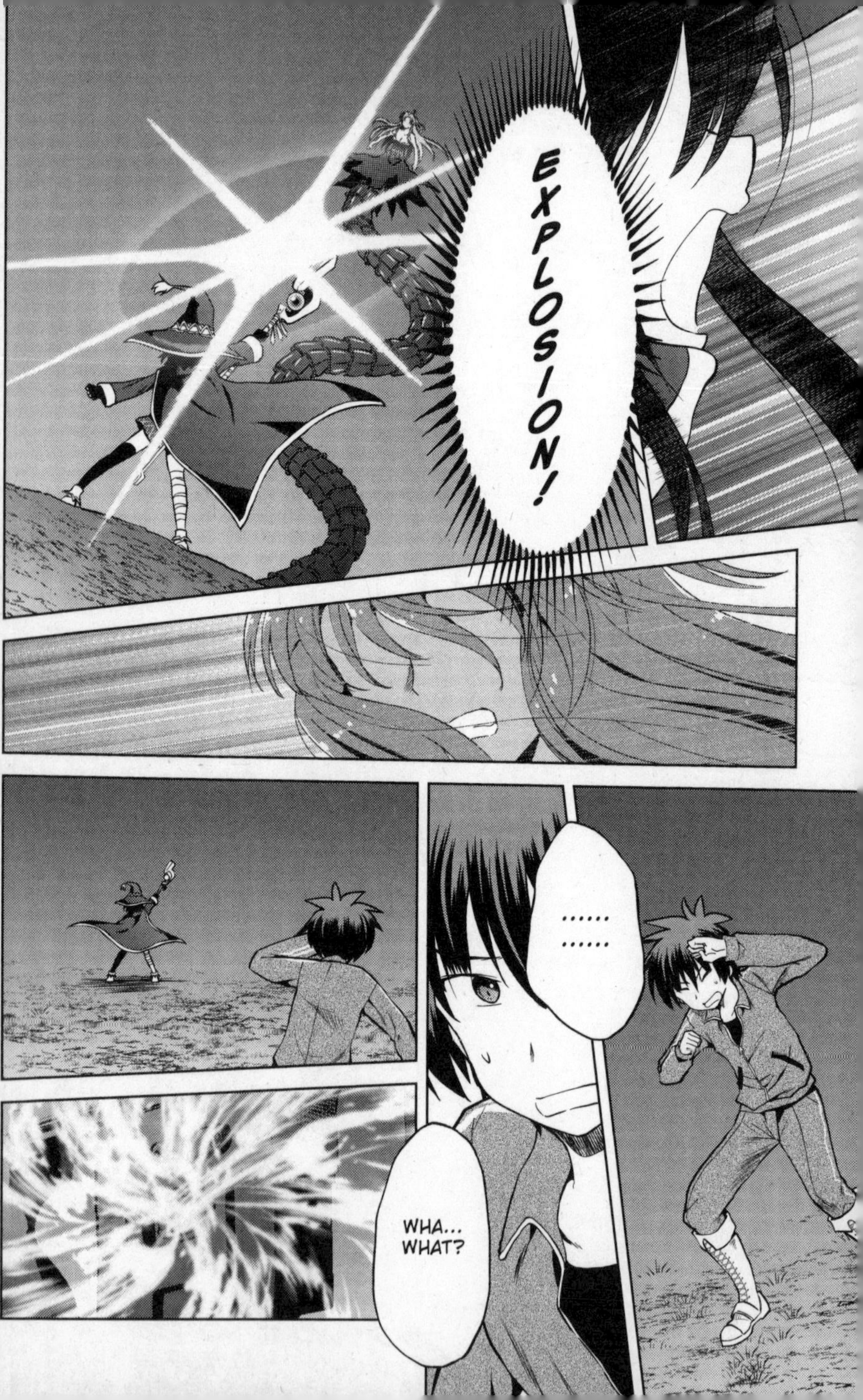
EXPLOSION!
......
......
WHA... WHAT?

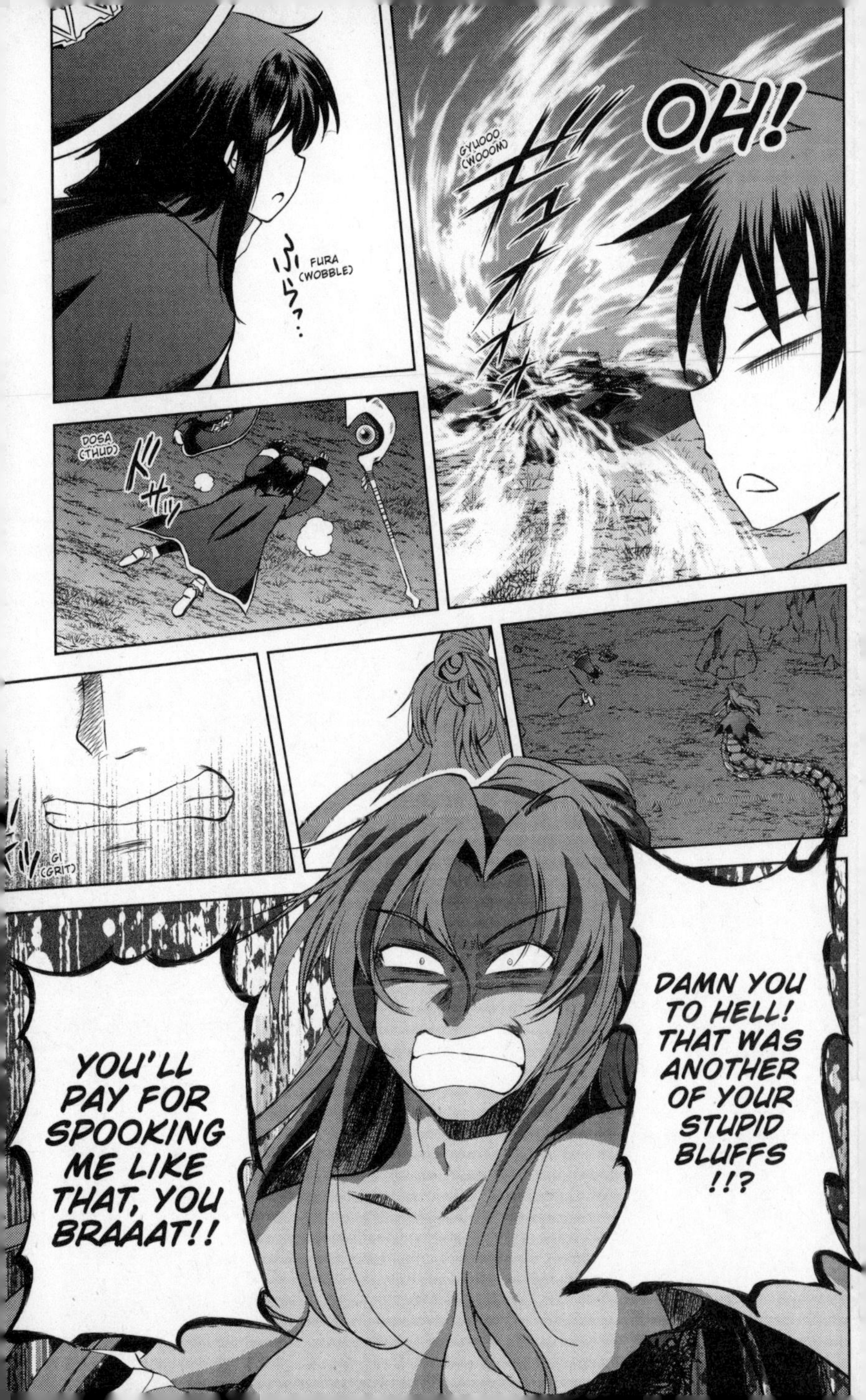
OH!
GYUOOO (WOOOM)
FURA (WOBBLE)
DOSA (THUD)
GI (GRIT)
DAMN YOU TO HELL! THAT WAS ANOTHER OF YOUR STUPID BLUFFS!!?
YOU'LL PAY FOR SPOOKING ME LIKE THAT, YOU BRAAAT!!

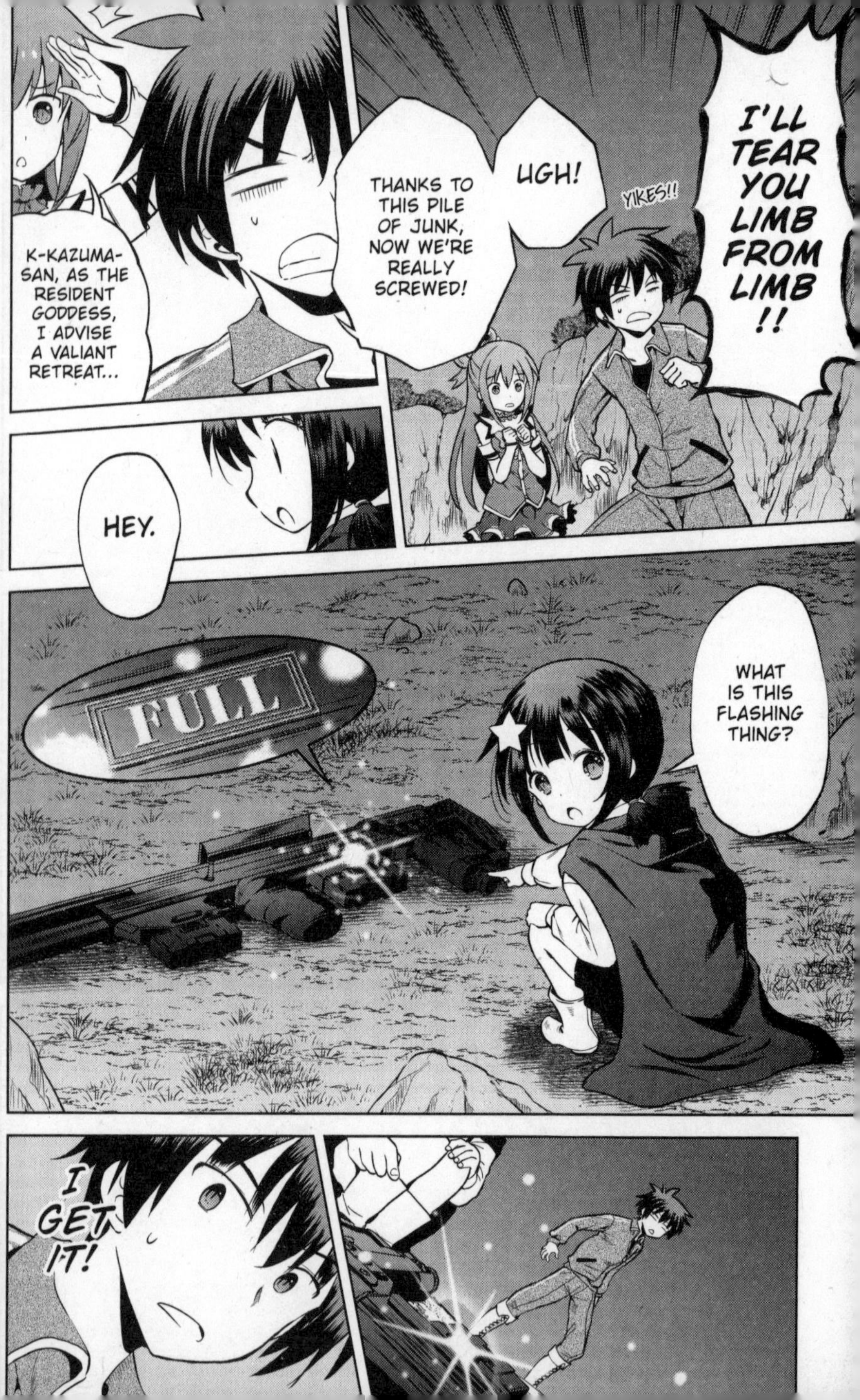
I'LL TEAR YOU LIMB FROM LIMB!!
YIKES!!
UGH!
THANKS TO THIS PILE OF JUNK, NOW WE'RE REALLY SCREWED!
K-KAZUMA-SAN, AS THE RESIDENT GODDESS, I ADVISE A VALIANT RETREAT...
HEY.
WHAT IS THIS FLASHING THING?
FULL
I GET IT!

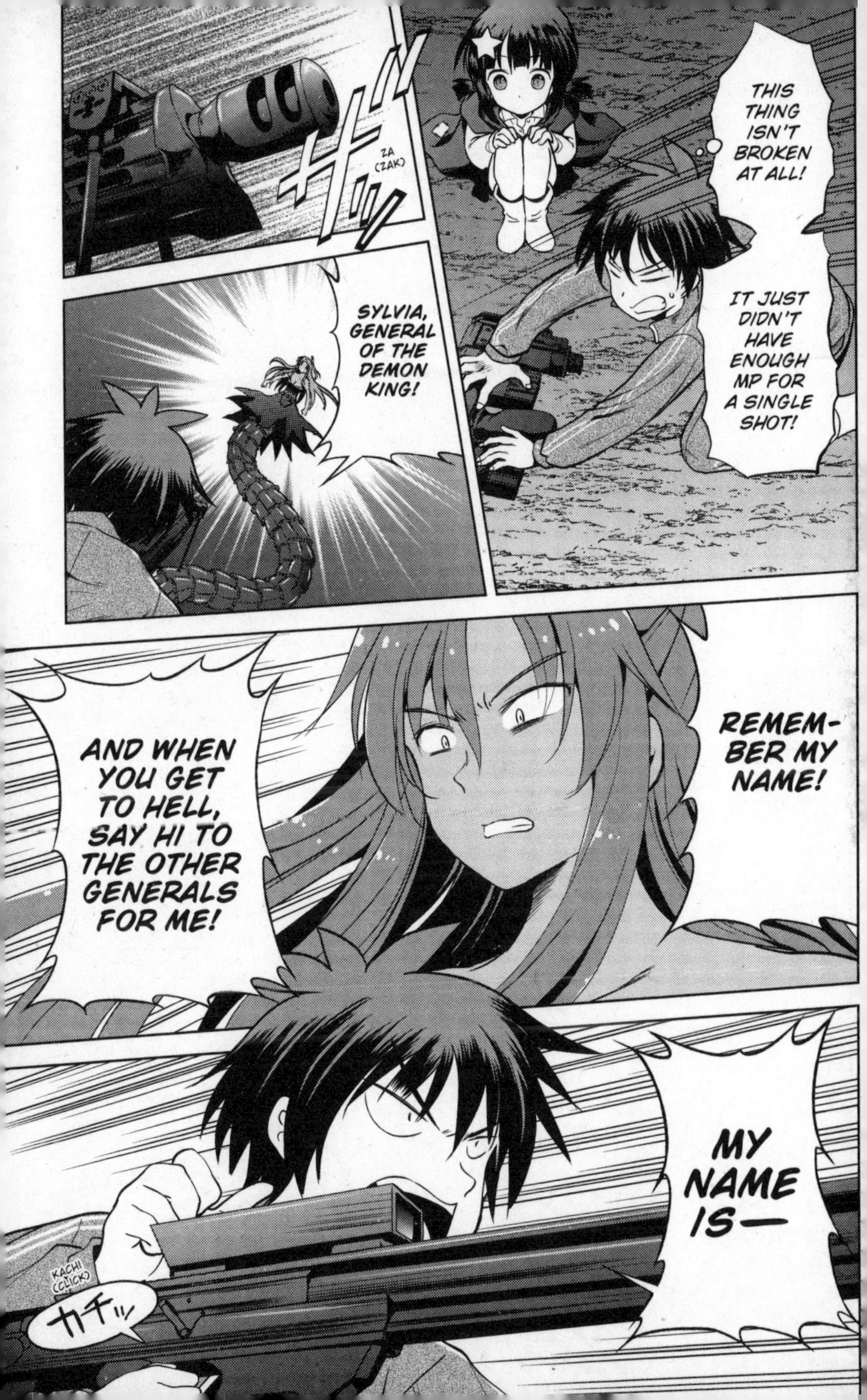
THIS THING ISN'T BROKEN AT ALL!
IT JUST DIDN'T HAVE ENOUGH MP FOR A SINGLE SHOT!
ZA (ZAK)
SYLVIA, GENERAL OF THE DEMON KING!
REMEM-BER MY NAME!
AND WHEN YOU GET TO HELL, SAY HI TO THE OTHER GENERALS FOR ME!
MY NAME IS—
KACHI (CLICK)
カチッ

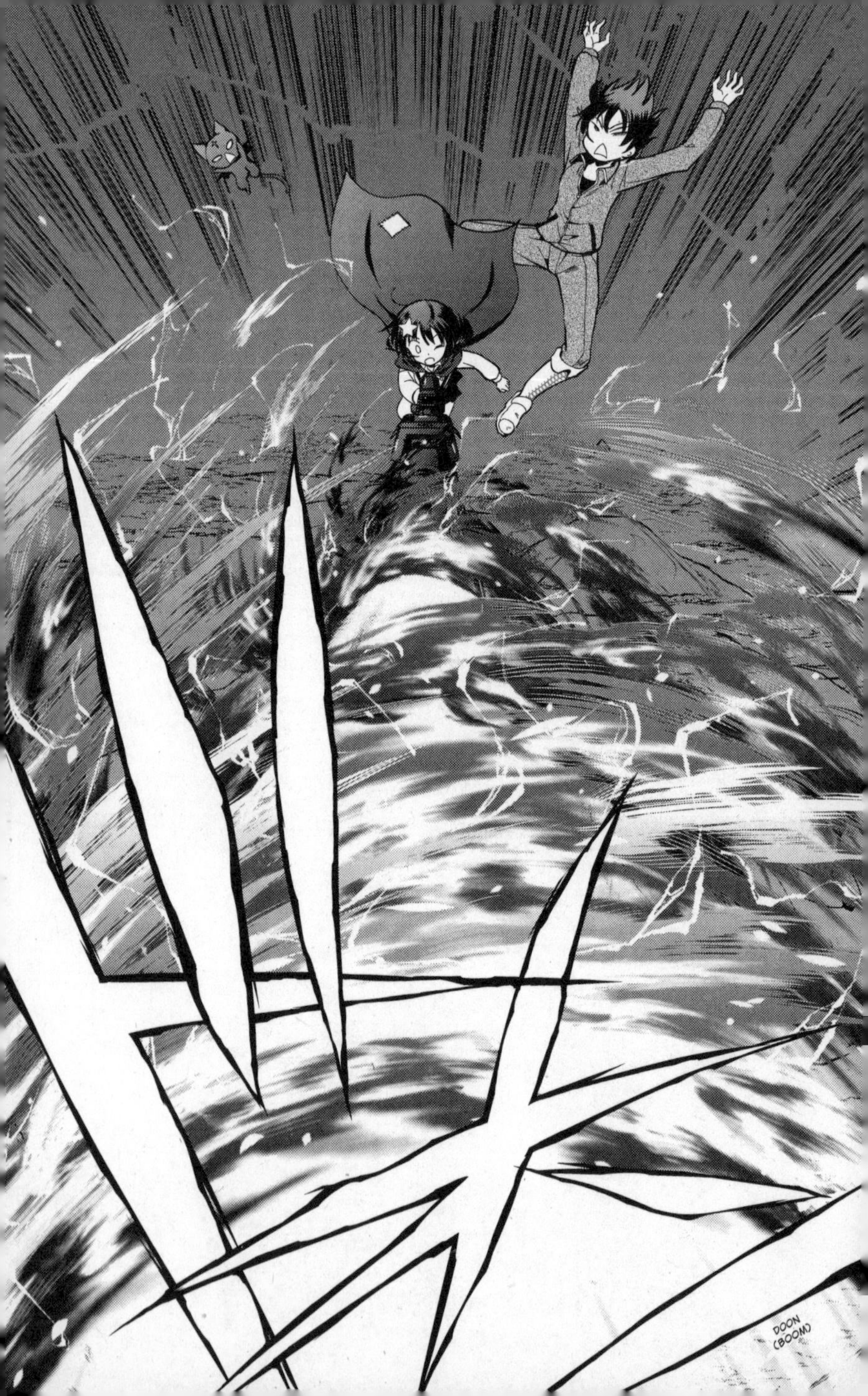
DOON
(BOOM)

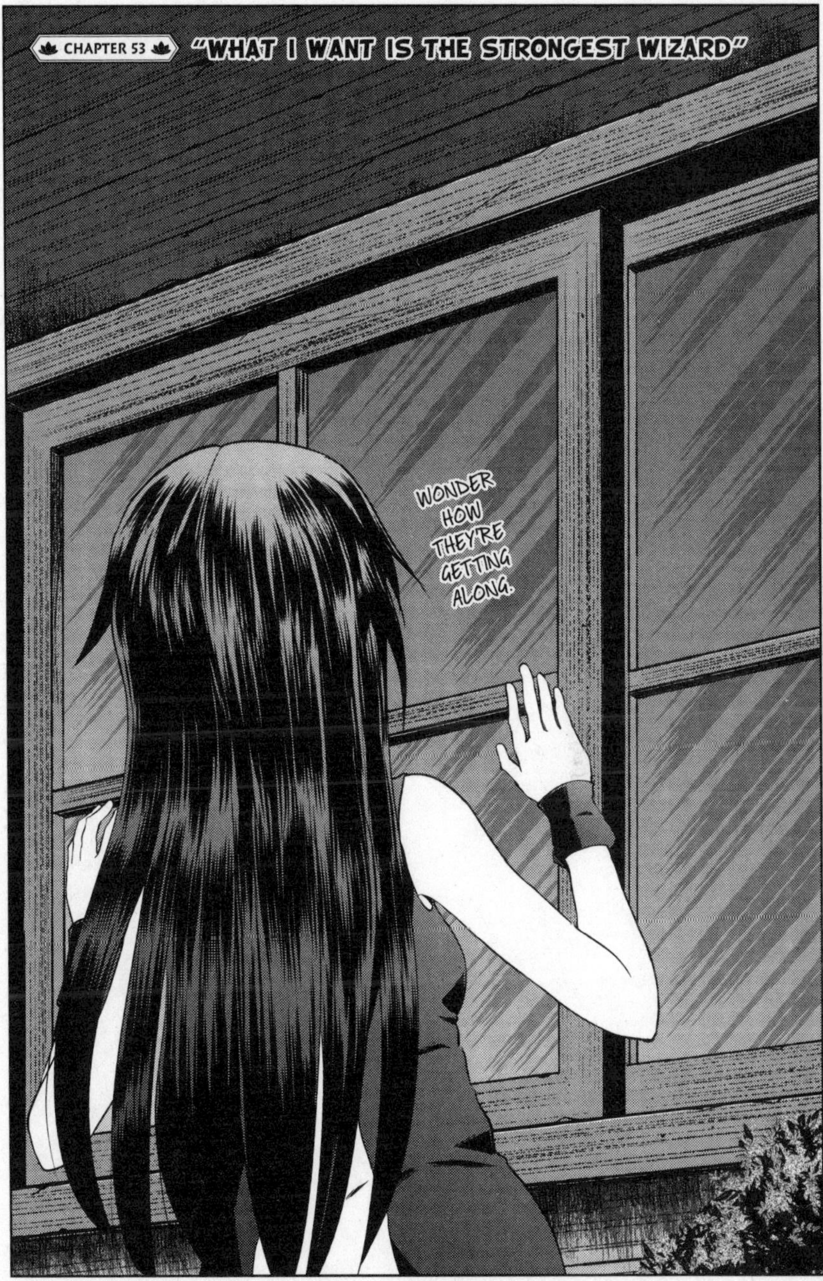
CHAPTER 53
"WHAT I WANT IS THE STRONGEST WIZARD"
WONDER HOW THEY'RE GETTING ALONG.

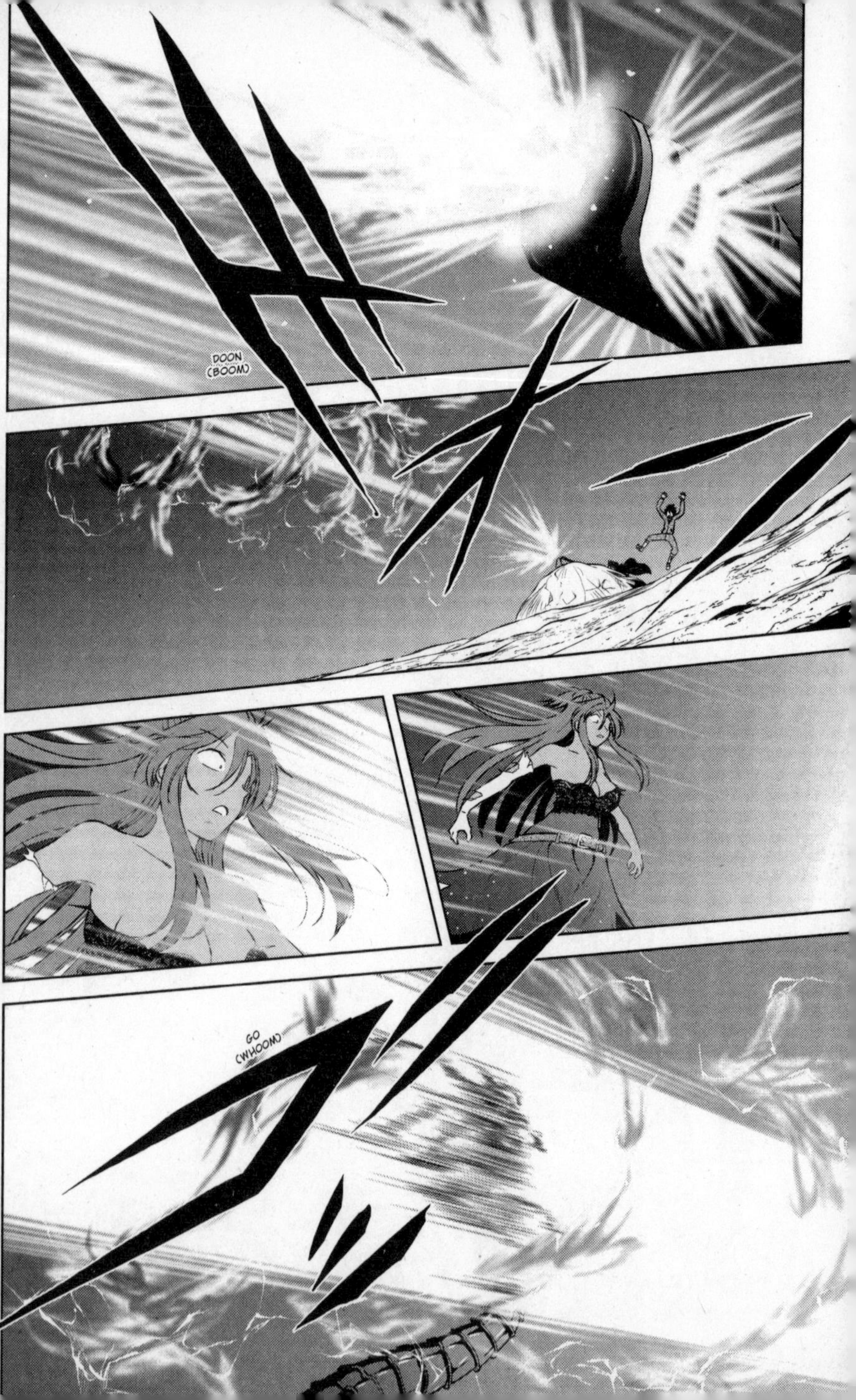
DOON
(BOOM)
GO
(WHOOM)

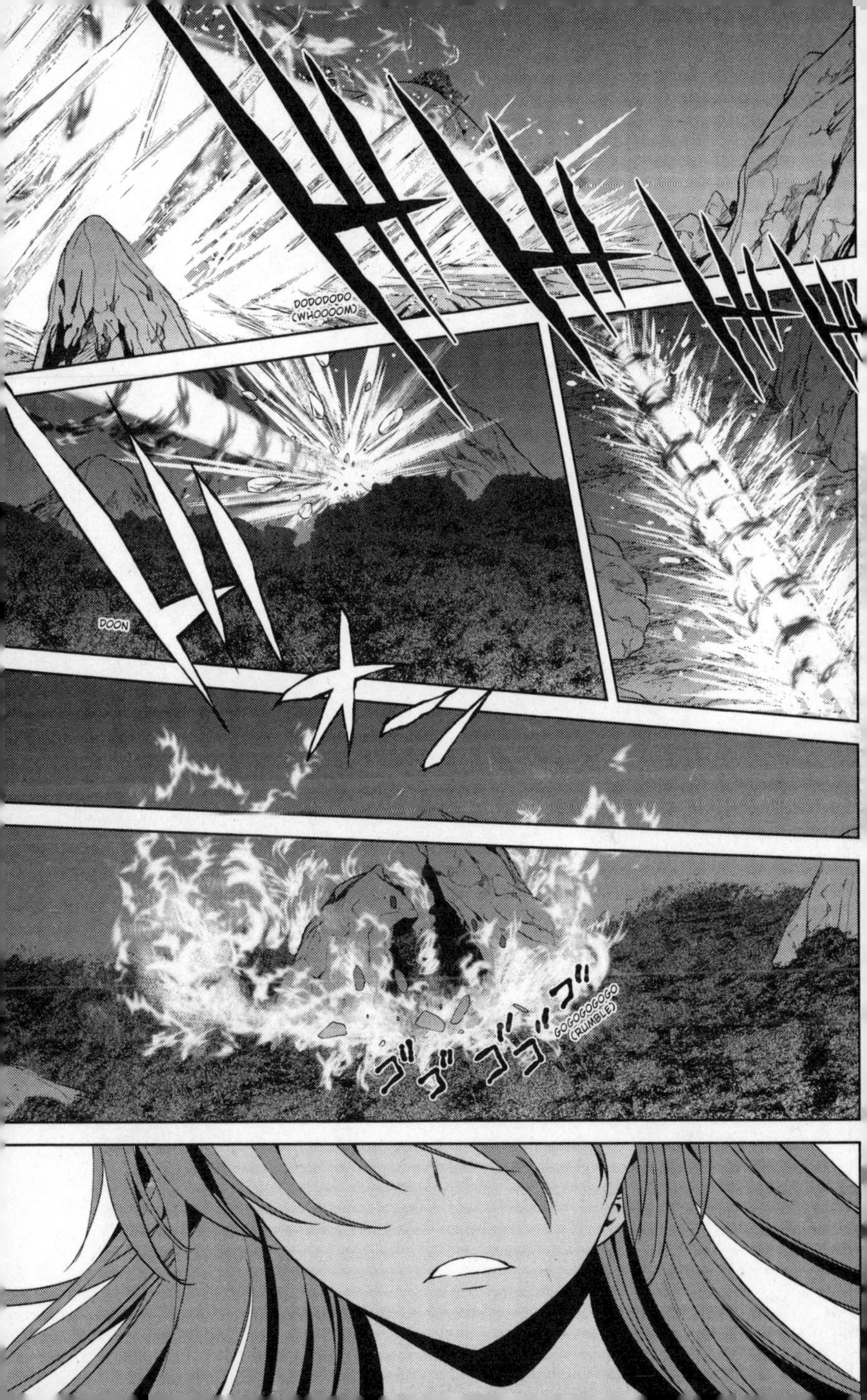
DODODODO
(WHOOOOM)
DOON
GOGOGOGOGO
(RUMBLE)

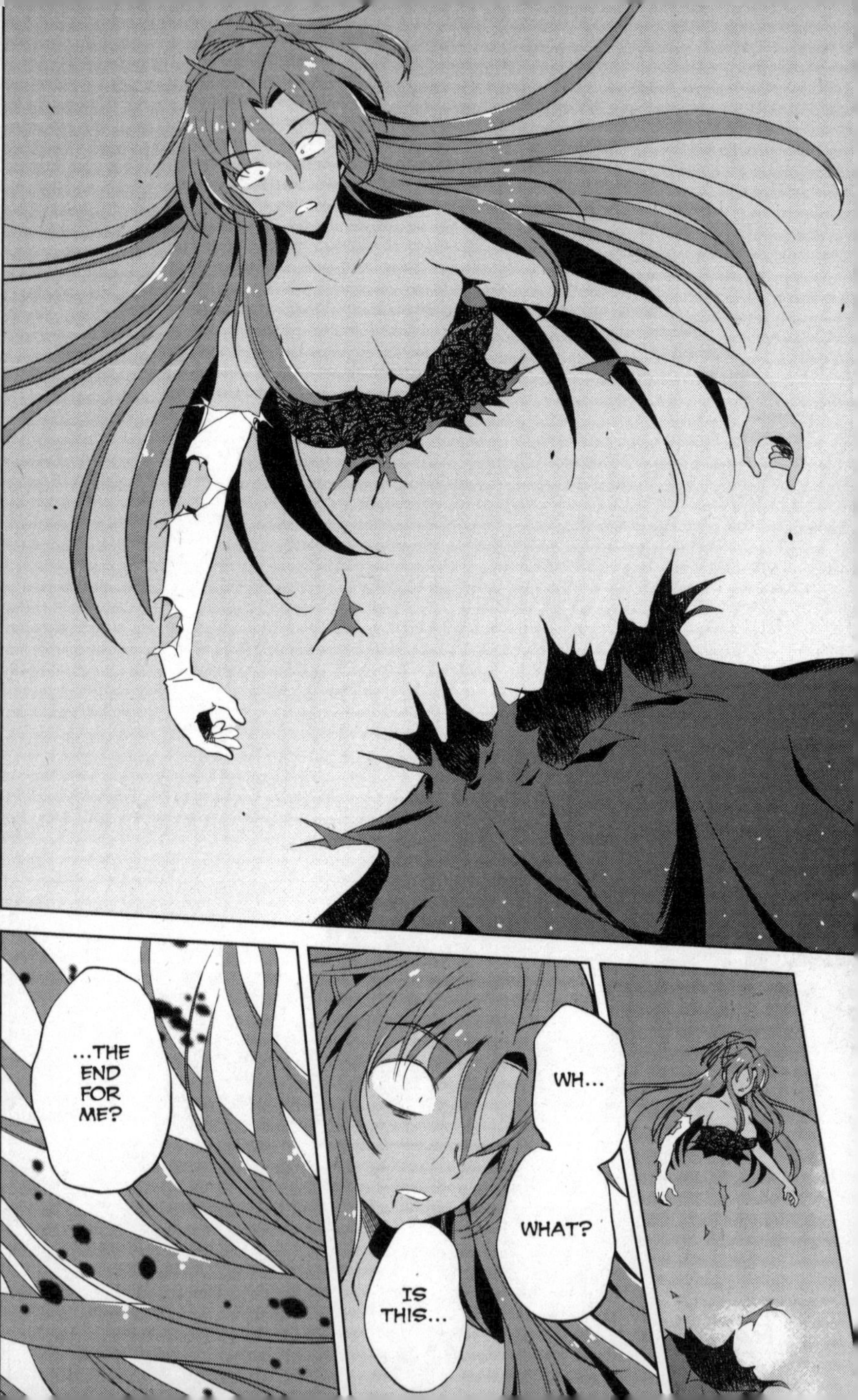
WH...
WHAT?
IS THIS...
...THE END FOR ME?

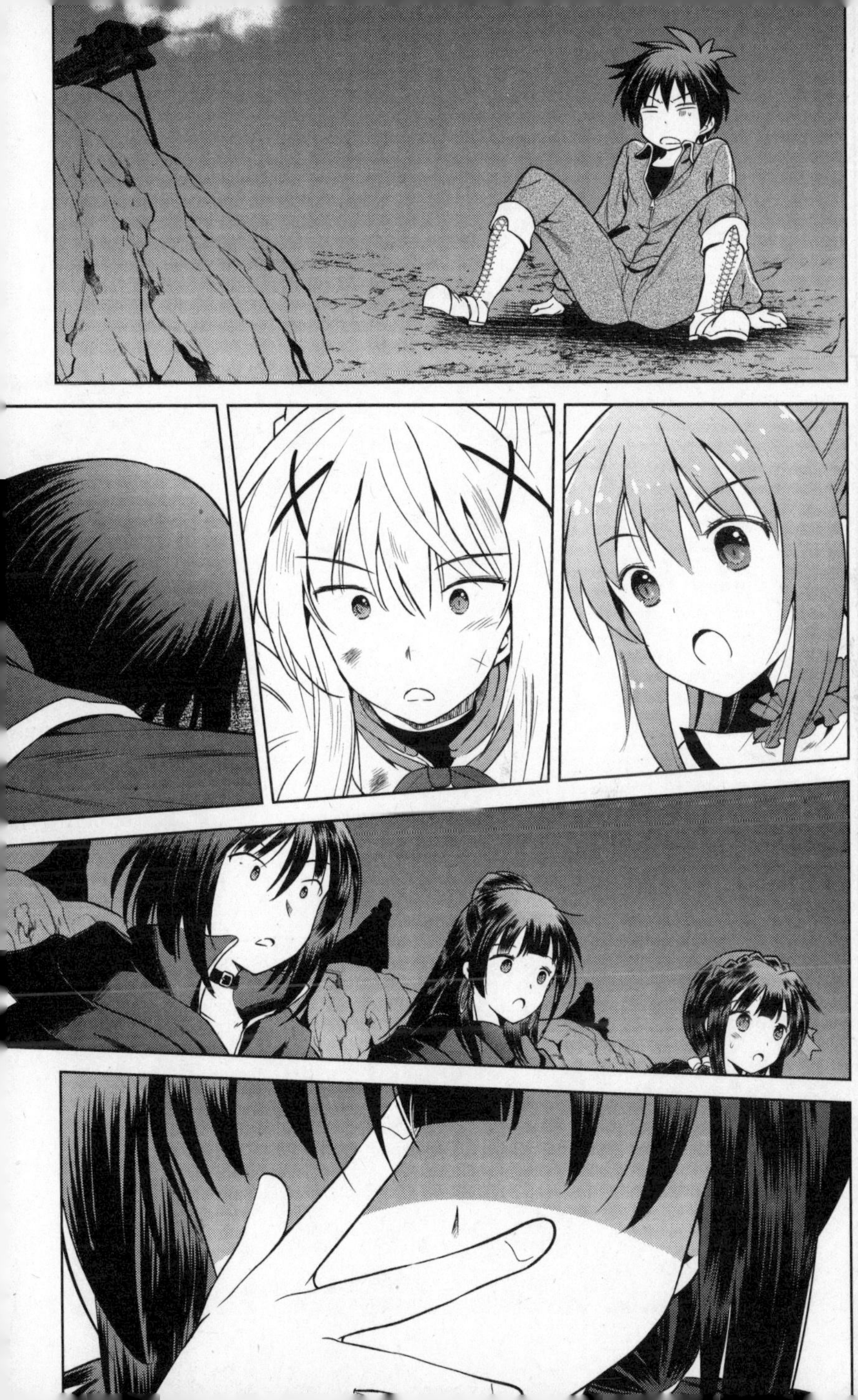

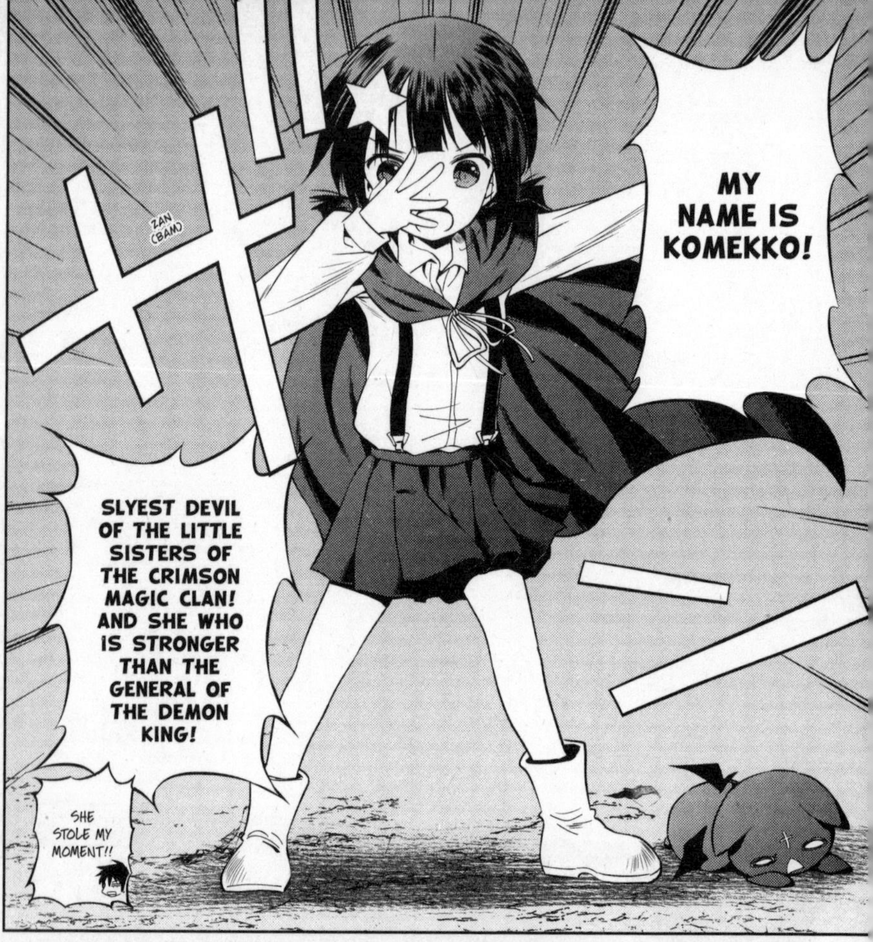
MY NAME IS KOMEKKO!
ZAN (BAM)
SLYEST DEVIL OF THE LITTLE SISTERS OF THE CRIMSON MAGIC CLAN! AND SHE WHO IS STRONGER THAN THE GENERAL OF THE DEMON KING!
SHE STOLE MY MOMENT!!
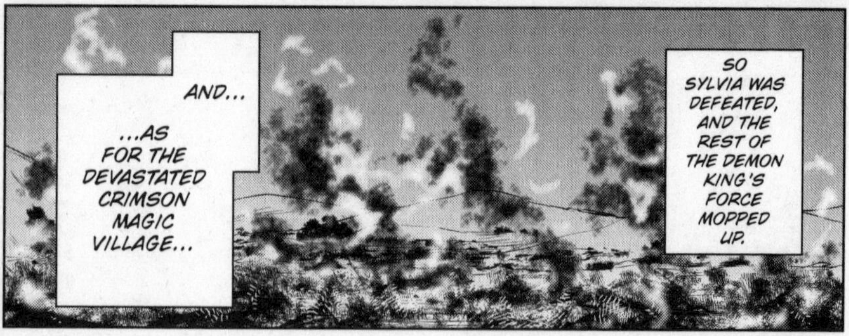
SO SYLVIA WAS DEFEATED, AND THE REST OF THE DEMON KING'S FORCE MOPPED UP.
AND...
...AS FOR THE DEVASTATED CRIMSON MAGIC VILLAGE...

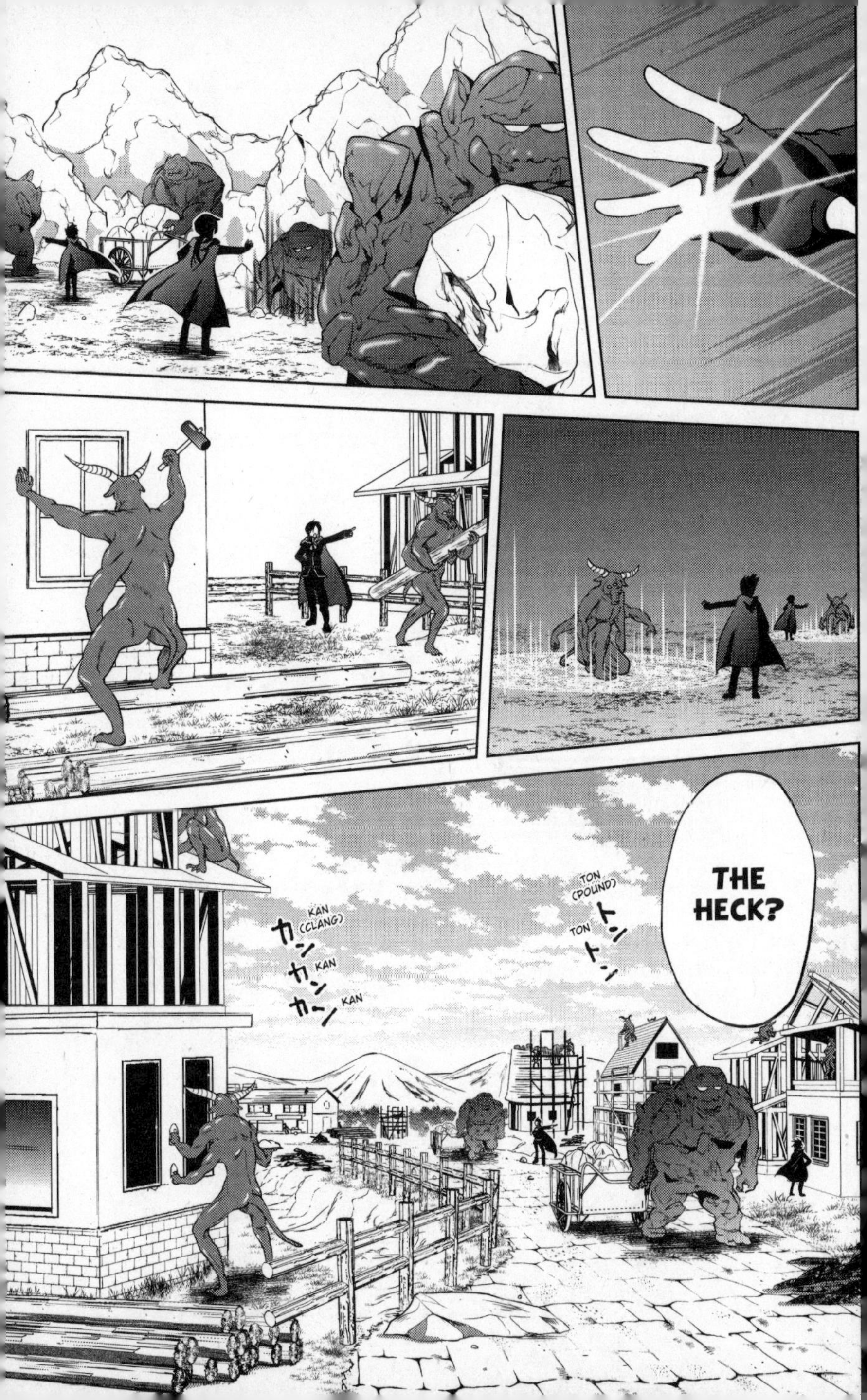
THE HECK?
TON (POUND) トン
TON トン
KAN (CLANG) カン
KAN カン
KAN カーン

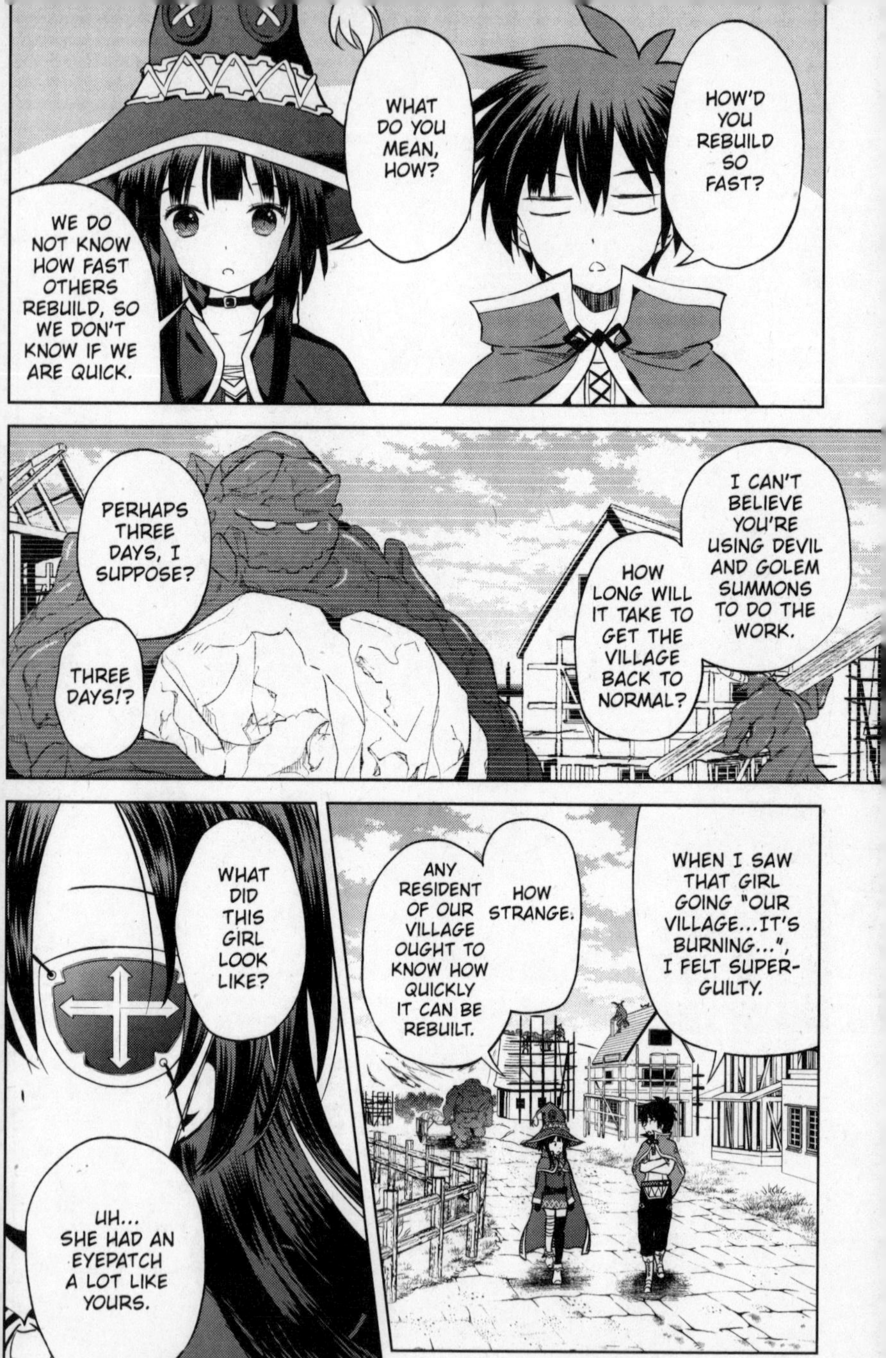
HOW'D YOU REBUILD SO FAST?
WHAT DO YOU MEAN, HOW?
WE DO NOT KNOW HOW FAST OTHERS REBUILD, SO WE DON'T KNOW IF WE ARE QUICK.
I CAN'T BELIEVE YOU'RE USING DEVIL AND GOLEM SUMMONS TO DO THE WORK.
HOW LONG WILL IT TAKE TO GET THE VILLAGE BACK TO NORMAL?
PERHAPS THREE DAYS, I SUPPOSE?
THREE DAYS!?
WHEN I SAW THAT GIRL GOING "OUR VILLAGE...IT'S BURNING...", I FELT SUPER-GUILTY.
HOW STRANGE.
ANY RESIDENT OF OUR VILLAGE OUGHT TO KNOW HOW QUICKLY IT CAN BE REBUILT.
WHAT DID THIS GIRL LOOK LIKE?
UH... SHE HAD AN EYEPATCH A LOT LIKE YOURS.

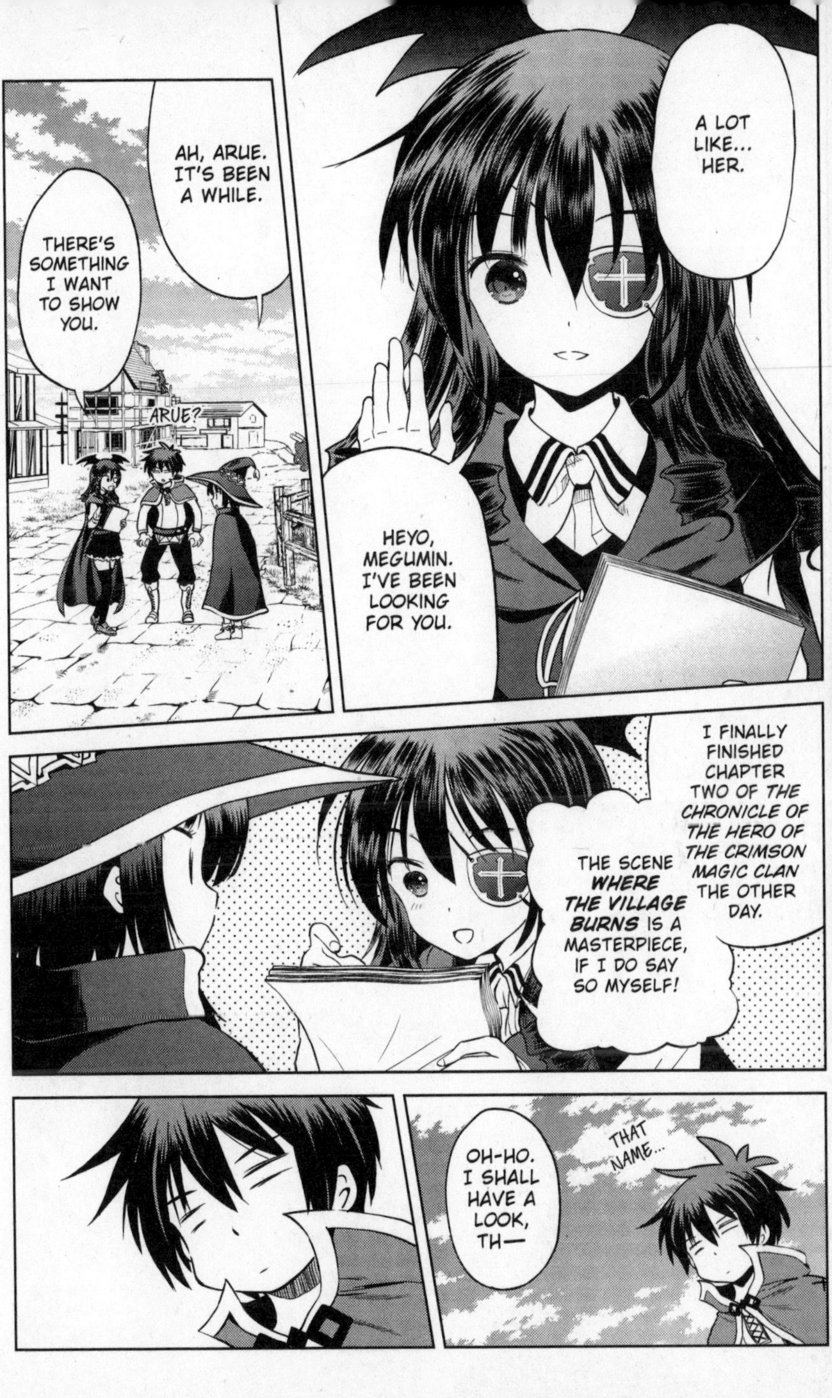
A LOT LIKE... HER.
HEYO, MEGUMIN. I'VE BEEN LOOKING FOR YOU.
AH, ARUE. IT'S BEEN A WHILE.
THERE'S SOMETHING I WANT TO SHOW YOU.
ARUE?
I FINALLY FINISHED CHAPTER TWO OF *THE CHRONICLE OF THE HERO OF THE CRIMSON MAGIC CLAN* THE OTHER DAY.
THE SCENE ***WHERE THE VILLAGE BURNS*** IS A MASTERPIECE, IF I DO SAY SO MYSELF!
THAT NAME...
OH-HO. I SHALL HAVE A LOOK, TH—

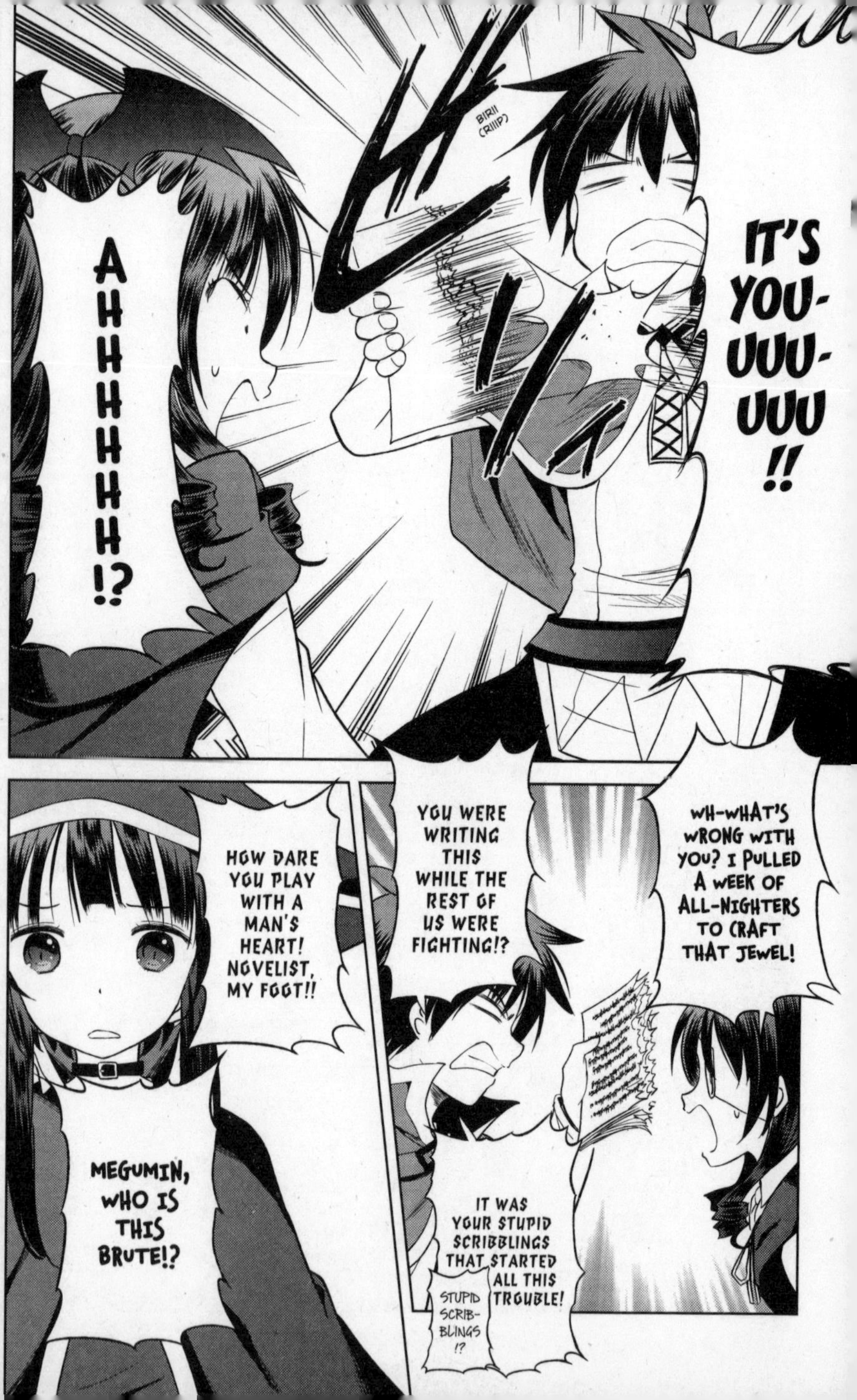
IT'S YOU-UUU-UUU!!
BIRII (RIIIP)
AHHHHHHH!?
WH-WHAT'S WRONG WITH YOU? I PULLED A WEEK OF ALL-NIGHTERS TO CRAFT THAT JEWEL!
YOU WERE WRITING THIS WHILE THE REST OF US WERE FIGHTING!?
IT WAS YOUR STUPID SCRIBBLINGS THAT STARTED ALL THIS TROUBLE!
STUPID SCRIB-BLINGS!?
HOW DARE YOU PLAY WITH A MAN'S HEART! NOVELIST, MY FOOT!!
MEGUMIN, WHO IS THIS BRUTE!?

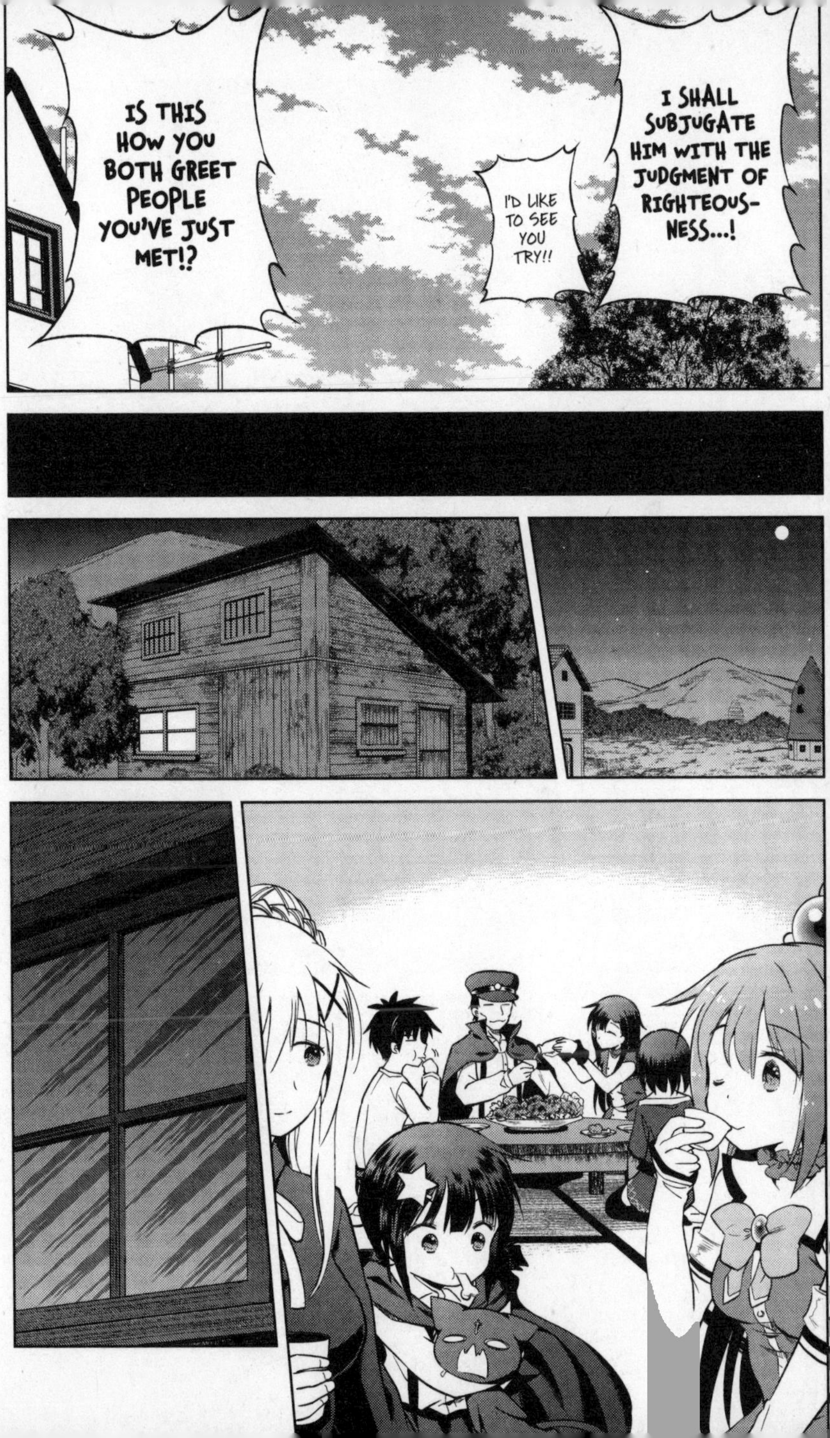
I SHALL SUBJUGATE HIM WITH THE JUDGMENT OF RIGHTEOUS-NESS...!
I'D LIKE TO SEE YOU TRY!!
IS THIS HOW YOU BOTH GREET PEOPLE YOU'VE JUST MET!?

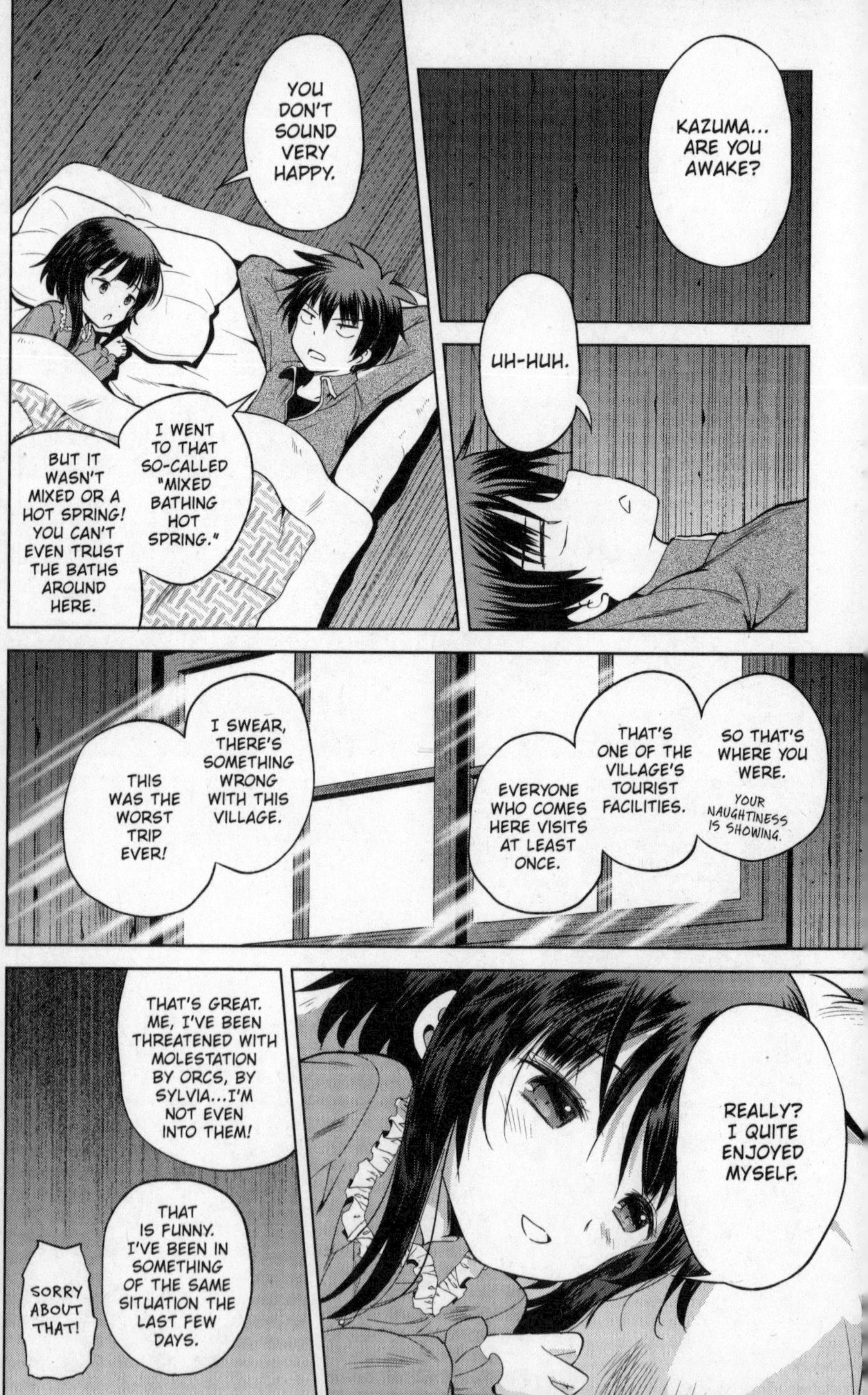
KAZUMA... ARE YOU AWAKE?
UH-HUH.
YOU DON'T SOUND VERY HAPPY.
I WENT TO THAT SO-CALLED "MIXED BATHING HOT SPRING."
BUT IT WASN'T MIXED OR A HOT SPRING! YOU CAN'T EVEN TRUST THE BATHS AROUND HERE.
SO THAT'S WHERE YOU WERE.
YOUR NAUGHTINESS IS SHOWING.
THAT'S ONE OF THE VILLAGE'S TOURIST FACILITIES.
EVERYONE WHO COMES HERE VISITS AT LEAST ONCE.
I SWEAR, THERE'S SOMETHING WRONG WITH THIS VILLAGE.
THIS WAS THE WORST TRIP EVER!
REALLY? I QUITE ENJOYED MYSELF.
THAT'S GREAT. ME, I'VE BEEN THREATENED WITH MOLESTATION BY ORCS, BY SYLVIA...I'M NOT EVEN INTO THEM!
THAT IS FUNNY. I'VE BEEN IN SOMETHING OF THE SAME SITUATION THE LAST FEW DAYS.
SORRY ABOUT THAT!

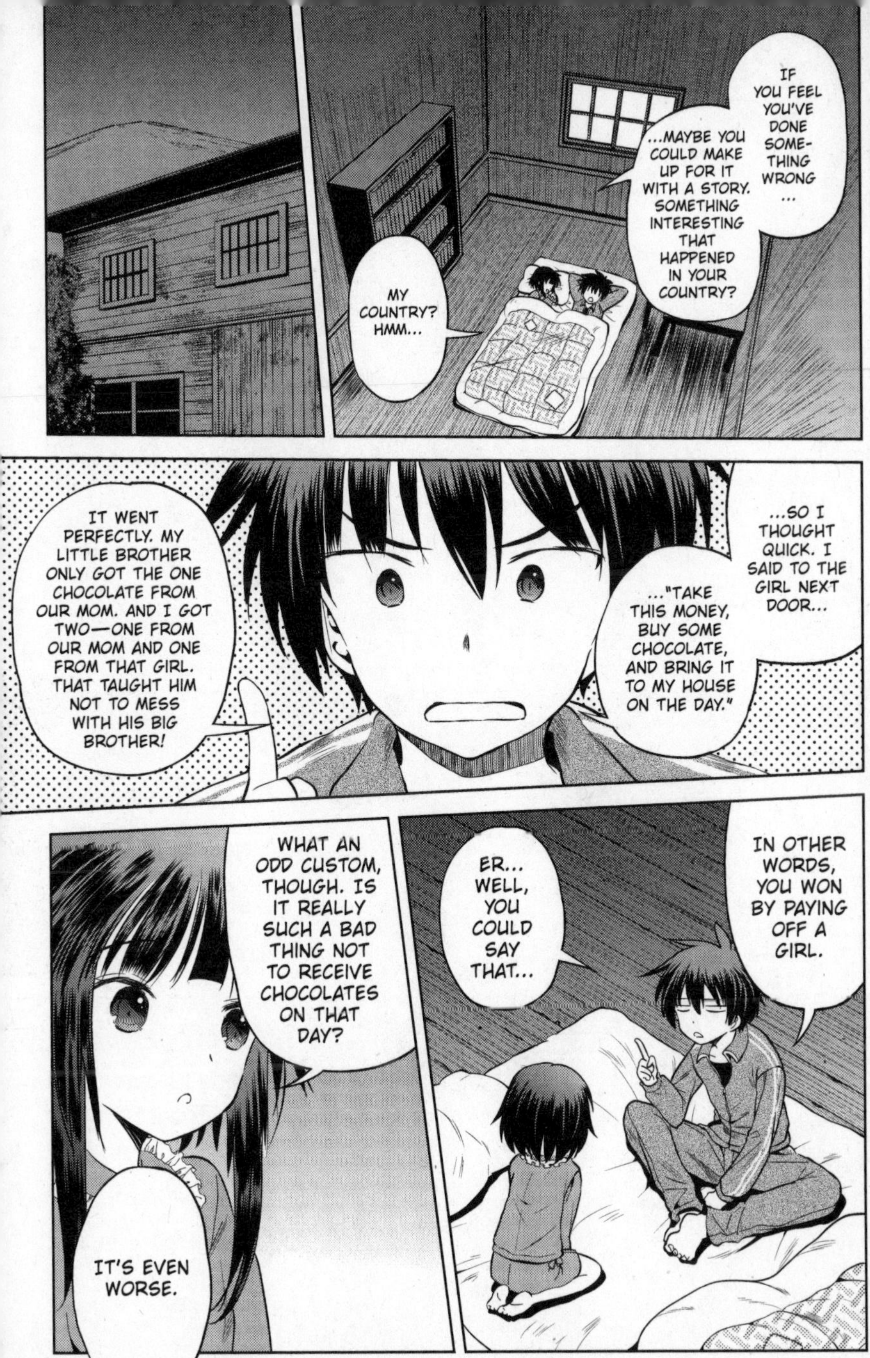
IF YOU FEEL YOU'VE DONE SOME-THING WRONG...
...MAYBE YOU COULD MAKE UP FOR IT WITH A STORY. SOMETHING INTERESTING THAT HAPPENED IN YOUR COUNTRY?
MY COUNTRY? HMM...
...SO I THOUGHT QUICK. I SAID TO THE GIRL NEXT DOOR...
..."TAKE THIS MONEY, BUY SOME CHOCOLATE, AND BRING IT TO MY HOUSE ON THE DAY."
IT WENT PERFECTLY. MY LITTLE BROTHER ONLY GOT THE ONE CHOCOLATE FROM OUR MOM. AND I GOT TWO—ONE FROM OUR MOM AND ONE FROM THAT GIRL. THAT TAUGHT HIM NOT TO MESS WITH HIS BIG BROTHER!
IN OTHER WORDS, YOU WON BY PAYING OFF A GIRL.
ER... WELL, YOU COULD SAY THAT...
WHAT AN ODD CUSTOM, THOUGH. IS IT REALLY SUCH A BAD THING NOT TO RECEIVE CHOCOLATES ON THAT DAY?
IT'S EVEN WORSE.

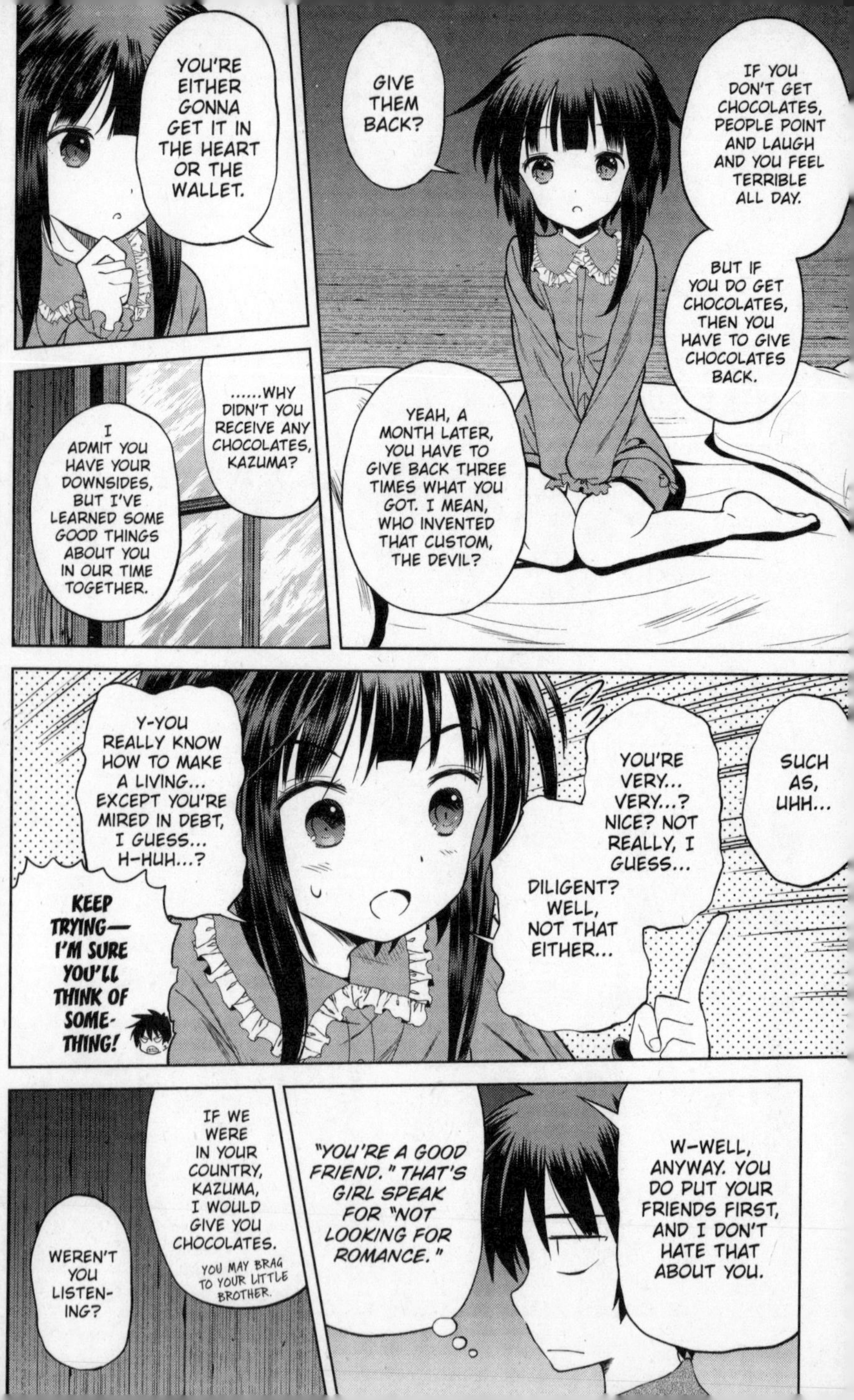
IF YOU DON'T GET CHOCOLATES, PEOPLE POINT AND LAUGH AND YOU FEEL TERRIBLE ALL DAY.
BUT IF YOU DO GET CHOCOLATES, THEN YOU HAVE TO GIVE CHOCOLATES BACK.
GIVE THEM BACK?
YEAH, A MONTH LATER, YOU HAVE TO GIVE BACK THREE TIMES WHAT YOU GOT. I MEAN, WHO INVENTED THAT CUSTOM, THE DEVIL?
YOU'RE EITHER GONNA GET IT IN THE HEART OR THE WALLET.
......WHY DIDN'T YOU RECEIVE ANY CHOCOLATES, KAZUMA?
I ADMIT YOU HAVE YOUR DOWNSIDES, BUT I'VE LEARNED SOME GOOD THINGS ABOUT YOU IN OUR TIME TOGETHER.
SUCH AS, UHH...
YOU'RE VERY... VERY...? NICE? NOT REALLY, I GUESS...
DILIGENT? WELL, NOT THAT EITHER...
Y-YOU REALLY KNOW HOW TO MAKE A LIVING... EXCEPT YOU'RE MIRED IN DEBT, I GUESS... H-HUH...?
KEEP TRYING—I'M SURE YOU'LL THINK OF SOME-THING!
W-WELL, ANYWAY. YOU DO PUT YOUR FRIENDS FIRST, AND I DON'T HATE THAT ABOUT YOU.
"YOU'RE A GOOD FRIEND." THAT'S GIRL SPEAK FOR "NOT LOOKING FOR ROMANCE."
IF WE WERE IN YOUR COUNTRY, KAZUMA, I WOULD GIVE YOU CHOCOLATES.
YOU MAY BRAG TO YOUR LITTLE BROTHER.
WEREN'T YOU LISTEN-ING?

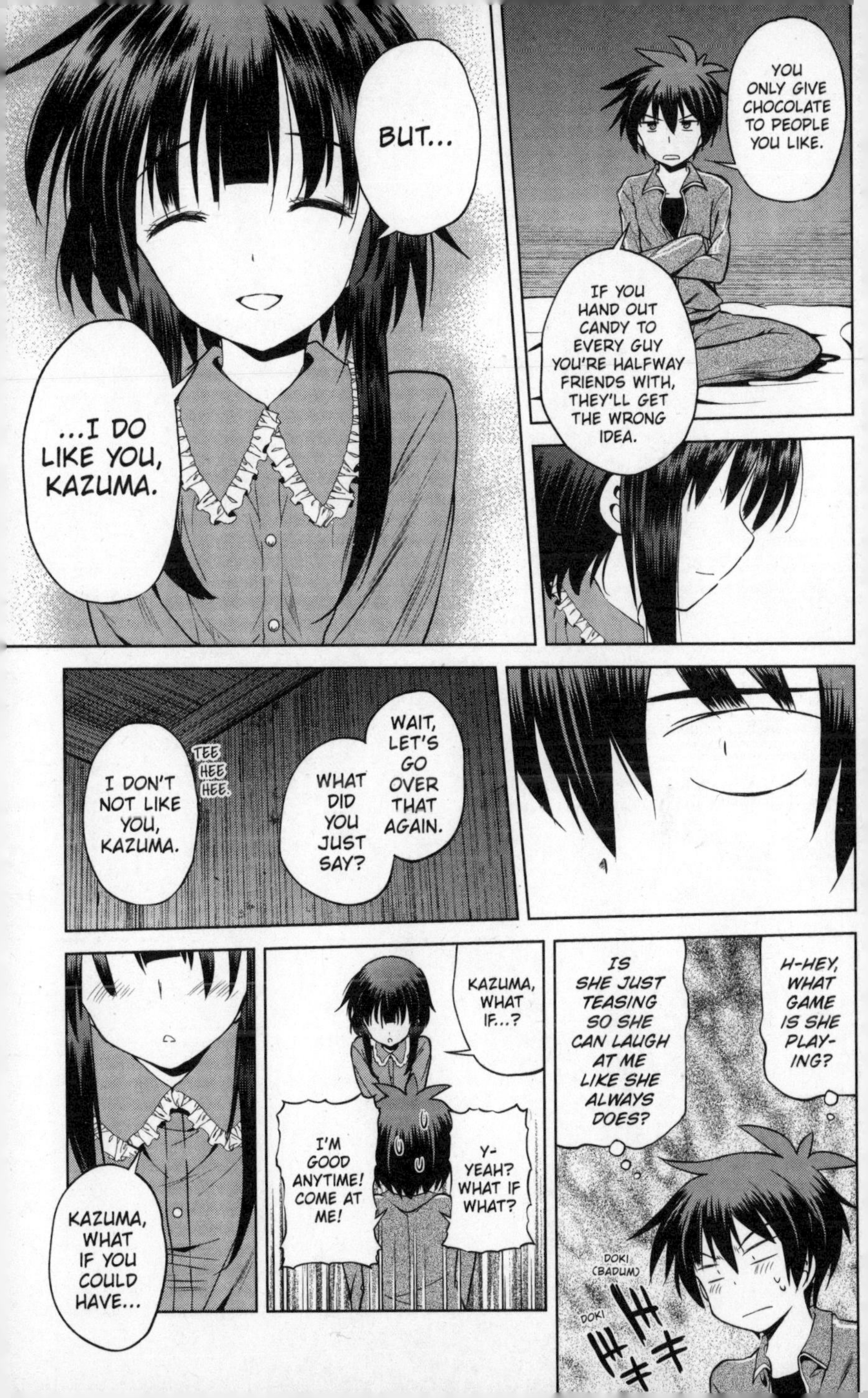
YOU ONLY GIVE CHOCOLATE TO PEOPLE YOU LIKE.
IF YOU HAND OUT CANDY TO EVERY GUY YOU'RE HALFWAY FRIENDS WITH, THEY'LL GET THE WRONG IDEA.
BUT...
...I DO LIKE YOU, KAZUMA.
WAIT, LET'S GO OVER THAT AGAIN.
WHAT DID YOU JUST SAY?
TEE HEE HEE.
I DON'T NOT LIKE YOU, KAZUMA.
H-HEY, WHAT GAME IS SHE PLAYING?
IS SHE JUST TEASING SO SHE CAN LAUGH AT ME LIKE SHE ALWAYS DOES?
DOKI (BADUM)
DOKI
KAZUMA, WHAT IF...?
Y-YEAH? WHAT IF WHAT?
I'M GOOD ANYTIME! COME AT ME!
KAZUMA, WHAT IF YOU COULD HAVE...

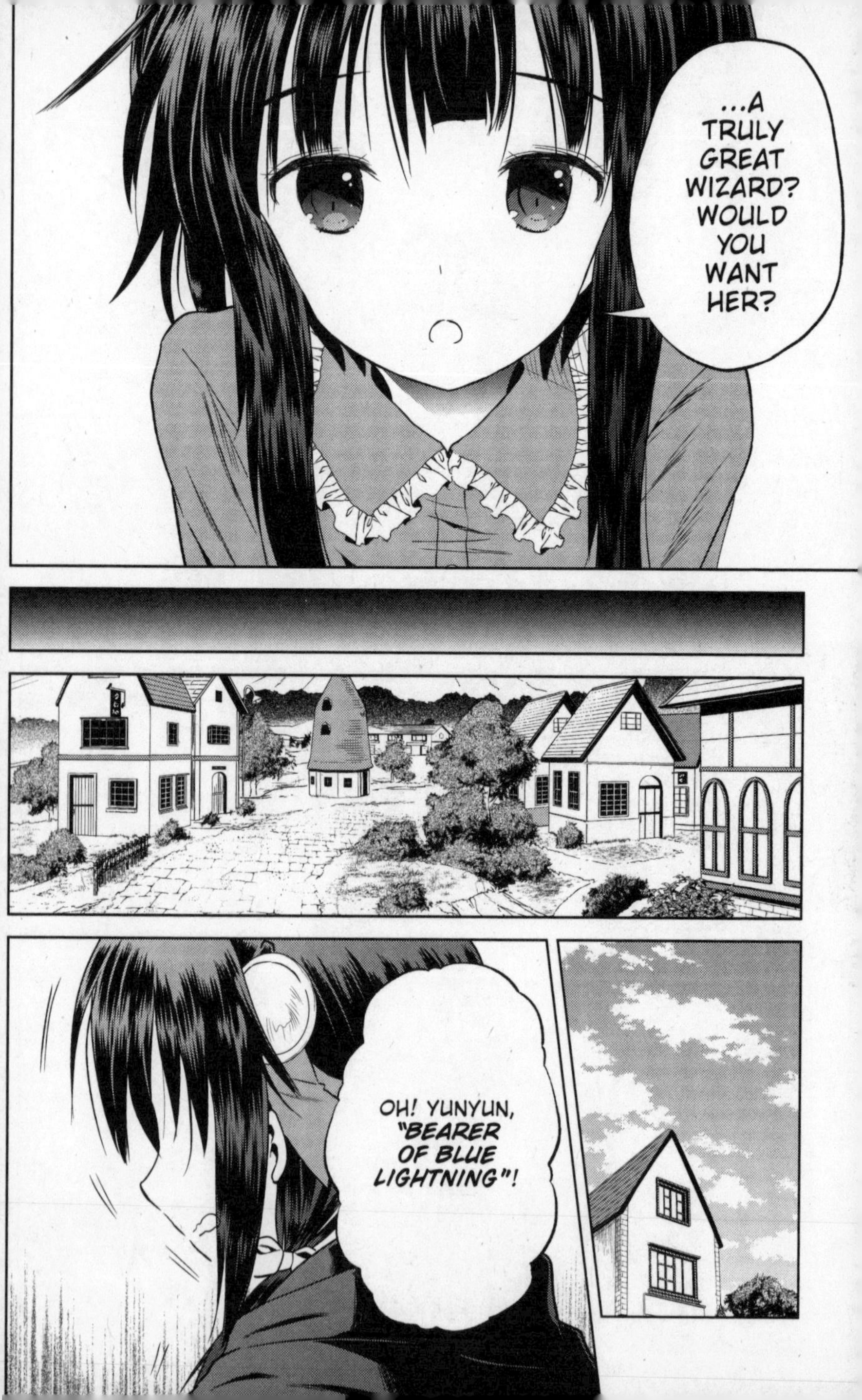
...A TRULY GREAT WIZARD? WOULD YOU WANT HER?
OH! YUNYUN, "BEARER OF BLUE LIGHTNING"!

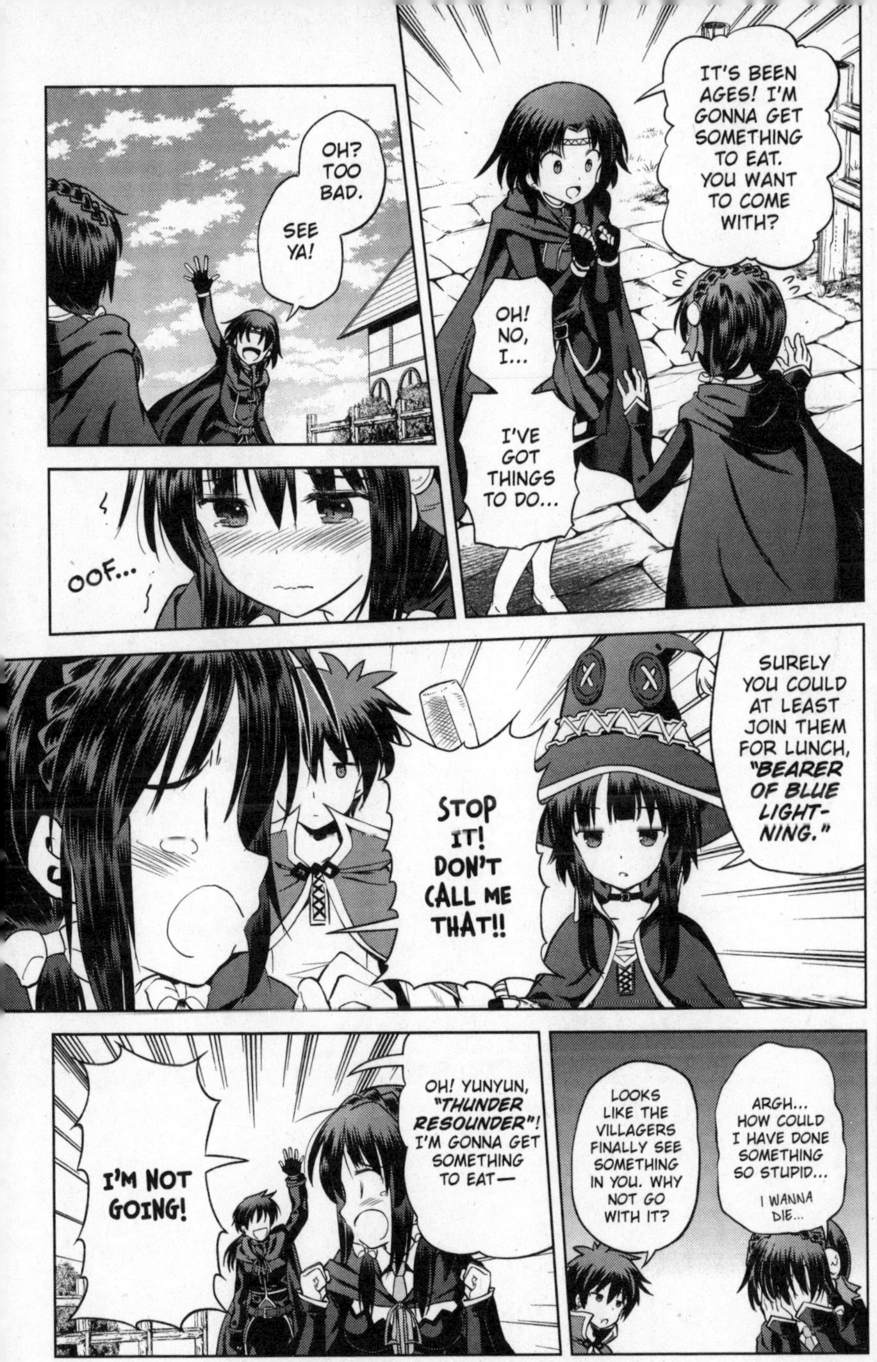
IT'S BEEN AGES! I'M GONNA GET SOMETHING TO EAT. YOU WANT TO COME WITH?
OH! NO, I...
I'VE GOT THINGS TO DO...
OH? TOO BAD.
SEE YA!
OOF...
SURELY YOU COULD AT LEAST JOIN THEM FOR LUNCH, *"BEARER OF BLUE LIGHTNING."*
STOP IT! DON'T CALL ME THAT!!
ARGH... HOW COULD I HAVE DONE SOMETHING SO STUPID...
I WANNA DIE...
LOOKS LIKE THE VILLAGERS FINALLY SEE SOMETHING IN YOU. WHY NOT GO WITH IT?
OH! YUNYUN, *"THUNDER RESOUNDER"*! I'M GONNA GET SOMETHING TO EAT—
I'M NOT GOING!

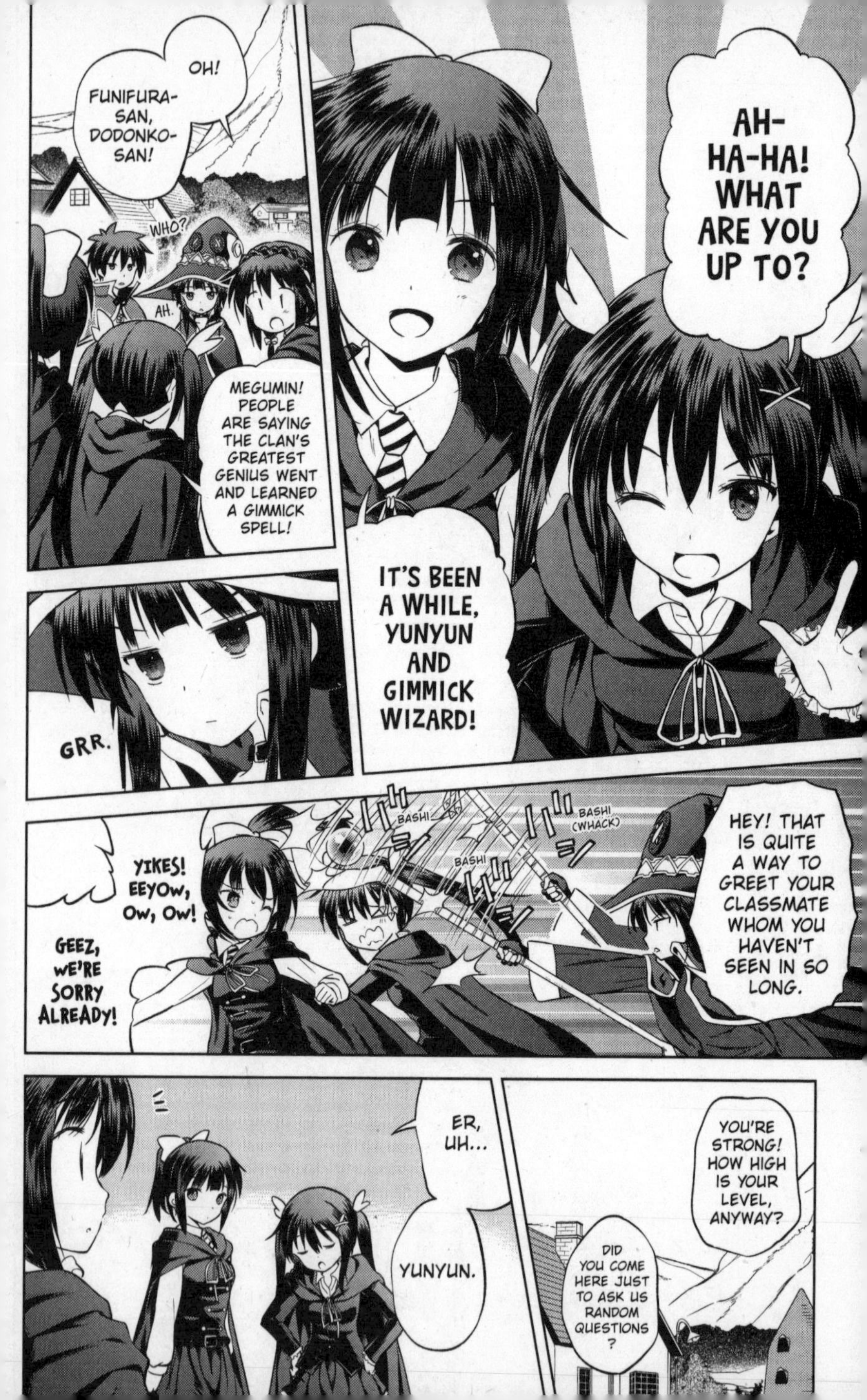
AH-HA-HA! WHAT ARE YOU UP TO?
IT'S BEEN A WHILE, YUNYUN AND GIMMICK WIZARD!
OH! FUNIFURA-SAN, DODONKO-SAN!
WHO?
AH.
MEGUMIN! PEOPLE ARE SAYING THE CLAN'S GREATEST GENIUS WENT AND LEARNED A GIMMICK SPELL!
GRR.
HEY! THAT IS QUITE A WAY TO GREET YOUR CLASSMATE WHOM YOU HAVEN'T SEEN IN SO LONG.
BASHI (WHACK)
BASHI
BASHI
YIKES! EEYOW, OW, OW!
GEEZ, WE'RE SORRY ALREADY!
YOU'RE STRONG! HOW HIGH IS YOUR LEVEL, ANYWAY?
DID YOU COME HERE JUST TO ASK US RANDOM QUESTIONS?
ER, UH...
YUNYUN.

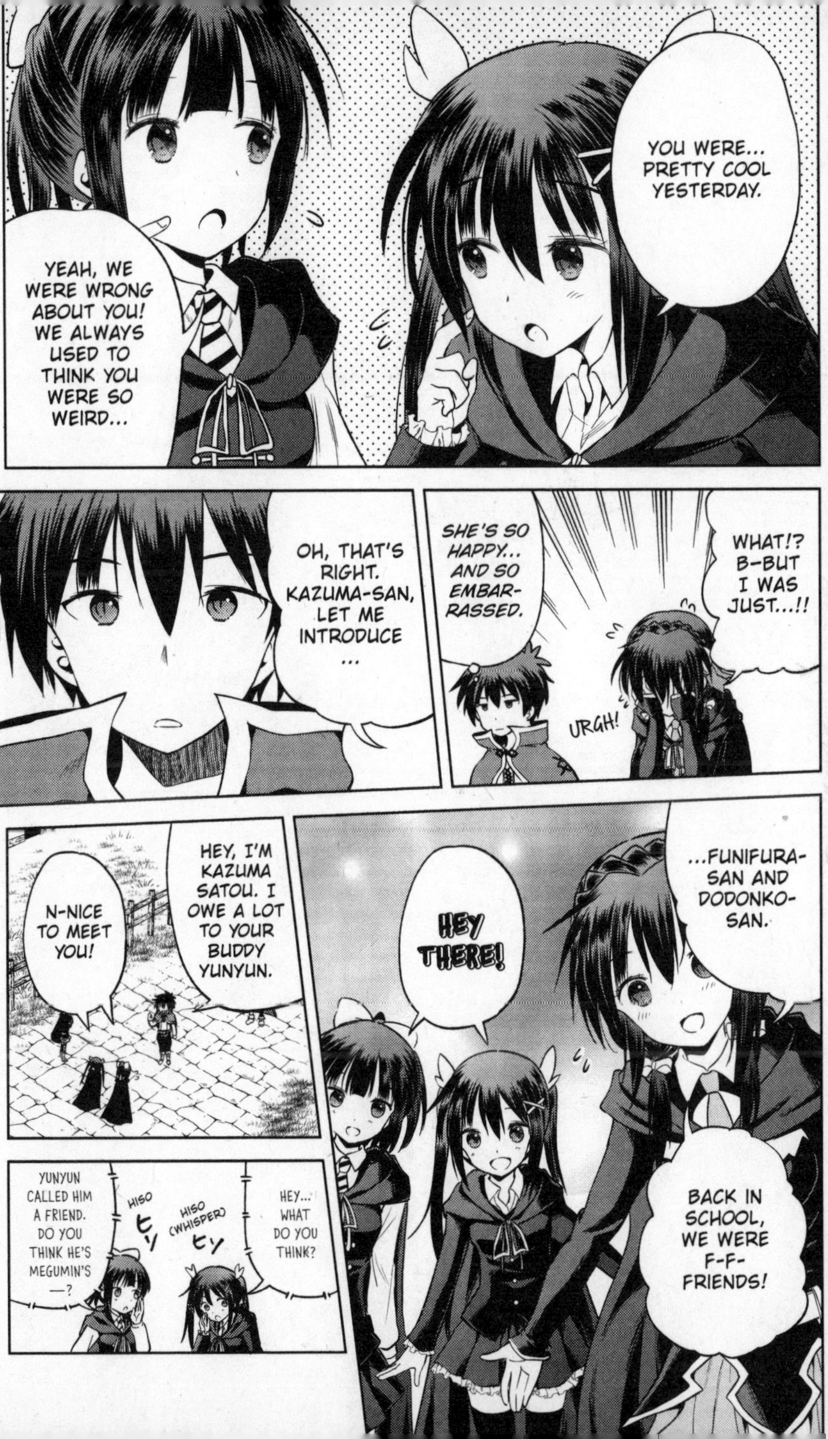
YOU WERE... PRETTY COOL YESTERDAY.
YEAH, WE WERE WRONG ABOUT YOU! WE ALWAYS USED TO THINK YOU WERE SO WEIRD...
WHAT!? B-BUT I WAS JUST...!!
SHE'S SO HAPPY... AND SO EMBAR-RASSED.
URGH!
OH, THAT'S RIGHT. KAZUMA-SAN, LET ME INTRODUCE ...
...FUNIFURA-SAN AND DODONKO-SAN.
HEY THERE!
BACK IN SCHOOL, WE WERE F-F-FRIENDS!
HEY, I'M KAZUMA SATOU. I OWE A LOT TO YOUR BUDDY YUNYUN.
N-NICE TO MEET YOU!
HEY... WHAT DO YOU THINK?
HISO (WHISPER) ヒソ
HISO ヒソ
YUNYUN CALLED HIM A FRIEND. DO YOU THINK HE'S MEGUMIN'S —?

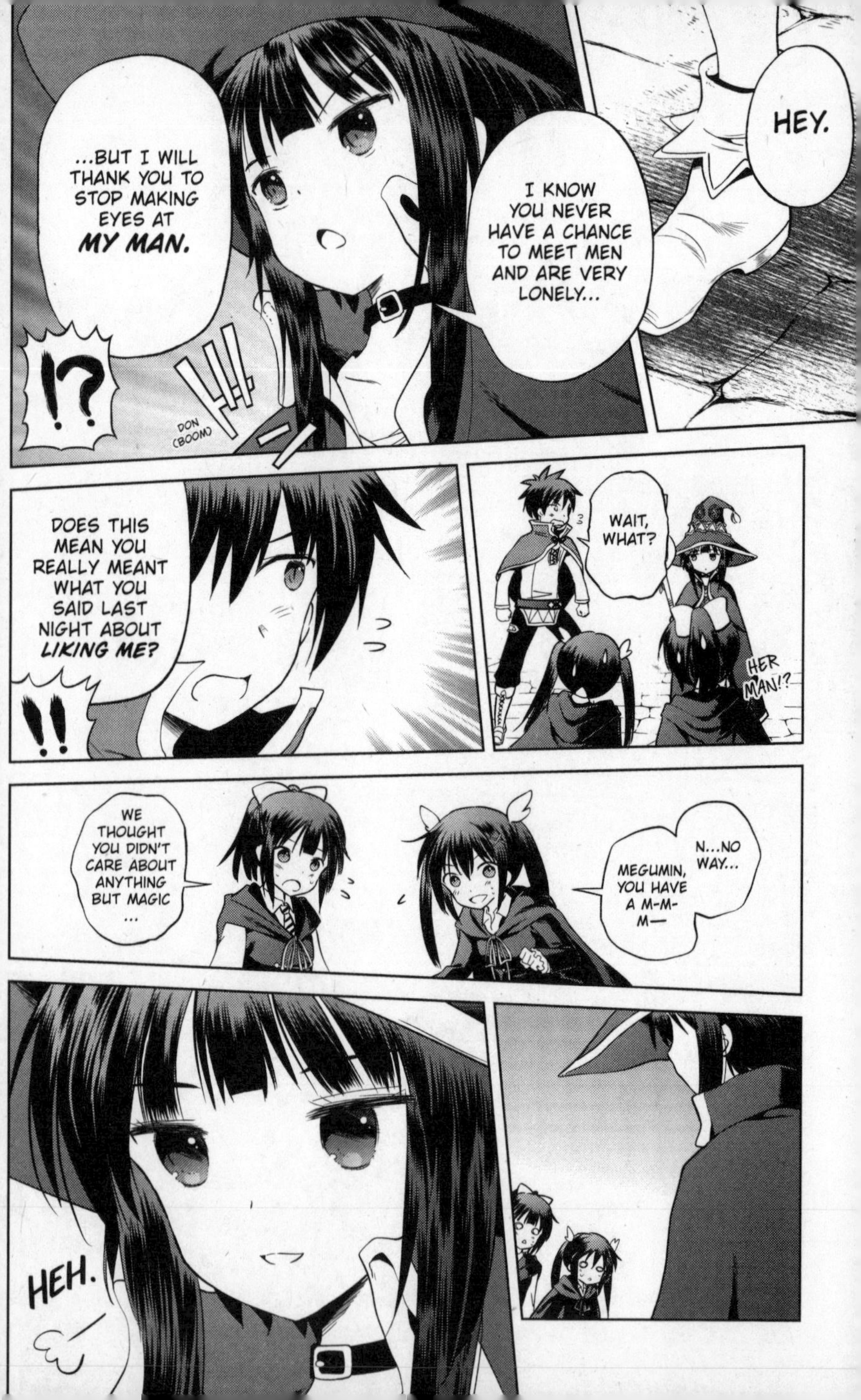
HEY.
I KNOW YOU NEVER HAVE A CHANCE TO MEET MEN AND ARE VERY LONELY...
...BUT I WILL THANK YOU TO STOP MAKING EYES AT **MY MAN.**
DON (BOOM)
!?
WAIT, WHAT?
HER MAN!?
DOES THIS MEAN YOU REALLY MEANT WHAT YOU SAID LAST NIGHT ABOUT ***LIKING ME?***
!!
N...NO WAY... MEGUMIN, YOU HAVE A M-M-M—
WE THOUGHT YOU DIDN'T CARE ABOUT ANYTHING BUT MAGIC...
HEH.

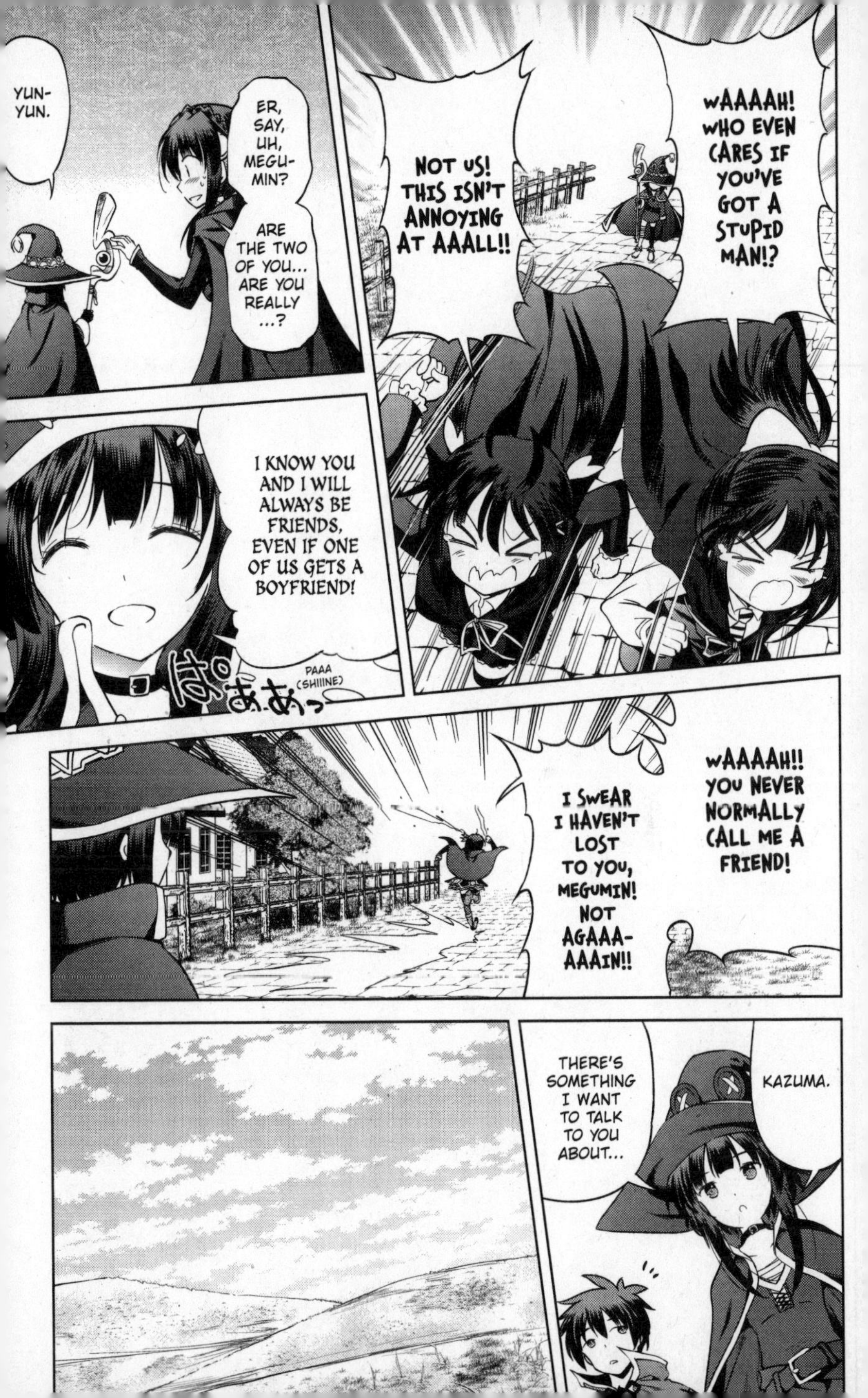
WAAAAH! WHO EVEN CARES IF YOU'VE GOT A STUPID MAN!?
NOT US! THIS ISN'T ANNOYING AT AAALL!!
ER, SAY, UH, MEGU-MIN?
ARE THE TWO OF YOU... ARE YOU REALLY ...?
YUN-YUN.
I KNOW YOU AND I WILL ALWAYS BE FRIENDS, EVEN IF ONE OF US GETS A BOYFRIEND!
ぱあぁっ
PAAA (SHIIINE)
WAAAAH!! YOU NEVER NORMALLY CALL ME A FRIEND!
I SWEAR I HAVEN'T LOST TO YOU, MEGUMIN! NOT AGAAA-AAAIN!!
KAZUMA.
THERE'S SOMETHING I WANT TO TALK TO YOU ABOUT...

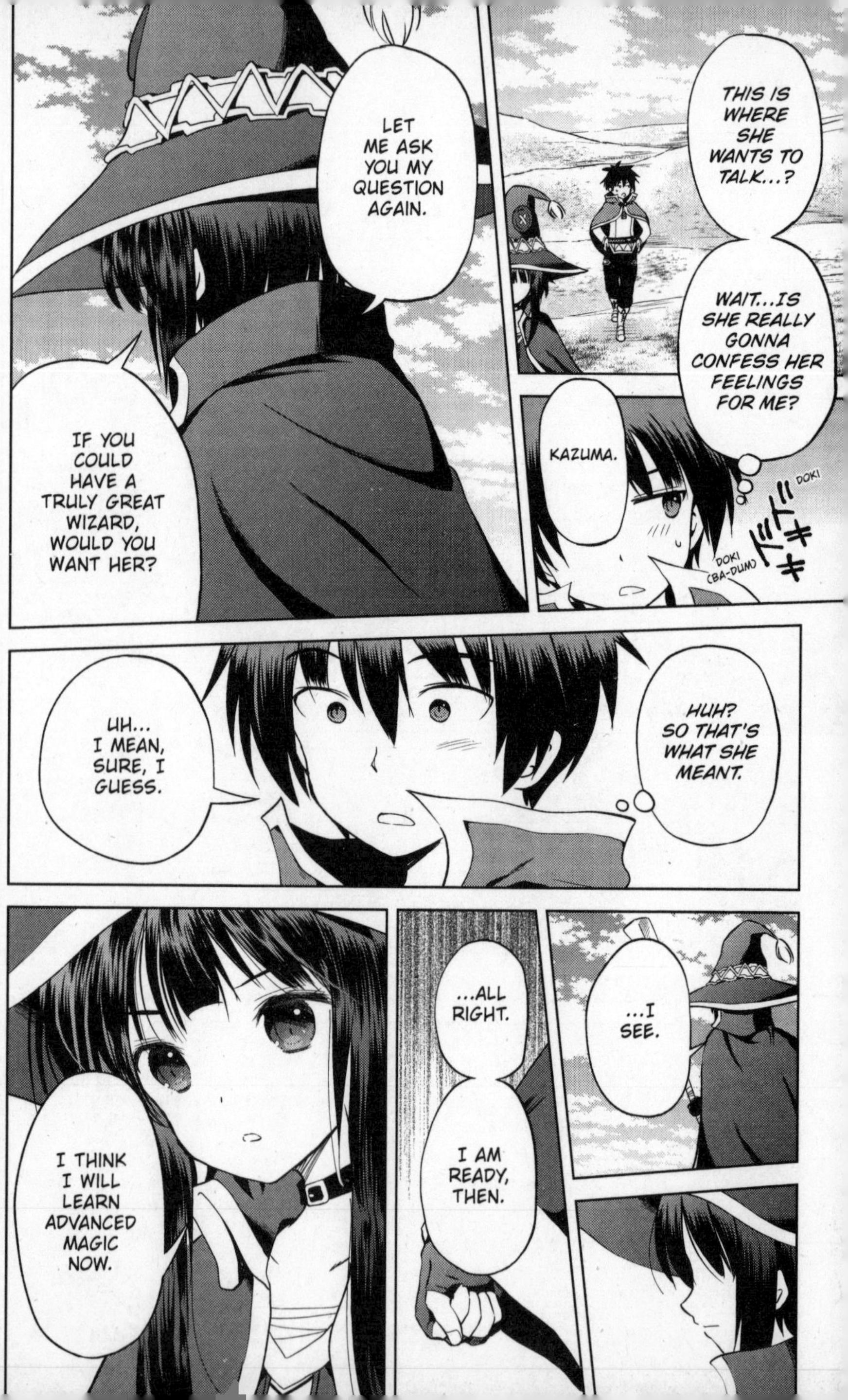
THIS IS WHERE SHE WANTS TO TALK...?
WAIT...IS SHE REALLY GONNA CONFESS HER FEELINGS FOR ME?
KAZUMA.
DOKI
DOKI (BA-DUM)
LET ME ASK YOU MY QUESTION AGAIN.
IF YOU COULD HAVE A TRULY GREAT WIZARD, WOULD YOU WANT HER?
HUH? SO THAT'S WHAT SHE MEANT.
UH... I MEAN, SURE, I GUESS.
...I SEE.
...ALL RIGHT.
I AM READY, THEN.
I THINK I WILL LEARN ADVANCED MAGIC NOW.

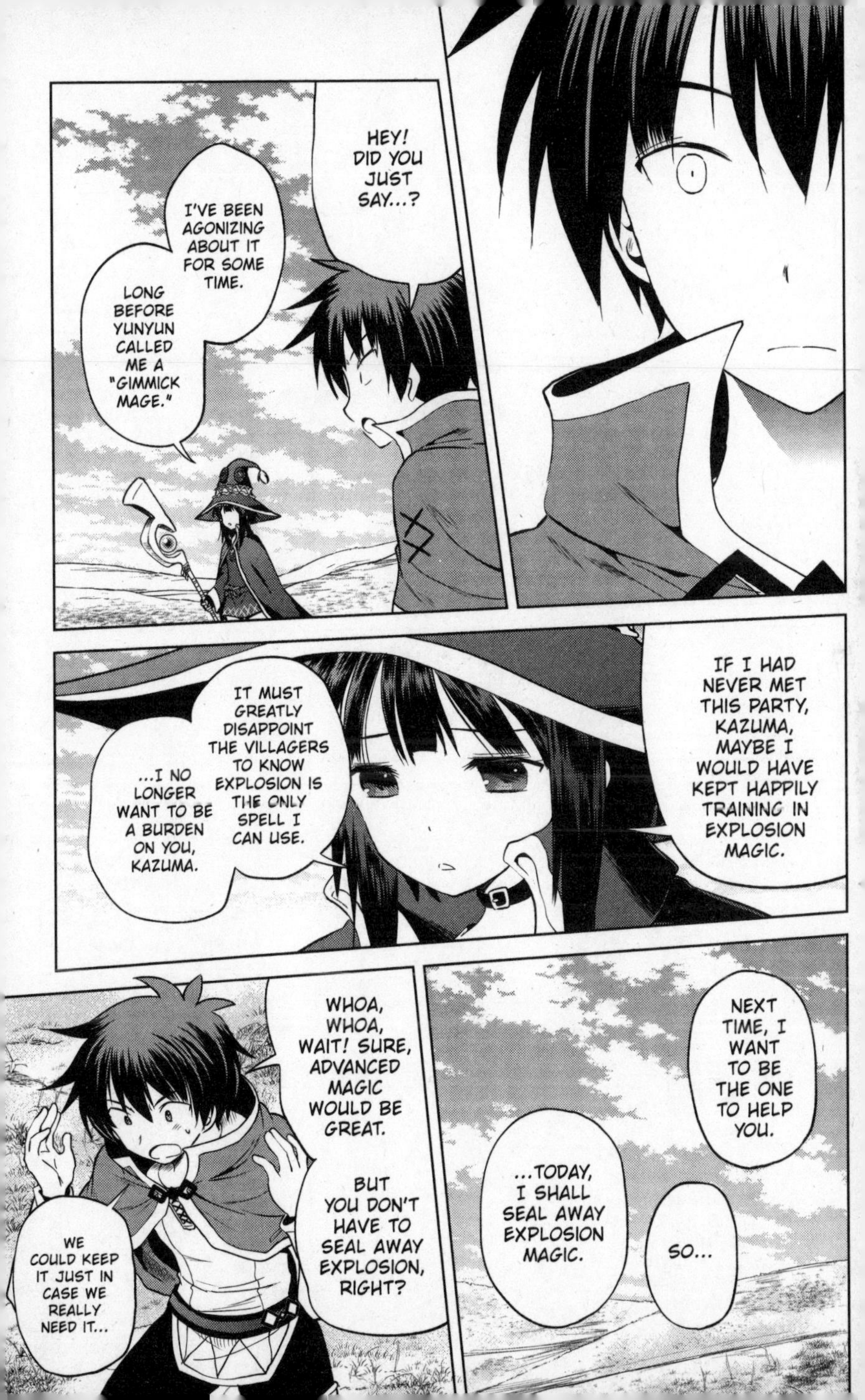
HEY! DID YOU JUST SAY...?
I'VE BEEN AGONIZING ABOUT IT FOR SOME TIME.
LONG BEFORE YUNYUN CALLED ME A "GIMMICK MAGE."
IF I HAD NEVER MET THIS PARTY, KAZUMA, MAYBE I WOULD HAVE KEPT HAPPILY TRAINING IN EXPLOSION MAGIC.
IT MUST GREATLY DISAPPOINT THE VILLAGERS TO KNOW EXPLOSION IS THE ONLY SPELL I CAN USE.
...I NO LONGER WANT TO BE A BURDEN ON YOU, KAZUMA.
NEXT TIME, I WANT TO BE THE ONE TO HELP YOU.
...TODAY, I SHALL SEAL AWAY EXPLOSION MAGIC.
SO...
WHOA, WHOA, WAIT! SURE, ADVANCED MAGIC WOULD BE GREAT.
BUT YOU DON'T HAVE TO SEAL AWAY EXPLOSION, RIGHT?
WE COULD KEEP IT JUST IN CASE WE REALLY NEED IT...

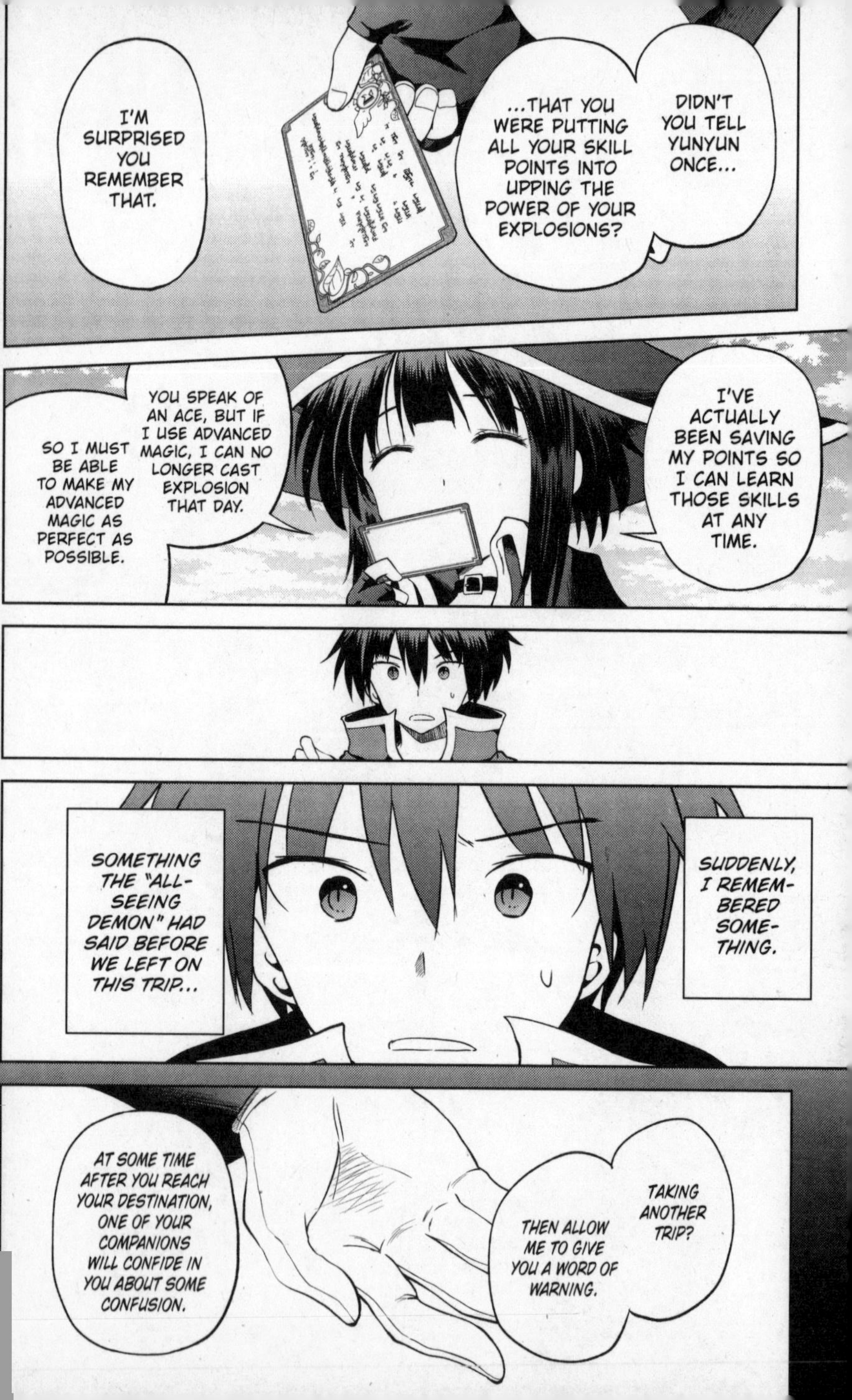
DIDN'T YOU TELL YUNYUN ONCE...
...THAT YOU WERE PUTTING ALL YOUR SKILL POINTS INTO UPPING THE POWER OF YOUR EXPLOSIONS?
I'M SURPRISED YOU REMEMBER THAT.
I'VE ACTUALLY BEEN SAVING MY POINTS SO I CAN LEARN THOSE SKILLS AT ANY TIME.
YOU SPEAK OF AN ACE, BUT IF I USE ADVANCED MAGIC, I CAN NO LONGER CAST EXPLOSION THAT DAY.
SO I MUST BE ABLE TO MAKE MY ADVANCED MAGIC AS PERFECT AS POSSIBLE.
SUDDENLY, I REMEMBERED SOMETHING.
SOMETHING THE "ALL-SEEING DEMON" HAD SAID BEFORE WE LEFT ON THIS TRIP...
TAKING ANOTHER TRIP?
THEN ALLOW ME TO GIVE YOU A WORD OF WARNING.
AT SOME TIME AFTER YOU REACH YOUR DESTINATION, ONE OF YOUR COMPANIONS WILL CONFIDE IN YOU ABOUT SOME CONFUSION.

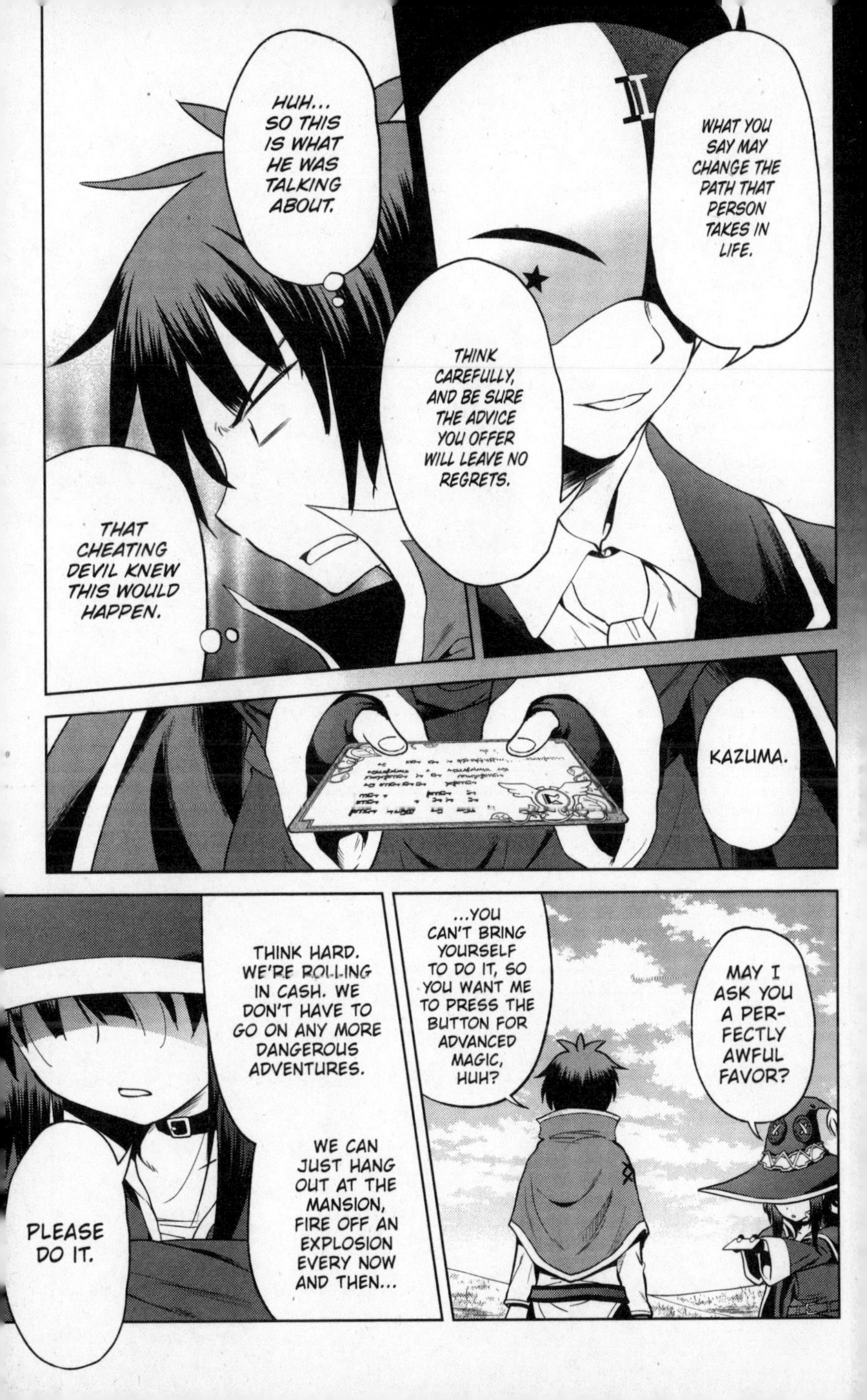
WHAT YOU SAY MAY CHANGE THE PATH THAT PERSON TAKES IN LIFE.
THINK CAREFULLY, AND BE SURE THE ADVICE YOU OFFER WILL LEAVE NO REGRETS.
HUH... SO THIS IS WHAT HE WAS TALKING ABOUT.
THAT CHEATING DEVIL KNEW THIS WOULD HAPPEN.
KAZUMA.
MAY I ASK YOU A PERFECTLY AWFUL FAVOR?
...YOU CAN'T BRING YOURSELF TO DO IT, SO YOU WANT ME TO PRESS THE BUTTON FOR ADVANCED MAGIC, HUH?
THINK HARD. WE'RE ROLLING IN CASH. WE DON'T HAVE TO GO ON ANY MORE DANGEROUS ADVENTURES.
WE CAN JUST HANG OUT AT THE MANSION, FIRE OFF AN EXPLOSION EVERY NOW AND THEN...
PLEASE DO IT.

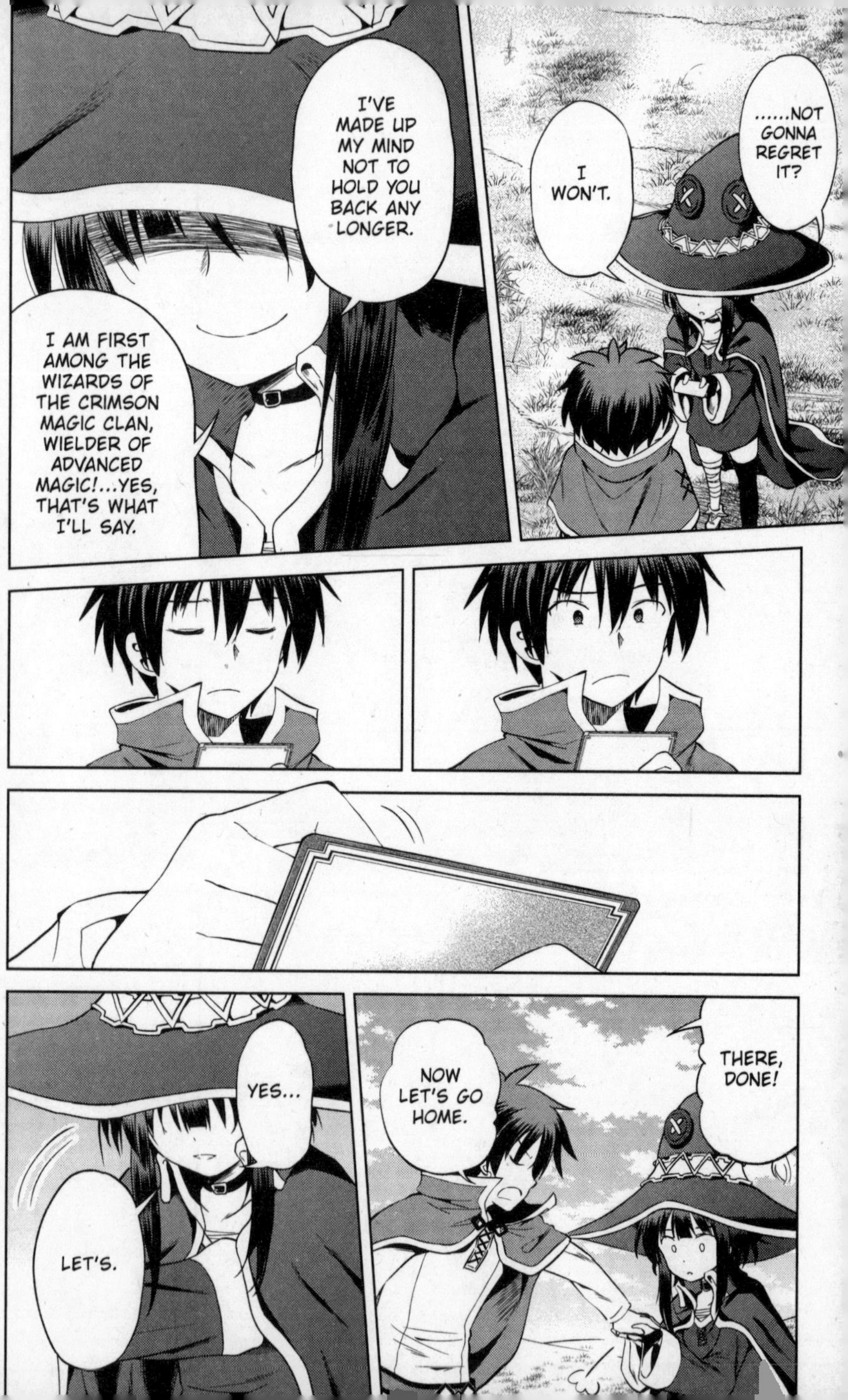

......NOT GONNA REGRET IT?
I WON'T.
I'VE MADE UP MY MIND NOT TO HOLD YOU BACK ANY LONGER.
I AM FIRST AMONG THE WIZARDS OF THE CRIMSON MAGIC CLAN, WIELDER OF ADVANCED MAGIC!...YES, THAT'S WHAT I'LL SAY.
THERE, DONE!
NOW LET'S GO HOME.
YES...
LET'S.

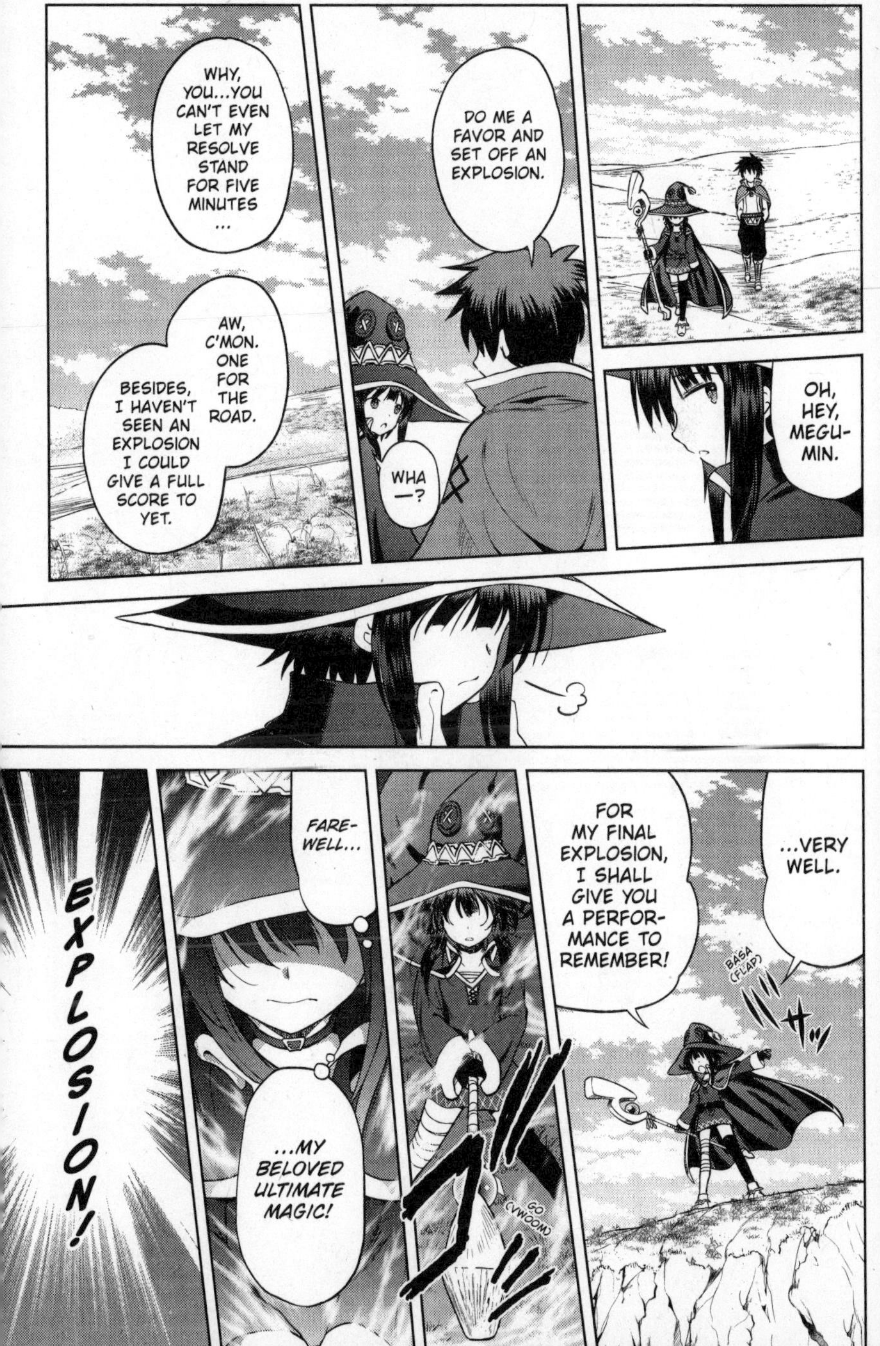
OH, HEY, MEGUMIN.
DO ME A FAVOR AND SET OFF AN EXPLOSION.
WHA—?
WHY, YOU...YOU CAN'T EVEN LET MY RESOLVE STAND FOR FIVE MINUTES...
AW, C'MON. ONE FOR THE ROAD.
BESIDES, I HAVEN'T SEEN AN EXPLOSION I COULD GIVE A FULL SCORE TO YET.
...VERY WELL.
BASA (FLAP)
FOR MY FINAL EXPLOSION, I SHALL GIVE YOU A PERFORMANCE TO REMEMBER!
GO (VWOOM)
FAREWELL...
...MY BELOVED ULTIMATE MAGIC!
EXPLOSION!

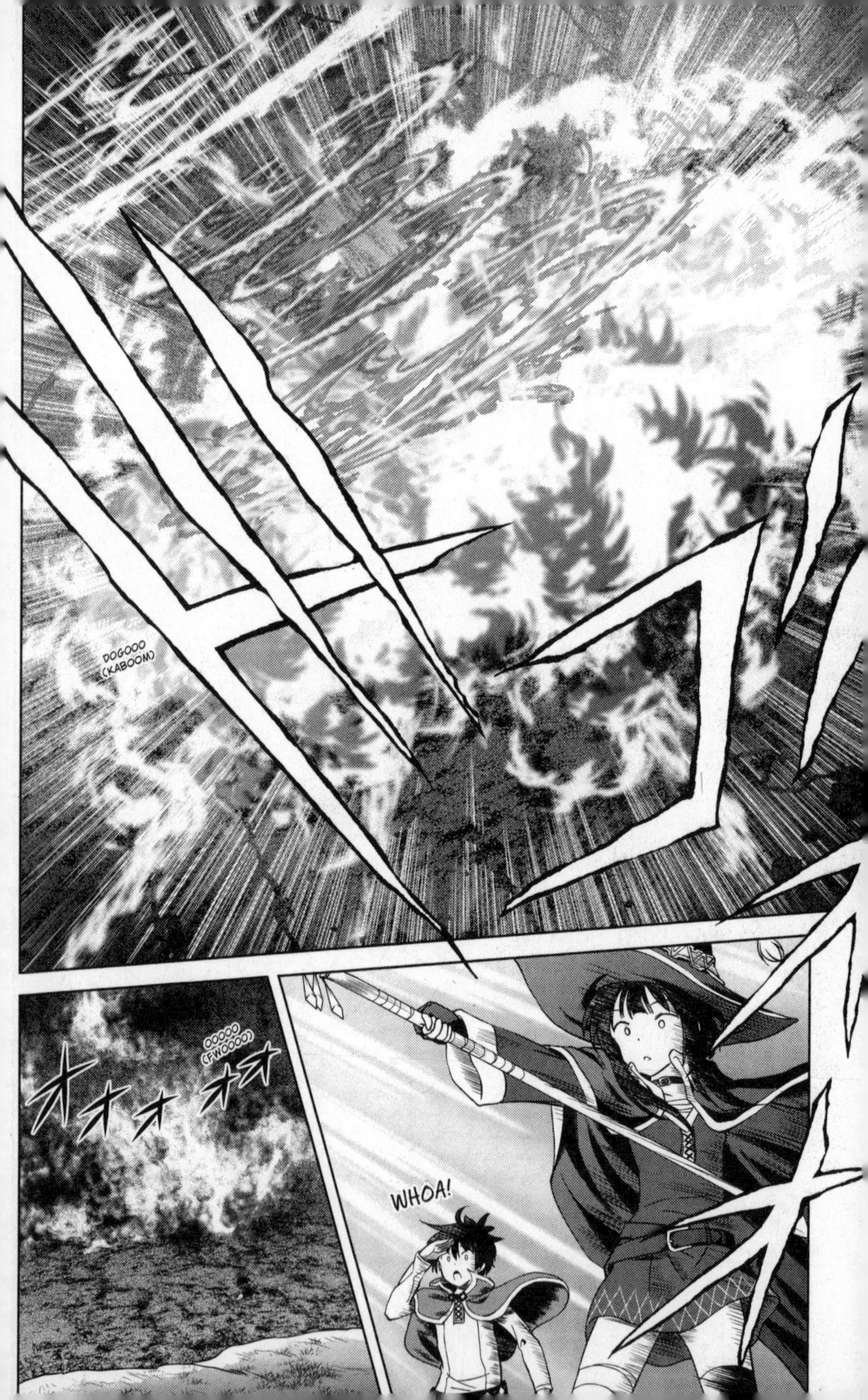
DOGOOO (KABOOM)
WHOA!
OOOOO (FWOOOO)

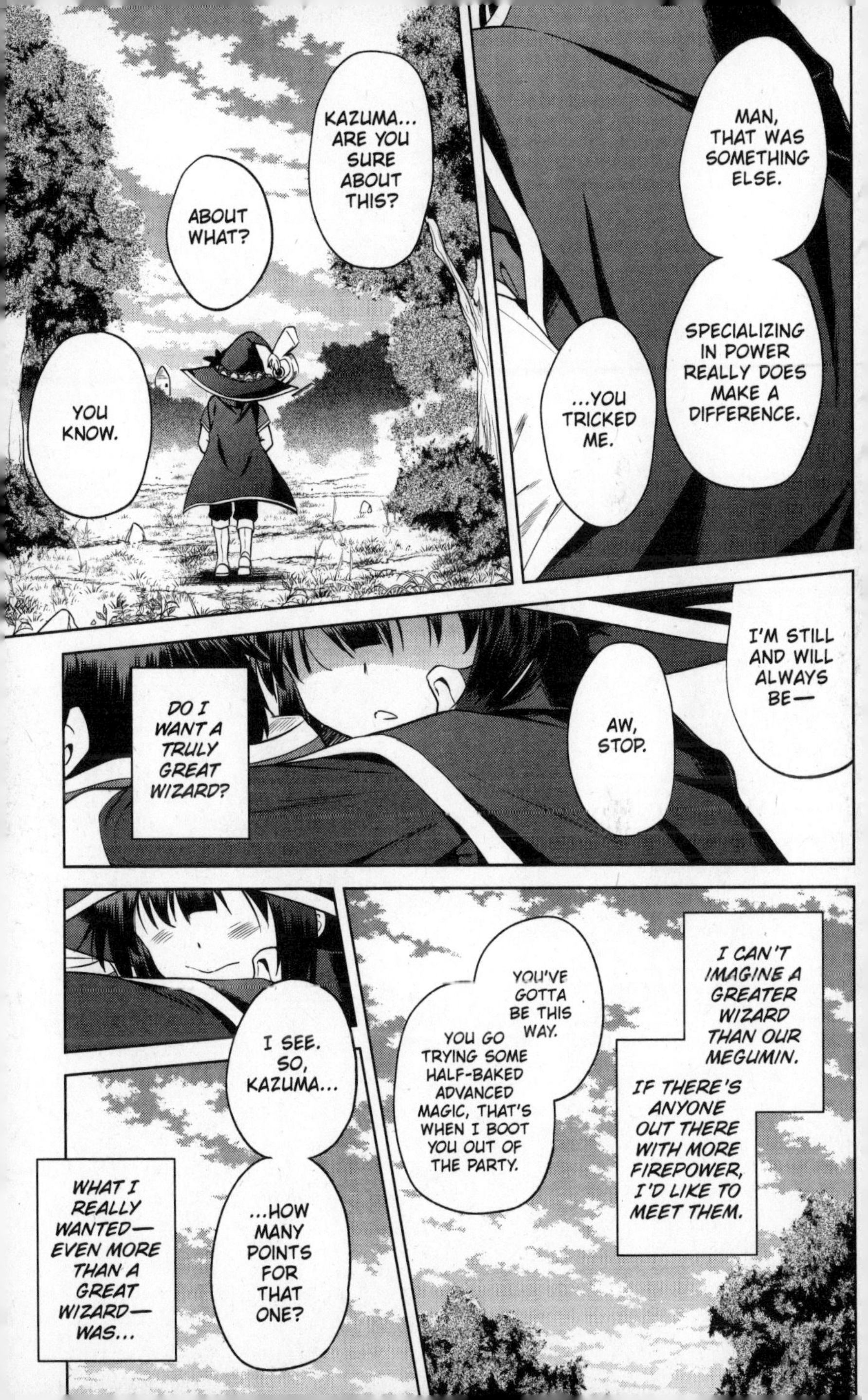
MAN, THAT WAS SOMETHING ELSE.
SPECIALIZING IN POWER REALLY DOES MAKE A DIFFERENCE.
...YOU TRICKED ME.
KAZUMA... ARE YOU SURE ABOUT THIS?
ABOUT WHAT?
YOU KNOW.
I'M STILL AND WILL ALWAYS BE—
AW, STOP.
DO I WANT A TRULY GREAT WIZARD?
I CAN'T IMAGINE A GREATER WIZARD THAN OUR MEGUMIN.
IF THERE'S ANYONE OUT THERE WITH MORE FIREPOWER, I'D LIKE TO MEET THEM.
YOU'VE GOTTA BE THIS WAY.
YOU GO TRYING SOME HALF-BAKED ADVANCED MAGIC, THAT'S WHEN I BOOT YOU OUT OF THE PARTY.
I SEE. SO, KAZUMA...
...HOW MANY POINTS FOR THAT ONE?
WHAT I REALLY WANTED—EVEN MORE THAN A GREAT WIZARD—WAS...

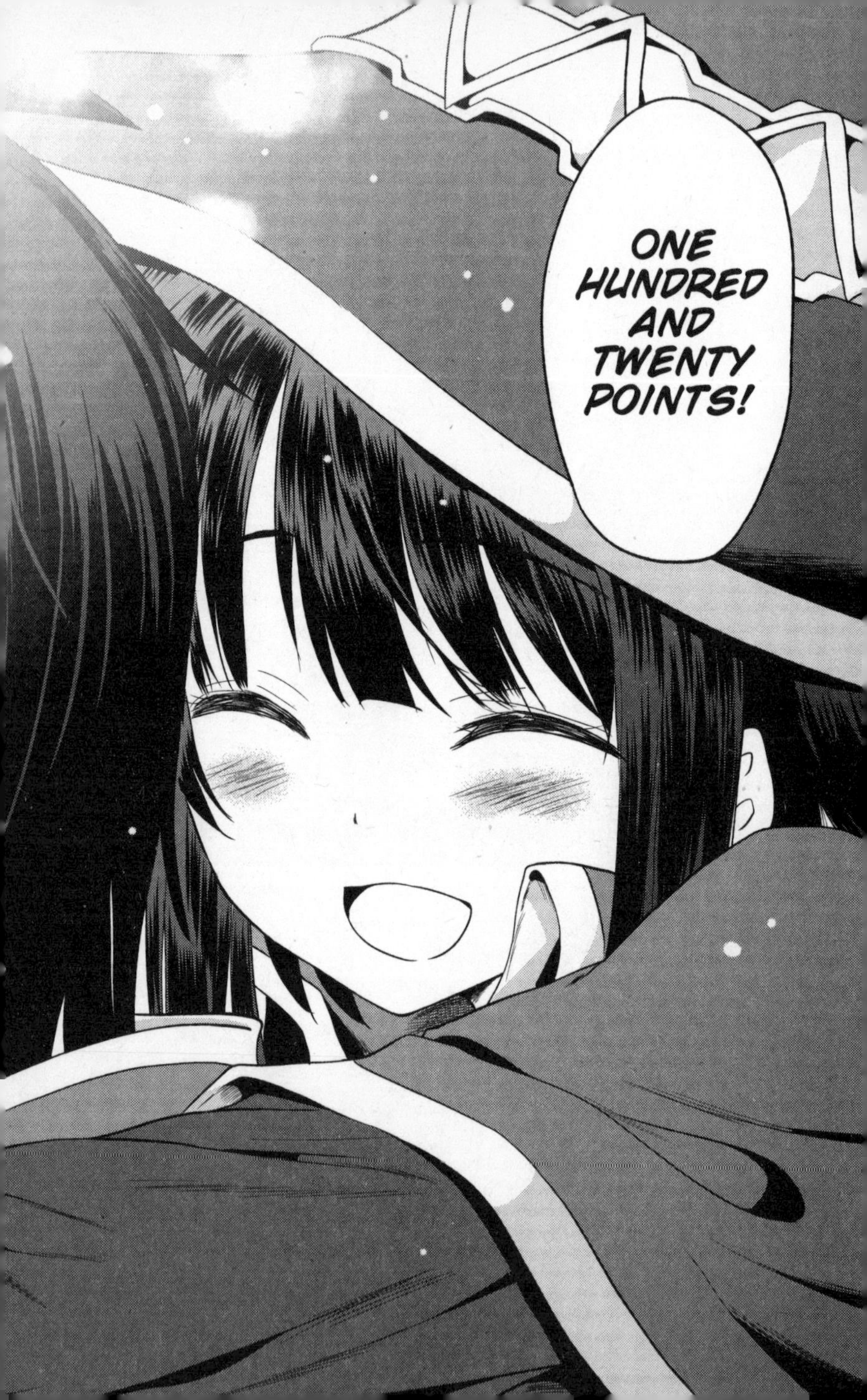
ONE HUNDRED AND TWENTY POINTS!

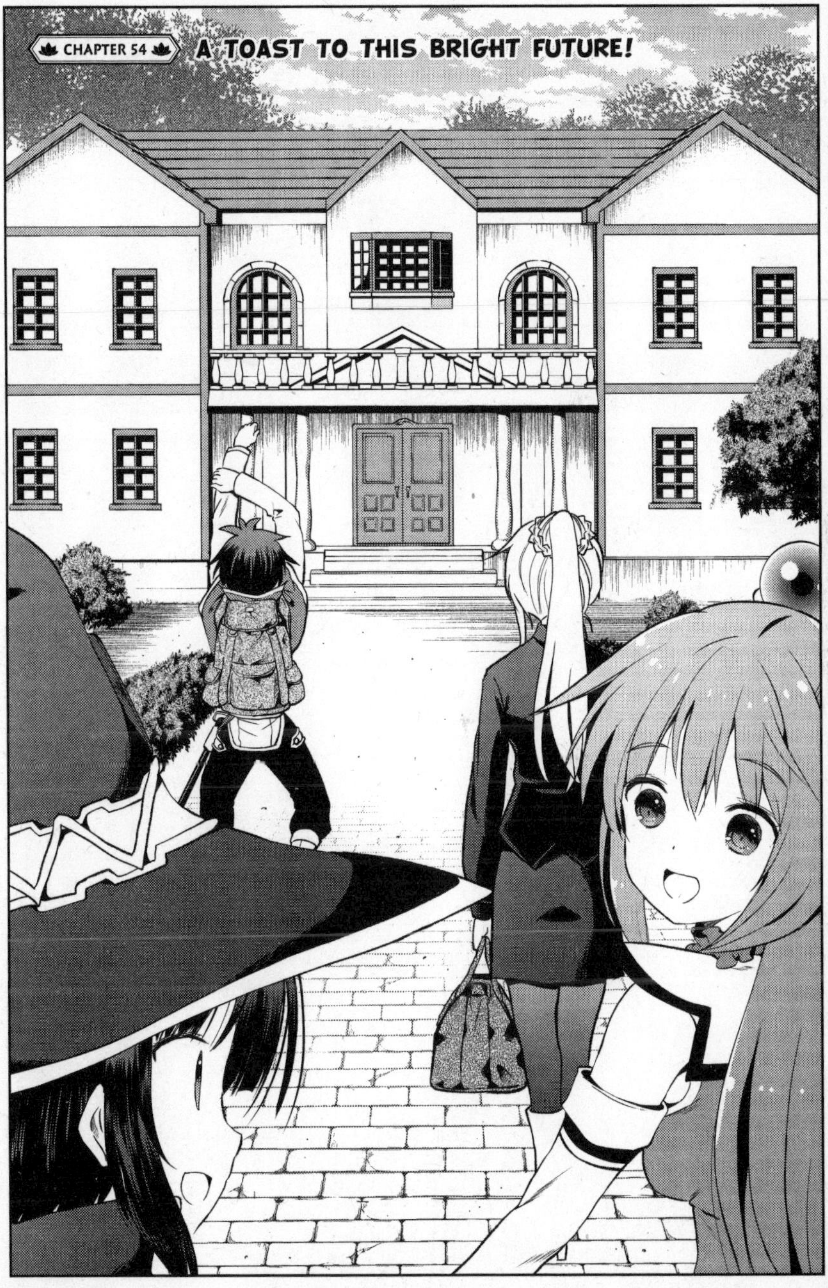
CHAPTER 54
A TOAST TO THIS BRIGHT FUTURE!

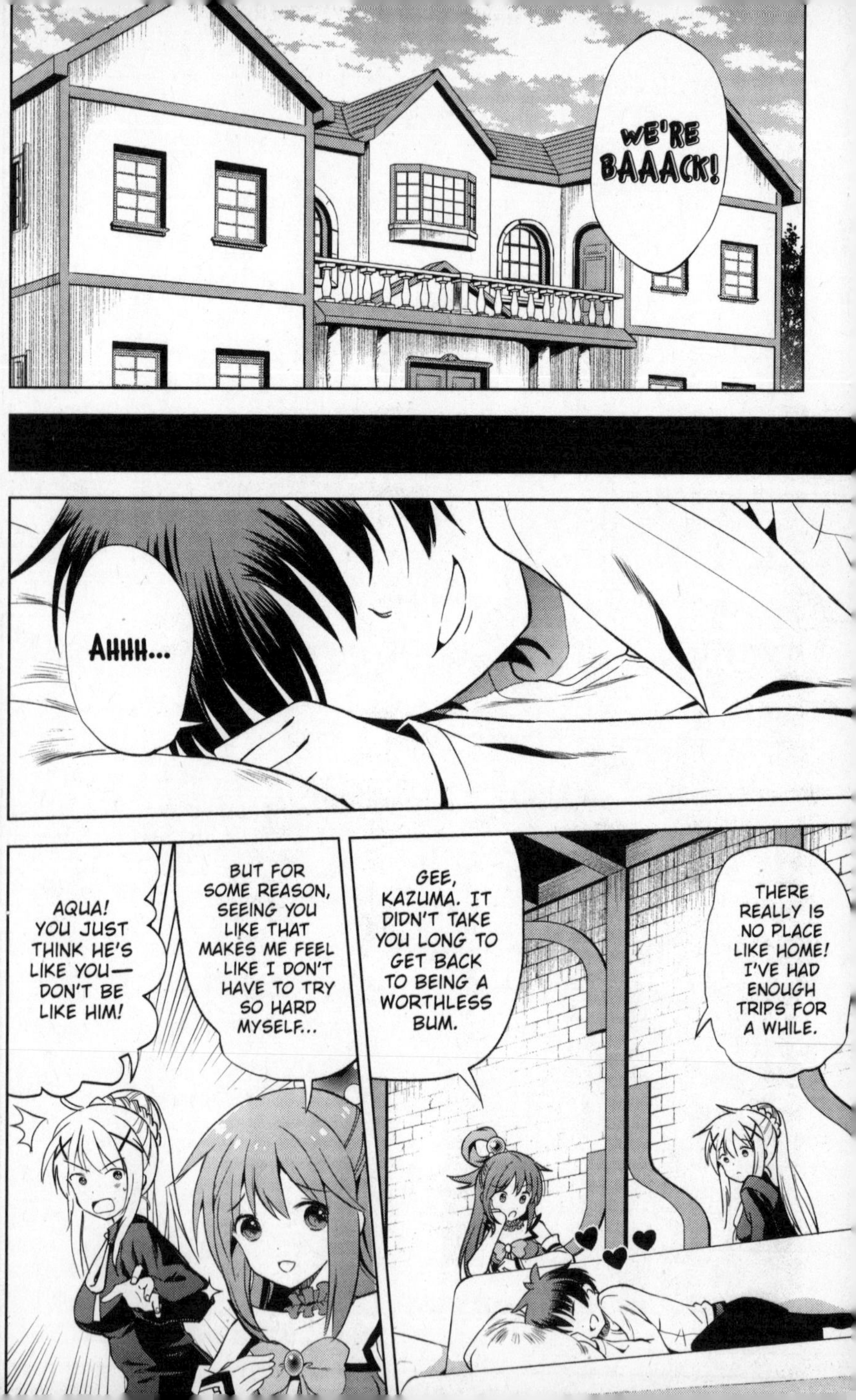
WE'RE BAAACK!
AHHH...
THERE REALLY IS NO PLACE LIKE HOME! I'VE HAD ENOUGH TRIPS FOR A WHILE.
GEE, KAZUMA. IT DIDN'T TAKE YOU LONG TO GET BACK TO BEING A WORTHLESS BUM.
BUT FOR SOME REASON, SEEING YOU LIKE THAT MAKES ME FEEL LIKE I DON'T HAVE TO TRY SO HARD MYSELF...
AQUA! YOU JUST THINK HE'S LIKE YOU—DON'T BE LIKE HIM!

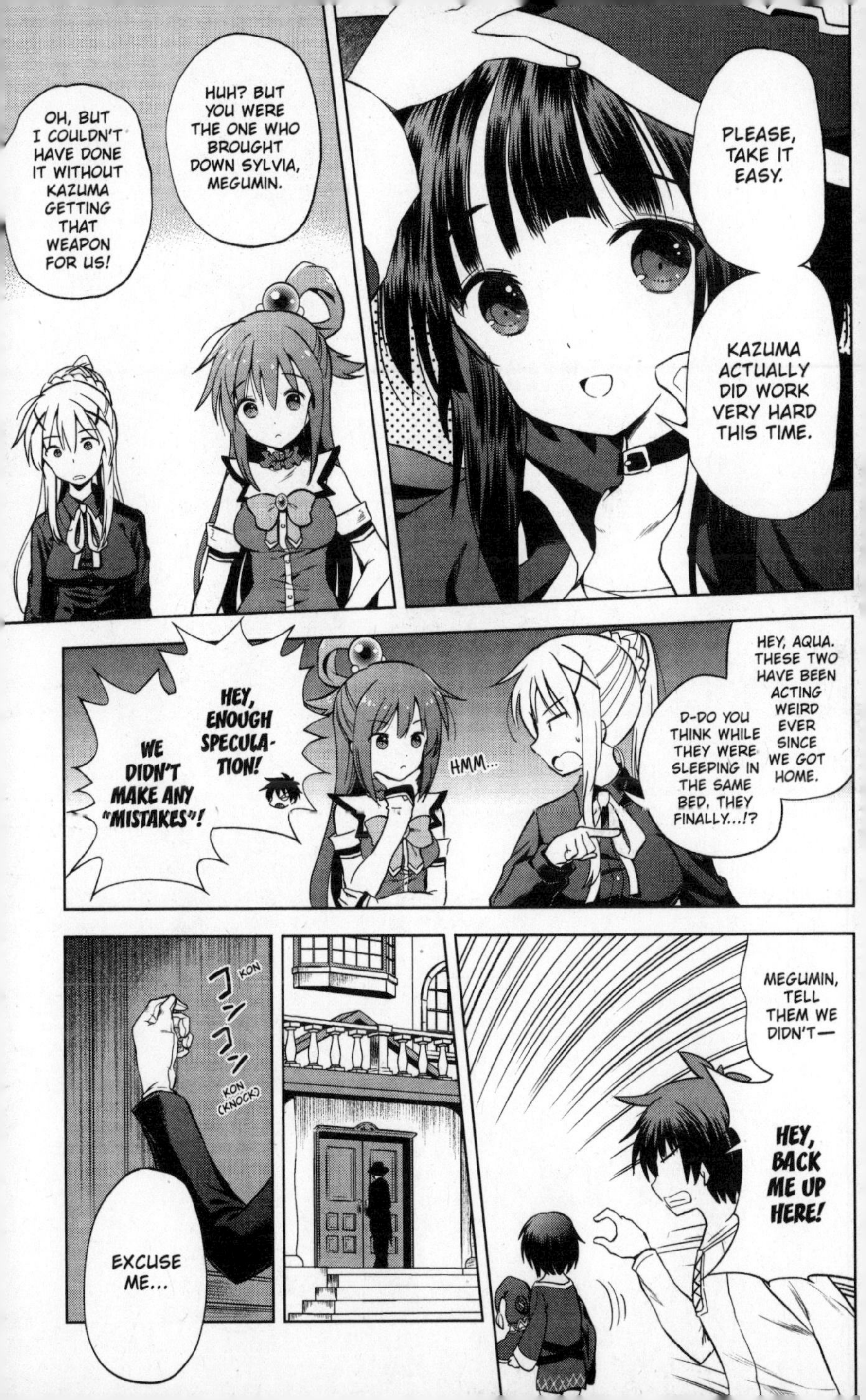
PLEASE, TAKE IT EASY.
KAZUMA ACTUALLY DID WORK VERY HARD THIS TIME.
HUH? BUT YOU WERE THE ONE WHO BROUGHT DOWN SYLVIA, MEGUMIN.
OH, BUT I COULDN'T HAVE DONE IT WITHOUT KAZUMA GETTING THAT WEAPON FOR US!
HEY, AQUA. THESE TWO HAVE BEEN ACTING WEIRD EVER SINCE WE GOT HOME.
D-DO YOU THINK WHILE THEY WERE SLEEPING IN THE SAME BED, THEY FINALLY...!?
HMM...
HEY, ENOUGH SPECULA-TION!
WE DIDN'T MAKE ANY "MISTAKES"!
MEGUMIN, TELL THEM WE DIDN'T—
HEY, BACK ME UP HERE!
コンコン
KON
KON (KNOCK)
EXCUSE ME...

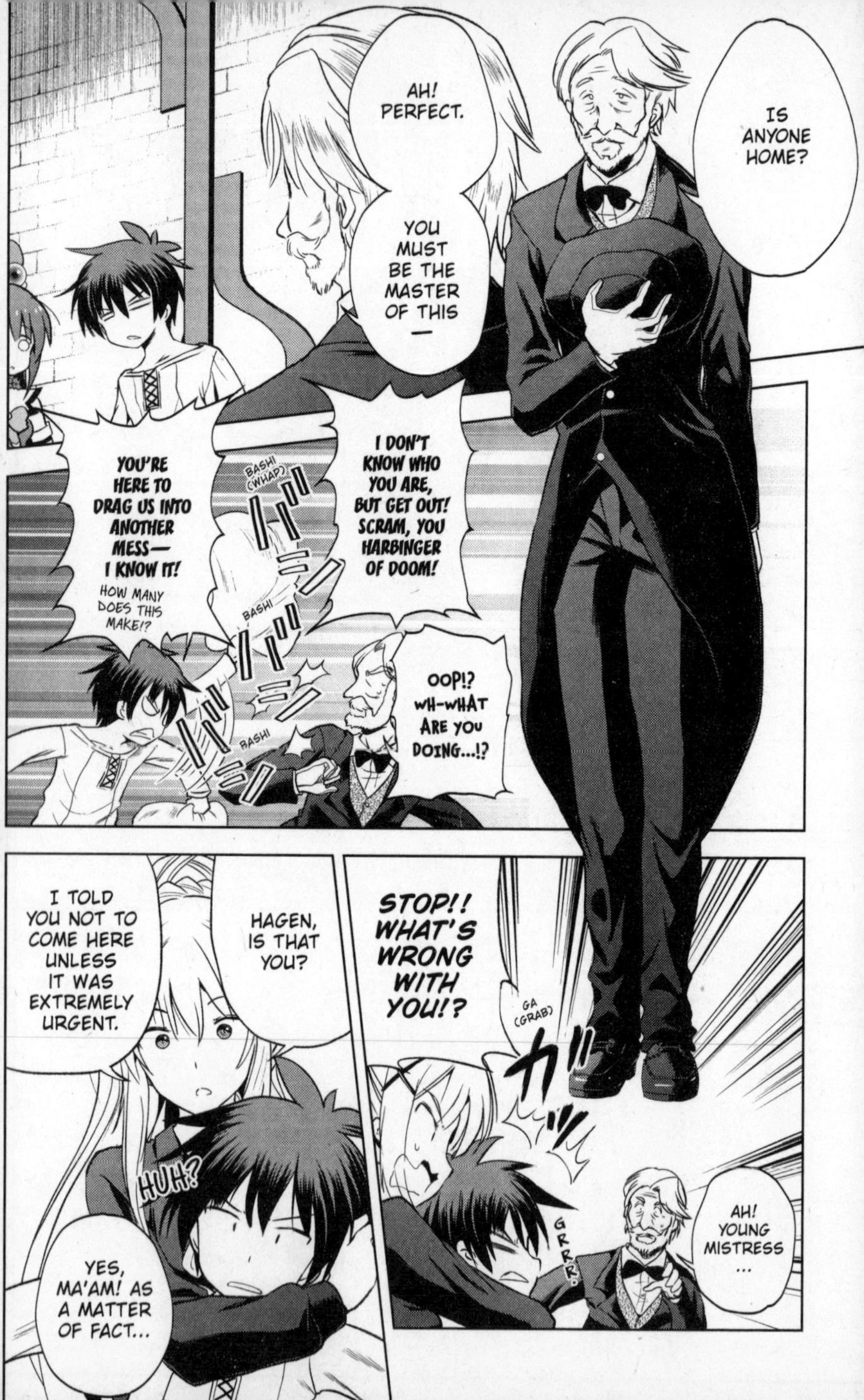
IS ANYONE HOME?
AH! PERFECT.
YOU MUST BE THE MASTER OF THIS—
I DON'T KNOW WHO YOU ARE, BUT GET OUT! SCRAM, YOU HARBINGER OF DOOM!
BASHI (WHAP)
YOU'RE HERE TO DRAG US INTO ANOTHER MESS— I KNOW IT!
HOW MANY DOES THIS MAKE!?
BASHI
BASHI
OOP!? WH-WHAT ARE YOU DOING...!?
AH! YOUNG MISTRESS...
GRRR
STOP!! WHAT'S WRONG WITH YOU!?
GA (GRAB)
HAGEN, IS THAT YOU?
I TOLD YOU NOT TO COME HERE UNLESS IT WAS EXTREMELY URGENT.
HUH?
YES, MA'AM! AS A MATTER OF FACT...

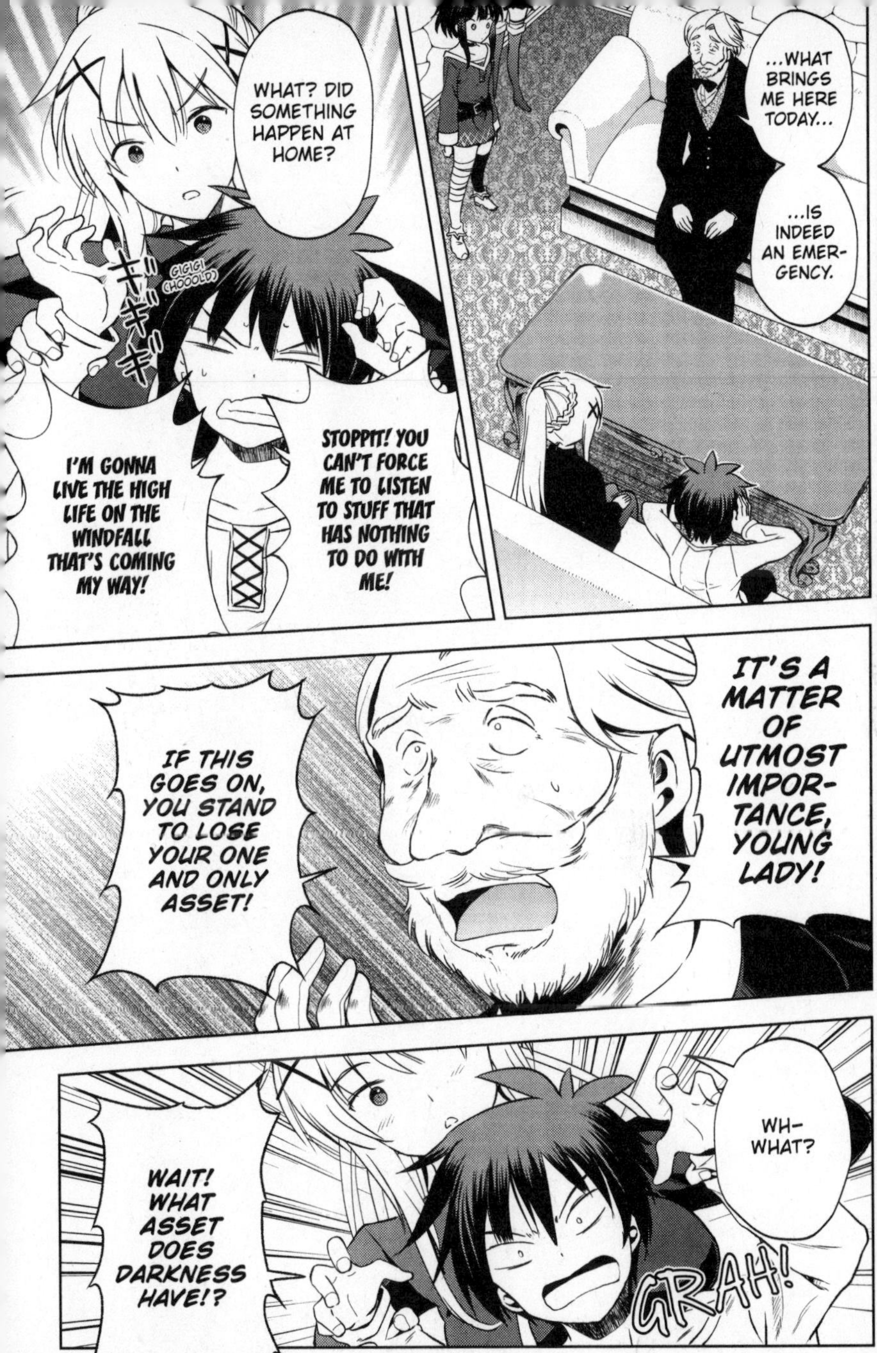
...WHAT BRINGS ME HERE TODAY...
...IS INDEED AN EMERGENCY.
WHAT? DID SOMETHING HAPPEN AT HOME?
GIGIGI (HOOOLD)
STOPPIT! YOU CAN'T FORCE ME TO LISTEN TO STUFF THAT HAS NOTHING TO DO WITH ME!
I'M GONNA LIVE THE HIGH LIFE ON THE WINDFALL THAT'S COMING MY WAY!
IT'S A MATTER OF UTMOST IMPORTANCE, YOUNG LADY!
IF THIS GOES ON, YOU STAND TO LOSE YOUR ONE AND ONLY ASSET!
WH-WHAT?
WAIT! WHAT ASSET DOES DARKNESS HAVE!?
GRAH!

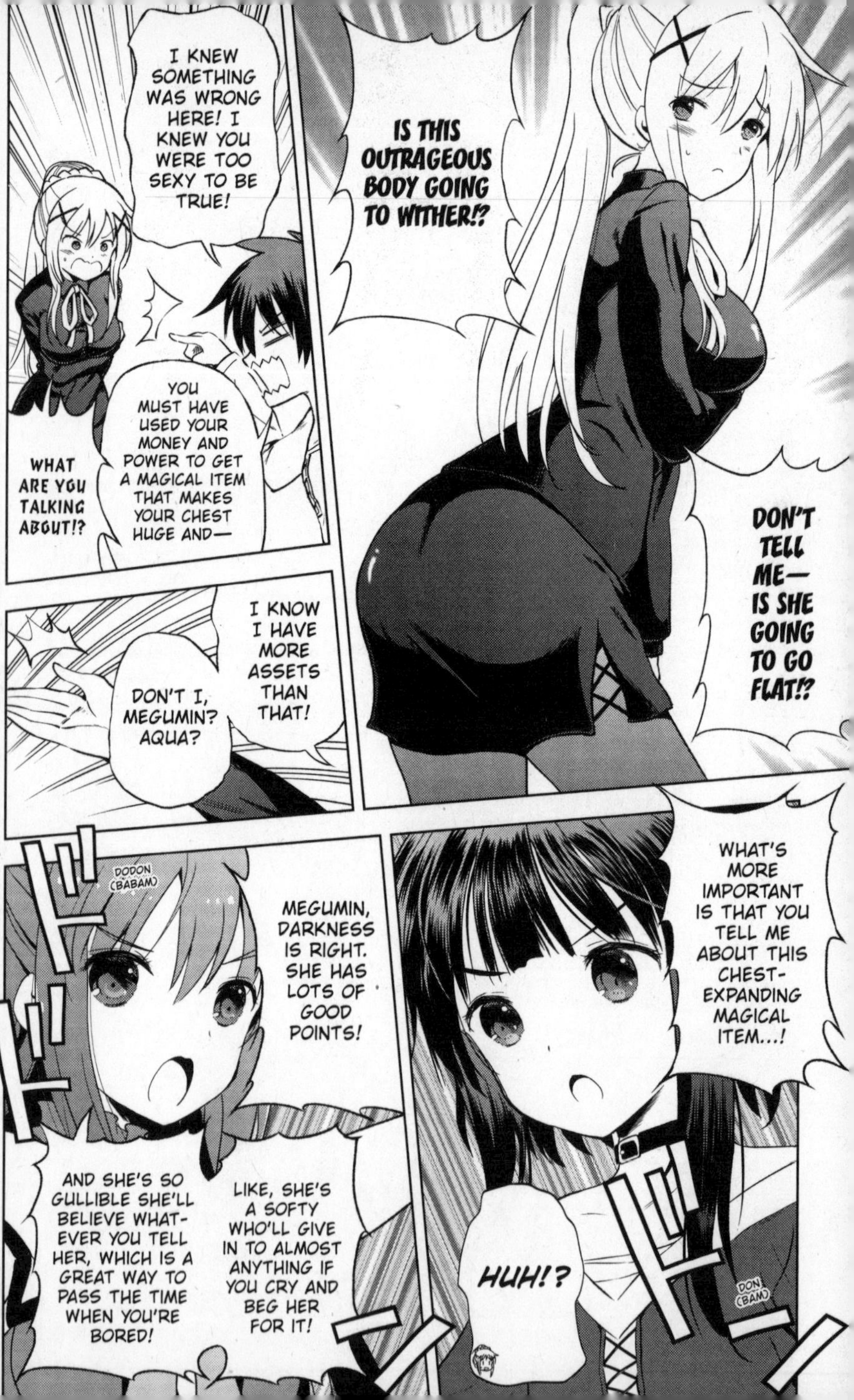
IS THIS OUTRAGEOUS BODY GOING TO WITHER!?
DON'T TELL ME— IS SHE GOING TO GO FLAT!?
I KNEW SOMETHING WAS WRONG HERE! I KNEW YOU WERE TOO SEXY TO BE TRUE!
YOU MUST HAVE USED YOUR MONEY AND POWER TO GET A MAGICAL ITEM THAT MAKES YOUR CHEST HUGE AND—
WHAT ARE YOU TALKING ABOUT!?
I KNOW I HAVE MORE ASSETS THAN THAT!
DON'T I, MEGUMIN? AQUA?
WHAT'S MORE IMPORTANT IS THAT YOU TELL ME ABOUT THIS CHEST-EXPANDING MAGICAL ITEM...!
HUH!?
DON (BAM)
DODON (BABAM)
MEGUMIN, DARKNESS IS RIGHT. SHE HAS LOTS OF GOOD POINTS!
LIKE, SHE'S A SOFTY WHO'LL GIVE IN TO ALMOST ANYTHING IF YOU CRY AND BEG HER FOR IT!
AND SHE'S SO GULLIBLE SHE'LL BELIEVE WHAT-EVER YOU TELL HER, WHICH IS A GREAT WAY TO PASS THE TIME WHEN YOU'RE BORED!

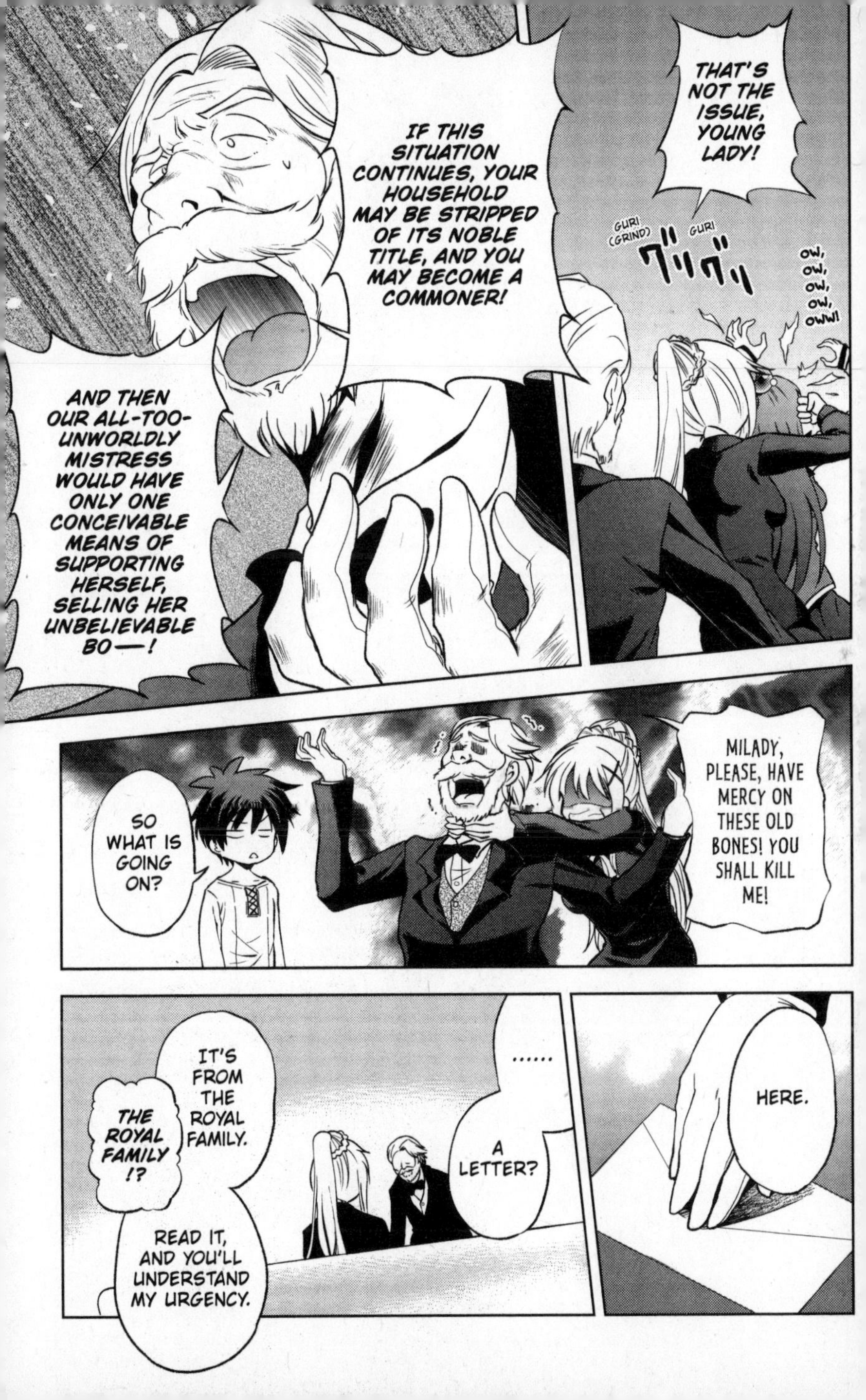
THAT'S NOT THE ISSUE, YOUNG LADY!
GURI (GRIND) GURI
グリグリ
OW, OW, OW, OW, OWW!
IF THIS SITUATION CONTINUES, YOUR HOUSEHOLD MAY BE STRIPPED OF ITS NOBLE TITLE, AND YOU MAY BECOME A COMMONER!
AND THEN OUR ALL-TOO-UNWORLDLY MISTRESS WOULD HAVE ONLY ONE CONCEIVABLE MEANS OF SUPPORTING HERSELF, SELLING HER UNBELIEVABLE BO—!
MILADY, PLEASE, HAVE MERCY ON THESE OLD BONES! YOU SHALL KILL ME!
SO WHAT IS GOING ON?
HERE.
......
A LETTER?
IT'S FROM THE ROYAL FAMILY.
THE ROYAL FAMILY!?
READ IT, AND YOU'LL UNDERSTAND MY URGENCY.

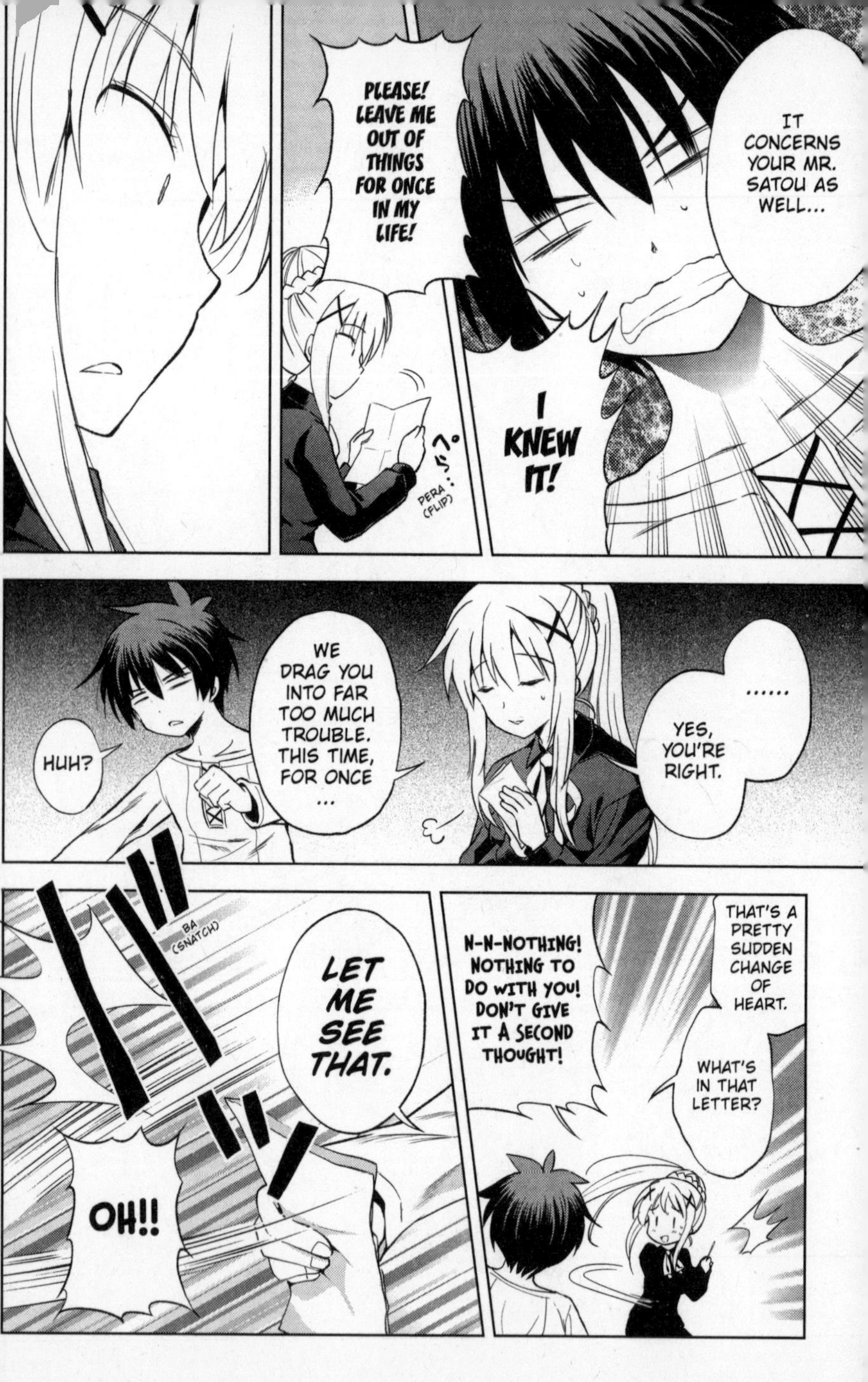
IT CONCERNS YOUR MR. SATOU AS WELL...
I KNEW IT!
PLEASE! LEAVE ME OUT OF THINGS FOR ONCE IN MY LIFE!
PERA (FLIP)
......
YES, YOU'RE RIGHT.
WE DRAG YOU INTO FAR TOO MUCH TROUBLE. THIS TIME, FOR ONCE ...
HUH?
THAT'S A PRETTY SUDDEN CHANGE OF HEART.
WHAT'S IN THAT LETTER?
N-N-NOTHING! NOTHING TO DO WITH YOU! DON'T GIVE IT A SECOND THOUGHT!
BA (SNATCH)
LET ME SEE THAT.
OH!!

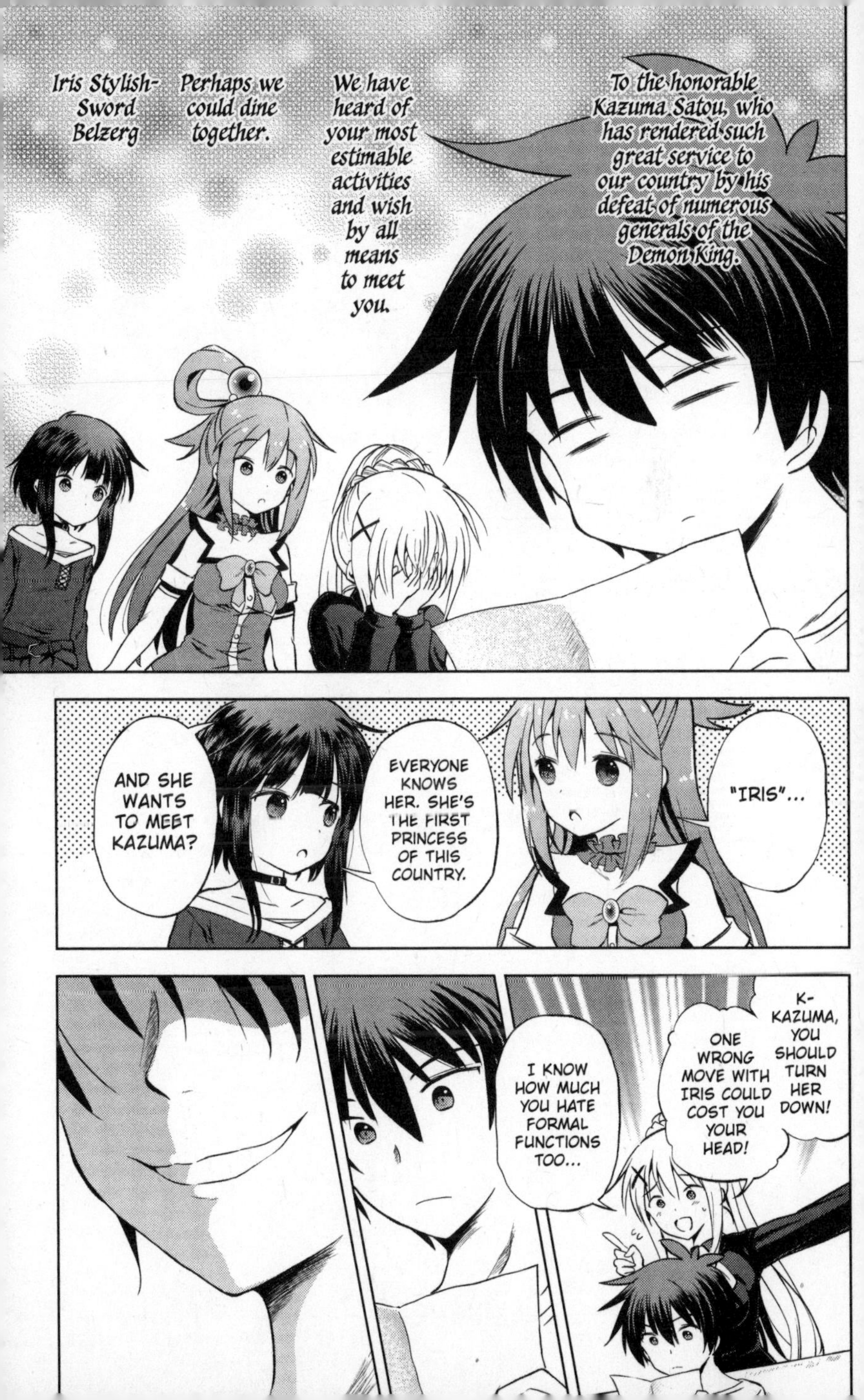
To the honorable Kazuma Satou, who has rendered such great service to our country by his defeat of numerous generals of the Demon King.
We have heard of your most estimable activities and wish by all means to meet you.
Perhaps we could dine together.
Iris Stylish-Sword Belzerg
"IRIS"...
EVERYONE KNOWS HER. SHE'S THE FIRST PRINCESS OF THIS COUNTRY.
AND SHE WANTS TO MEET KAZUMA?
K-KAZUMA, YOU SHOULD TURN HER DOWN!
ONE WRONG MOVE WITH IRIS COULD COST YOU YOUR HEAD!
I KNOW HOW MUCH YOU HATE FORMAL FUNCTIONS TOO...

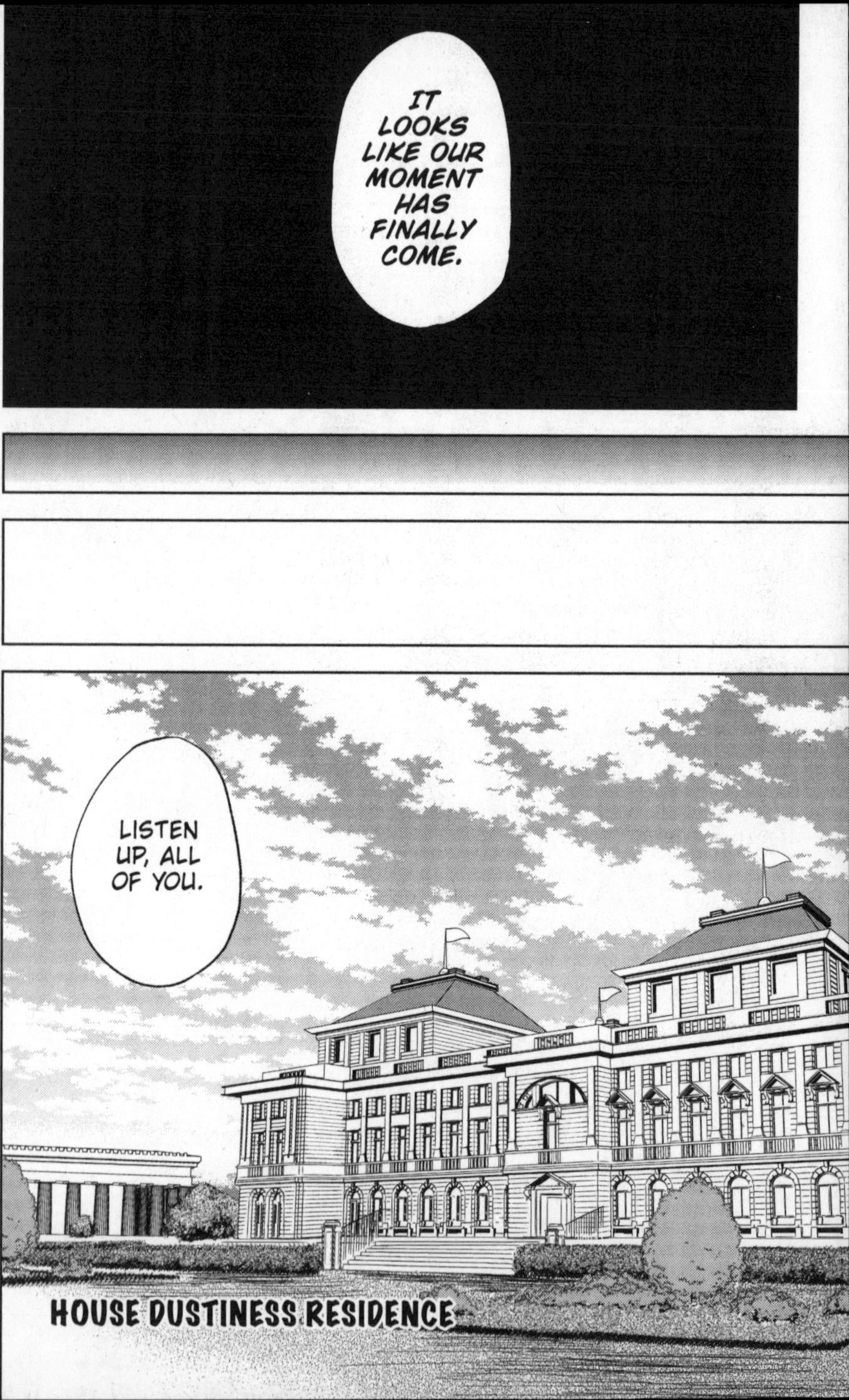
IT LOOKS LIKE OUR MOMENT HAS FINALLY COME.
LISTEN UP, ALL OF YOU.
HOUSE DUSTINESS RESIDENCE

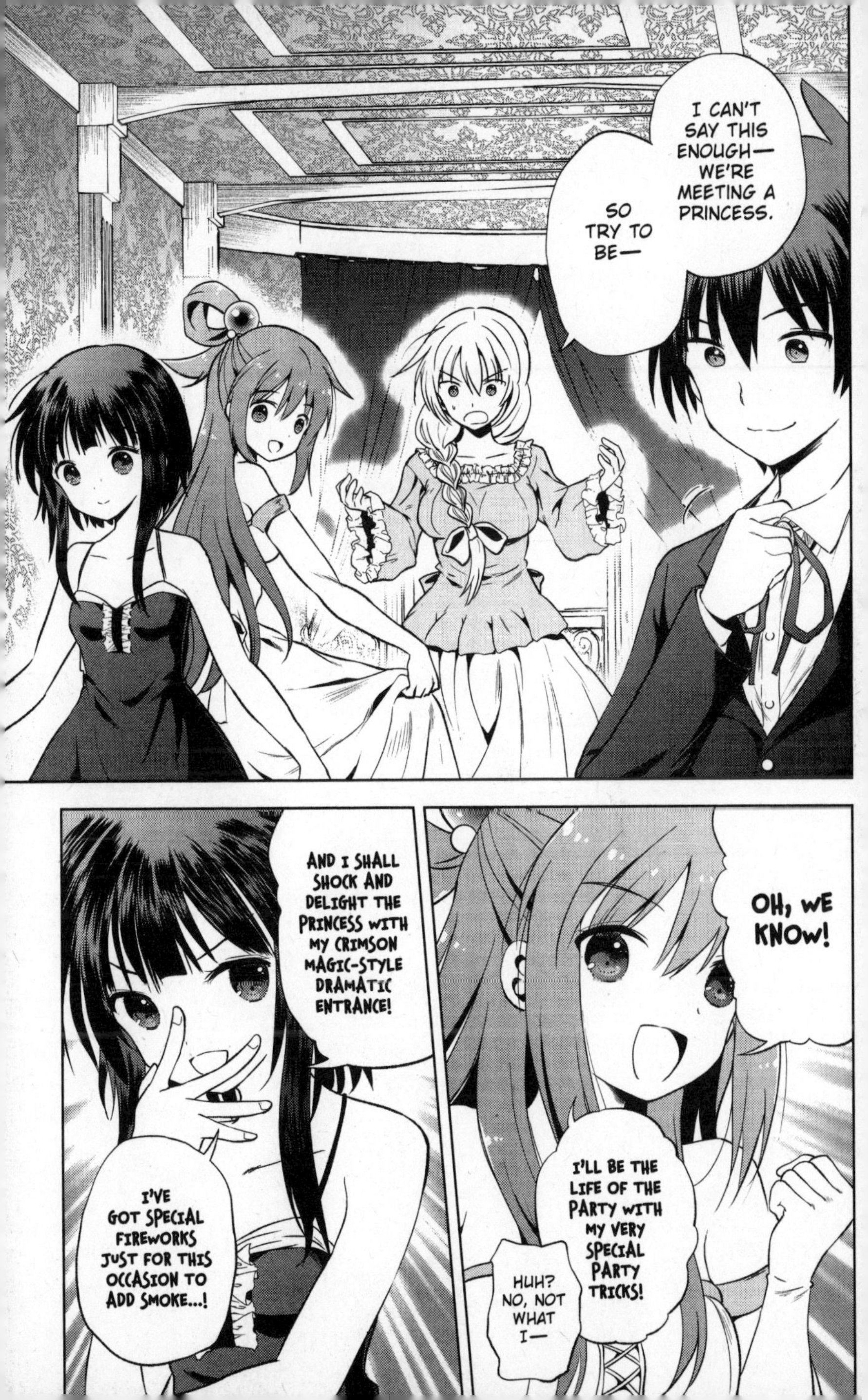
I CAN'T SAY THIS ENOUGH—WE'RE MEETING A PRINCESS.
SO TRY TO BE—
OH, WE KNOW!
I'LL BE THE LIFE OF THE PARTY WITH MY VERY SPECIAL PARTY TRICKS!
HUH? NO, NOT WHAT I—
AND I SHALL SHOCK AND DELIGHT THE PRINCESS WITH MY CRIMSON MAGIC-STYLE DRAMATIC ENTRANCE!
I'VE GOT SPECIAL FIREWORKS JUST FOR THIS OCCASION TO ADD SMOKE...!

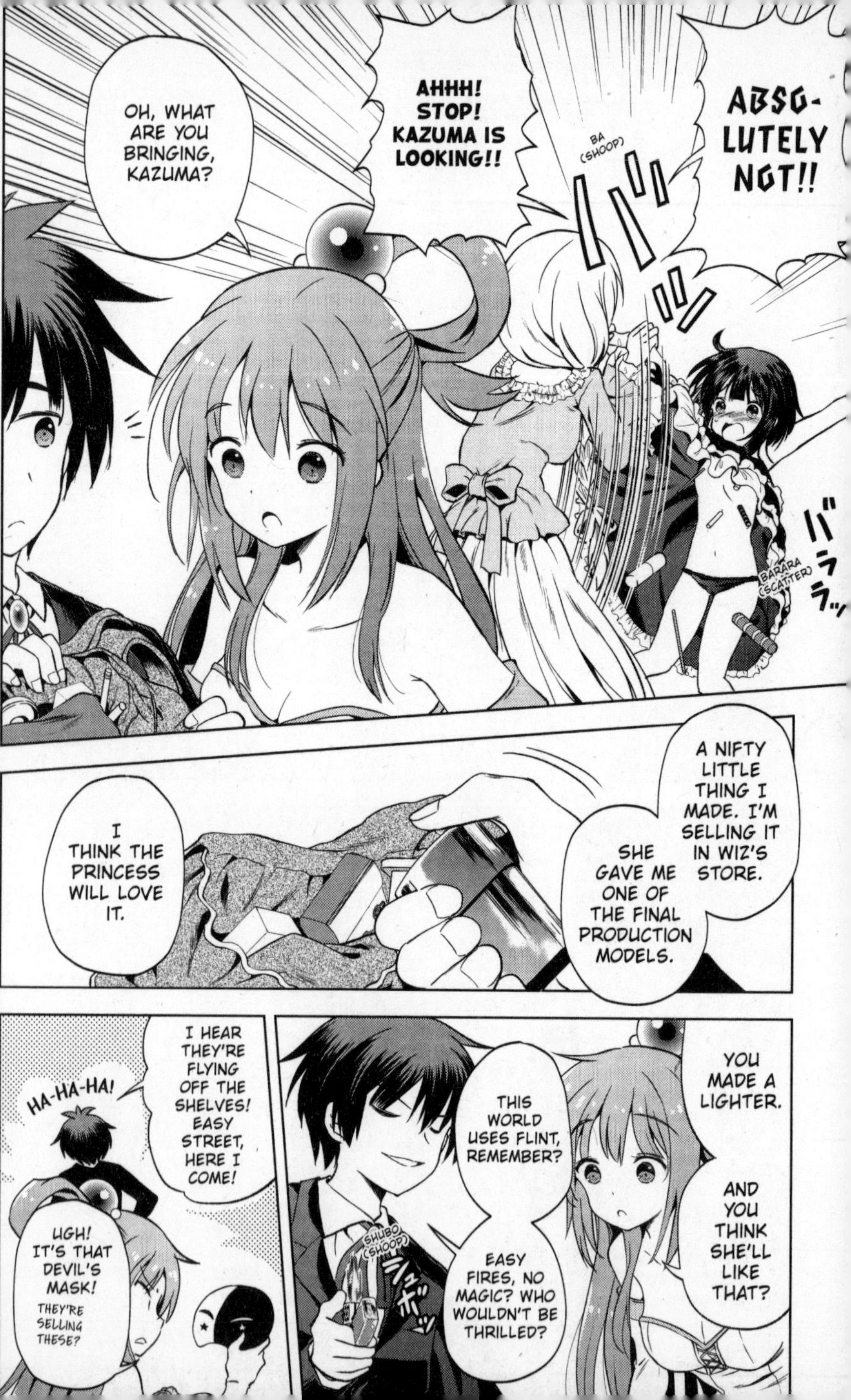
ABSO-LUTELY NOT!!
BA (SHOOP)
AHHH! STOP! KAZUMA IS LOOKING!!
OH, WHAT ARE YOU BRINGING, KAZUMA?
BARARA (SCATTER)
A NIFTY LITTLE THING I MADE. I'M SELLING IT IN WIZ'S STORE.
SHE GAVE ME ONE OF THE FINAL PRODUCTION MODELS.
I THINK THE PRINCESS WILL LOVE IT.
YOU MADE A LIGHTER.
AND YOU THINK SHE'LL LIKE THAT?
THIS WORLD USES FLINT, REMEMBER?
SHUBO (SHOOP)
EASY FIRES, NO MAGIC? WHO WOULDN'T BE THRILLED?
I HEAR THEY'RE FLYING OFF THE SHELVES! EASY STREET, HERE I COME!
HA-HA-HA!
UGH! IT'S THAT DEVIL'S MASK!
THEY'RE SELLING THESE?

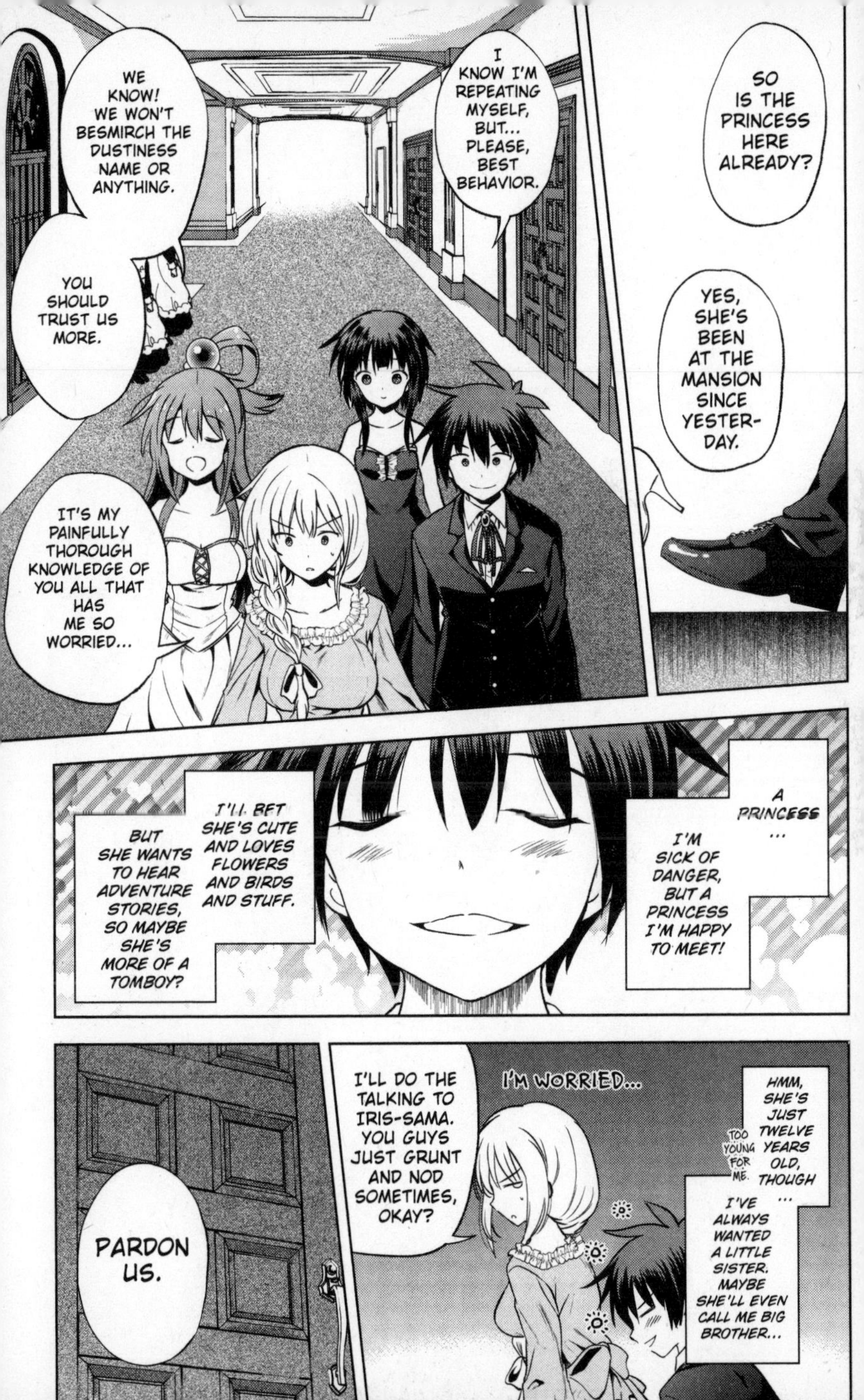
SO IS THE PRINCESS HERE ALREADY?
YES, SHE'S BEEN AT THE MANSION SINCE YESTER-DAY.
I KNOW I'M REPEATING MYSELF, BUT... PLEASE, BEST BEHAVIOR.
WE KNOW! WE WON'T BESMIRCH THE DUSTINESS NAME OR ANYTHING.
YOU SHOULD TRUST US MORE.
IT'S MY PAINFULLY THOROUGH KNOWLEDGE OF YOU ALL THAT HAS ME SO WORRIED...
A PRINCESS...
I'M SICK OF DANGER, BUT A PRINCESS I'M HAPPY TO MEET!
I'LL BET SHE'S CUTE AND LOVES FLOWERS AND BIRDS AND STUFF.
BUT SHE WANTS TO HEAR ADVENTURE STORIES, SO MAYBE SHE'S MORE OF A TOMBOY?
HMM, SHE'S JUST TWELVE YEARS OLD, THOUGH...
TOO YOUNG FOR ME.
I'VE ALWAYS WANTED A LITTLE SISTER. MAYBE SHE'LL EVEN CALL ME BIG BROTHER...
I'M WORRIED...
I'LL DO THE TALKING TO IRIS-SAMA. YOU GUYS JUST GRUNT AND NOD SOMETIMES, OKAY?
PARDON US.

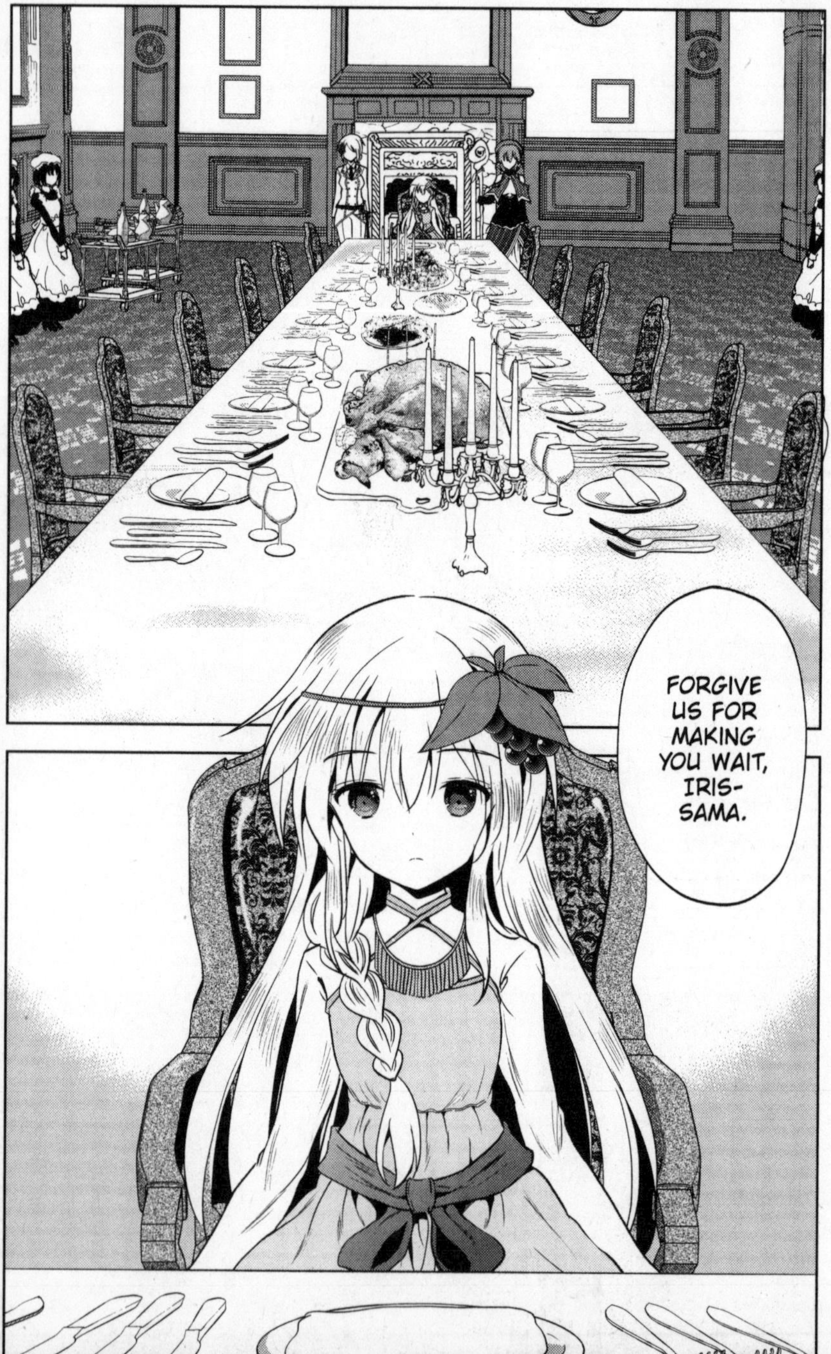
FORGIVE US FOR MAKING YOU WAIT, IRIS-SAMA.

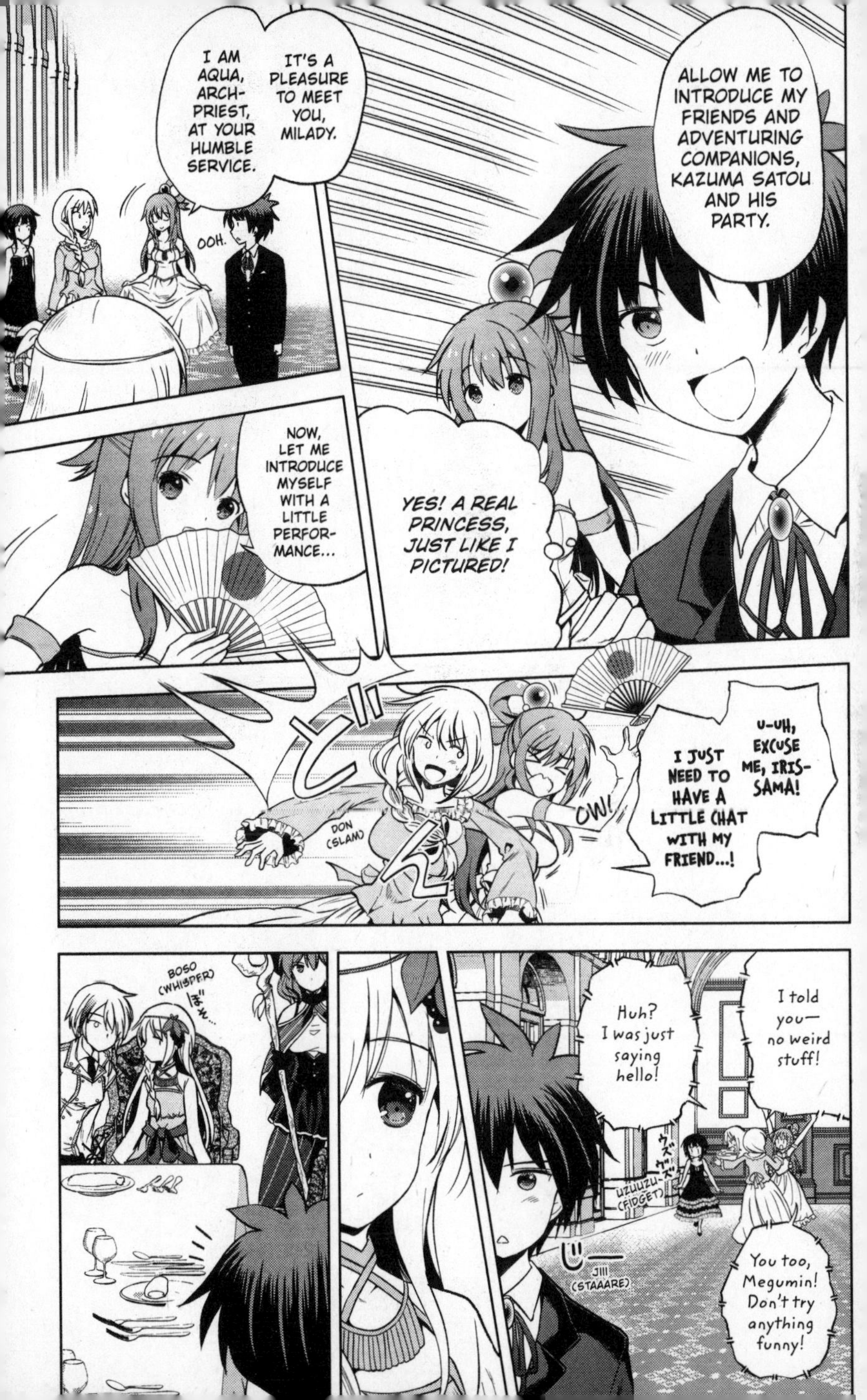
ALLOW ME TO INTRODUCE MY FRIENDS AND ADVENTURING COMPANIONS, KAZUMA SATOU AND HIS PARTY.
YES! A REAL PRINCESS, JUST LIKE I PICTURED!
IT'S A PLEASURE TO MEET YOU, MILADY.
I AM AQUA, ARCH-PRIEST, AT YOUR HUMBLE SERVICE.
OOH.
NOW, LET ME INTRODUCE MYSELF WITH A LITTLE PERFORMANCE...
U-UH, EXCUSE ME, IRIS-SAMA!
I JUST NEED TO HAVE A LITTLE CHAT WITH MY FRIEND...!
OW!
DON (SLAM)
I told you— no weird stuff!
Huh? I was just saying hello!
You too, Megumin! Don't try anything funny!
UZUUZU (FIDGET)
JIII (STAAARE)
BOSO (WHISPER)

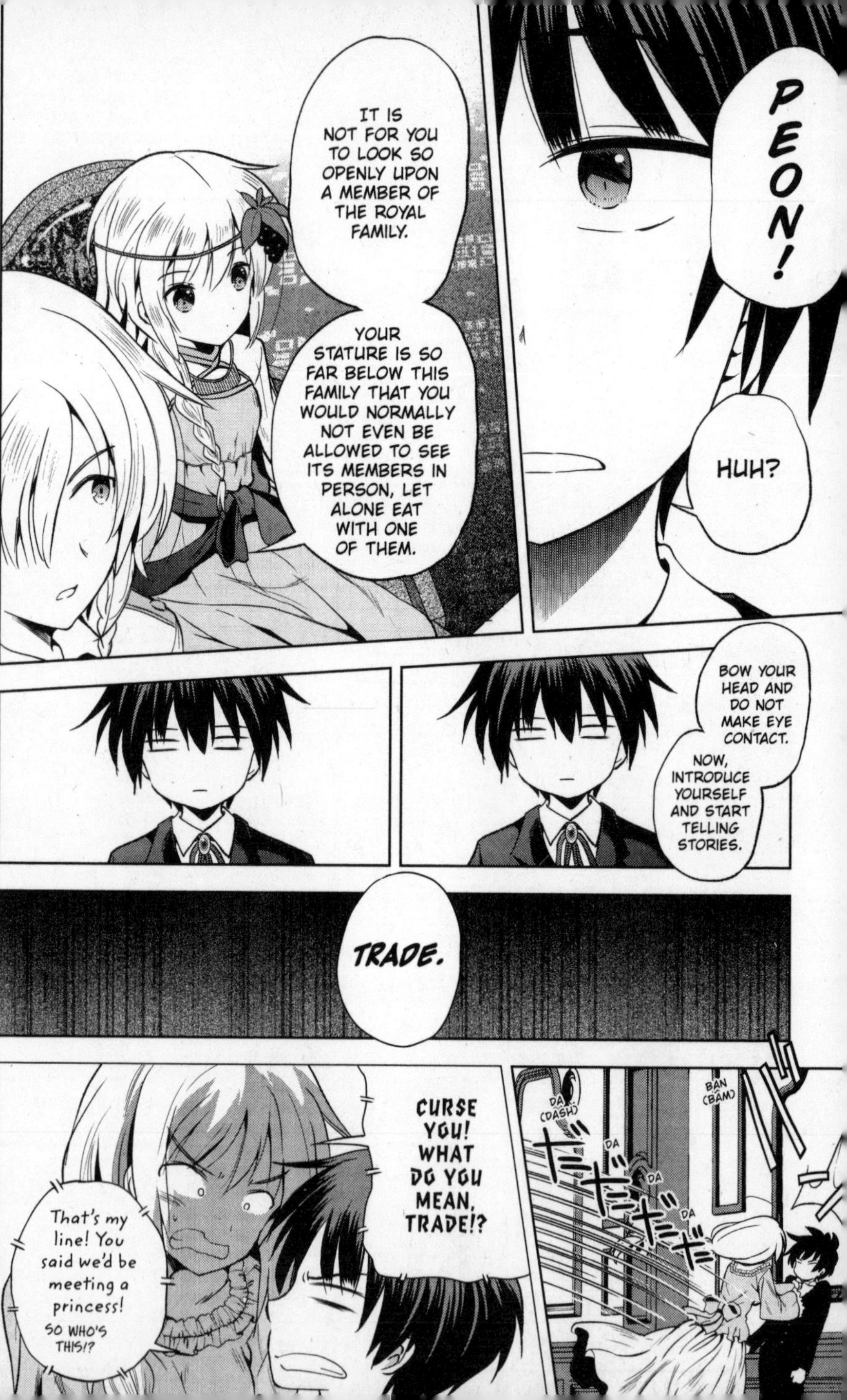
PEON!
HUH?
IT IS NOT FOR YOU TO LOOK SO OPENLY UPON A MEMBER OF THE ROYAL FAMILY.
YOUR STATURE IS SO FAR BELOW THIS FAMILY THAT YOU WOULD NORMALLY NOT EVEN BE ALLOWED TO SEE ITS MEMBERS IN PERSON, LET ALONE EAT WITH ONE OF THEM.
BOW YOUR HEAD AND DO NOT MAKE EYE CONTACT.
NOW, INTRODUCE YOURSELF AND START TELLING STORIES.
TRADE.
BAN (BAM)
DA (DASH)
DA
DA
DA
CURSE YOU! WHAT DO YOU MEAN, TRADE!?
That's my line! You said we'd be meeting a princess!
SO WHO'S THIS!?

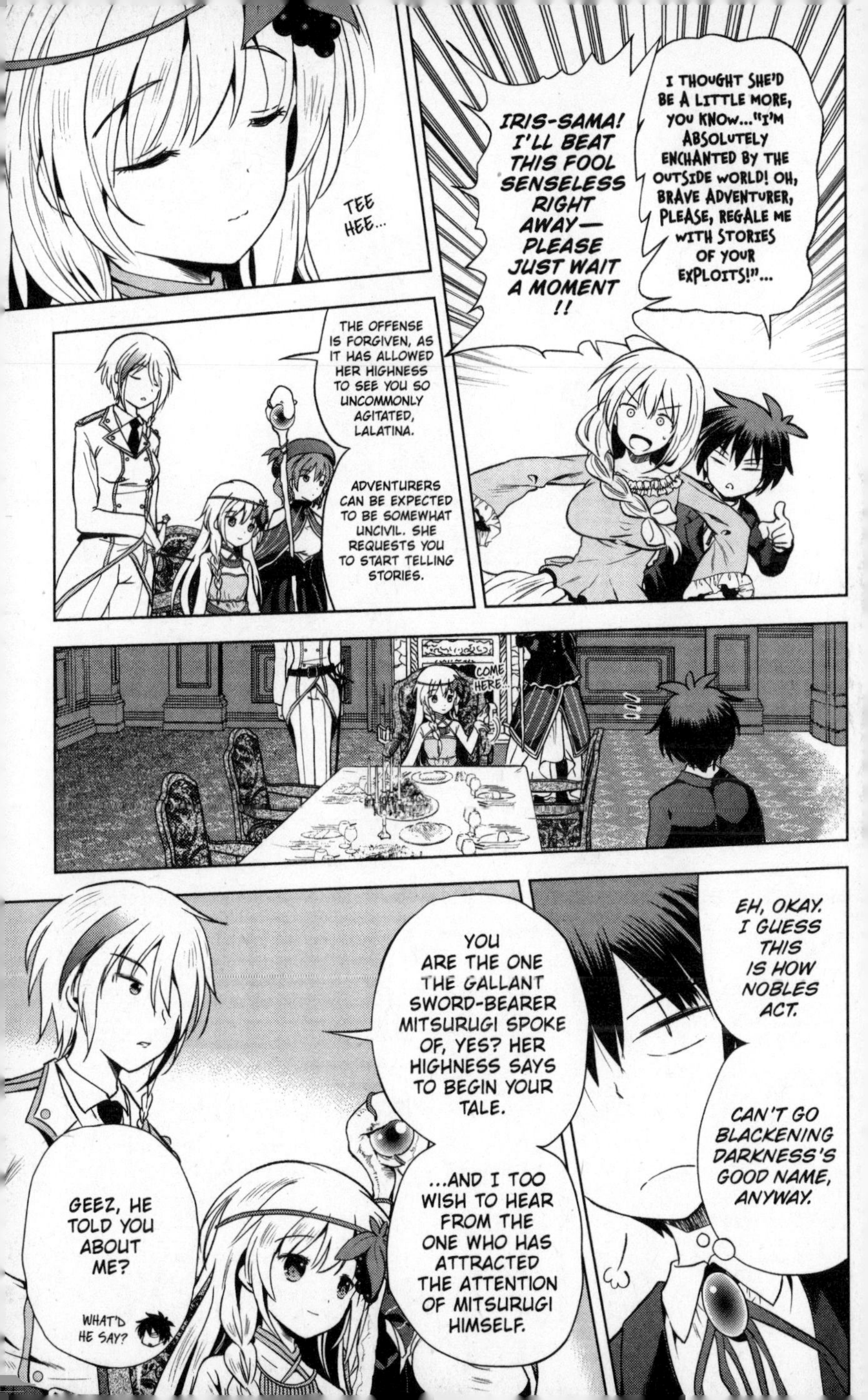
I THOUGHT SHE'D BE A LITTLE MORE, YOU KNOW..."I'M ABSOLUTELY ENCHANTED BY THE OUTSIDE WORLD! OH, BRAVE ADVENTURER, PLEASE, REGALE ME WITH STORIES OF YOUR EXPLOITS!"...
IRIS-SAMA! I'LL BEAT THIS FOOL SENSELESS RIGHT AWAY—PLEASE JUST WAIT A MOMENT!!
TEE HEE...
THE OFFENSE IS FORGIVEN, AS IT HAS ALLOWED HER HIGHNESS TO SEE YOU SO UNCOMMONLY AGITATED, LALATINA.
ADVENTURERS CAN BE EXPECTED TO BE SOMEWHAT UNCIVIL. SHE REQUESTS YOU TO START TELLING STORIES.
COME HERE...
EH, OKAY. I GUESS THIS IS HOW NOBLES ACT.
CAN'T GO BLACKENING DARKNESS'S GOOD NAME, ANYWAY.
YOU ARE THE ONE THE GALLANT SWORD-BEARER MITSURUGI SPOKE OF, YES? HER HIGHNESS SAYS TO BEGIN YOUR TALE.
...AND I TOO WISH TO HEAR FROM THE ONE WHO HAS ATTRACTED THE ATTENTION OF MITSURUGI HIMSELF.
GEEZ, HE TOLD YOU ABOUT ME?
WHAT'D HE SAY?

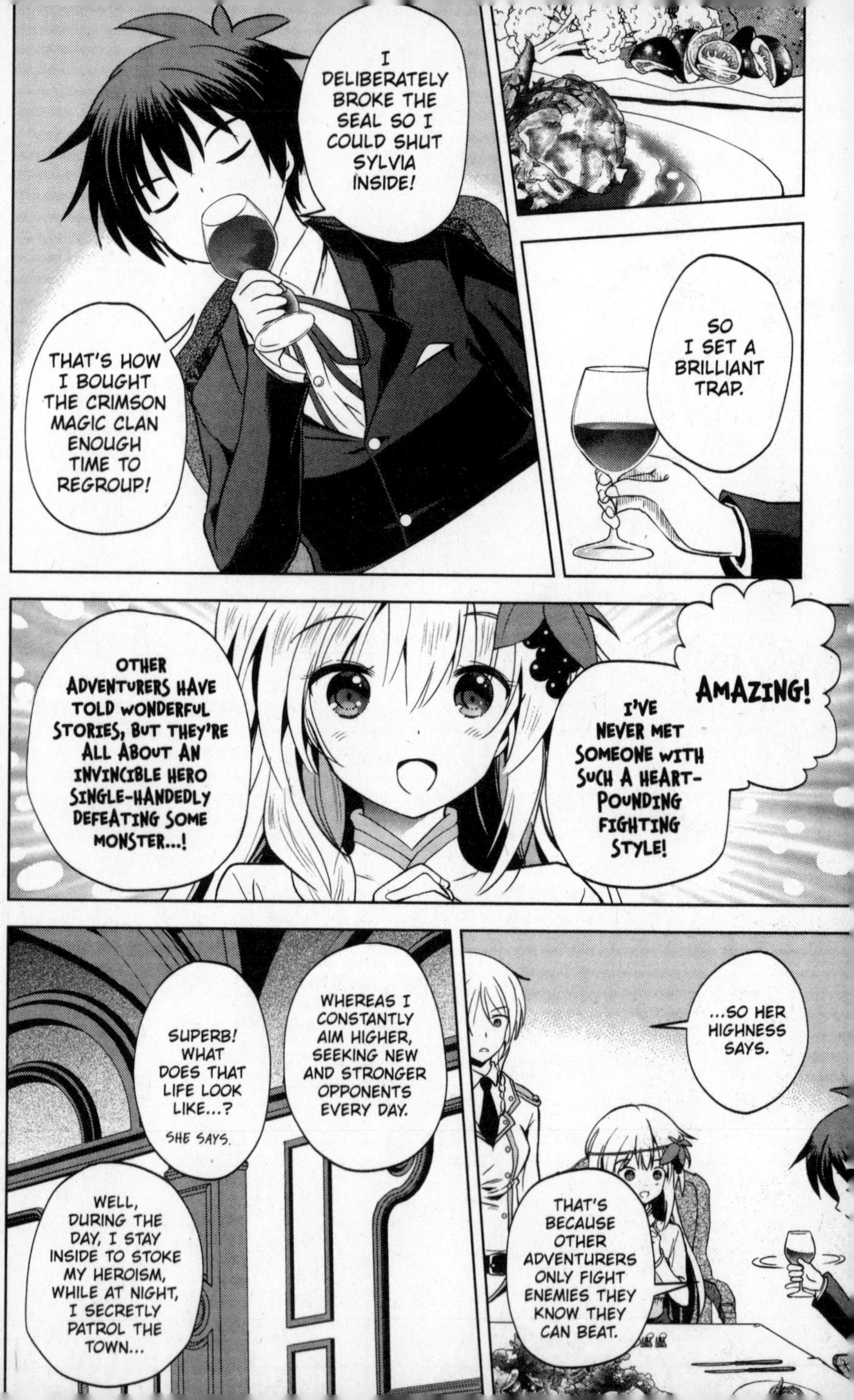
SO I SET A BRILLIANT TRAP.
I DELIBERATELY BROKE THE SEAL SO I COULD SHUT SYLVIA INSIDE!
THAT'S HOW I BOUGHT THE CRIMSON MAGIC CLAN ENOUGH TIME TO REGROUP!
AMAZING!
I'VE NEVER MET SOMEONE WITH SUCH A HEART-POUNDING FIGHTING STYLE!
OTHER ADVENTURERS HAVE TOLD WONDERFUL STORIES, BUT THEY'RE ALL ABOUT AN INVINCIBLE HERO SINGLE-HANDEDLY DEFEATING SOME MONSTER...!
...SO HER HIGHNESS SAYS.
THAT'S BECAUSE OTHER ADVENTURERS ONLY FIGHT ENEMIES THEY KNOW THEY CAN BEAT.
WHEREAS I CONSTANTLY AIM HIGHER, SEEKING NEW AND STRONGER OPPONENTS EVERY DAY.
SUPERB! WHAT DOES THAT LIFE LOOK LIKE...?
SHE SAYS.
WELL, DURING THE DAY, I STAY INSIDE TO STOKE MY HEROISM, WHILE AT NIGHT, I SECRETLY PATROL THE TOWN...

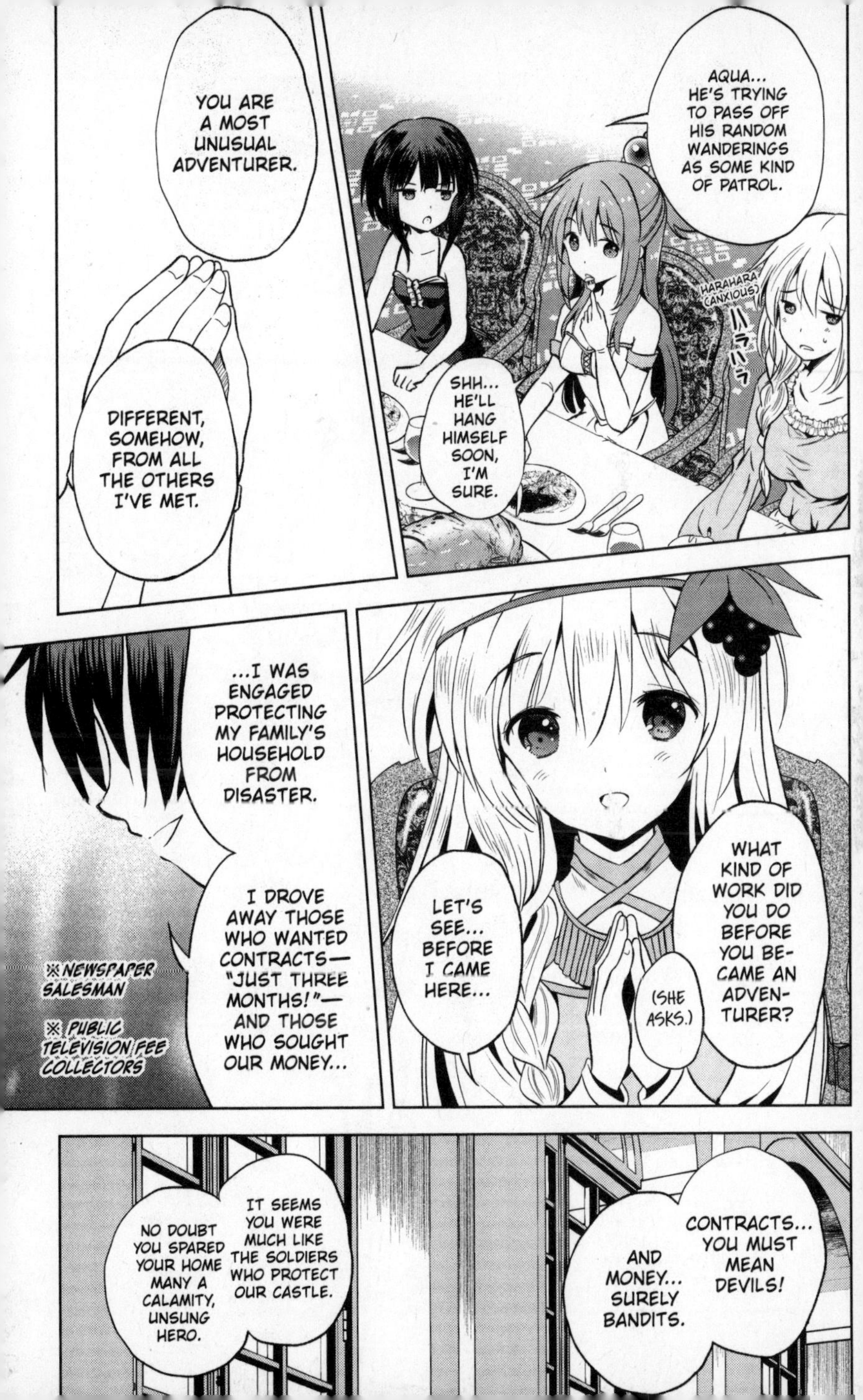
AQUA... HE'S TRYING TO PASS OFF HIS RANDOM WANDERINGS AS SOME KIND OF PATROL.
HARAHARA (ANXIOUS)
ハラハラ
SHH... HE'LL HANG HIMSELF SOON, I'M SURE.
YOU ARE A MOST UNUSUAL ADVENTURER.
DIFFERENT, SOMEHOW, FROM ALL THE OTHERS I'VE MET.
WHAT KIND OF WORK DID YOU DO BEFORE YOU BE-CAME AN ADVEN-TURER?
(SHE ASKS.)
LET'S SEE... BEFORE I CAME HERE...
...I WAS ENGAGED PROTECTING MY FAMILY'S HOUSEHOLD FROM DISASTER.
I DROVE AWAY THOSE WHO WANTED CONTRACTS—"JUST THREE MONTHS!"—AND THOSE WHO SOUGHT OUR MONEY...
※NEWSPAPER SALESMAN
※ PUBLIC TELEVISION FEE COLLECTORS
CONTRACTS... YOU MUST MEAN DEVILS!
AND MONEY... SURELY BANDITS.
IT SEEMS YOU WERE MUCH LIKE THE SOLDIERS WHO PROTECT OUR CASTLE.
NO DOUBT YOU SPARED YOUR HOME MANY A CALAMITY, UNSUNG HERO.

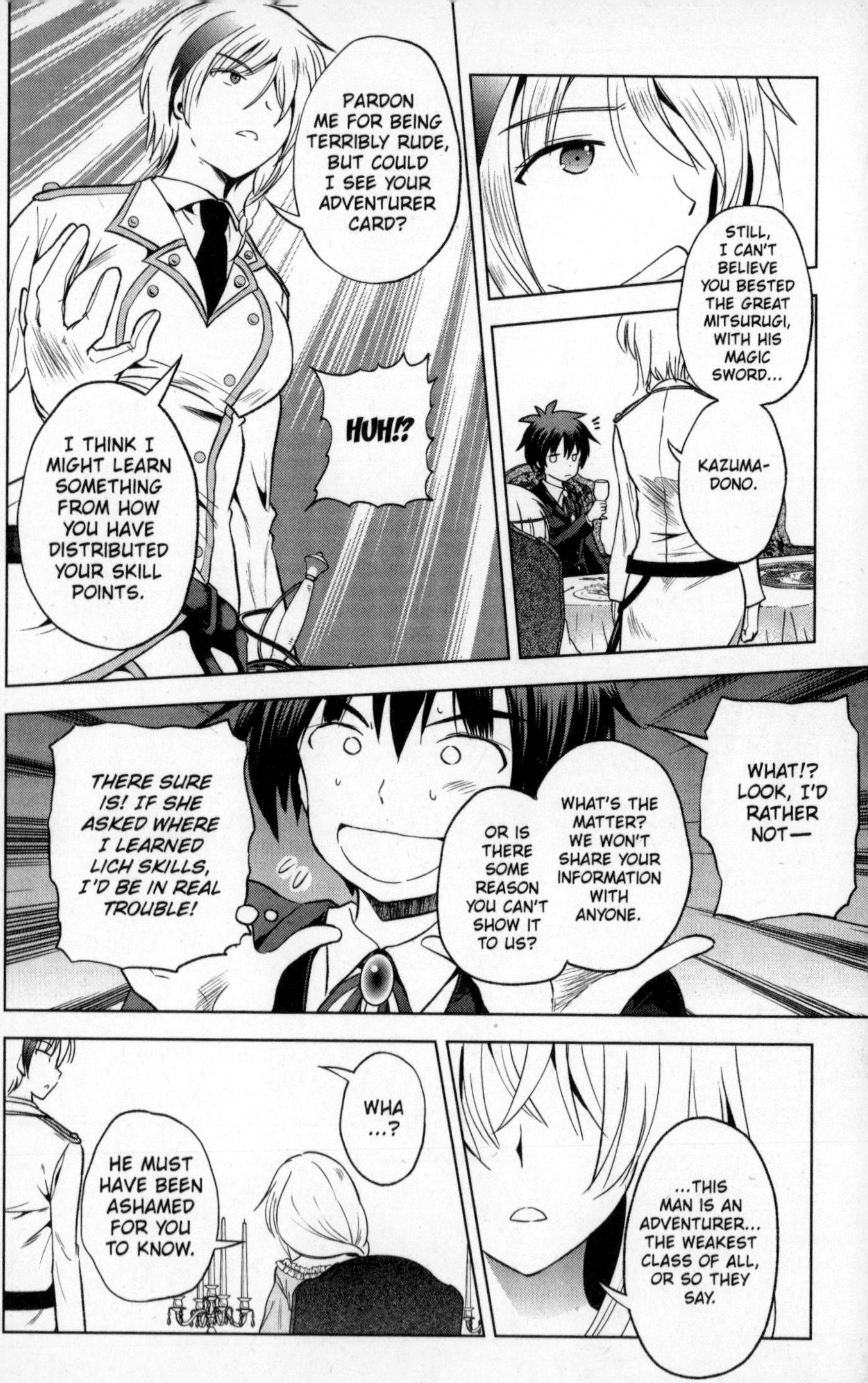
STILL, I CAN'T BELIEVE YOU BESTED THE GREAT MITSURUGI, WITH HIS MAGIC SWORD...
KAZUMA-DONO.
PARDON ME FOR BEING TERRIBLY RUDE, BUT COULD I SEE YOUR ADVENTURER CARD?
HUH!?
I THINK I MIGHT LEARN SOMETHING FROM HOW YOU HAVE DISTRIBUTED YOUR SKILL POINTS.
WHAT!? LOOK, I'D RATHER NOT—
WHAT'S THE MATTER? WE WON'T SHARE YOUR INFORMATION WITH ANYONE.
OR IS THERE SOME REASON YOU CAN'T SHOW IT TO US?
*THERE SURE IS! IF SHE ASKED WHERE I LEARNED LICH SKILLS, I'D BE IN REAL TROUBLE!*
...THIS MAN IS AN ADVENTURER... THE WEAKEST CLASS OF ALL, OR SO THEY SAY.
WHA ...?
HE MUST HAVE BEEN ASHAMED FOR YOU TO KNOW.

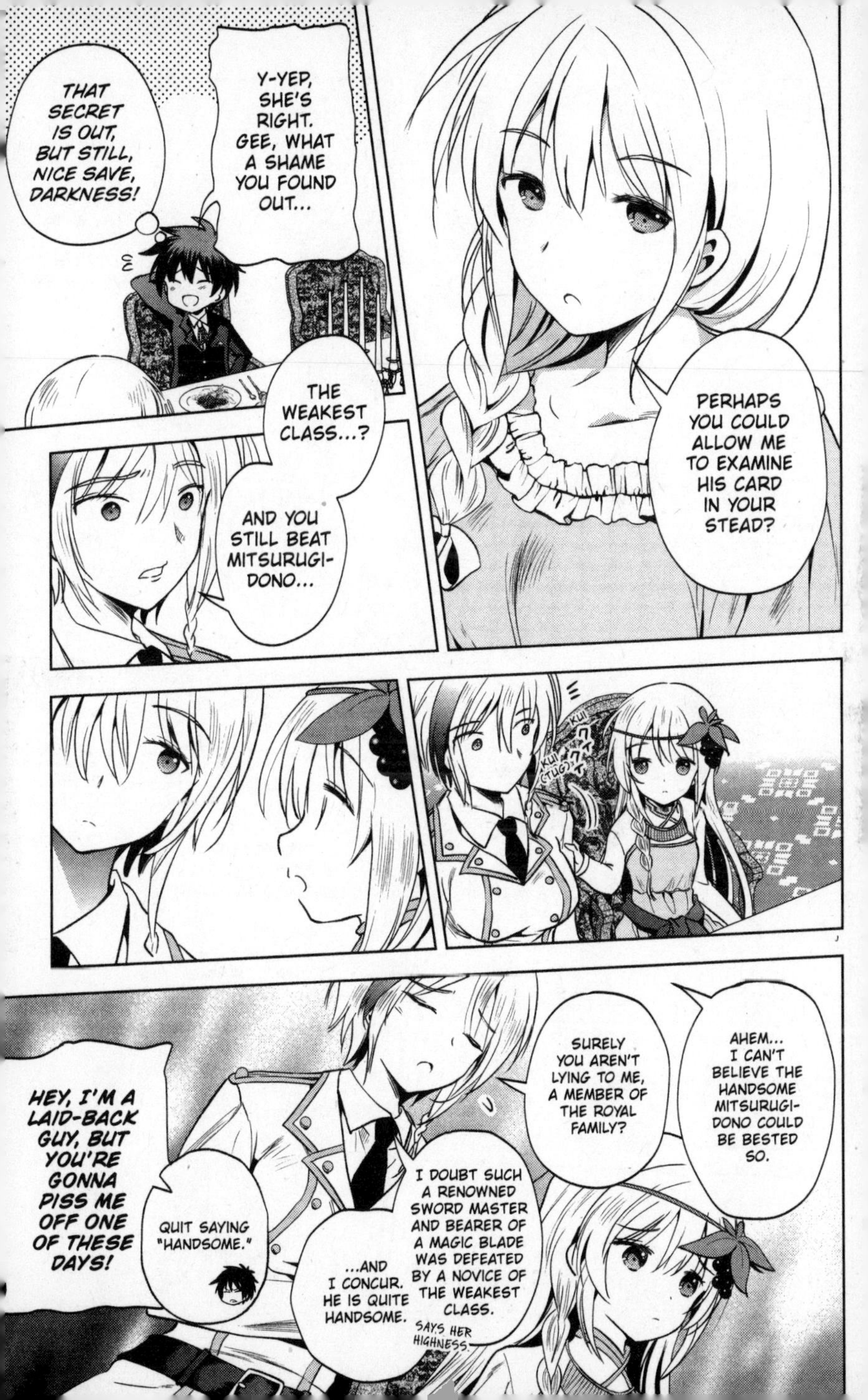
PERHAPS YOU COULD ALLOW ME TO EXAMINE HIS CARD IN YOUR STEAD?
Y-YEP, SHE'S RIGHT. GEE, WHAT A SHAME YOU FOUND OUT...
THAT SECRET IS OUT, BUT STILL, NICE SAVE, DARKNESS!
THE WEAKEST CLASS...?
AND YOU STILL BEAT MITSURUGI-DONO...
KUI KUI (TUG)
AHEM... I CAN'T BELIEVE THE HANDSOME MITSURUGI-DONO COULD BE BESTED SO.
SURELY YOU AREN'T LYING TO ME, A MEMBER OF THE ROYAL FAMILY?
I DOUBT SUCH A RENOWNED SWORD MASTER AND BEARER OF A MAGIC BLADE WAS DEFEATED BY A NOVICE OF THE WEAKEST CLASS.
SAYS HER HIGHNESS.
...AND I CONCUR. HE IS QUITE HANDSOME.
QUIT SAYING "HANDSOME."
HEY, I'M A LAID-BACK GUY, BUT YOU'RE GONNA PISS ME OFF ONE OF THESE DAYS!

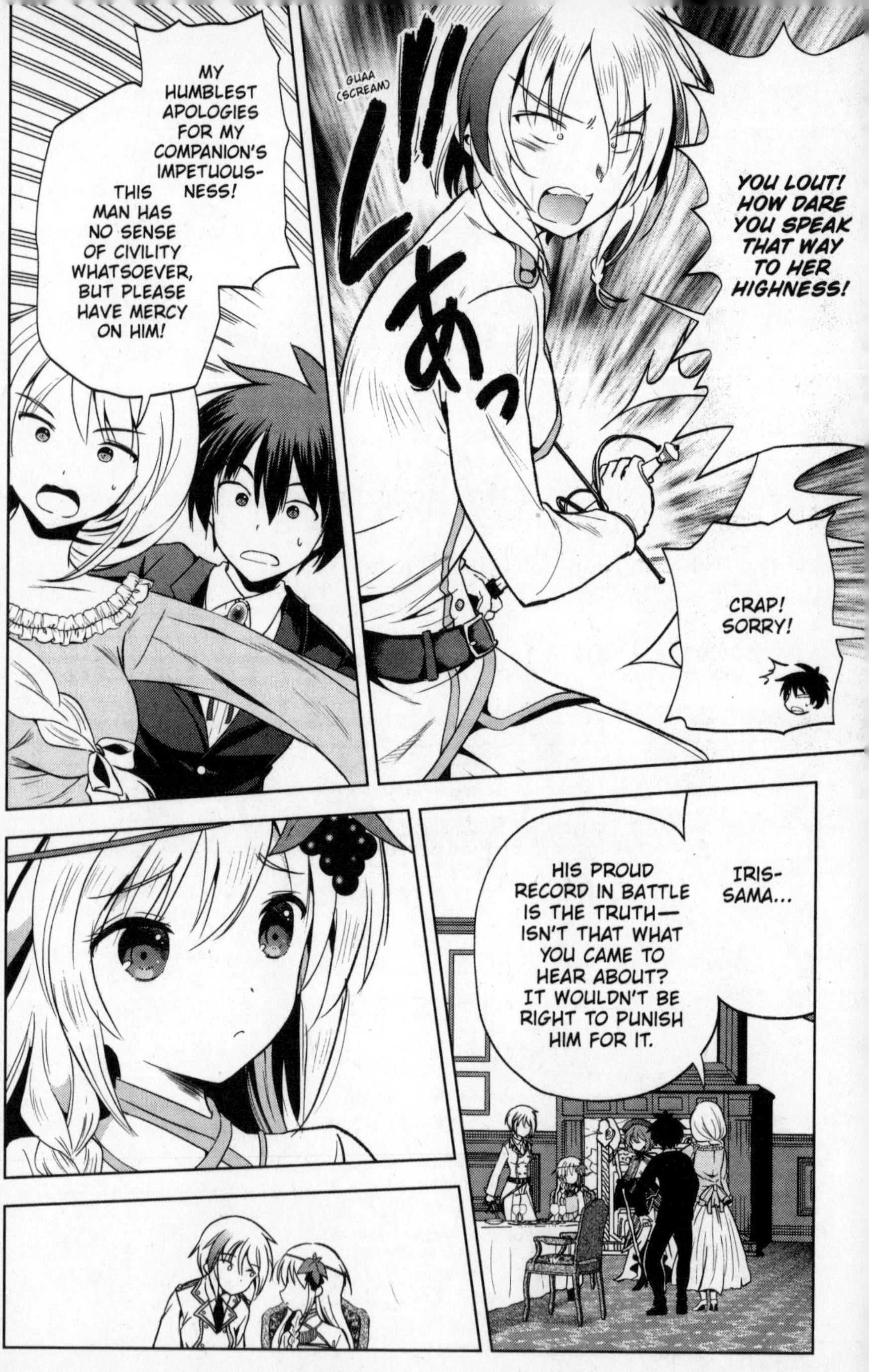
GUAA (SCREAM)
YOU LOUT! HOW DARE YOU SPEAK THAT WAY TO HER HIGHNESS!
CRAP! SORRY!
MY HUMBLEST APOLOGIES FOR MY COMPANION'S IMPETUOUSNESS! THIS MAN HAS NO SENSE OF CIVILITY WHATSOEVER, BUT PLEASE HAVE MERCY ON HIM!
IRIS-SAMA...
HIS PROUD RECORD IN BATTLE IS THE TRUTH— ISN'T THAT WHAT YOU CAME TO HEAR ABOUT? IT WOULDN'T BE RIGHT TO PUNISH HIM FOR IT.

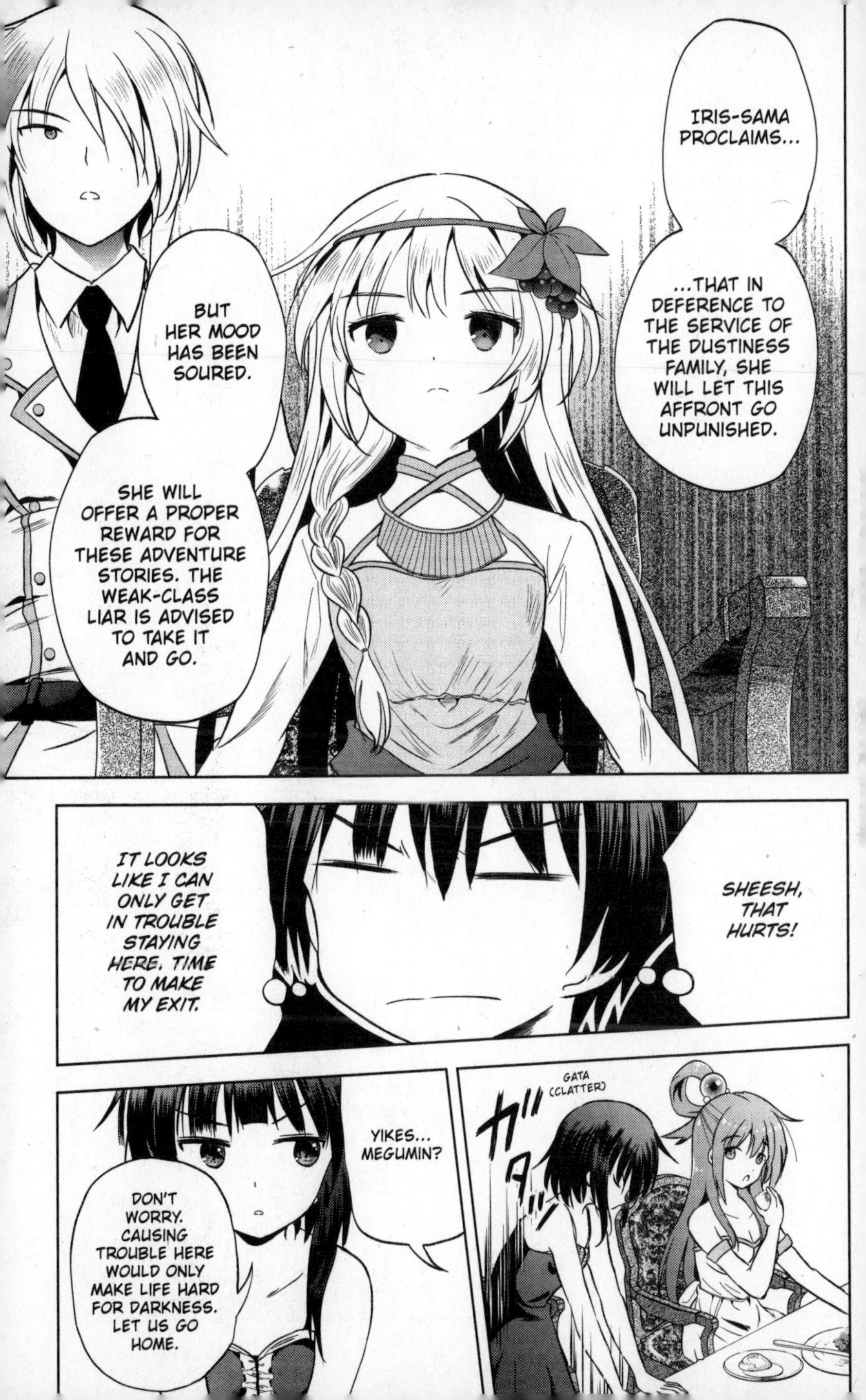
IRIS-SAMA PROCLAIMS...
...THAT IN DEFERENCE TO THE SERVICE OF THE DUSTINESS FAMILY, SHE WILL LET THIS AFFRONT GO UNPUNISHED.
BUT HER MOOD HAS BEEN SOURED.
SHE WILL OFFER A PROPER REWARD FOR THESE ADVENTURE STORIES. THE WEAK-CLASS LIAR IS ADVISED TO TAKE IT AND GO.
SHEESH, THAT HURTS!
IT LOOKS LIKE I CAN ONLY GET IN TROUBLE STAYING HERE. TIME TO MAKE MY EXIT.
GATA (CLATTER)
YIKES... MEGUMIN?
DON'T WORRY. CAUSING TROUBLE HERE WOULD ONLY MAKE LIFE HARD FOR DARKNESS. LET US GO HOME.

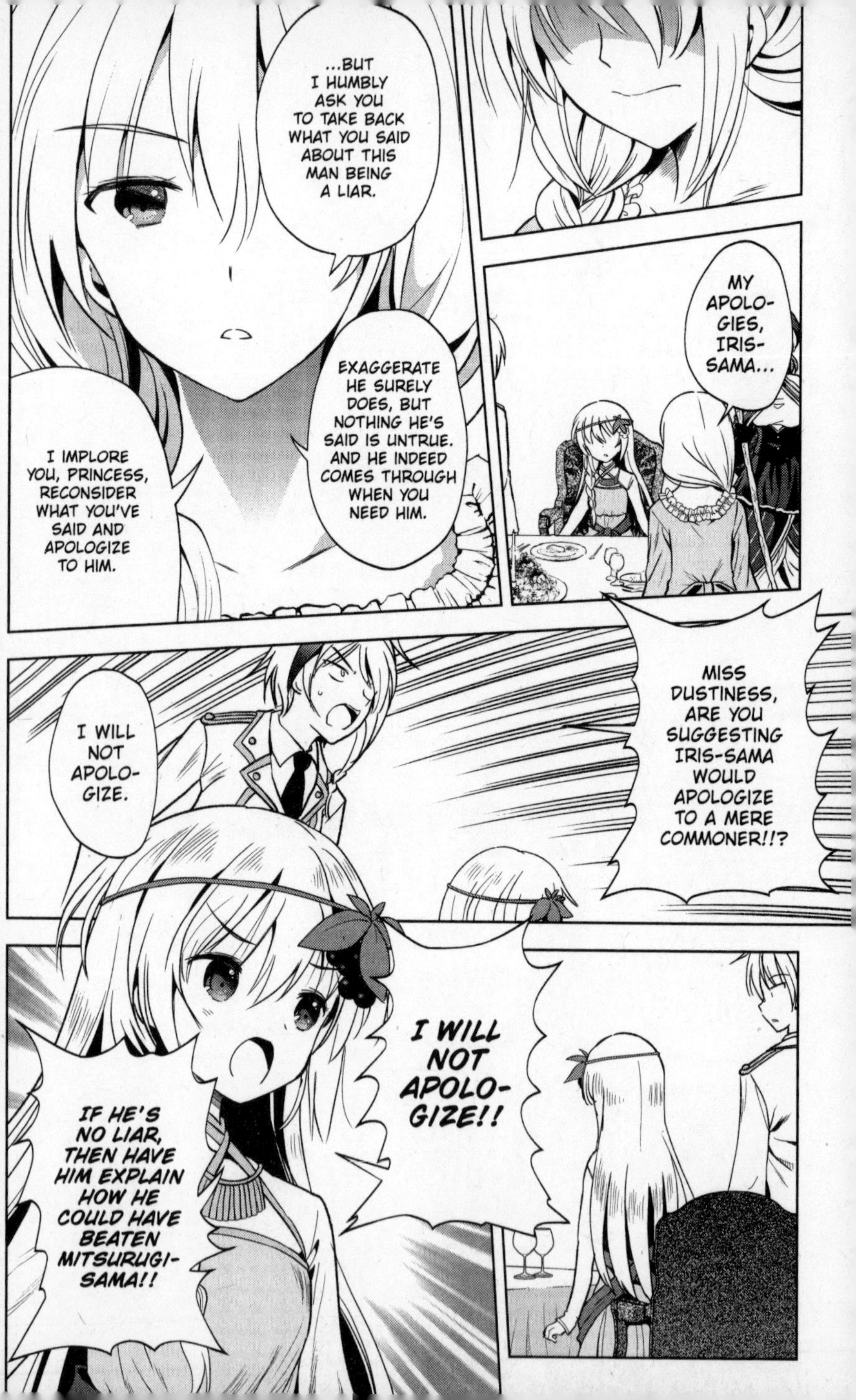
MY APOLOGIES, IRIS-SAMA...
...BUT I HUMBLY ASK YOU TO TAKE BACK WHAT YOU SAID ABOUT THIS MAN BEING A LIAR.
EXAGGERATE HE SURELY DOES, BUT NOTHING HE'S SAID IS UNTRUE. AND HE INDEED COMES THROUGH WHEN YOU NEED HIM.
I IMPLORE YOU, PRINCESS, RECONSIDER WHAT YOU'VE SAID AND APOLOGIZE TO HIM.
MISS DUSTINESS, ARE YOU SUGGESTING IRIS-SAMA WOULD APOLOGIZE TO A MERE COMMONER!!?
I WILL NOT APOLOGIZE.
I WILL NOT APOLOGIZE!!
IF HE'S NO LIAR, THEN HAVE HIM EXPLAIN HOW HE COULD HAVE BEATEN MITSURUGI-SAMA!!

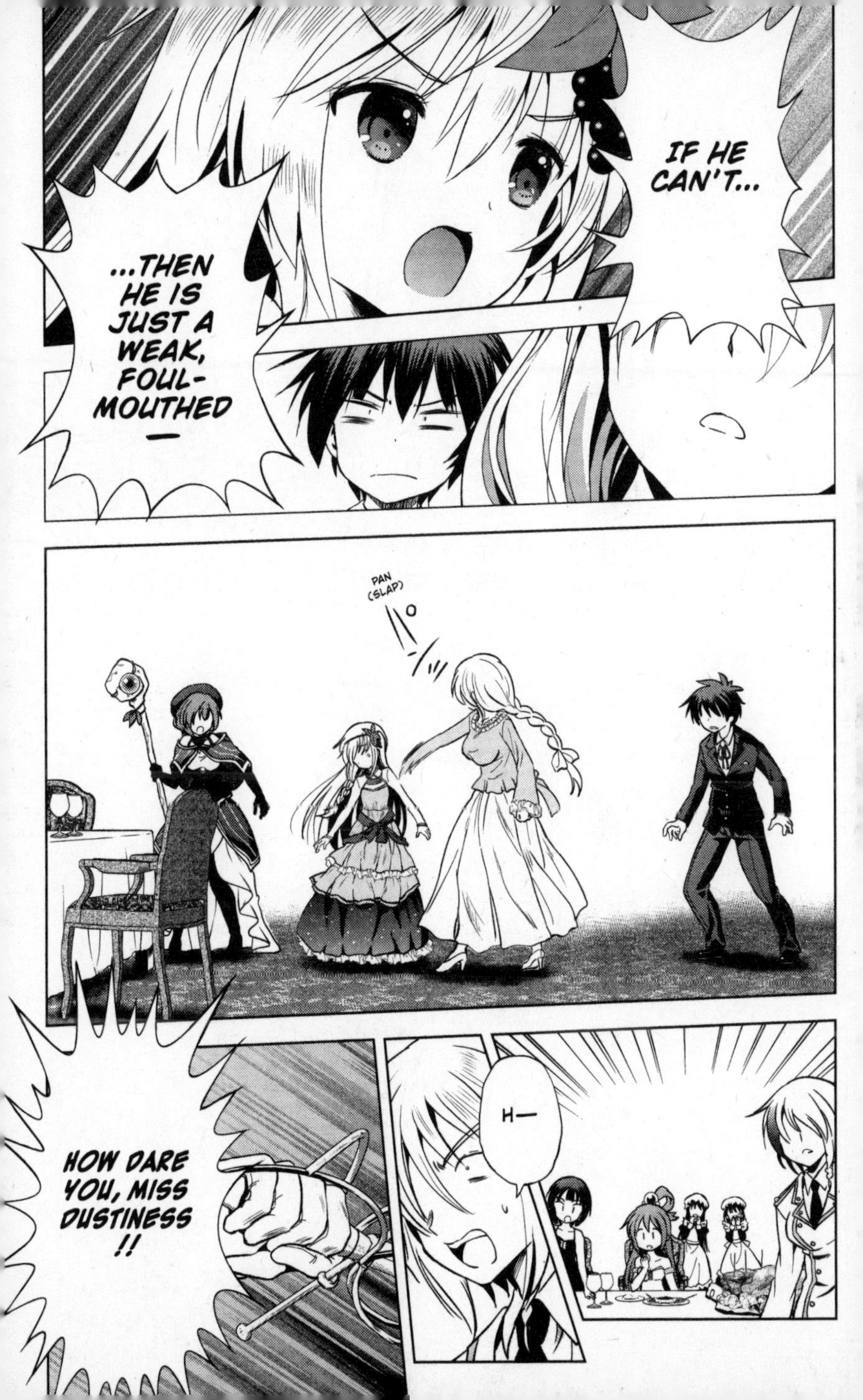
IF HE CAN'T...
...THEN HE IS JUST A WEAK, FOUL-MOUTHED —
PAN (SLAP)
H—
HOW DARE YOU, MISS DUSTINESS!!

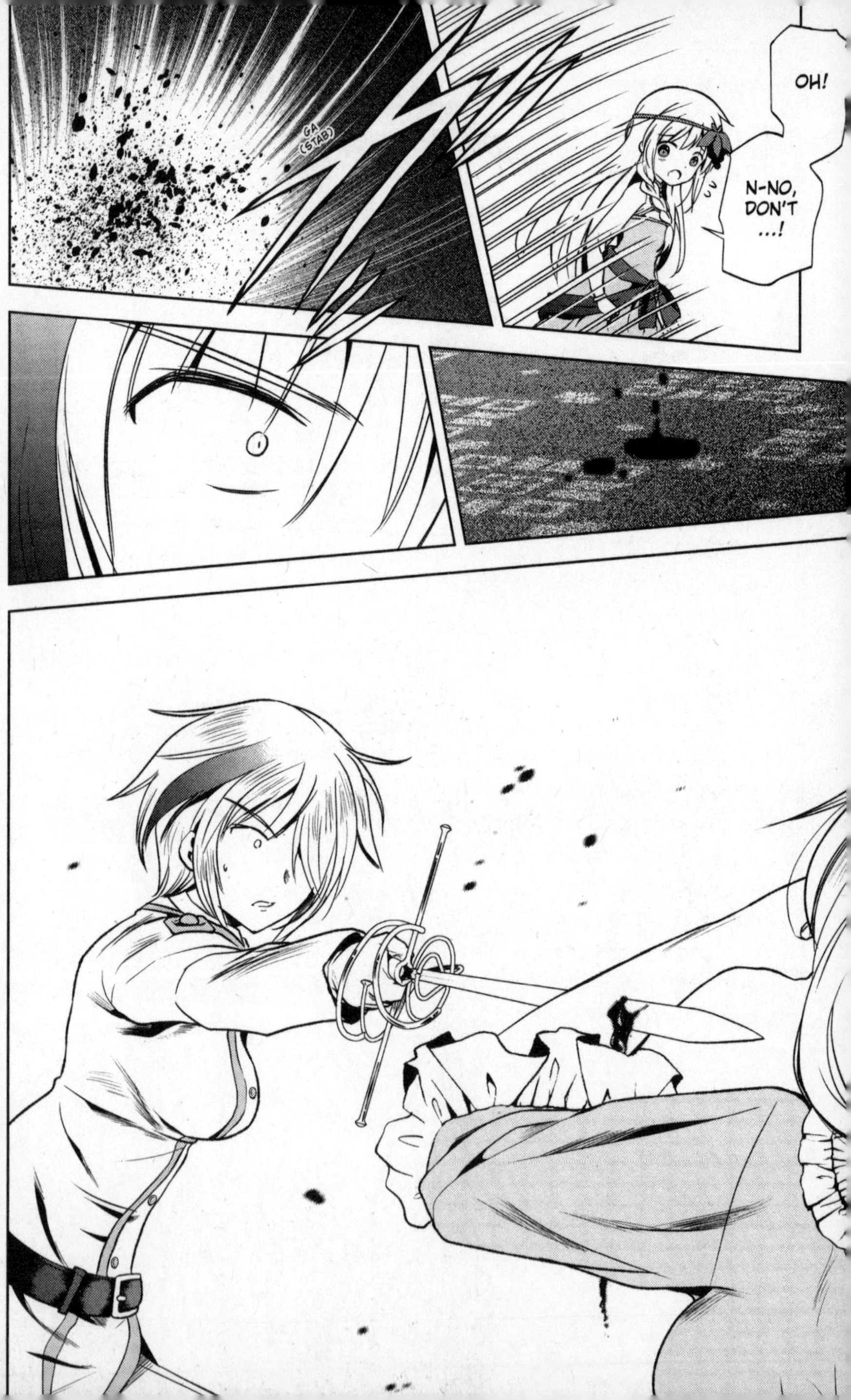
OH!
N-NO, DON'T ...!
GA (STAB)

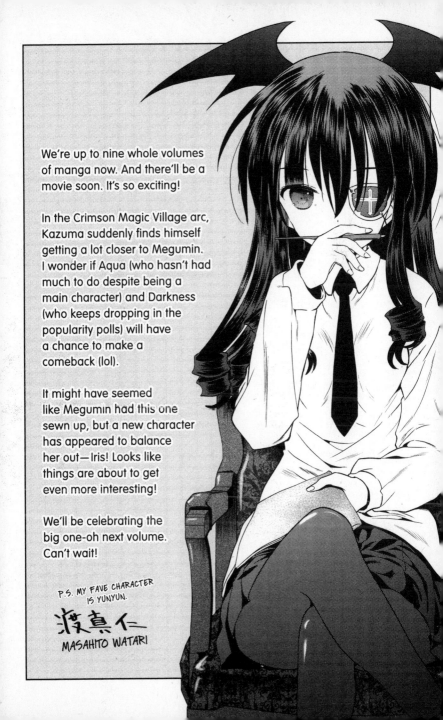

We're up to nine whole volumes of manga now. And there'll be a movie soon. It's so exciting!

In the Crimson Magic Village arc, Kazuma suddenly finds himself getting a lot closer to Megumin. I wonder if Aqua (who hasn't had much to do despite being a main character) and Darkness (who keeps dropping in the popularity polls) will have a chance to make a comeback (lol).

It might have seemed like Megumin had this one sewn up, but a new character has appeared to balance her out—Iris! Looks like things are about to get even more interesting!

We'll be celebrating the big one-oh next volume. Can't wait!

P.S. MY FAVE CHARACTER IS YUNYUN.

渡真仁

MASAHITO WATARI

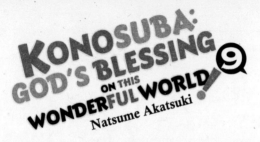

# KONOSUBA: GOD'S BLESSING ON THIS WONDERFUL WORLD! ⑨

Natsume Akatsuki

**TRANSLATION:** Kevin Steinbach ● **LETTERING:** Rochelle Gancio

KONO SUBARASHII SEKAI NI SYUKUFUKU WO! Volume 9
©MASAHITO WATARI 2019
©NATSUME AKATSUKI, KURONE MISHIMA 2019
First published in Japan in 2019 by Kadokawa Corporation, Tokyo. English translation rights arranged with KADOKAWA Corporation, Tokyo through Tuttle-Mori Agency, Inc., Tokyo.

Yen Press
150 West 30th Street, 19th Floor
New York, NY 10001

Visit us at yenpress.com
facebook.com/yenpress
twitter.com/yenpress
yenpress.tumblr.com
instagram.com/yenpress

First Yen Press Edition: December 2019

Yen Press is an imprint of Yen Press, LLC.
The Yen Press name and logo are trademarks of Yen Press, LLC.

Library of Congress Control Number: 2016946112

ISBNs: 978-1-9753-5954-6 (paperback)
       978-1-9753-0659-5 (ebook)

10 9 8 7 6 5 4 3 2 1

WOR

Printed in the United States of America